APPROACHES
TO
ART THERAPY
Theory and Technique

APPROACHES TO ART THERAPY

Theory and Technique

Edited by

Judith Aron Rubin

Brunner/Mazel, *Publishers* • **New York**

Library of Congress Cataloging-in-Publication Data

Approaches to art therapy.

Includes bibliographies and index.
1. Art therapy. I. Rubin, Judith Aron.
RC489.A7A67 1987   616.89'1656   86-26376
ISBN 0-87630-452-8

Published by
BRUNNER/MAZEL, INC.
19 Union Square
New York, New York 10003

Contents

Preface

In October 1983, I wrote the following letter to the colleagues whose chapters comprise this book . . .

> While lying on a raft in a pond last summer, I found myself reviewing an idea for a book. The notion had popped into my head years ago, but I had never really thought it through or had time to implement it. . . .
>
> The idea stems from my conviction that only someone who knows and understands a theory well can teach it to others. While I think this is true for any kind of therapy, I think it is especially true when the theory must be modified in some way in order to be applied to a specific form of treatment with its own intrinsic qualities, such as art therapy.
>
> The plan for the book is quite simple: to have a series of chapters, each one written by an author who is familiar with the theory of personality and/or psychotherapy involved, and who has worked out a way of making it applicable to art therapy. In order for the book to have a coherent and orderly form, I think it necessary for each author to follow a similar format for explaining and demonstrating a particular theoretical approach to art therapy.
>
> I think such a book would be a significant contribution to the field, and hope that you will want to be a part of it. If everyone I have invited accepts, you will be in excellent company. I look forward eagerly to hearing your response.

By the middle of November, I was able to write the following letter, which should give the reader an idea of what I had hoped this book would look like . . .

> First, let me thank you for agreeing to participate in writing a chapter for a book on different theoretical approaches to art therapy. I am delighted to be able to report that everyone I had invited has accepted, so that you are part of a rather impressive group. Everyone I have spoken to about the project, especially those involved in educating art therapists, has confirmed the need for such a book.

As I indicated in the first letter, I think it essential that each author follow the same general framework or outline, which I hope will not be felt as constricting or inhibiting; but which will serve to give the book an overall feeling of continuity, predictability, and aesthetic coherence. After consulting with several colleagues, I should like to suggest the following general outline for each chapter:

1. Definition of and Orientation to the Particular Theory (or Area of Emphasis), including some historical information and references to the literature for those who want to read more fully in the area.
2. The Particular Relevance of the Theory (or Concept) to Art Therapy in General, from the point of view of both diagnosis and treatment.
3. Case Example(s): One or two brief case vignettes, which clarify the way in which the theory helps the art therapist to understand and to execute the treatment. Make the connections explicit; don't take for granted the reader's ability to see the links which are obvious to you.

I went on to suggest a consistent number of pages and illustrations for each chapter, and I am pleased that the contributors were largely able and willing to keep to the guidelines. I finished that letter with the following statement which I still hope will be the case: "I think that, with each person sharing his/her expertise, we will be supplying a much-needed and qualitatively fine resource for art therapists."

Since that time, over two years have elapsed. I have left full-time work at the University of Pittsburgh, where I was codirector of a creative arts therapy program in a psychiatric hospital, and have gone into the full-time private practice of art therapy.

I first saw the need for a book like this one largely from my perspective as teacher, supervisor, and part-time clinician. Now, though I still do some teaching and supervision, the majority of my time is spent doing art therapy with patients of all age levels and a variety of disorders. As a full-time clinician, the need for the kind of thinking illustrated in this book has become even more vivid, in the press of trying to do my best to help my patients to recover and to grow.

What has also become clear is that, although the primary audience for this book is probably art therapists, it may also have value for other kinds of clinicians who do psychotherapy, and who also struggle with the daily dilemma of translating theory into technique: psychiatrists, psychoanalysts, psychologists, social workers, counselors, psychiatric nurses, child life specialists, play therapists, etc. Of course, other creative arts therapists may also find the book useful, those working in dance, music, drama, and poetry therapy where the same issues arise, and where the problems of translation and application of theory are similar to those in the visual arts.

I hope that readers, whatever their discipline, will remember that the following descriptions of what is always a heavily nonverbal or paraverbal process should be understood as mere approximations of therapeutic reality. As John Locke wrote in his *Essay on Human Understanding*, "We should have a great many fewer disputes in the world if words were taken for what they are, the signs of our ideas only, and not for things themselves." And as far as I am concerned, the last word on that issue was said by Lewis Carroll in *Through the Looking Glass*:

> "The question is," said Alice, "whether you *can* make words mean so many different things?"
> "The question is," said Humpty Dumpty, "which is to be master— that's all."

Hopefully, this book, though far from perfect, will help the reader to be "master" of his or her work as a therapist . . . "that's all."

Pittsburgh, Pennsylvania   *Judith A. Rubin*
January 1986

Acknowledgments

There are always many who have helped directly and indirectly with a project as complex as this book. This was my first attempt at an edited volume, and it turned out to be surprisingly free of stress, despite the warnings of others. My cooperative colleagues, the authors of the chapters to follow, were by and large prompt and agreeable, even when the changes I suggested in their first drafts were more than minimal. My deepest thanks, then, to each and every one, not only for writing a chapter apiece, but also for making my editorial job so pleasant and rewarding. I am especially grateful to those who actually met all deadlines, and who have been most patient with their less-speedy colleagues and this tardy editor.

Specific thanks go to many. First, to Elinor Ulman, former publisher and now executive editor of the *American Journal of Art Therapy*, for permission to reprint all or part of Chapters 2, 3, 11, and 15, and for permission to reproduce photographs that had previously appeared in that periodical.

My thanks, too, to the Western Psychiatric Institute and Clinic and the Department of Psychiatry of the University of Pittsburgh. Because of the splendid word-processing equipment and fine media services available at WPIC, the majority of the work on this book was made considerably easier and qualitatively better. Thanks especially to photographer Norman Snyder, who either took or transformed into black-and-white glossies the majority of the illustrations in the book.

Perhaps the person most responsible for this volume after myself is my loyal and dependable typist, Mari Dulgeroff, who in her capacity as secretary to the Creative and Expressive Arts Therapy Program did most of the typing and correcting on the book, and who continued in a private capacity after I left WPIC.

Finally, I thank my family, especially my perenially patient husband, who has tolerated the many at-home hours spent on this volume. And my gratitude to Ann Alhadeff and Bernie Mazel, whose receptivity to the idea resulted in a stress-free contract signing and patient support throughout all stages of production.

Judith A. Rubin

Contributors

SUSAN AACH-FELDMAN, M.Ed., ATR
Special Educator, Western Pennsylvania School for Blind Children, Pittsburgh; Adjunct Faculty, Art Therapy Preparation Program, Carlow College, Pittsburgh; Consultant, Arts in Special Education Project of Pennsylvania

MALA G. BETENSKY, Ph.D., ATR
Psychologist and Art Therapist in Independent Practice, Washington, D.C.; Author, *Self-Discovery Through Self-Expression* (1973)

MICHAEL EDWARDS, R.A.Th., H.L.M.*
Director and Associate Professor, Graduate Art Therapy, Concordia University, Montreal, Canada; Analytic Candidate, C. G. Jung Institute, Zürich, Switzerland; Honorary Curator, The C. G. Jung Picture Archives

JOSEF E. GARAI, Ph.D., ATR
Professor Emeritus, Pratt Institute, Brooklyn, N.Y.; Art Therapist and Psychologist in Private Practice, New York City; Former Chairman, Creative-Expressive Arts Therapies Program, Pratt Institute

ROSE GARLOCK, M.A., ATR
Art Therapist in Private Practice, New York City; Former Director, Therapeutic Social Club, Alfred Adler Clinic, New York City

EDITH KRAMER, ATR, HLM
Adjunct Professor of Art Therapy, New York University and George Washington University; Author, *Art Therapy in a Children's Community* (1958), *Art as Therapy with Children* (1971), and *Childhood and Art Therapy* (1979)

CAROLE KUNKLE-MILLER, Ph.D., ATR
Art Therapist and Psychologist in Private Practice, Pittsburgh, PA; Art Therapist, Western Pennsylvania School for the Deaf; Consultant, Arts in Special Education Project of Pennsylvania

MILDRED LACHMAN-CHAPIN, M.Ed., ATR
Art Therapist in Private Practice (C.C.M.H.C. †), Deerfield, IL; Former Director, Adjunctive Therapies, Barclay & Pritzker Hospitals, Chicago; Former Acting Director, Art Therapy Program, Vermont College of Norwich University

JANIE RHYNE, Ph.D., ATR, HLM
Assistant Professor of Art Therapy, Vermont College of Norwich University; Adjunct Assistant Professor, Graduate School of Social Work, University of Iowa; Private Practice, Gestalt Art Experience, Iowa City, IA; Author, *The Gestalt Art Experience* (1973)

ARTHUR ROBBINS, Ed.D., ATR
Professor, Art Therapy, Pratt Institute, Brooklyn, N.Y.; Director, Institute for Expressive Analysis, New York City; Faculty, National Psychological Association for Psychoanalysis; Private Practice of Art Therapy and Psychoanalysis, New York City; Author, *Creative Art Therapy* (1976) and *Expressive Therapies* (1980)

ELLEN A. ROTH, Ph.D., ATR
Research Consultant, Western Psychiatric Institute & Clinic, University of Pittsburgh, PA; Contributing Editor, *Art Therapy*; Editor, *Perspectives on Art Therapy* (1978)

JUDITH A. RUBIN, Ph.D., ATR, HLM
Clinical Assistant Professor of Psychiatry, University of Pittsburgh; Faculty-by-Invitation, Pittsburgh Psychoanalytic Institute; Art Therapist and Psychoanalyst in Private Practice, Pittsburgh, PA; Author, *Child Art Therapy* (1978), and *The Art of Art Therapy* (1984)

RAWLEY A. SILVER, Ed.D., ATR, HLM
Art Therapist and Consultant in Private Practice, Mamaroneck, N.Y.; Former Director, National Institute of Education Project and Associate Professor, College of New Rochelle, N.Y.; Author, *Developing Cognitive & Creative Skills Through Art* (1978, 1986) and *The Silver Drawing Test* (1983)

ELINOR ULMAN, D.A.T. (Honorary), ATR, HLM
Founder and Executive Editor, *American Journal of Art Therapy*; Adjunct Professor of Art Therapy, George Washington University, Washington, D.C.; Editor, *Art Therapy in Theory and Practice* (1975) and *Art Therapy Viewpoints* (1980)

HARRIET WADESON, Ph.D., ATR
Director, Art Therapy Graduate Program, University of Illinois, Chicago; Former Director, Art Therapy Program, University of Texas; Author, *Art Psychotherapy* (1980)

EDITH WALLACE, M.D., Ph.D.
Faculty, C. G. Jung Foundation and Institute for Expressive Analysis, New York City; Painter, Seminar and Workshop Leader, "Opening Channels to the Creative"; Jungian Analyst and Psychiatrist in Private Practice, New York City

LAURIE WILSON, Ph.D., ATR
Director, Graduate Art Therapy Program, New York University; Research Candidate, Psychoanalytic Institute, New York University Medical Center; Art Therapist in Private Practice, New Jersey; Sculptor; Collaboration with Edith Kramer, *Childhood and Art Therapy* (1979); Author, *Louise Nevelson's Iconography and Sources* (1980)

Key

ATR: Registered Art Therapist, American Art Therapy Association
HLM: Honorary Life Member, American Art Therapy Association
*R.A.Th. and H.L.M.: Registered Art Therapist and Honorary Life Member, British Association of Art Therapists
†C.C.M.H.C.: Certified Clinical Mental Health Counselor

Introduction

One decade ago (December 1975), I wrote a paper for a graduate course in which I described, in somewhat more detail than I later put into print (Rubin, 1978, p. 18), my personal quest for a sound theoretical framework to guide my work as an art therapist. "I, like my chosen field, have been shopping for a theory. Each time I have looked for a 'goodness of fit,' wondering whether I have at last found the 'right' theoretical framework for therapeutic growth in and through art. At first, I worked with people on a largely intuitive basis. Later, I looked for ways to understand what was going on and ideas about how best to proceed."

In 1963, Margaret Naumburg had suggested that, since I was dealing with children, I should read Clark Moustakas (1953) on play therapy. I did, and fell in love with his warmth, his concern, and his respect for the youngsters with whom he worked. For a while, his basically humanistic approach seemed sufficient, and it was appealingly unintrusive.

Later, however, working at the Pittsburgh Child Guidance Center (1969ff), I found that the more disturbed youngsters did not automatically get better just by providing the sort of permissive child-centered context recommended by Moustakas. I therefore had to look further, and in the course of a search for additional training, I realized that my most helpful supervisors had been those who had a psychoanalytic orientation. Attracted to this framework, largely through those espousing it, I decided to study it in depth.

And it *has* been helpful, especially in understanding and working with the dynamics of the more complicated cases that have crossed my path. But (and this is still valid today, despite having completed full training in both adult and child analysis) Freudian theory does not adequately explain for me all of the richness, mystery, and beauty of the creative process which is at the heart of art therapy. In search of a theory that could shed light on that realm, I have delved briefly into analytic (Jung), Gestalt, existential, and humanistic psychotherapy. And I have found that each of these approaches, these different sets of lenses, illuminates slightly different aspects of human personality and growth.

I have enjoyed the reading I have done in most theories, usually finding something with which to resonate, even if I have not always been able to respond positively to all aspects of each. At first, I had thought that the solution to my problem would be a kind of patchwork, a mosaic, a collage of different facets from different theories, which together would account for what happens in art therapy. Although this kind of additive eclecticism may yet be the answer, I have doubts about the inevitable inconsistencies of such an attempt. I question the feasibility, in other words, of mixing theoretical apples, oranges, raisins, and nuts.

What seems more probable is that a theory about art therapy will eventually emerge from art therapy itself. It will no doubt partake of elements from other perspectives, but will need to have its own inner integrity in terms of the creative process of which it consists. Many concepts—from Freudian psychoanalysis and Jungian analytic therapy, from Gestalt psychology and Gestalt therapy, from humanistic and existential thought, from aestheticians like Susanne Langer, and from studies of creativity by academic psychologists—will no doubt prove ultimately to be relevant. And no doubt many will not, perhaps even some of those that now seem most seductive and appealing. What seems best is to proceed by looking with what has variously been called "free-floating," "even-hovering," "desireless," or "nonjudgmental" attention—with an openness that does not categorize or label—at the experience of art therapy, until the central themes, issues, constructs, and concepts begin to take shape.

I continued to espouse this viewpoint in a more recent book (1984), suggesting that "what is needed now is the development of meaningful theoretical constructs from the matrix of art therapy itself" (p. 190) and devoting an entire chapter to a beginning attempt to do just that. Nevertheless, I also continue to believe in "the possible relevance of theories from other disciplines and their application to our own," despite my "uneasiness about the possibility that we may be forcing art therapy into theoretical molds that do not quite 'fit' " (*Ibid.*).

Even more pertinent to the present volume, I feel certain that "in order to be able to converse and to communicate with students and other professionals, it is necessary to know and understand the similarities and differences between things like Gestalt psychology and Gestalt therapy, or classical psychoanalytic drive theory and the recent developments in object relations" (*Ibid.*). In other words, it is vital—if art therapists are to function as sophisticated members of any clinical or educational team— that our comprehension of any theoretical stance be as deep and clear as that of other professionals. It is distressing to read or hear presentations by art therapists that reflect incomplete and confused notions about different theoretical perspectives.

And it is not only important to know what one is talking about in order to gain the respect of others; it is also best for the eventual development of theory in our own discipline. "Being familiar with different theories of how and why people function in general, and particularly in art, cannot but deepen our understanding of the phenomena with which we deal" (*Ibid*.). I also believe that "it is especially useful, where possible, to read the original (not just someone else's translation of meaning) in order to fully grasp Freud's (1900) theory of dream formation as well as its technical implications (Altman, 1975)" (*Ibid*.).

In the chapters that comprise this volume, individuals who have read the original theorists recommend selected readings and also try to describe those aspects of the theory they find relevant to their work. They then present clinical examples of art therapy conducted according to their understanding of the particular model, so that the reader can more easily bridge the gap between the original theory and its possible application to our own discipline.

> Theory is only meaningful and worthwhile if it helps to explain the phenomena with which it deals in a way that enables us to work better with them. To learn or to develop theories of personality, psychotherapy, or creativity without actually applying them to real life situations is to grasp neither their meaning nor their significance. Theory and technique should go hand in hand: the one based on and growing out of the other, each constantly modifying the other over time. Although this may sound too intellectual for most art therapists, it may be as important to the continued development of our field as defining the "basics" (Rubin, 1984, pp. 191–192).

The intimate relationship between theory and practice is the main reason why a book like this one is needed. To do things with patients or clients in art therapy without knowing why one does them is simply irresponsible. A good therapist has some notion of what is "wrong," as well as some ideas about how to facilitate a process of getting "better." Since many different approaches seem to work, it is foolish to debate which is the "correct" one. Rather, it seems most sensible to try to understand *each* of the common approaches in depth, especially the link between theory and practice.

Professional maturation in any clinical field usually involves "trying on" or experimenting with different approaches, as much to find which one "fits" the therapist as which one "works" with the patient. In fact, I'm quite convinced that only if an approach is comfortable for a therapist is it at all useful in his or her hands. As Susan Deri, also quoted by Ulman, points out, "one seldom hears acknowledgement that the organizational symbols behind one's outlook are, to some extent, subjectively chosen. We select our conceptual framework not only on the basis of intellectual judgment but also because it is congenial to our way of thinking and because the type of clinical work that follows from it suits our personality'' (Deri, 1984, p. 181).

As I reread Deri's words, I was reminded of another paper I wrote for a graduate course (in 1974) on the connection between my own values and my reactions to different theories of personality and psychotherapy. At the time, I felt—and still do—

> that my work as an art therapist is based on certain strongly-held convictions about human beings: that all have genuine creative potential; that most have one or more preferred creative modalities which must be identified in order for each to fulfill that potential; and that all have a natural tendency toward growth, toward actualizing that potential at increasingly mature levels. I see that growth process as characteristically cyclical—both regressive and progressive—with a general tendency toward and preference for something like "order," "homeostasis," or "balance," with both dynamic and static elements. All of these assumptions concern human capacities, positive tendencies—toward creativity, growth, and balance—which seems to me to be potential in all creatures. It is not surprising, then, that I have often found myself attracted to theories whose picture of man resonates with such optimistic notions . . . ideas about self-actualization, for example, which form the core of humanistic approaches to personality and psychotherapy.
>
> Despite my conviction that all human beings are internally propelled in the direction of growth, however, the provision of facilitating conditions for creativity often seemed insufficient [as noted earlier]. Those positive tendencies were often blocked or distorted, and in their stead were destructive or disorderly behaviors. The theory of personality and development which [still] makes the most sense to me in explaining the blocks and distortions, as well as their genesis, is that derived from Freudian psychoanalysis. This is especially true of the developmental aspects of psychoanalytic theory, which explain to me how individuals can be "stuck" at earlier phases . . . , and thus be unable to fulfill their potential. The Freudian theory of personality structure and psychodynamics has also been most useful. Learning to recognize different adaptive modes and defensive mechanisms for dealing with intrapsychic conflict, has helped me to better understand the forms the blocking or distortions take [e.g., "symptoms"].
>
> Structurally, the Freudian notion of conscious, preconscious, and unconscious portions of the mental apparatus also makes sense to me. The Jungian idea of a "collective unconscious," while aestheti-

cally appealing, does not fit the data of my clinical work, at least not through my by now rather Freudian eyes. The universality of certain themes and symbols seems to me to be related to the universal aspects of the human experience, still largely personal to each individual. The importance of the symbol, of that powerful form of expression and communication, is central to my work. To the extent that both Freud and Jung concerned themselves with this aspect of human thought and expression, they have both been helpful.

As we continue to struggle toward greater clarity and more coherent theory in the field of art therapy, it is essential that we not abandon the parallel task of truly comprehending different theoretical and technical approaches to psychotherapy. It is equally important to go on with the challenging attempt to apply existing theories to art therapy, a task begun by the contributors to this volume.

In 1980 I was asked to review a collection of papers on art therapy for a journal that subsequently discontinued publication. In that unpublished review, I noted that the articles selected for the book shared a common bias, openly stated by the editors at the outset (Ulman & Levy, 1980, p. ix). That volume, and others available in our field, represented a single theoretical point of view. Most have been written by individuals and are attempts to organize and express the writer's understandings after a period of work as an art therapist. I have written two books of that sort myself, and I think that such personal statements are necessary and understandable in a youthful discipline, which is working hard to define its identity for itself as well as for others. I also wrote in that unpublished book review

there is a crying need in this young and divergent field for a single volume which attempts to clarify and articulate genuinely *different* points of view. . . .

In imagining such a volume, I find myself remembering a film much-used in the training of psychotherapists, in which a woman named Gloria is interviewed successively by three clinicians with different theoretical and technical perspectives (Carl Rogers, Fritz Perls, and Albert Ellis). What is most fascinating about this film, in addition to the very different personalities of the three men (consonant with their stated views), is that each of them evokes a somewhat distinct aspect of the client. While clearly the same person throughout, Gloria expresses different facets of herself in response to each of the three interviewers. The question of which approach would be most useful to her in ongoing treatment is implicit in asking her at the end which therapist she might want to visit again; suggesting that the "right" approach for any individual is in part a function of what that person responds to most positively at that moment in time.

This book is my attempt to provide a similar kind of glimpse, for art therapists, of different ways of working and the theories on which they are based. I hope that the chapters in this volume will help both students and practitioners to make the leap from any general theory of personality and psychotherapy to the theory and practice of art therapy.

As for the selection of theories and authors, there is no question that psychoanalytic theory was dominant in art therapy, as it was in American psychiatry and psychology, during the early years of its development (Kramer, 1958; Naumburg, 1947, 1950, 1953). In university psychology departments, however, there was a heated debate between those espousing dynamic approaches and those enamored of Watsonian behaviorism, which, like Freudian theory, had developed in the beginning of the century. In some places the tension was so great that the two could not coexist under one administrative roof, as at Harvard with its separate Departments of (experimental) Psychology and (clinical) Social Relations.

In response to the determinism inherent in both psychoanalysis and behaviorism, a variety of other approaches were proposed; these became known as "humanistic" and were seen as a "third force" in psychology. Most of them stressed the positive, "self-actualizing" elements in man's nature, as well as his ability to take charge of his fate and not be at the mercy of either his invisible unconscious or his learning experiences. The three divisions of this book, then, parallel the three major orientations in psychology and psychotherapy, at least conceptually: the psychodynamic, the humanistic, and the behavioral/cognitive/developmental approaches.

Although the latter group is rapidly growing in popularity among "talking cure" specialists of all disciplines, psychodynamic approaches still seem dominant in art therapy. Perhaps this is simply an inevitable "developmental lag" because of the time required to translate theory into application. On the other hand, the continuing popularity of psychodynamic approaches may be due to the very nature of art, which makes theories assuming the existence of a dynamic unconscious intrinsically appealing. Artists, after all, often feel as if "inspiration" comes mysteriously from their own depths, and most art therapists are artists themselves, as well as trying to inspire creativity in others.

Probably a close second in popularity among art therapists are those orientations known as humanistic. I believe this is due to the pleasure, sense of autonomy, and possibility of self-definition that are all inherent in a satisfying creative process. Least popular among art therapists are the "stars" of the current psychotherapy scene: behavioral and cognitive approaches. Since developmental approaches often involve more education and "prescription" than either dynamic or humanistic ones, I have arbitrarily included them in the third section of the book, though one might argue that they belong equally well in the first or second grouping.

The reader may wonder at the absence of some familiar approaches usually included in textbooks on theories of psychotherapy. Although known to art therapists, it seems fair to say that reality, primal, and rational-emotive therapies have simply not "caught on" with many, and transactional analysis, though mentioned by some (Keyes, 1974), has also not been proposed by anyone in the field as a general framework. Finally, though family and systems dynamics are important to practicing art therapists, much of whose work is done with groups, they seem to me of a different order from the approaches included in the book, all of which involve a particular frame of reference for viewing the individual—whether treated alone, with family members, or in a group.

Since any selection process is somewhat arbitrary, I apologize to those readers who feel that important theories have been overlooked or misrepresented. Art therapy in the eighties is really no different from contemporary psychotherapy, in that "the reason why there are so many different definitions . . . is that there is lively disagreement about most of the issues central to the therapy process" (Belkin, 1980, p. 1). And, "although therapy is conceived of as a helping process, there is wide disagreement about how the helping is done, and the respective roles of the therapist and patient . . . " (*Ibid.*, p. 2).

Although the contributors to this book were asked to briefly describe the theories they were advocating, they were, of necessity, selective. What you will find are their personal interpretations of the theories they have chosen, which not only involve some decisions about which aspects "fit" art therapy, but may also include some distortion, albeit unintentional. My advice, then, is to read these chapters with the awareness that, in order to fully understand any particular approach, one must read the original theorists and practitioners for oneself. The references and suggested readings at the end of each chapter should serve as a beginning for those wishing to be more broadly informed.

To put it another way, the reader will not encounter a complete or scholarly introduction to any of the theories; rather, each chapter represents one art therapist's sincere attempt to apply what seems relevant from a particular theoretical position to his or her work with patients. You or I might well disagree with the selectivity of some authors or the inclusiveness of others. We might also disagree with the particular way in which an author has interpreted a theory, in terms of the technique described. What I hope the reader will gain is an introduction to different perspectives and a notion of how one might go about translating theory into technique. If I and my colleagues have accomplished that, we have done at least part of what seemed to be needed. If we also stimulate further theoretical thinking in others, then we have done even more for the future of our discipline.

I recently came across a presentation I had made as a member of a panel at the 1979 Conference of the American Art Therapy Association. The topic was "The Future of Art Therapy: Fantasy vs. Reality," and the chairman had asked that we address ourselves specifically to the areas of *theory* and *practice*. I wrote then what I still believe, that "theory in a clinical field is best built and tested through practice," and that my "nightmares" in this area—which are, sadly, sometimes a reality—were of "half-digested hodgepodges, built on poorly-understood and inadequately-integrated ideas from various sources. They also include[d] visions of superficial, oversimplified, and shallow propositions—seductively appealing because of their surface shine, but having little substance underneath."

Lest this fearsome imagery sound unduly harsh and pessimistic, I also shared some of "my most ecstatic dreams about the future of our theory," which began with the hope "that clinicians will be trained not only to practice well, but also to think clearly; and will be able to begin the hard work of exploring the art therapy process itself, developing a theory with appropriate constructs, the precise shape of which is still a mystery to me at this time." In order to do that, I suggested that we *begin* by looking at the "many good models in other fields and the few outstanding ones in our own," referring to both Freud and Kramer, who was also on that panel and was one of the first to seriously think through some implications of psychoanalytic theory for the work of an art therapist.

I hoped then, and continue to hope, "that we will have the frustration tolerance to sustain us as we struggle towards greater clarity and synthesis. I believe that we must be willing to take risks, to debate openly, and to continually go back to the data of our clinical work in order to decide how viable—not how attractive—any particular construct seems to be." I went on to suggest in that brief talk that "we will need to train our students and supervisees to think theoretically and, hopefully, to find it both enjoyable and highly relevant to their work. Only when people see the intimate relationship between theory and practice can it be a lively area, and only then will we be able to progress constructively. As long as it is viewed as an unessential, abstract form of 'mental masturbation,' which I think it is by many clinicians, we won't get very far."

Although that presentation was relatively informal, the convictions expressed still seem valid: "The vision of a superficial mishmash in theory and/or practice is horrendous; but the image of greater refinement and depth in both is quite a lovely picture. Only if we work together for quality in both theory and practice, will the wishful dream replace the nightmare as the reality of the future." This volume, with all its imperfections, is meant to be a contribution to such work.

REFERENCES

Altman, L. L. *The dream in psychoanalysis*, 2nd ed. New York: International Universities Press, 1975.

Belkin, G. S. (Ed.). *Contemporary psychotherapies*. Chicago: Rand McNally College Pub. Co., 1980.

Deri, S. K. *Symbolization and creativity*. New York: International Universities Press, 1984.

Freud, S. The interpretation of dreams (1900). *Standard Edition*, Vol. 4–5. London: Hogarth Press, 1955.

Keyes, M. F. *The inward journey: Art as psychotherapy for you*. Millbrae, CA: Celestial Arts, 1974.

Kramer, E. *Art therapy in a children's community*. Springfield, IL: Charles C Thomas, 1958.

Moustakas, C. E. *Children in play therapy*. New York: Ballantine Books, 1953.

Naumburg, M. Studies of the "free" art expression of behavior problem children and adolescents as a means of diagnosis and therapy. *Nervous & Mental Disease Monograph* No. 71, 1947.

Naumburg, M. *Schizophrenic art: Its meaning in psychotherapy*. New York: Grune & Stratton, 1950.

Naumburg, M. *Psychoneurotic art: Its function in psychotherapy*. New York: Grune & Stratton, 1953.

Rubin, J. A. *Child art therapy: Understanding and helping children grow through art*. New York: Van Nostrand Reinhold, 1978 (2nd ed., 1984).

Rubin, J. A. *The art of art therapy*. New York: Brunner/Mazel, 1984.

Ulman, E., & Levy, C. (Eds.) *Art therapy viewpoints*. New York: Schocken Books, 1980.

APPROACHES
TO
ART THERAPY
Theory and Technique

SECTION I

PSYCHODYNAMIC APPROACHES

As noted in the Introduction, the chapters in this section reflect the origins as well as many of the current trends in art therapy. Freudian psychoanalytic theory, contrary to popular prejudice, has never been rigid or static. Its founder was an inquiring explorer whose own notions about human beings changed considerably over the course of his many productive years, during which he continually modified his theoretical formulations. Similarly, his followers have continued to question, to debate, and to reformulate ideas about both theory and technique, in both psychoanalysis and psychoanalytic psychotherapy. The first five chapters in this section are all based on Freudian theory, each with a slightly different focus.

If Margaret Naumburg (1947, 1950, 1953, 1966) were alive today, she would have been the logical choice to write the first chapter, with its emphasis on Freud's early goal of "making the unconscious conscious," leading eventually to insight ("where id was there shall ego be"). I have written that chapter myself, after considerable internal debate about the propriety of being both editor and author, but having been trained at an orthodox Freudian institute in classical psychoanalytic technique, which I have tried to apply to art therapy, I felt as well qualified as most of my colleagues to speak as a descendant of our first pioneer.

In the following two chapters, Edith Kramer and Laurie Wilson concentrate on the implications for art therapy of psychoanalytic ego psychology, with particular attention to sublimation and symbolization. Kramer, the originator of one of the earliest and most widely used theories of art therapy, here further clarifies a position expressed in an already impressive list of contributions (1958, 1971, 1979). Wilson has written a most stimulating chapter, in which she looks at the clinical phenomena

3

of art therapy, through eyes sharpened by recent psychoanalytic formulations on the development and dynamics of symbolization.

The last two chapters influenced by Freud and his descendants involve still other facets of psychoanalytic theory. Arthur Robbins sees much of value to the art therapist in the various understandings of "object relations," which he elucidates through vivid clinical examples. Mildred Lachman-Chapin then focuses our attention on recent developments in self psychology and some possible implications for work in our field. Both are realms of lively debate among contemporary psychoanalysts, as studies of early development and work with an increasingly broad range of patients lead to an expansion of theory and technique in realms only touched on by Freud himself.

The other major depth psychologist is Jung, whose popularity among art therapists has always been high in Great Britain (cf. Dalley, 1984), but is only recently rising among American practitioners. Because Jung himself painted and used art with his patients, those trained in analytic psychology are more likely than Freudian analysts to include creative processes in their treatment, such as drawing in the process of "active imagination" or creating imaginary worlds in a tray of sand. Unable to decide between inviting a Jungian analyst who used art or an art therapist trained in analytic psychology to write the chapter, I resolved my dilemma in a rather cowardly way, but one which I think turns out well for the reader. I invited *both* an experienced artist/analyst (Edith Wallace) and an art therapist in Jungian training (Michael Edwards), and each has written a fascinating chapter which I believe complement one another quite nicely. Despite a good deal of literature by Jungians *about* art (Campbell, 1974; Jung, 1950; Neumann, 1959), as well as some of the use of art in analytic psychotherapy (Baynes, 1940; Jung, 1934), these chapters represent a welcome addition to the sole book available on the application of Jungian theory to the practice of art therapy (Lyddiatt, 1971).

As noted earlier, those "depth" psychologies which value internal imagery appeal to the artist in every art therapist. The task of trying to comprehend symbolic communication through art is so great that we are constantly challenged to find new and better ways to understand the messages our patients send us. Psychodynamic approaches, all of which are rooted in the seminal analytic work of Freud and Jung, are still probably the most attractive to the majority of workers in our field. They are, however, only part of the truth for many and are even aversive to some, as Elinor Ulman acknowledges in her discussion of three Freudian approaches to art therapy, which is found in the last section of the book on applications of theory.

REFERENCES

Baynes, H. G. *Mythology of the soul*. Baltimore: Williams & Wilkins, 1940.

Campbell, J. *The mythic image*. Princeton, NJ: Princeton University Press, 1974.

Dalley, T. (Ed.) *Art as therapy*. New York: Tavistock Publications, 1984.

Jung, C. G. A study in the process of individuation (1934). In *Mandala symbolism*. Princeton, NJ: Princeton University Press, 1972, pp. 6–70.

Jung, C. G. Concerning mandala symbolism (1950). In *Mandala symbolism*. Princeton, NJ: Princeton University Press, 1972, pp. 71–100.

Lyddiatt, E. M. *Spontaneous painting and modelling*. London: Constable & Co., 1971.

Kramer, E. *Art therapy in a children's community*. Springfield, IL: Charles C Thomas, 1958.

Kramer, E. *Art as therapy with children*. New York: Schocken Books, 1971.

Kramer, E. *Childhood and art therapy*. New York: Schocken Books, 1979.

Naumburg, M. Studies of the "free" art expression of behavior problem children and adolescents as a means of diagnosis and therapy. *Nervous and Mental Disease Monograph* No. 71, 1947 (2nd ed., *An introduction to art therapy*, New York: Teachers College Press, 1973).

Naumburg, M. *Schizophrenic art: Its meaning in psychotherapy*. New York: Grune & Stratton, 1950.

Naumburg, M. *Psychoneurotic art: Its function in psychotherapy*. New York: Grune & Stratton, 1953.

Naumburg, M. *Dynamically oriented art therapy: Its principles and practices*. New York: Grune & Stratton, 1966.

Neumann, E. *The archetypal world of Henry Moore*. New York: Pantheon Books, 1959.

1

Freudian Psychoanalytic Theory: Emphasis on Uncovering and Insight

Judith A. Rubin

Freud recognized early in his work that many of his patients' most important communications were descriptions of visual images. In fact, for several years he actively requested images, using what he called a "pressure" or "concentration" technique to evoke forgotten memories:

> I placed my hand on the patient's forehead or took her head between my hands and said: "You will think of it under the pressure of my hands. At the moment at which I relax my pressure you will see something in front of you or something will come into your head. Catch hold of it. It will be what we are looking for—well, what have you seen or what has occurred to you?" (Freud & Breuer, 1893–1895, p. 110).

Of one of his analysands, he said, "It was as though she were reading through a lengthy book of pictures" (*Ibid.*, p. 193). Even when he had abandoned this method in favor of free association, he couched his instructions in visual terms, asking the patient to "act as though you were a traveler sitting next to the window of a railway carriage and describing to someone inside the carriage the changing views which you see outside" (1913, p. 135). He cautioned his followers not "to deny that it is possible for thought-processes to become conscious through a reversion to visual residues, and that in many people this seems to be the favored method" (1923, p. 21).

It is well known that Freud's discovery of the importance of dream images as rich with meaning became the source of further developments in both theory and technique. Several years after he published his "dream book" (1900), he wrote a passage frequently quoted by pioneer art therapist Margaret Naumburg: "We experience it [a dream] predominantly in visual images. . . . Part of the difficulty of giving an account of dreams is due to our having to translate these images into words. 'I could draw it,' a dreamer often says to us, 'but I don't know how to say it'" (1916–1917, p. 90). As Naumburg was fond of pointing out, Freud did not pursue this notion by including drawing as part of classical technique, even though "the wolf-man," one of his analysands, did draw a dream during his treatment. What is not clear from the text is whether the patient produced the drawing spontaneously or at Freud's request: "He added a drawing of the tree with the wolves, which confirmed his description" (1918, p. 30).

Freud also reported a drawing by another famous patient, Little Hans— the first case of child analysis. After his father drew a picture of a giraffe, Hans made "a short stroke, and then added a bit more to it, remarking 'Its widdler's longer!'" (1905, p. 13, Fig. 1). Indeed, drawing and other creative media were, from the first, well accepted as part of child analytic technique. This was due primarily to what Anna Freud referred to as the "absence of the child's readiness for free association" (1927, p. 35). She went on to say: "A further technical aid, which besides the use of dreams and daydreams comes very much to the fore in many of my analyses of children, is drawing; in three of my cases this almost took the place of all other communications for some time" (*Ibid.*, p. 30). And, in a later book by a French analyst, there is a whole chapter on "the use of drawings as a technique in child psychoanalysis" (Rambert, 1949).

Despite the fact that child analysts were comfortable with art expression, few who treated adults utilized drawing or painting as part of classical analysis. There were, however, some notable exceptions. One was Marcinowski, who reportedly "studied dreams of his patients in connection with their pictorial representation" (Bychowski, 1947, p. 34). Another, Pfister, tried to "psychoanalyze an artist by means of free association to his own pictures, but had little success in treating this patient" (Naumburg, 1950, p. 12). He wrote enthusiastically, however, of his work with an 18-year-old who "presented a number of oil paintings and drawings which I, in accordance with good analytic procedure, had him at once exhibit and explain to me" (Pfister, 1917, p. 390). In fact, the analysis "dealt almost exclusively with drawings and poems" (*Ibid.*, p. 399).

In 1925 Nolan D. C. Lewis, an American psychiatrist/psychoanalyst, noted that "the interpretation of the art productions has long been recognized as part of the psychoanalytic technique" (p. 317). He also suggested that "frequently the basic unconscious difficulties of certain patients are through this manner of objectification brought to consciousness with greater facility than through dream analysis" (*Ibid.*). Lewis played a key role in the development of art therapy, since he was not only representative of those who saw art productions as relevant to psychoanalysis, but also facilitated the early clinical work of Margaret Naumburg, art therapy pioneer.

Throughout the thirties, forties, and fifties, there were individual clinicians who described the incorporation of art into psychoanalytic treatment. In some instances, drawings or paintings were offered spontaneously by the patient and utilized by the analyst (Bychowski, 1947; Hulse, 1949; Liss, 1936; Milner, 1969; Sechehaye, 1951). In others, analysts suggested that patients create art. Schilder, for example, engaged an artist to help patients draw pictures, which they then brought to group analytic sessions (Schilder & Levine, 1942). And Spitz hired an art teacher to help severely depressed, inhibited patients to create products, which they then brought to their analytic hours (Naumburg, 1966, p. 16; Spitz, 1954).

Some analysts even asked adults to work with art media in the treatment setting, like Mosse (1940), who encouraged patients in psychotherapy to fingerpaint and then associate to the pictures, or Auerbach (1950), who invited patients on the couch to doodle on a pad. Stern (1952), also doing classical analysis, encouraged a freely associative painting process at home. The paintings were then brought into analytic sessions for use in the treatment. And chances are that many an analyst has done what Slap recently reported: asking "a patient [to] draw a dream detail he is having trouble describing" (1976, p. 455).

The integration of Freudian insights about unconscious communication through imagery and the use of art in therapy was brought about, however, largely through the efforts of Margaret Naumburg. She began her long and productive career as an educator. In 1914, she founded Walden, a school that was based on psychoanalytic principles and emphasized the arts (Naumburg, 1928). She was also one of the first Americans to undergo analysis, working with both Jungian and Freudian analysts. She urged all of her teachers to be analyzed and insisted that the art expression of the children be as "spontaneous" as possible. She began her work during the early Freudian era of "id psychology," when "making the unconscious conscious" was seen as a primary therapeutic goal; the "release" of unconscious imagery was therefore central to her approach to art education as well as to her later development of art therapy.

Freud's earliest model of the mind was known as the "topographic" theory (cf. Gedo & Goldberg, 1973). As if the human mind were a geological entity, Freud postulated layers or levels of consciousness—from the deepest and most inaccessible (the unconscious), to that which is accessible but not in awareness (the preconscious), to that which is "on one's mind" (consciousness). Central to his theory was also the idea of the "id" as the source of repressed (forbidden) wishes (impulses, ideas). These impulses (the "instinctual drives") constantly strive for discharge (satisfaction) and are expressed in a disguised form, because only in that way can they bypass the "censor" (the force serving to keep unwelcome ideas out of awareness). The "compromise" effected by the "ego" consists of finding some way to satisfy or discharge the impulse, without offending either the environment (reality) or the individual's moral code ("superego"). This theory helped Freud to explain the compromises found in psychological symptoms, slips of the tongue, and the nightly reveries embodied in dreams.

The decoding of the wishes behind symbolic products was an especially fascinating enterprise for the early psychoanalysts, with all of the excitement of a voyage into unknown and potentially dangerous realms. No wonder so much of their time and interest centered on deciphering the messages sent by the mystical unconscious, through dreams and daydreams and images, all of which are largely visual. The first psychoanalytic therapists also modeled their work in part on Freud's earliest treatments, in which he strove for "catharsis," for the "abreaction" of "strangulated affect." Uncovering traumatic events that had been repressed ("making the unconscious conscious") was therefore thought to be the key to recovery from neurotic illness.

Margaret Naumburg, excited by the "spontaneous" art expressions of the young children at Walden, also felt liberated by her personal experience of psychoanalysis, which had included making pictures of her dreams and fantasies. It makes sense, therefore, that she saw "releasing" the repressed (unconscious) through imagery as curative, in a cathartic as well as a communicative sense. She was not alone in her enthusiasm for the healing potential of symbolic artistic expression. This conviction was shared by many analytic therapists (Arlow & Kadis, 1946; Baruch & Miller, 1951; Bender, 1952; Elkisch, 1948; Harms, 1948; Meares, 1958; Milner, 1957; Pickford, 1967; Sechehaye, 1951). Nor was she isolated in valuing the rich projective possibilities of art as a diagnostic tool, a conviction also shared by others (Alschuler & Hattwick, 1947; Bell, 1948; Elkisch, 1945, 1948; England, 1943; Harms, 1948; Hulse, 1952; Kadis, 1950; Machover, 1949; Schmidl-Waehner, 1946; Shaw, 1934).

Although Naumburg was not unique in her use of art for either diagnostic or therapeutic purposes, she was one of the few who stressed its role as a primary agent, rather than an auxiliary tool. A "critical incident" in the synthesis of art and psychoanalytic therapy took place some years after Naumburg had resigned from the directorship of Walden and had done some creative work of her own in art and poetry (Frank, 1984). She attended a meeting of occupational therapists, where she met Dr. Lewis, already cited as pioneering the use of art in psychoanalysis (Naumburg, 1975). He was most interested in her ideas about the potential of art in therapy. He encouraged her and provided a setting in which she could explore the use of art with disturbed youngsters—the New York State Psychiatric Institute, of which he was then the director. Naumburg subsequently published a series of case studies, in which she reviewed the literature on art in diagnosis and therapy and presented her work with the children. These were collected into a monograph (1947) and were followed by books on her work with schizophrenic (1950) and neurotic adolescents and adults (1953, 1966).

Naumburg called her approach "dynamically oriented art therapy," which meant one based primarily on Freudian understandings of psychological dynamics. She was also sympathetic to Jung's (1964) notions of universal symbolism (the "collective unconscious") and Sullivan's (1953) ideas about object relations, both of which she incorporated into her work. As an artist and a scholar, knowledgeable about many schools of thought regarding symbolism, she insisted that the only valid meaning of anyone's art was one which came from the person himself. She was skeptical about simplistic or rigid approaches to decoding symbolic meaning, a position that was consistent with Freud's teachings regarding dream analysis.

Most analysts still agree that the only valid way to understand the latent meaning of a dream is for the dreamer to associate as freely as possible to the dream and its elements (Altman, 1975). Only such idiosyncratic associations to the manifest content can lead to the hidden significance of the dream, disguised by what Freud called the "dream work" (e.g., symbolization, condensation, displacement, reversal, and other mechanisms of defense). In addition, most analysts believe that there are probably some symbols that have "universal" meanings. This appears to be true because certain symbols appear in so many cultures, usually referring to some property of the object or idea being represented. However, as Freud himself pointed out, "Sometimes a cigar is only a cigar," and one must learn to regard all such translations of symbolic meaning from manifest content as hypotheses, to be confirmed or refuted by the dreamer's own associations. More recently, attention has been paid by analysts to what can be learned from the manifest content of a dream, especially some of the formal (pictorial and spatial) elements (Erickson, 1954).

Naumburg modeled her approach to the use of art in therapy largely on what the psychoanalysts did. Technically, she attempted to stimulate free association, utilized then and now by most psychoanalytically trained clinicians. The technique grows logically out of Freud's theory of how the mind works, but it was also the method by which he made his discoveries (cf. A. Kris, 1982). As Lewis had described in his early (1925) paper on the use of art during psychoanalysis: "The drawing of the patient may be considered subject to an analytical attack similar to that employed in dealing with dream material, regardless of the nature of the releasing cause . . . " (p. 317).

In her role as a therapist who saw the patient's art as a form of "symbolic speech" (1955), Naumburg remained within the communicative framework of her more verbal model. In psychoanalysis or psychoanalytic therapy, the method is, first, for the patient to express himself as freely as possible. Then, both therapist and patient work together toward an understanding of what is interfering with the patient's ability to function more effectively, presumably internalized conflicts. An important tool in this kind of treatment is the transference: the symbolic ways in which the patient perceives and responds to the therapist. It helps both participants to identify distorted perceptions based on unresolved conflicts from the past.

The therapist helps the patient to understand and gain control over maladaptive patterns of thought and behavior by questions, clarifications, confrontations, and other forms of intervention—especially interpretations, in which connections are made explicit (Hammer, 1968). Psychoanalytic psychotherapy, then, has as its goals: first, uncovering repressed material (presumably internalized conflicts that are causing problems), and second, helping the patient to gain insight into the meaning of his behavior in terms of these formerly hidden ideas and feelings. If this process is lived through in a relationship charged with affective as well as cognitive meaning for the patient (the transference), he can be helped to change considerably, especially when the problem is a neurotic one (Brenner, 1976).

Naumburg had already demonstrated the intensity of her belief in Freudian theory by founding a school based on psychoanalytic principles. As someone who began my work many years later, I have often wondered why I have been so attracted to Freud's psychoanalytic theories and so interested in the direction first taken by Margaret Naumburg. Although I value and utilize other frames of reference in my work, I find the use of art in an insight-oriented approach to be the most powerful and exciting kind of art therapy for myself, as well as for most of my patients.

At this point, having spent almost a decade in classical psychoanalytic training, I am probably far from objective about the values of the theory. I continue to be excited by the developments in ego psychology, object relations, and self-psychology, as described in the other chapters in this section. But the organizing principle for most of my clinical work remains a psychoanalytic understanding of what is going on in the patient, from the point of view of both development and dynamics. Although few patients today fit a classical neurotic picture, these concepts are still clinically useful, as the following illustrations from art therapy with an adult indicate.

CASE EXAMPLE: MRS. L.

Some years ago, I had the opportunity to work with a young woman of 27, Mrs. L., in individual art therapy. A look at her first art session and at a later one may be helpful in illustrating how a psychoanalytic approach can facilitate understanding material and making technical decisions. She was invited to choose freely from among the available art media and to create whatever she wished. This is, like free association, an open, unstructured approach, designed to help patients to express what troubles them as freely as possible (Rubin, 1973). My minimal comments during her spontaneous verbalization were designed primarily to facilitate a comfortable flow of thought in words, as well as a relaxed process of creating with materials.

I listened to the patient's spontaneous remarks and observed her behavior. I asked only for specific "associations" to the art productions themselves, similar to what analysts often do with dreams. And, in making sense of the material, I thought in terms of the kinds of issues highlighted in a psychoanalytical diagnostic "profile" (A. Freud, 1965; Freud, Nagera, & Freud, 1965). Such a profile first notes the reason for referral, the history, and possible environmental stressors. In this case, the referral of Mrs. L. and her 4 ½-year-old daughter was prompted by a separation between the parents, followed by depressive symptomatology in the child. Mrs. L. also became increasingly anxious about her ability to parent either of her two children. The referral for art therapy came after two months of verbal therapy, in which she tended to deny all affects.

Although Mrs. L.'s depression and anxiety were clearly "reactive" to her situation, her unresolved conflicts and copying mechanisms had to be understood in order to help her to master the current stress. A psychoanalytic understanding includes not only the external "facts," but also an assessment of the internal "situation" of the patient, in regard to the developmental level at which the person is functioning (in terms primarily of libidinal and aggressive drive development and object relations), and whether there are any evident fixation points or regressions. And, since psychoanalysis is a psychology that assumes that unresolved conflict of some sort is at the root of most neurotic difficulty, potential sources of conflict are also examined. Conflict may be primarily with the external world (e.g., with other people), "internal" within the individual (e.g., ambivalence), or "internalized" in a structural sense (e.g., between or within one of the metaphorical parts of the mind—id, ego, or superego). In order to determine the person's potential for psychoanalytic therapy, attention is also given to frustration tolerance, sublimation potential, overall attitude to anxiety, and the general picture of progressive forces versus regressive tendencies.

In an oversimplified sense, a psychoanalytic understanding helps the therapist to know *where* an individual is "stuck" developmentally and gives clues about *what* is being defended against (feared impulses) and *how* (favored coping and defense mechanisms). Mrs. L.'s first art session will be examined psychoanalytically, in order to translate some of this terminology into the clinical "data" of art therapy. As in all forms of dynamic therapy, initial hypotheses need to be continually tested and revised in the light of further emergent material, as will become apparent when we review a later session with the same patient.

Mrs. L.'s First Art Session

Mrs. L. nervously selected 12″ × 18″ white drawing paper and thin chalk and proceeded to draw a vase filled with flowers of different colors (Figure 1). While she worked, she alternated between voicing concern about her picture (confessing that she had practiced drawing at home) and commenting on her good grades in art being due to the teacher's clear directions. Although critical of her product, calling it "terrible" and "lopsided," she was able to look at it on the easel and react to it associatively. She said she loved flowers, loved both growing and arranging them, and that in this interest as in all ways, she was "just like" her mother. Focusing on the red flowers, she said she liked red roses, but that they gave her a sad feeling because they reminded her of a hospital.

Her second drawing was a "scribble," suggested by me because of her intense discomfort about what to choose and to make in the time remaining. She said it reminded her of a "rolled-up wire fence" (Figure 2). She then tearfully recalled the times she had fenced her children in during the past summer. This was necessary, she said, in order for her to accomplish all the chores falling on her shoulders since the separation, such as mowing and caring for the lawn. She confessed that she had feared my disapproval of her use of the fencing. Although she asserted its necessity, she clearly felt guilty and was openly worried about having harmed her daughter. She was visibly relieved and ready to leave at the end of her first 45-minute art therapy session. She had behaved throughout the interview in a fairly controlled way, consistent with the description of the

Figure 1

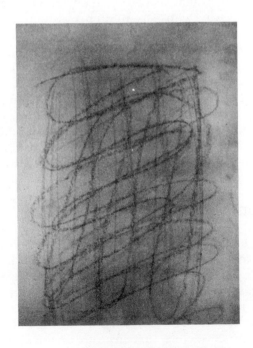

Figure 2

referring psychiatrist, that she was highly defended against feelings and ideas that might be threatening.

A psychoanalytic understanding of the communications (both verbal and nonverbal) of any patient, even in the first session, involves the notion of *transference*: the projection by the patient onto the therapist of ideas, feelings, and expectations stemming from unresolved past conflicts. I therefore "heard" Mrs. L.'s comments about the art teacher who gave good directions as an indirect rebuke to me for not telling her what to make and thus making her feel inadequate. She let me know what she wanted from me—clear directions about what to do—and also what she expected—criticism. I heard her critical comments about her product as an expression of negative feelings about herself, an indication of little healthy narcissism. I also heard them as a clue to the existence of a severe, punitive superego.

Mrs. L.'s initial associations to the superficially pleasant manifest content of her drawing—that she "loved" growing and arranging flowers— paralleled her surface presentation of herself as smiling, in charge, and pleased with life. Her statement that she was, in this, as in all else "just like" her mother, suggested possible problems with separation and individuation. The psychoanalytic theory regarding the "repetition-compulsion" also led me to assume that her own unresolved problems would be replayed in some way with her children (Anthony & Benedek, 1970; Brocher, 1971).

Manifest art content and initial associations are, like the manifest dream, a deceptive disguise for a less obvious (latent) meaning (cf. Vaccaro, 1973). Mrs. L.'s subsequent associations to red roses and the sad feeling they gave her, along with her allusion to a hospital, was her first (indirect) communication of her own (masked) depression. It wasn't clear *who* might be ill, e.g., whether this association indicated anxiety over her own health— now that she had been abandoned—or a worried (disguised) hostility toward someone else (mother? husband? children?). However, it appeared that behind the cheerful smile on her face and the colorful stereotyped flowers in the vase lay a good deal of anxiety, suggesting her use of reaction-formation as a defense.

When Mrs. L. blocked, unable to choose or to initiate a second creation, I understood that event in terms of the psychoanalytic assumption of "psychic determinism" and the consequent notion that any series of behaviors (thoughts, words, actions, art) is linked in some meaningful way. Her blocking was similar to a child's "play disruption" (Erikson, 1950), an indication that the anxiety aroused (presumably by the discussion of flowers, sadness, and hospitals) was sufficient to interfere with her associative processes (e.g., to constitute an unconscious *resistance*).

I therefore suggested a "scribble drawing," which offers the patient his own unstructured stimulus upon which to project further imagery, an approach developed independently by a child analyst (Winnicott, 1971) and a therapeutic art teacher with a Jungian orientation (Cane, 1951). Margaret Naumburg welcomed this approach to projection developed by her sister (the art teacher), since it could help to "release" that imagery felt to be dormant in the artist's unconscious (Naumburg, 1966). Mrs. L. labeled her rapidly drawn image a "rolled-up wire fence." My first thought was of how tightly "wound" she herself seemed to be, tensely controlling her feelings. This idea, surfacing from my own "evenly hovering attention," seemed related to her subsequent associations to the fencing in of her children during the summer so that she could work in the yard. Her openly expressed anxiety about my disapproval, and her fear that she might be responsible for her daughter's depression, were further indications of a severe superego and strong sense of guilt. That she would see herself as harmful suggested that her earlier associations to the roses of sickness and death may have stemmed from unconscious death wishes toward primary objects, perhaps her mother whom she had mentioned previously as identical to herself. This, in turn, suggested the possibility that she used identification as a defense, something that emerged later in therapy in regard to her hostility toward her daughter.

Despite a defensive idealization of me as a "good mother," Mrs. L. was able to use weekly art therapy to explore her feelings of rage and hurt toward both her parents and her husband, as well as to accept her ambivalence toward her children. She soon became able to use her artwork as a valuable source of information about herself. During most sessions, like the one to be described, she would work almost casually with the materials—preconsciously it seemed—while telling me the significant events of the previous week. Then she would put her picture on the easel and look at it with interest, curiosity, and a desire to learn from it, often regarding it with puzzlement, as if it had come from elsewhere.

Mrs. L.'s Penultimate Art Session (After 10 Months of Treatment)

Mrs. L. chose to use acrylic paints, putting them directly onto a small (9″ × 12″) canvas with a palette knife. As she spoke of her current concerns, including sadness about termination, she made a series of separate oval shapes, some green and some yellow. As if she were regressing to her earlier dependent behavior, she asked if it would be "all right to mix the colors together." Reminded that she could do whatever she wished, she mixed them first slowly, then vigorously, smearing almost the entire surface, creating a large mass of thick yellow-green paint. She finished by painting a solid white border surrounding the mass, effectively "containing" it (Figure 3).

As was characteristic by then, she was sure she was finished, and she placed the painting on the easel where we both looked at it. Her first thought was of the ocean, and her spontaneous title was "Sea Mist." She was surprised by her association and went on to say that she doesn't *like* the sea, that she's afraid to go in the water, afraid of fish, a fear she can't seem to conquer. "Whenever . . . anything brushes my leg, I really, you know, go crazy! Jellyfish, shark—what is it?" Laughing nervously, she went on to talk of her fear of horses, and of being bitten by a dog, recalling that she'd grown up "in a neighborhood with a lot of vicious dogs" and reflecting that so many of her problems go back to her childhood. She returned to her fear of swimming in the sea and being bitten by a shark. When asked how she felt about the picture, she called it "a big round blob," and said—as she often did in regard to her artwork—"I don't know how it got like that. I didn't intend for it to be like that." Again, she said the painting reminded her of the sea, of "ripples in the water," and that "it looks kind of *wild*, but I don't think I *intended* for it to be." She said she was thinking of "something calmer," that "the sea is kind of peace-

Figure 3

Figure 4

ful,'' and that she likes wide-open spaces. ''I don't like congestion, you
know, or being congested or hindered in any way.''

She then decided to do another picture, this time using her by-then-
favorite medium, thick poster chalk on a small 9'' × 12'' piece of white
paper (Figure 4). While she drew rapidly, she spoke of her plan to take
art classes after termination. Looking at her picture on the easel, she first
thought that it looked ''like something you'd see under a microscope, like
an amoeba. . . . It looks like it might just be a watery mass around it, as
if you're taking something out of water and putting it under a microscope,
although the water isn't brown, unless it's very muddy water.''

At this point she paused for a long time, and as she seemed to be
blocked, I asked: ''If they were people, who would they be?'' She laughed,
and said, ''Here we go—three again! I always end up with three shapes
of some kind. I don't know why that is. I do that very unconsciously, but
for some reason or other, it always ends up that way. Oh well, I guess
that's me in the middle again. That always seems to be me in the middle.''
She identified the shape below as her daughter and the one above as her
son, saying that it looked like she was ''trying to protect'' her little girl,
probably because ''she *feels* things'' more than the boy.

Mrs. L. then spoke of her daughter as sensitive and fearful, especially at night, and told how last night she couldn't sleep because "she kept visualizing a man crawlin' up on a ladder to her bedroom, or to my bedroom." She named the picture "Mother Love." She then thought of how the child would ruminate obsessively about fears, and how she does that too; but that "I try to push it out of my mind, like I do anything that I'm afraid of." I wondered if all of this imagery about fear of attack (sharks, dogs, male intruders) was in any way related to the impending termination and her anxiety about being more vulnerable, less "protected" (as she saw herself protecting her daughter). Mrs. L. agreed that, although she tends to try to deny or disavow her anxiety, it was heightened by anticipating the separation from her therapist.

Mrs. L.'s artwork from this later session is more directly reflective of her impulses than that from the first one, in the process employed and in her associations to both products. Her surprise in response to both pictures and associations reflects her enhanced ability not only to express herself more freely, but also to acknowledge some of the affect involved in what she sees and thinks. Her "observing ego" is stronger, enabling her to "see" more frightening imagery, as well as to acknowledge uncomfortable feelings like sadness and anxiety in response to termination. Her anger was less accessible to her in this session than in others, perhaps because her hostility toward me at that time was too frightening to contemplate. I had the sense that she was expressing it indirectly through the aggressive smearing of the acrylic paint, which she saw as "breaking" some kind of "rule" (not to mix colors), as well as in her choice of brown and black chalk for the second picture, first seen as dirty, "muddy water."

Although she rarely worked representationally, she enjoyed projecting images onto what she had created and was often excited and surprised by what she "saw." This viewing of an image—which she realized came from within herself—had the affectively charged quality of what Kris (1956) has called "id insight." Such discoveries of something about the self are seen as critical in psychoanalytic treatment (Shapiro, 1976). Although many question whether insight alone is sufficient for healing, its value in conjunction with affective experiences and a sense of conviction is acknowledged by all analysts (Freud, Kennedy, Neubauer, & Blum, 1980).

CONCLUSION

Having worked in a variety of modes with a variety of patients over the past 10 years—ranging from strictly verbal adult psychoanalysis, to the use of art in adult analysis, to child analysis where art is frequent, to art therapy with adults and children—I am convinced that art can greatly enhance the analytic experience of insight ("seeing in"). This is probably true because art is concrete and visual, in addition to its value in "uncovering" unconscious imagery stressed by Naumburg. The psychoanalytic approach to art therapy, in the hands of a trained clinician, offers an extremely rich vehicle for change with many patients. My own conviction, by the way, shared by most practitioners trained in the Freudian tradition, is that classical psychoanalysis is neither appropriate nor necessary for most, but that the theory which informs it is useful in understanding and guiding all therapeutic work, whether the clinician behaves in a supportive/ego-building or in an interpretive/uncovering manner.

In psychoanalytic art therapy, it is often necessary to shift one's stance as a therapist, sometimes supporting defenses, at other times analyzing them. The shifts are often rapid and the relevant cues subtle, so that it is necessary to be flexible in one's clinical behavior, within certain stable conditions—what has been referred to as the "frame" (Langs, 1979) or "framework" (Rubin, 1984). However one conceptualizes that constant, dependable "holding environment" (Winnicott, 1971), it does not mean rigidity. Rather, in psychoanalytic art therapy, the clinician shifts his/her stance in accord with what he/she perceives as most needed by that particular patient at that moment in time.

For example, I have found myself recently recommending the "least restrictive" (most facilitating, least intrusive) intervention as a way of helping a patient who, in some way, indicates a need for the activity of the therapist. For a person who is stuck, like Mrs. L. in her first session, I might suggest a "scribble drawing," or perhaps a series of images, done as freely as possible (Rubin, 1981), thus lending my "auxiliary ego" to the patient's blocked efforts at expression. On the other hand, if it seemed that the person might be able to handle a more insight-oriented approach, I might wonder what in the previous image or associations could have led to the current "disruption" (e.g., analyzing the resistance).

Similarly, if a patient were producing chaotic imagery, I would probably try to find some way to help him sort out and organize his confused images (e.g., supporting defenses). I might suggest that he frame and view one image at a time, or that he select several to put together in a more related fashion in a new picture. If that person was generally able to function at a higher level, however, and the confusion seemed a momentary response to stress, I might ask him to stop and to consider just what in the preceding images or statements had created tension.

In either case, I would be lending my support where it seemed most critical—either intervening constructively in the creative/expressive process or, where appropriate, inviting the patient's "observing ego" to look with me at what was happening in order to better understand it. In both, I would try to understand the blocking or the regression from a psychoanalytic perspective and would intervene in such a way as to provide what seemed most useful therapeutically to that patient at that particular moment in time.

In that regard, as in most issues one faces in conducting diagnosis or therapy through art, the psychoanalytic approach to understanding and to intervening has been most helpful to me. Although an art therapist cannot possibly behave in the passive, neutral manner of a classical analyst, I have come to feel that in most cases sufficient neutrality for a transference to develop is helpful, whether or not one chooses to analyze it with the patient (Rubin, 1984). And, as psychoanalysts have stressed (Greenspan, 1965; Zetzel, 1956), an "alliance" with the patient is essential to good therapeutic work, something as true for art therapy as for analysis. Both the patient and his art have become less mysterious, the more I have understood of psychoanalytic theory over time. I have no question that the training has made me a more effective art therapist than would have been possible without it.

REFERENCES

Alschuler, R., & Hattwick, L. W. *Painting and personality*, Vols. 1 & 2. Chicago: University of Chicago Press, 1947 (rev. ed. 1969).

Altman, L. L. *The dream in psychoanalysis*, rev. ed. New York: International Universities Press, 1975.

Anthony, E. J., & Benedek, T. *Parenthood: Its psychology and psychopathology*. Boston: Little, Brown & Co., 1970.

Arlow, J. A., & Kadis, A. Fingerpainting in psychotherapy with children. *American Journal of Orthopsychiatry*, 1946, *16*, 134–146.

Auerbach, J. G. Psychological observations on "doodling" in neurotics. *Journal of Nervous & Mental Disease*, 1950, *3*, 304–332.

Baruch, D. W., & Miller, H. The use of spontaneous drawings in group therapy. *American Journal of Psychotherapy*, 1951, *5*, 45–58.

Bell, J. E. *Projective techniques: A dynamic approach to the study of the personality*. New York: Longmans Green, 1948.

Bender, L. (Ed.) *Child psychiatric techniques*. Springfield, IL. Charles C Thomas, 1952.

Brenner, C. *Psychoanalytic technique and psychic conflict*. New York: International Universities Press, 1976.

Brocher, T. Parents' schools. *Psychiatric Communication* (WPIC), 1971, *13*, 1–9.

Bychowski, G. The rebirth of a woman. *Psychoanalytic Review*, 1947, *34*, 32–57.

Cane, F. *The artist in each of us*. 1951, Reprint Craftsbury Common, VT: Art Therapy Publications, 1983.

Elkisch, P. Children's drawings in a projective technique. *Psychological Monographs*, 1945, *50*, #1.

Elkisch, P. The scribbling game—A projective method. *Nervous Child*, 1948, 7, 247–256.

England, A. O. A psychological study of children's drawings: Comparison of public school, retarded, institutionalized and delinquent children's drawings. *American Journal of Orthopsychiatry*, 1943, *13*, 525–531.

Erikson, E. H. *Childhood and society*. New York: Norton, 1950.

Erikson, E. H. The dream specimen of psychoanalysis. In Knight, R. P., & Friedman, C. R. (Eds.) *Psychoanalysis, psychiatry, and psychology*. New York: International Universities Press, 1954, 131–171.

Frank, T. Margaret Naumburg, pioneer art therapist. A son's perspective. *American Journal of Art Therapy*, 1984, *22*, 112–115.

Freud, A. *Normality and pathology in childhood. Assessments of development*. New York: International Universities Press, 1965.

Freud, A. The methods of child analysis. In "Four lectures on child analysis." (1927). *The writings of Anna Freud, Vol. 1*. New York: International Universities Press, 1974, 19–35.

Freud, A., Kennedy, H., Neubauer, P., & Blum, H. P. Papers on: The role of insight in psychoanalysis and psychotherapy. In Blum, H. P. (Ed.) *Psychoanalytic explorations of technique: Discourse on the theory of therapy*. New York: International Universities Press, 1980, 3–69.

Freud, A., Nagera, H., & Freud, W. E. Metapsychological assessment of the adult personality. The adult profile. *Psychoanalytic Study of the Child*, 1965, *20*, 9–41.

Freud, S. *The interpretation of dreams* (1900). Standard edition, Vols. 4–5, London: Hogarth Press, 1955.

Freud, S. *Analysis of a phobia in a five year-old-boy* (1905). Standard edition, Vol. 10, London: Hogarth Press, 1955, 3–149.

Freud, S. *On beginning the treatment* (1913). Standard edition, Vol. 12, London: Hogarth Press, 123–144.

Freud, S. *Introductory lectures on psycho-analysis* (1916–1917). Standard edition, Vol. 12, London: Hogarth Press.

Freud, S. *From the history of an infantile neurosis* (1918). Standard edition, Vol. 17, London: Hogarth Press, 1955, 3–124.

Freud, S. *The ego and the id* (1923). Standard edition, Vol. 19, London: Hogarth Press, 1964.

Freud, S., & Breuer, J. *Studies in hysteria* (1893–1895). Standard edition, Vol. 2, London: Hogarth Press, 1955.

Gedo, J. E., & Goldberg, A. *Models of the mind: A psychoanalytic theory*. Chicago: University of Chicago Press, 1973.

Greenspan, R. R. The working allliance and the transference neurosis. *Psychoanalytic Quarterly*, 1965, *34*, 155–181.

Hammer, E. (Ed.) *Use of interpretation in treatment: Technique and art*. New York: Grune & Stratton, 1968.

Harms, E. Play diagnosis. *Nervous Child*, 1948, 7, 233–246.

Hulse, W. C. Symbolic painting in psychotherapy. *American Journal of Psychotherapy*, 1949, *3*, 559–584.

Hulse, W. C. Childhood conflict expressed through family drawings. *Journal of Projective Techniques*, 1952, *16*, 66–79.

Jung, C. G. *Man and his symbols*. New York: Doubleday, 1964.

Kadis, A. L. Finger-painting as a projective technique. In Abt, E. L., & Bellack, L. (Eds.) *Projective psychology*. New York: Knopf, 1950, 403–431.

Kris, A. O. *Free association: Method and process*. New Haven, CT: Yale University Press, 1982.

Kris, E. On some vicissitudes of insight in psychoanalysis. *International Journal of Psychoanalysis*, 1956, *37*, 445–455.

Langs, R. J. *The therapeutic environment*. New York: Aronson, 1979.

Lewis, N. D. C. The practical value of graphic art in personality studies. *Psychoanalytic Review*, 1925, *12*, 316–322.

Liss, E. Play techniques in child analysis. *American Journal of Orthopsychiatry*, 1936, *6*, 17–22.

Machover, K. *Personality projection in the drawing of the human figure*. Springfield, IL: Charles C Thomas, 1949.

Meares, A. *The door of serenity*. London: Faber & Faber, 1958.

Milner, M. *On not being able to paint*. New York: International Universities Press, 1957.

Milner, M. *The hands of the living god*. New York: International Universities Press, 1969.

Mosse, E. P. Painting analyses in the treatment of neuroses. *Psychoanalytic Review*, 1940, *27*, 65–81.

Naumburg, M. *The child and the world*. New York. Harcourt, Brace, 1928.

Naumburg, M. *Schizophrenic art: Its meaning in psychotherapy*. New York: Grune & Stratton, 1950.

Naumburg, M. *Psychoneurotic art: Its function in psychotherapy*. New York: Grune & Stratton, 1953.

Naumburg, M. Art as symbolic speech. *Journal of Aesthetics and Art Criticism*, 1955, *12*, 435–450.

Naumburg, M. *Dynamically oriented art therapy: Its principles and practices*. New York: Grune & Stratton, 1966.

Naumburg, M. Studies of the "free" art expression of behavior problem children and adolescents as a means of diagnosis and therapy. *Nervous and Mental Disease Monograph*, 1947, No. 17 (2nd ed.: *An introduction to art therapy*. New York: Teachers College Press, 1973).

Naumburg, M. Unpublished Transcript, "Interview with Judith Rubin" for film *Art Therapy: Beginnings*, 1975 (American Art Therapy Association).

Pfister, O. Analysis of artistic production (1913). In *The psychoanalytic method*. New York: Moffat, Yard, 1917.

Pickford, R. W. *Studies in psychiatric art*. Springfield, IL: Charles C Thomas, 1967.

Rambert, M. Drawings as a method in child psychoanalysis. In *Children in conflict*. New York: International Universities Press, 1949, 173–190.

Rubin, J. A. A diagnostic art interview. *Art Psychotherapy*, 1973, *1*, 31–43.

Rubin, J. A. Art and imagery: Free association with art media. In DiMaria, A. E. (Ed.) *Art therapy: A bridge between worlds*. Falls Church, VA: American Art Therapy Association, 1981.

Rubin, J. A. *The art of art therapy*. New York: Brunner/Mazel, 1984.

Schilder, P., & Levine, E. L. Abstract art as an expression of human problems. *Journal of Nervous & Mental Disease*, 1942, *95*, 1–10.

Schmidl-Waehner, R. Interpretation of spontaneous drawings and paintings. *Genetic Psychology Monographs*, 1946, *33*, 3–70.

Sechehaye, M. *Symbolic realization*. New York: International Universities Press, 1951.

Shapiro, S. L. *Moments of insight*. New York: International Universities Press, 1976.

Shaw, R. F. *Finger painting*. Boston: Little, Brown & Co., 1934.

Slap, J. W. A note on the drawing of dream details. *Psychoanalytic Quarterly,* 1976, *45,* 455–456.

Spitz, R. Review of *Psychoneurotic art* by M. Naumburg. *Psychoanalytic Quarterly,* 1954, *23,* 279–282.

Stern, M. M. Free painting as an auxiliary technique in psychoanalysis, In Bychowski, G. & Despert, L. (Eds.) *Specialized techniques in psychotherapy.* New York: Basic Books, 1952.

Sullivan, H. S. *The interpersonal theory of psychiatry.* New York: W. W. Norton, 1953.

Vaccaro, V. M. Specific aspects of the psychology of art therapy. *Art Psychotherapy,* 1973, *1,* 81–89.

Winnicott, D. W. *Therapeutic consultations in child psychiatry.* New York: Basic Books, 1971.

Zetzel, E. R. Correct concepts of transference. *International Journal of Psychoanalysis,* 1956, *37,* 369–376.

2

Sublimation and Art Therapy

Edith Kramer

My understanding of the process of sublimation is based on Freudian psychoanalytic thinking. It has been broadened and confirmed by the study of the findings of ethologists, in particular by the writing of Konrad Lorenz, and by clinical observations made in the course of my work as an art therapist.

According to Freudian psychoanalytic theory, we use the term *sublimation* to designate processes whereby primitive urges emanating from the id are transformed by the ego into complex acts that do not serve direct instinctual gratification. In the course of this transformation primitive behavior, necessarily asocial, gives way to activities that are ego-syntonic and are also as a rule *socially productive* although they may not always be *socially acceptable*. We need only to recall the fate of Socrates, Rembrandt, Freud, and innumerable others to realize how frequently achievements that undoubtedly came about through processes of sublimation were rejected by society.

Sublimation is no simple mental act; it embraces a multitude of mechanisms. These include displacement, symbolization, neutralization of drive energy, identification, and integration. Always there is a threefold change: of the object upon which interest centers, of the desired goal, and of the kind of energy through which the new goal is attained. Sublimation invariably implies some element of renunciation. Yet sublimation somehow remains so linked to the urges that set the process in motion that the individual attains through it at least partial gratification and partial relief

Parts of this chapter have been published in a different context in *Art as Therapy with Children* by Edith Kramer (New York: Schocken Books, 1971) and in *Childhood and Art Therapy: Notes on Theory and Application* by Edith Kramer in collaboration with Laurie Wilson (New York: Schocken Books, 1979). Reproduced by permission of the publisher.

from the pressure of these libidinal and aggressive drives. Inasmuch as sublimation implies postponement of instinctual gratification and channeling of drive energy, we can perceive it as one of the mechanisms of defense. Implied in this concept is the awareness that man's instincts are in a state of disarray, so that they can no longer be relied on to safely regulate behavior.

We assume that the atrophy of the instinctive programming that largely regulates the behavior of the lower species occurred in conjunction with and as a consequence of the advent of the faculty for conceptual thinking. This enabled man to judge situations on their own merit, rendering the more global do's and don't's of the ancient instinctual organization obsolete. Psychoanalytic psychology also assumes that the dissolution of this mindless (yet exquisitely balanced) organization has brought into existence the accumulation of unregulated forces with undifferentiated libidinal and aggressive energies pushing toward immediate discharge, oblivious of time, place, and circumstance, in nonrational, potentially lethal behavior.

Man's survival as a species thus depended on the concomitant advent of a new psychic organization holding the key to all goal-directed behavior, capable of taming and directing drive energy. This new organization, the ego, constitutes man's indispensable organ of survival. Infinitely more flexible and efficient, it is also more fragile and less dependable than the ancient instinctive programming it supplants.

Inasmuch as we are still inclined to describe unbridled, impulse-ridden behavior as animal-like, we adhere to obsolete, nineteenth-century notions about the nature of animals. The uninhibited human seeking immediate gratification is actually further removed from our nonhuman ancestors than is civilized man. The healthy animal functioning in its natural habitat does not eat, mate, or fight incessantly and indiscriminately. Instead, behavior is very precisely regulated to assure that the right thing is likely to occur at the right time under the right circumstances with the right partner. Even though animal behavior must be aimed toward essential consummatory goals, such as mating or ingesting food or protecting offspring, it consists in the main of a multitude of preparatory activities. Each of these must command energy commensurate with the work to be accomplished by it, and evidently much more energy must be expended in preparatory behavior than in consummatory acts.

As the ego replaces instinctive programming, an analogous redistribution of drive energy must be achieved. Within the array of mechanisms that effect this redistribution, often at the price of much psychic suffering, sublimation stands apart by its unequaled economy. The amount of energy lost in unproductive maneuvers is exceptionally small and the pleasure generated in the new activity exceptionally great. The question arises:

How can pleasure be experienced in acts that depend on the inhibition of drive gratification, which indeed are instrumental in inhibiting it? How can complex, demanding, often farfetched substitute activities afford pleasure that is at all comparable to the pleasure of immediate fulfillment of passionate physical and emotional urges? Can we find any analogous mechanisms among the lower species?

Ethology teaches us that in the parliament of instincts that govern the life of animals, arbitrary—even nonsensical—kinds of behavior may attain key positions, endowed with absolute power over the release or inhibition of essential acts. This occurs particularly in relation to social behavior such as mating, rearing of young, and control of intraspecific aggression, where each species can evolve reliable signals for releasing or inhibiting behavior along with the corresponding faculty to react to them. I suggest that certain behavior that has evolved within this realm is analogous to some aspects of the mechanism of sublimation in man. All these behaviors evolved in the service of social cohesion. For even though much social signaling unrolls automatically, it is in this area that we first encounter behavior that seems to be accompanied by subjective experiences that may be analogous to man's emotions of pleasure and grief.

According to Konrad Lorenz (1966), the capacity to experience subjective states of mind, in which attention is passionately directed toward a limited number of specific individuals, has evolved only among those species which, in the course of evolution, resolved the following dilemma: how to form individual bonds among sexual mates and conspecifics such as offspring, leaders, or companions, even though the inclination to act aggressively against other conspecifics persists. Aggressive energy is not reduced, since it is essential for survival that each individual shall remain ready and eager to vigorously defend its companion against hostile conspecifics as well as against other intruders.

Konrad Lorenz describes the greeting ceremonial among friendly individuals of the Anatidae family (ducks, geese, swans) as a classical example of the successful solution of this problem. The pattern consists of an initial threatening gesture performed by the stronger and more aggressive partner that corresponds to one which would ordinarily initiate a serious battle. The gesture is, however, pointedly redirected past the friend and against another bird, a person, an inanimate object such as a twig, or even into empty space. After a real or fictitious victory, the bird turns to its partner, greeting it loudly and triumphantly, whereupon the partner joins in the celebration. The greater the social cohesiveness of a particular species, the less the need for an actual enemy in order for the greeting ceremony to be successfully completed. In the more fully socialized species, where the enemy may become entirely fictitious, the gestures of the redirected attack are correspondingly more ceremonial— exaggerated, abbreviated, or both, so that they lose their practical usefulness in favor of their function as social signals.

The behavior constitutes a bond between the partners. It is charged with emotions analogous to the pleasures of friendship and of love. Correspondingly, the loss of the partner causes emotions analogous to grief. And so we find that ritualized behavior that has no immediate practical value can become an end in itself, charged with pleasures that are independent of the gratification of simple biological needs. These pleasures came into existence in conjunction with actions that had the function of establishing cohesive social behavior, without loss of sexual and aggressive energy. These actions entailed a reversal of meaning, so that an originally asocial aggressive act becomes a component part of an act of love and friendship. The change of meaning came about through the confluence of two contradictory instinctive tendencies: on the one hand, *mutual antagonism* between members of the same species in the service of equitable distribution of territory, and on the other, *mutual attraction* in the service of procreation. Behavior originally evolved to serve practical purposes acquired new functions. This came about through change of direction, ritualization, and ceremonial abbreviations and exaggerations. The intensity and frequency with which such behavior occurs and the entirely new kind of rewards and punishment it offers through subjective feelings of joy and grief are a measure of the enormous amount of energy that must be expended to establish and maintain social cohesion.

That analogous behavior patterns came into existence among territorial fish, social birds, and socially living mammals testifies to the effectiveness of these mechanisms. We find that nothing we have described runs counter to the mechanisms we associate with the idea of sublimation. But naturally there are fundamental differences. Animal behavior is genetically determined while sublimation is achieved by the individual. Furthermore, sublimation entails partial renunciation of simple drive gratification. In nonhuman beings, which are not pressured by drives that demand immediate gratification, there exists neither the need for renunciation nor a psychic apparatus comparable to man's ego that could bring it about. Also, even though we find among animals behavior that has the power to influence the partner or the group, these actions do not carry symbolic meaning. They remain signals. Behavior and message are identical, response is automatic, and there is no leeway for individual inventions. Modifications of behavior occur only through the evolution of new species.

In contrast, sublimation entails establishing a *symbolic linkage* between some primitive need and another more complex cluster of ideas and actions. This presupposes the capacity to evoke ideas and perceive analogies, a faculty involving both primary- and secondary-process thinking. The ability to perceive analogies belongs to primary-process thinking. As secondary-process thinking takes over, symbolic representations lose their protean, driven quality and become stable. Imagination replaces fantasy. We must presume that the faculties of primary-process and secondary-process mental functioning, as well as the capacity of conceptual thinking, evolved simultaneously and interdependently. Evidently, sublimation in the full sense of the word could not occur among any species lacking these mental faculties.

However, we discern among the lower species certain phenomena sufficiently analogous to sublimation to assure us that the process as we conceive of it is not totally without precedent and does not constitute a biological impossibility. It seems reasonable to postulate: that man's subjective experiences can be linked to the physiological process of tension reduction; that actions which are linked only by a long chain of modification to the gratifications of basic urges can have the power to generate emotions of pleasure and pain, and to reduce tension; and that man's biological heritage includes the faculty to channel considerable energies into such processes.

SUBLIMATION IN ART THERAPY

Sublimation is not limited to the arts. A ubiquitous process, it permeates man's entire life. In this presentation, however, we must focus on sublimation as we observe it in the course of art therapy. We must distinguish sublimation from catharsis, from simple displacement, and from the highly sexualized and/or aggressively charged imagery that we encounter in the art work of psychotics.

Catharsis

When Mrs. Smith, after a day's vacation, found the cottage where she worked as a house parent in an unbelievable mess, she relieved her feelings by covering a white paper entirely with red paint. She then painted a tiny figure with hands upraised in despair on the bottom of the page. After she finished, she had calmed herself sufficiently to resume her duties. Mrs. Smith had found a symbol for her situation: the white sheet of paper upon which the symbol of her all-pervasive rage, the red color, was spread. She had experienced the relief that catharsis affords the strong individual who, after such an outburst, is able to return to the task at hand in an invigorated mood.

Failure of Neutralization

When 20-year-old Jim, an ambulatory paranoid psychotic, attempted to draw a tomato using colored pencils, it took on an unmistakably breast-like shape rendered sinister by a dark, blood-red spot that gave the impression of a wound or bruise. The product told of his longing for nurturance, of the pressure of his sexuality, of sadistic perception of the sexual act, and of his anxiety. The picture remained unfinished and appeared misshapen, an unsuccessful attempt at displacement. Sublimation was not attained.

Sublimation Induced and Supported

Sublimation is a complex process requiring a modicum of ego strength and intelligence, yet with some assistance, 18-year-old Jack, an educable retarded man, was able to experience the power of sublimation during a memorable art therapy session. When Jack was informed that his favorite art therapy student would leave the program before his birthday, he stormed out of the art room in a rage. After a little while he returned and began systematically and angrily to tear up a stack of drawing paper, one by one. Thereupon the chief art therapist took the two halves of a torn sheet and commented, "Now you made two sheets. Will you give me one of them as a present?" Jack was startled. His eyes lit up. He laboriously printed the art therapist's initials on one half of the torn sheet and his initials on the other half, and proffered the half that was inscribed with her initials to the art therapist.

He then began to ask all the people in the room for their initials. He tore paper into even smaller pieces, printed initials onto each of these fragments and proudly went around distributing the many gifts to everyone in sight. His mood had changed dramatically. He had found a way of continuing to give symbolic vent to his pain about being torn from his beloved art therapist. He was still tearing paper; however, he was no longer only destroying it, but was also making more of it. And he was working very hard—as the task of remembering the many initials and of forming the letters was taxing his limited intelligence to the utmost. The episode lasted for approximately 20 minutes, until the end of the session. The next day, however, left to himself, Jack broke a number of clay pieces he had made with the student's help. Without continual support, sublimation could not be maintained.

Sublimation and Other Mechanisms of Defense *

Faced with anxiety and emotional turbulence, the ego is likely to mobilize a variety of defenses. Thus, more often than not, sublimation emerges in conjunction with other defensive mechanisms.

Eight-year-old Kenny had sustained second-degree burns on his back, neck, and hands, requiring plastic surgery. A fire had broken out while his mother had absented herself from home for two days, leaving him and his two younger siblings unattended. She was subsequently charged with criminal neglect. After his physical recovery, Kenny was admitted to the child psychiatric ward for observation. An art therapy evaluation session was held as part of the psychological workup.

The session was conducted by the ward's art therapist, whom Kenny had met previously. Also present was an art therapy student, a newcomer. When Kenny perceived a bright-red birthmark on this student's cheek, he was visibly upset and commented on her "ugly scar."

When asked to make a drawing, he immediately set out to draw the student's portrait. Observing her intensely, he produced a figure, paying special attention to the detailed rendering of her spectacles and her birthmark. As he drew, he became visibly calmer. Faced with a frightening reminder of his own stigmatized condition, he had at first responded by projection: "Not I, but the *student* is ugly." However, as he began drawing, healthier defenses came into play. Changing passive into active by creating her image, he had also found a way of keeping a watchful eye on this dangerous individual. By keeping himself busy drawing, he managed to look at her without being overwhelmed by anxiety and revulsion. The mature and detailed drawing that resulted testified to considerable ego strength.

However, when Kenny was introduced to clay, he regressed. Smearing and smelling the unfamiliar substance, he dropped it on the floor, yelling: "The floor is bad. It made the doo-doo fall." The intensity and irrationality of his protests signaled the necessity for intervention. Demonstrating that clay had other possibilities, the art therapist attracted Kenny's attention by modeling a clay figure of a little boy. Kenny soon began to play with the figure. Placing him on a clay bed, he declared that the boy

---

*The following case history has been published in somewhat different form in the *American Journal of Art Therapy* (Vol. 23, No. 1) as part of an article on "An Art Therapy Evaluation Session for Children" by Edith Kramer and Jill Scherr.

was "bad because he peed in bed" (Kenny was enuretic). This led to a discussion of both the clay-boy's and Kenny's own feelings about not being able to control his urination. Hope was expressed that the doctors would be able to help.

The clay-boy safely at rest, Kenny resumed modeling. Pounding out a flat pancake shape and producing a number of clay balls, he discovered that he could make an apple tree by adding a trunk. When he was encouraged to paint his tree with tempera paints,* he became deeply concerned about the choice of colors. "Apples are red," he mused, "but aren't they brown sometimes?" Kenny asserted that he would have no brown apples because "it would mean they are wormy." Furthermore, he declared that he would use neither brown nor black paint on his tree because they were "bad" colors. He was overjoyed when he discovered that he could make a brilliantly bright green by mixing turquoise blue and yellow, and he initially painted the whole tree including the trunk with this green, while all the apples were painted red. But the result did not satisfy him. He found that black would be a better color for a realistic trunk. He also discovered that he had forgotten to make stems for his apples. He added stems and painted them brown, declaring, "They can be brown but not the apples." The finished work with the stems not attached to the tree resembled a long-handled frying pan holding apples. Kenny was delighted. The clay brought forth both Kenny's most disturbed and his most mature and healthy functioning. The material's anal connotations led initially to massive regression and loss of reality testing. But when the possibility of forming the clay into symbolic objects was demonstrated, Kenny could respond to the invitation to enact his trouble in symbolic play rather than via delusional behavior. Symbolic play enabled him to ventilate anxiety and obtain reassurance. This sufficed to inspire him to the creation of a good apple tree. Initially, he attempted to rigidly separate good from bad, rejecting brown and black as "bad" colors. He was about to constrict and impoverish his range of action. However, he transcended the inclination to resort to splitting. Instead, he found a way to integrate the colors in a realistic fashion and still create a good apple tree. Sublimation was attained.

The session, however, did not end with this victory, for Kenny was next asked to use the tempera paints to make a picture. Quickly dipping his brush into the black paint, he produced a simple version of his first

---

*Ordinarily, children would have to wait until their sculptures have been fired before painting them. But since the choice of color often yields important information about the emotional meaning of the sculpture, an exception is made during the first evaluation session, and the child is encouraged to paint the wet clay.

pencil portrait of the art therapy student and wrote her name above it. But when he used red paint to fill in her scar, he suddenly burst into tears. Covering up her name he replaced it with his own, exclaiming, "I am ugly, my face is ugly, and that's why I want to kill myself." Then, with black paint he added a large stop sign to the picture.

The desperate message naturally required a direct response. Since the art therapist knew of Kenny's ongoing psychotherapy, she could reassure him by reminding him that his doctor was there to help him with his feelings, and by pointing out that he had been able to paint a powerful stop sign, to remind himself that he wanted to get over these dangerous feelings.

The session ended on a hopeful note, as Kenny checked on his apple tree and reassured himself that it would be kept safely—a gesture that confirms that the brief episode of healthy symbolic living had been precious to him, even though sublimation alone had not sufficed to stave off the upsurge of suicidal ideation. Indeed, inasmuch as sublimation tends to reduce the power of rigid defenses, it might have contributed to it. Faced with the full impact of his despair, Kenny had needed to resort to a stark, prohibitive command borrowed from the outside world of law and order. This measure was nevertheless healthier than his initial projection and splitting. Thus, the undisguised communication of his despair opened the way to effective psychotherapy, while the completed apple tree gave hope for continued and fruitful art therapy. More often than not, art therapy and psychotherapy complement each other in such a manner.

Projection, Pornography, and Sublimation

Twelve-year-old Gordon, an ardent and gifted painter, and his friend, John, shared an art therapy session. In the course of the session, the two boys embarked on a bout of so-called "slipping" or "playing the dozens," a ritual of mutual insult where each boy accuses the other's mother and grandmother of every conceivable and inconceivable kind of sexual perversion and promiscuity.

The exchange of vituperation constitutes a conventional social pattern among slum children, whose mothers are in fact promiscuous. It can be embellished with all sorts of colorful inventions, but the crowning insult remains the disdainful declaration "You don't even have no mother." Both partners to the abusive exchange get relief through projection. The child could not possibly accuse his own mother of desertion and immorality, but he can freely accuse another child's mother and have the accusation thrown back at him. Such loaded banter may remain playful among friends, but more often it ends up in a fistfight.

This time peace prevailed. While insults were passed back and forth almost mechanically, Gordon began a large painting of Moby Dick (Figure 1; its actual size is 1½ × 4 feet). The subject gave occasion for additional obscenity over the double meaning of the word "dick." One might expect that a painting created while such talk was in the air would at best be crudely obscene. Instead, there emerged a powerful, beautifully executed image of evil, which comes close to embodying the symbolic meaning of Melville's masterpiece.

The white whale is floating on the surface of a light-blue sea, spouting a blue jet of water. The sky is indicated by loose blue brush strokes. The whale's body is painted in subtle shades of gray, with dark-gray accents. The light, silvery atmosphere of the painting contrasts sharply with the whale's evil expression. His mouth is open in a crooked sneer, baring a dark-red cavity surrounded by sharp, white teeth. There is a sly, evil look in his small, black eye. The whole body conveys a feeling of nakedness.

The sexual symbolism of the painting is obvious. We see a composite of male and female elements. The whole whale can be interpreted as one gigantic penis, conceived as a dangerous weapon with teeth. The whale's mouth, on the other hand, can also be interpreted as a vagina dentata, devouring the male organ. The whale as a whole also recalls a woman's body, with the forked tail standing for her thighs and vulva. Most striking are the proportions, roughly 3 : 8, an unusual, extravagant length suitable for the whale, which indeed fills the paper completely. Equally impressive is the painting's tactile quality. This whale is no decorative symbol; it is a three-dimensional, living thing. Gordon had been intensely absorbed as he painted the whale's body. Again and again, he brushed over its surface adding more and more subtle shading. Although his way of painting was reminiscent of masturbation, it did not become obsessive or purely

Figure 1

repetitive. Gordon never lost command over paint and brush; he knew what he was doing and when to stop. He was proud of the completed painting, and his friend and slipping partner was filled with admiration. The session ended in a spirit of contentment.

If we compare the meaning of the talk that had accompanied the making of Moby Dick with the symbolic meaning of the painting, we find that they both relate to the same painful situation: the boys' unfulfilled longing for mother, their rage over her unfaithfulness, shame over her behavior, and guilt and shame over their own degraded desires and fantasies.

On the surface this all seems to be expressed more directly in the boys' talk. "Your mother," it implies, "is promiscuous. She is indeed no mother at all; furthermore, you, her son, are ready to degrade her by attacking her sexually." When we listen closely to the merciless words, we find that the abuse is quite impersonal, uttered so mechanically that it becomes meaningless. Talk circles endlessly around the boys' more profound longing and grief, but it brings no insight or relief. The longing for mother is denied, drowned in the flood of mutual abuse.

When Gordon painted a gigantic image, half fish, half mammal, frightening, fascinating, and unfathomable, he created it out of the same ambivalent feelings, the same fears and pressures that drove him and his schoolmates to relentless vituperation, threats, and fights, but he was no longer obsessed, forced to repeat stereotyped behavior with no will of his own. By finding a symbol that transposed his conflicts from the narrow confines of his life into the wider world of imagination and adventure, he freed himself from meaningless repetition. Painting did not alter the nature of his trouble. He was too deeply injured to make an image of goodness. He could only make a monstrous composite of love and hate, male and female, but in making it he had ceased, at least for the duration of the creative act, to be the helpless victim of his conflicts.

The serendipitous event could not have occurred without the many preceding art therapy sessions during which Gordon discovered his gift and learned to trust himself and to have confidence in the art therapist. During the crucial session the art therapist did not need to intervene. At this juncture her tolerance for the obscene banter and her supportive presence sufficed to establish an atmosphere in which the painting could materialize.

Displacement and Sublimation

In my next example, we can observe the transition from displacement to sublimation. Twelve-year-old Donald, a bright, emotionally troubled child, suffered a psychotic breakdown triggered by a minor operation on his genitals. During one period of his acute illness he developed an obsessive interest in noses. It became his ambition to learn to sculpture ''a perfect human nose.'' During many art therapy sessions he modeled nothing but noses.

Later he tried to sculpture human heads. At first they all looked alike, a huge nose dominating a rudimentary face (Figure 2). He became quite distressed by this repetition. He could see very well that people had different faces and noses, but try as he might, he could only make the same nose and the same face over and over again. Finally, he made up his mind

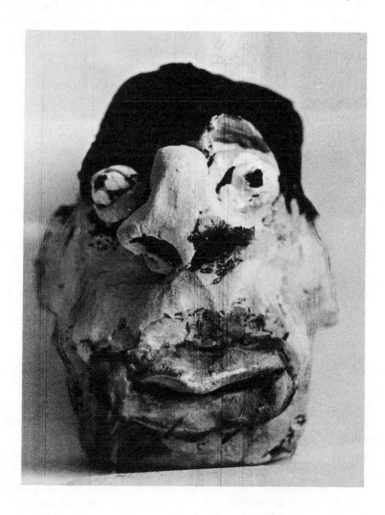

Figure 2

to get out of this impasse by devoting himself seriously to making a self-portrait in a more adult manner.

He was taught how to build an armature of wood and plaster and how to apply the clay systematically around this solid core. Built in this manner, the finished sculpture could be cut into halves, detached from its armature, reassembled, fired in a kiln, and finally painted with poster paint. To look at himself, Donald used a reversible shaving mirror with both an enlarging and reducing side. That by simply reversing the sides he could get very close to his face or move further away was endlessly fascinating to him. It seemed to help him to establish the right distance from himself and to perceive himself as a whole. When the sculpture had been fired, Donald spent much time carefully mixing the colors for skin, hair, eyes, mouth, and sweatshirt to match his own (Figure 3). The sculpture marked a turning point in both his self-perception and his perception of others. He blossomed into a sensitive portraitist able to produce excellent self-portraits in charcoal. This dramatic increase of energy and heightened productivity constitutes one of the hallmarks of sublimation.

Only a short time before, any complex procedure in making sculpture would have been beyond Donald's capacities. He could have used a shaving mirror only for endlessly repetitive play—casting light reflections on walls or making the world larger or smaller at will. It was essential that material, tools, and instruction in using them were available when Donald emerged from his withdrawn and fragmented state. At this juncture the workmanlike logic of building a substantial sculpture in clay paralleled and confirmed the psychic process of reintegration. Moving further away and closer could be practiced, in order to study detail and totality, with the aim of achieving unity. We see in Donald's story the difference between symptom and sublimation, but we also see how closely linked these two may be, and how inextricably they may at times be intertwined.

Sublimation Achieved

The understanding of the process of sublimation is as important in working with adults as it is in art therapy with children.

When Carmine Lombardi, a gifted self-taught artist, had conquered his dependency on drugs and alcohol, he became engrossed in sculpting a huge teardrop in marble. Many mishaps occurred. The stone cracked, the shape had to be modified. Somehow the piece resisted completion. At this juncture art therapist Vera Zilzer suggested that he go out and draw all the trees of his native South Bronx. A large collection of exquisitely composed drawings resulted. They celebrated the impressive ruins of early twentieth-century architecture as it persisted among the rubble and the

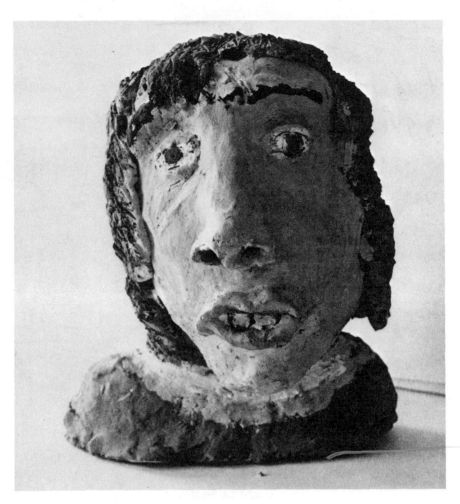

Figure 3

irrepressive growth of weeds, flowers, and Ailanthus trees (Figure 4).
Lombardi had neither been encouraged to immerse himself continuously
in his grief, nor to escape the tragedy of his environment. Rather, he had
been inspired both by works and by example (Vera Zilzer was an excellent
artist and thus a suitable object of identification) to integrate his past and
present: his inner world and his external situation. Lombardi's work
became a source of pride to the community. The process of sublimation
initiated in this series of drawings provided energy for artwork of ever-
broadening scope.

Figure 4

CONCLUSION

The art therapist's attitude toward the concept of sublimation must fundamentally influence both practice and theoretical outlook. Art therapists who recognize in it a powerful source of energy will approach their task differently from those who perceive it as little more than icing on the cake. Sublimation cannot be planned or plotted. All we can do is establish an atmosphere wherein the group of processes of which it is born can unfold. The prototype of this situation has been beautifully described by Winnicott (1965) as one in which the child is in contact with a mother who is benignly available but not at all intrusive. Because the child can be calmly certain of her continued availability, the infant reaches a state of relaxed tension. Experiences belonging to the realm of impulsive, instinctual living, or, to use Winnicott's terminology, *id experiences*, can occur within the framework of a relationship anchored in the ego, rather than arising from the id, serene rather than passionate. Instead of being overwhelmed, the ego is strengthened by the experience.

Such processes are characterized by a benign contact with the primitive mind that enriches and energizes the ego. Repressions are lifted and older modes of functioning activated. Ideas and memories belonging to the ego's realm are briefly subjected to the mechanisms of primary-process thinking. To be beneficial rather than destructive, this dipping into the domain of the id must occur when the individual is able to resist the pull toward permanent regression, so that even though prelogical primary process thinking prevails and ancient libidinal and aggressive strivings are reactivated, the ego continues to function on a mature level. If all goes well, this brings about new maturational spurts. Ernst Kris, who in 1952 described these processes from a psychoanalytic viewpoint, coined the term "regression in the service of the ego," while Silvano Arieti (1976) suggested the term "tertiary process" for this creative synthesis. However, we must be aware of the risk entailed, for if the ego should be unable to withstand the pressures arising from the id, there may be regression in the pathological sense.

Undoubtedly, the companionable solitude that Winnicott describes in terms of psychoanalytic understanding constitutes the ideal situation for producing art or for vicariously experiencing it. In the practice of art therapy we must frequently be much more active than the mother Winnicott envisions. At times we must directly participate in the patient's creative efforts. At other times we may be the first to provide the essential catalyst that had been missing in the patients' lives, Kohut's (1966) "gleam in the mother's eye" encouraging ego functioning. As we strive to libidinize the creative process, we must nevertheless maintain a balance between ego support and respect for the patient's need for unmolested introspection. We must remember that only what emerges within an ambience of supportive, but nonintrusive contact can feel real to the person who brings it forth. Enforced productions or information obtained through coercion can rarely be fully assimilated and can have no lasting effect on the individual's life.

Neither intrapsychic conflict nor the conflict between man's drives and the demands of the environment permit final solutions. Sublimation in art remains a continuous task, but one that never becomes stale or empty as does the repetition born of emotional deadlock. Rather, each new endeavor constitutes a fresh beginning leading to another partial solution so that, if all goes well, each new work becomes more powerful and interesting than the preceding one.

Is there any difference between art and other forms of sublimation? The contemplation of all outstanding feats of sublimation can inspire feelings that are similar to those evoked by works of art. When we admire a bridge, a beautiful carpet, a precision instrument, a heroic deed, a mathematical equation, or any other valuable achievement, it is not only its usefulness that evokes admiration. All of us have experienced the difficulties of taming the instincts, of building ego structure, of becoming human. Therefore, we can experience something of the struggle and of the triumph of sublimation even when we do not personally benefit from its results and when we have no technical understanding of the specific difficulties that had to be surmounted. Most products of sublimation, however, are in themselves emotionally neutral, even though they arouse aesthetic pleasure or even inspire awe.

Art, on the other hand, retells the story of transformation; it offers primarily the pleasure of witnessing the process. Art's value to society consists in stimulating sublimation and influencing its direction. Artist and audience travel together in two directions, from the primitive source of the creative impulse toward its final form, and again from the contemplation of form to the depth of complex, contradictory, and primitive emotions. In this adventure conscious, preconscious, and unconscious processes complement each other. It is thus probable that affect, which is contained but not neutralized, is essential to art, whereas other forms of sublimation would be disrupted by similar quantities of raw libidinal or aggressive drive energies.

The art therapist who sees in sublimation a process essential to emotional health will be inclined to shield it from untimely interference, and this will influence the nature and timing of therapeutic intervention. In work with the severely disturbed and the retarded, much depends on the art therapist's perception of the boundaries of sublimation and of the role of precursory activities. The theoretical orientation presented in this paper encourages a search for the vestiges of sublimation even where, in the full sense, it is out of reach.

As we recognize its powers we must guard against any starry-eyed belief in salvation through sublimation, and we must avoid oversimplification. We must remember that art and sublimation are not identical. Art serves a great many purposes, both in the life of individuals and in the cultural and practical lives of peoples, all of them likely to become the art therapist's concern. Kenny's story is a good example of the many functions art therapy may serve within the confines of a single session. Premature insistence on sublimation in the face of other pressing needs can be as destructive as failure to recognize its value.

REFERENCES

Arieti, S. *Creativity: The magic synthesis*. New York: Basic Books, 1976.
Kohut, H. Forms and transformations of narcissism. *Journal of the American Psychoanalytic Association*, 1966, *14*, 243–272.
Kris, E. *Psychoanalytic explorations in art*. New York: Schocken, 1952.
Lorenz, K. *On aggression*. New York: Harcourt, Brace, Jovanovich, 1966.
Winnicott, D. W. *Maturational processes and the facilitating environment*. New York: International Universities Press, 1965.

3

Symbolism and Art Therapy:
Theory and Clinical Practice

Laurie Wilson

The capacity to form and to use symbols is seen by many as the feature that distinguishes man from other species. In his classic work on symbolism the philosopher Ernst Cassirer said, "Instead of defining man as an animal rationale, we should define him as an animal symbolicum. By so doing we can designate his specific difference, and we can understand the new way to man—the way to civilization" (1974, p. 26). Psychologists, psychoanalysts, linguists, art historians, anthropologists, and theologians have all pondered and continue to debate the nature of symbolism and symbol formation. In my opinion, a consideration of symbolism should be equally central in the daily work of art therapists since visual imagery, the quintessential stuff of symbolism, is the raw material of our work with patients. In this chapter I shall attempt to demonstrate that, by encouraging production of artwork, we are promoting the development of the capacity to symbolize, and that this capacity is linked to a number of critically important ego functions.

Observations and hypotheses that offer some very fruitful ways for art therapists to understand the symbolic products of their patients are found in the writings of David Beres, a psychoanalyst who wrote a number of papers concerning symbolism from the perspective of psychoanalytic ego psychology. In his most extensive paper on this theme, "Symbol and Object" (1955), Beres finds that the psychoanalytic definition differs from other definitions. The dictionary defines symbolism as "something that stands for, represents, or denotes something else (not by exact resem-

Parts of this chapter have been published in somewhat different form in two articles in *The American Journal of Art Therapy*, 1985, *23*, 79–88, 129–133.

blance, but by vague suggestion, or by some accidental or conventional relation).'' Beres finds this definition too broad to be useful in differentiating various types of indirect representation.

In his view, something that substitutes for something else and is experienced in every sense as equal to the original object is not a symbol. It may serve as a sign or a signal, but a symbol must *stand for* and *not stand in for* the thing it represents. Thus, the infant responding to a nurturing adult other than its mother *as* it would to its mother is responding to an equally good *substitute* object, not a *symbolic* object. A time will come when the infant has developed the mental capacity to know the difference between his mother and a substitute. At about this same time (around 16–18 months), the child will also be able to think of or *evoke* a *representation* of his mother *in her absence*. Beres repeatedly emphasizes that symbolism, as understood by psychologists and philosophers, includes more than an immediate response to a signal. A key part of his definition is that a symbol ''is a representational object that can be evoked in the absence of an immediate external stimulus'' (1968, p. 509).

The capacity to evoke an absent object requires a level of cognitive functioning that enables the symbol former to perceive and to hold an image in the mind. Piaget (1951) uses the term ''object permanence'' for this capacity to evoke an absent object; it is seen as a necessary step on the way to what psychoanalysts call ''libidinal object constancy'' (Fraiberg, 1969).

In order for both these capacities to develop, the child must be able to distinguish reality from fantasy. In fact, this capacity has to be in place in order for the infant to be able to perceive the difference between the substitute object and the symbolic object. He has to be able to see that the *substitute object* stands as equal to the original object, and that the *symbolic object* represents the original object, but is known to be different from it. Beres suggests that Winnicott's (1953) concept of the *transitional object* refers to the *transition from substitute to symbolic object*. Thus, Linus' blanket is at first experienced *as* mother's comforting presence, and later serves as a *reminder* of mother sufficient to give comfort.

SYMBOL FORMATION

Beres asserts ''that the symbolic process is not present at birth . . . it develops along with the growth of ego functions'' (1965, p. 8). This is consistent with his ego psychological approach to psychoanalytic thought, which emphasizes developmental principles. According to Beres, the following ego functions must be sufficiently developed for symbol formation to be possible: perception, memory, learning, conceptualization, and the reality and organizing functions. Supporting Beres' developmental approach to symbol formation is research that has found that the earliest symbolic functioning occurs in a syncretic, concrete fashion; only later does it progress to an abstract conceptual mode. Thus, an infant who is trying to open a box may reveal his understanding of openness by opening and closing his mouth; some months later the same infant can replace the concrete, gestural act with the *word* "open" (Piaget, 1951; Werner & Kaplan, 1963).

In his paper, "Perception, Imagination and Reality" (1960, p. 328) Beres describes a hierarchy of perceptual experiences that he postulates underlie all complex mental functioning—such as thinking and fantasizing. At the first level he places sense data: the response of the sensory nerve endings (to temperature, pain, touch, proprioception, and pressure), vision, hearing, taste, and smell. It should be remembered that sensory data may impinge on the organism both from within the body and from the external environment. At this level sensation is a neurophysiological phenomenon and should be considered preperceptual.

At the second level these primary sensations are organized into percepts. These percepts are recognized by the responses they produce in animals as well as in man. They are registered in the brain as Gestalts or configurations of space, form, and color. Dependent on immediate, direct sensory stimulation, they are comparable to signals or cues. At this level they may also be called mental registrations or memory traces.

Only at the third level is perception independent of immediate sensory stimulation. It becomes a mental representation of something not actually present to the senses. As Beres puts it, " . . . there are several different aspects of reality. There is an 'outer' reality (which includes the body), whose existence and nature we can only assume from indirect evidence; there is a reality of direct perception of immediate sensation; there is a reality of organized gestalt configurations, and finally, there is a reality of abstraction and conceptualization. Only in man is there this last kind of reality, and it is the one we understand the least" (Beres, 1960, p. 329).

What does all this have to do with symbolism? According to Beres, symbolism is one type of *mental representation* among several, but a crucial one since it provides the building blocks for other, more complex mental representations: images, fantasies, thoughts, concepts, dreams, hallucinations, symptoms, and language. I cannot here explore all the ramifications of this idea but ask the reader to accept for the moment Beres' idea that the symbol is one of the earliest mental representations of an absent stimulus, internal or external.

Another concept fundamental to psychoanalytic psychology is that psychic functioning is mediated through mental representations. Responses to stimuli are mediated, as the child develops and his ego functions mature, almost exclusively through mental representations. Mental functioning takes on its characteristic and unique human quality—perceptions of the external world, perceptions of inner drives and affects, are all somehow registered in the mind by psychic representations, and it is to these representations that the energies of the instinctual drives are directed in the process that we recognize as "cathexis" (Beres, 1960, p. 329). If the two ideas are taken together, one sees how the symbol (defined earlier as "a representational object that can be evoked in the absence of an immediate external stimulus") is a critical link between the world of reality (as stimulus) and human behavior, thought, and fantasy (as response).

PATHOLOGY OF THE SYMBOLIC PROCESS

Keeping developmental aspects in mind, I turn now to a consideration of the pathology of the symbolic process. It is well known that dysfunction in symbol formation characterizes severe disabilities ranging from schizophrenia to aphasia. If we take a brief look at some specific forms of pathology, we may gain a better understanding of the value and usefulness of making visual images in treating those pathologies. Beres notes three clinical areas in which pathology of the symbolic process may be seen: retarded ego development in the child, schizophrenia, and organic brain disease. In all three "the essential element is a concurrent disturbance of the reality function of the ego" (Beres, 1965, p. 16).

Retarded Ego Development

In retarded ego development the child does not develop the capacity to distinguish the representative object from the real object—Linus' blanket *is* mother. We see this clearly with the mentally retarded, whose crippling incapacity in this area (among others) interferes with normal development of language, thought processes, and object relations.

I have elsewhere described the case of Elena, a severely retarded, 22-year-old woman with an IQ of 20 who had been living in institutions for 18 years (Wilson, 1977). Institutional records documented Elena's prolonged fixation at the oral phase. She could not be weaned from a bottle until the age of five, and shortly thereafter she developed a habit of collecting and chewing or swallowing bits of string and buttons. In adolescence Elena still collected such objects but she no longer put them in her mouth. By age 22 she had abandoned this habit; instead she constantly carried or wore around her neck on a chain a ball-like clump of metal jingle bells. Elena herself wove the bells together with wire and from time to time would increase or decrease the size of the cluster. If the bells were taken from her or she accidentally left them behind, she would cry inconsolably or angrily hit or overturn tables or chairs.

In addition to this fixation, Elena had a repertoire of gestures that included rubbing her hands together, stroking her cheeks, mouth, and nose, and holding and rubbing her breasts. When she began to make these gestures she often looked distressed, but this pained expression would usually give way to signs of pleasure or comfort. Elena appeared to be attempting to comfort herself with caresses that had in the past been given her by others.

When Elena began art therapy sessions, she was fixated to one image: a circle with a pattern of radial lines imposed on it. She repeated this pattern steadily in her artwork for a year and a half, covering sheet after sheet with numerous examples of it, almost always using red. Although she willingly varied the medium (using crayon, paint, or chalk), she would rarely alter the image or the color. At the same time she was very clinging and demonstrated a need for constant reassurance and praise.

Over the course of two years' work Elena gradually progressed in both her art expression and general behavior from an infantile dependency to greater maturity. The key to helping Elena was understanding the psychological meaning of her art. By partially satisfying some of her needs, both artistic and personal, and by leading her toward small, but appropriate changes in these two areas, Elena was gradually helped to become more flexible and independent, becoming in time able to travel unassisted to the art room. Her graphic vocabulary expanded to include concentric circles, images of bodies, squares, and ultimately a relatively rich combination of circles, triangles, squares, and hybrid shapes that she used to depict full figures, clothing, and ornaments. She gradually became able to modify her radial schema and to include it in different configurations as eyes (Figure 1) and breast.

As I came to discover that Elena's perseverative radial schema stood equally for breast, mother, and bell, I understood the clump of jingle bells to be her transitional object. I would now describe this young woman's desperate attachment to her bells as a *failure of the symbolic function* in that at the beginning of treatment the bells stood for her as a *substitute*, not a *symbolic* object.

I now see Elena as having developed through her art therapy a capacity for symbolization, whereby the function of the transitional object shifted from substitute (*standing as equal*) to symbol (*standing as representation*) for the original object—mother. I also suggest that it was the persistent making of visual images in art therapy sessions that served to spur the development of her ability to symbolize. It seems that while

Figure 1

the clump of bells and the radial schema functioned as a *substitute* for mother, they were experienced as essential and could not be given up or altered. When finally Elena developed the capacity to *symbolize* and thereby evoke the absent mother, she was freed to function more flexibly in a world where security consisted now of symbolic rather than concrete reminders of an absent object. Thus, she became able to leave her bells behind in the residence of the institution and to come to sessions unaccompanied either by this transitional object or by an actual attendant. In time we saw her replace the bells with a pocketbook—another symbolic transformation of the original substitute object.

Schizophrenia

Loss of or difficulty with reality function is characteristic of schizophrenia. Beres describes this second malfunction of the symbolic process as a loss of the capacity to recognize and differentiate between the real object and its representation. Making visual images can play a critical role

for psychiatric patients, facilitating an increased capacity for symbolization and associated reality resting. Many art therapists could produce
examples in which a schizophrenic child or adult has regained the capacity
to symbolize and increased his sense of reality through the regular production of artwork. Most often, there is repeated expression of key symbols, with a gradual recognition of their meaning, and a consequent ability
to differentiate reality from fantasy. The case of Dorothy (Rubin, 1984),
in which a schizophrenic girl moved from *being* a bird to *painting* birds—
and eventually people—is a typical example of such a process (cf. Wilson,
1985a, pp. 81–84).

Organic Brain Disease

Partial or total loss of the ability to articulate ideas, resulting from brain
damage, is known as aphasia. Observations and theoretical propositions
on the therapeutic effect of art with this population must be considered
quite tentative at this time. Too little is understood about recovery and
rehabilitation in aphasia (Sarno, 1981), and the use of imagery—specifically the production of artwork—with aphasics has not been sufficiently
explored to allow for more than the raising of questions.

I have selected for discussion the case of an aphasic patient seen in art
therapy for three months by Irene Rosner, an art therapist who specializes
in work with the physically ill and disabled. David, a 65-year-old aphasic
man, had suffered a stroke—a left-sided cerebrovascular accident. An
injury to the left hemisphere of the brain causes paralysis of the right side
of the body (hemiplegia) and usually of the speech center as well. David
had a history of hypertension as well as residual left-sided weakness due
to poliomyelitis in childhood. His speech disorder manifested itself in the
form of expressive aphasia; that is, he was unable to talk intelligibly. He
had been retired for three years from his position as a Social Security
examiner and had maintained a private business in accounting before his
stroke. His wife was disabled with cerebral palsy, as was one of their five
children. The family appeared to be supportive and nurturing.

When first admitted to the hospital, David was extremely lethargic. His
yes/no responses (by means of head movement) were unreliable, and he
appeared to be exhausted by any attempts at communication on his part
or that of others. The psychologist reported that David was only spo-
radically alert but when alert did respond to visual stimuli by nodding.
Despite his global expressive disability, he retained minimal receptive
capacity. His attention span, however, was very limited. He emitted a
repetitive, grating cry and was very demanding.

A treatment plan was devised that included daily physical and occupational therapy, speech therapy two or three days a week, and art therapy every other day. Initially art therapy sessions lasted 20 minutes. They were increased to between 45 minutes and an hour as he became able to concentrate longer.

David's first drawings in art therapy are similar to a child's early spontaneous scribbles. Although his marks looked as if they had been placed randomly on the paper, there was evidence in his drawing process of a struggle to gain motor control. The paralysis of his right side meant that David had to use his left hand—not his dominant hand—and it was weakened by his bout with polio in childhood. Thus, he was doubly handicapped in terms of control. David was focused and attentive while he drew. Although his drawings were incomprehensible to an observer, they appeared to have specific meaning for him. Thus, his art therapist focused on attempting to help him to achieve more recognizable forms.

David's progress in art paralleled the development of drawing in young children. In time, his perseverative vocalization decreased, and he slowly regained the ability to say some words; he then reached the stage of naming his scribbles, although they were still unrecognizable. Like a young child, the name David supplied for a given drawing might shift as the associational current flowed on. Thus, at times he called an early scribble "ice chips" and other times "fish." At this time the psychologist reported that David was more alert and attentive, was communicating his needs with nonverbal cues, and was responding well to directions.

The next stage in David's development marked an advance in two areas. He began to produce recognizable forms and to name them appropriately, and he became able to place his marks on the paper in a way that indicated his awareness of the entire page. We can easily pick out the tree in Figure 2, entitled by David "Fish, Tree, and Amoeba."

In contrast to his earlier efforts, David's work now gave evidence of planning and deliberation. He created numerous intentional enclosures: circles of various sizes, elongated triangles, and irregular shapes. Because of the shakiness of his hand, the shapes were barely discernible amid the scribbled lines on the same page, as with young children's drawings. Nevertheless, on close inspection, forms became apparent in David's drawings from this period—in one a face schema, a crude circular shape with two eyes.

Soon after, when asked to draw a person, David combined his face schema with body parts to create Figure 3. As he drew this human figure, it took on personal meaning for him. He began to cry and, in response to gentle questioning, said, "My wife—she's short and fat and ugly and wonderful." Up to this time David had been responding to the environment without signs of emotion; now he had begun to register personal,

Figure 2

Figure 3

emotional involvement. His reaction, brought forth by his own artistic expression, seemed a pivotal event in his psychological recovery. He went on to produce better integrated pictures and to invest them with personal meaning, as well as to make further strides in speech and movement.

In view of the various therapies David received, it is impossible to say to what extent his work with imagery precipitated or merely coincided with a longer attention span, more coherent speech, and appropriate affect. But the moving sequence of events just described suggests that, just as the development of visual images by young children promotes their capacity to engage in symbolic processes; so can brain-damaged people be helped to recover symbolic functioning in all areas—including language—by a similar development of visual images.

David seemed to reflect progress first in his drawings and only afterward in his language and object relations. With each advancing step of visual symbol formation—scribbles, named scribbles, schemas, recognizable images, and human figure drawing—we can postulate the return of impaired ego functions. Perception, memory, conceptualization, reality function, and organizing function all unite to once again permit mental representations—symbols of absent objects. With the return of this capacity affect and object relations are reinstated—a lost love has taken on new life.

Conclusion

The lesson to be learned from these two cases is that patients with an impaired symbolic function (and consequent defective ego functioning) can be helped, by the making of visual images, to *develop* their capacity to symbolize—an ability fundamental to almost all civilized activity. Elena's and David's pathologies resulted from developmental irregularities. Elena, a case of arrested development, was spurred by making images to develop a capacity to recall and relate to an absent object. This step, in turn, promoted increased freedom on Elena's part to explore the world and to develop autonomous functioning. Severe regression characterized David's developmental pathology. His production of images at the level of a young child promoted higher-level functioning of the capacity to symbolize and ultimately led to the restoration of object relations.

Language, a shared symbolic system, is central in individual development and human experience. In cases of developmental pathology where the use of language is too challenging—and also for those patients who find the use of words too frightening—practice in symbolizing by manipulating visual images rather than words can serve to further development. Developmentally impaired patients, like young children, can be helped by exercising the visual-motor function to achieve higher-level functioning—the capacity to symbolize in the form of language. Thus, as art therapists learn to appreciate the particulars of symbol formation and their relationship to the development of ego functions, we can hope to arrive at interventions that will better promote the desired development.

MENTAL REPRESENTATION

In order to understand more fully the part played by symbolism in *psychic functioning*, we need to return to Beres' discussion on *mental representation*; a difficult and subtle concept, but an essential one for our purposes.

> The symbol is the conscious derivative of the unconscious mental representation, the psychic reality of Freud. There is considerable evidence for the postulation of organized unconscious mental representations which may be spoken of as unconscious symbols. In this sense symbolism gives conscious expression to unconscious mental content and serves both adaptation and communication (1968, p. 510).

The concept of mental representation may be known to art therapists by some of its other names: self-representation, object representation, body image, memory schema, introjected object, internal object, representational world, etc.

Returning to Beres for a definition, we find one in a paper devoted to the subject: "a mental representation is a postulated unconscious psychic organization capable of evocation in consciousness as symbol, image, fantasy, thought, affect, or action" (Beres & Joseph, 1970, p. 2). The actual nature of unconscious mental representation is unknown. No anatomical, biochemical, or physiological correlate has been discovered; however, there is abundant evidence that such phenomena do indeed exist. The data are provided by the conscious derivatives that are familiar to us as symbols, images, fantasies, dreams, thoughts, feelings, and actions. Beres and Joseph contend that "mental representations form the unconscious basis for all conscious psychic activity" (*Ibid.*, p. 4).

Furthermore, they argue that mental representations shape our perception of reality in significant ways. The process of perception in humans is such that individuals respond not to the external stimulus that initiates perception, but to the mental representation activated by it. This mental representation is by no means an exact reproduction of the original stimulus, but is the product of many distorting and mediating forces, including feeling states, memories of past experiences, and cognitive states. An individual's "reality" is thus relative and indeterminate, a fact long known to artists. Most psychoanalytic clinicians accept this notion, and I would guess most art therapists might agree. It is in the nature of our work to avidly seek the meaning behind or beneath the pictures our patients and clients produce. All of us would accept the idea of hidden feelings, fears, or fantasies that are revealed by the form and content of the artwork. For psychoanalysts the unconscious is equivalent to a mental representation.

I turn now to another important function provided by symbolization—delay in the response to stimulation, also relevant for art therapy. To understand this we must first understand the concept of *psychic energy* as it is postulated by psychoanalysts. Psychic energy is a hypothetical force in mental functioning, derived mainly from the instinctual drives that impel the mind to activity. Beres explains that "in the human being, stimuli whether from the external world or from the organs of the body, arouse the instinctual drive forces to the development of a need" (Beres, 1965, p. 13). He sees this as a neurophysiological state, occurring prior to the transformation of the need into a wish, which adds the psychological component.

It is in the nature of drive energies to seek discharge through mental or physical activity. Mental activity of any sort is accompanied by a transfer or flow of psychic energy. The amount of psychic energy invested in a mental process or mental representation is called its *cathexis*. *Freely mobile* mental energy accompanies the *primary process* and presses for immediate discharge. Energy that accompanies the *secondary process* is generally more or less *bound*. Its discharge can be delayed temporarily or longer. The capacity to bind psychic energy increases as the individual matures. It is closely related to the capacity for deinstinctualization or neutralization. With neutralization, energy is deflected from its original pleasure-seeking aims and becomes available for use in ego functioning. To explain the delay of discharge, Beres and Joseph observe that

. . . it is necessary to postulate an unconscious psychic organization that will provide the basis for binding the energies which otherwise would be immediately discharged. In accordance with the hypothesis that it is the mental representation upon which cathexes are focused, it follows that the mental representations would serve to contain the "quiescent" drive energies, to "bind" them and thus to facilitate delay of discharge (1970, p. 4).

These mental representations

. . . can be evoked to consciousness as images, fantasies, or thoughts. The building blocks of these conscious manifestations are the symbols. Symbol formation in this sense is an ego function involved in a reciprocal relationship to other ego functions. It requires for its activity the aid of those functions and, in turn, it enters into every manifestation of ego activity (Beres, 1965, p. 13).

It seems to me that this theoretical formulation partially accounts for the effectiveness of art therapy. By asking our patients to make pictures or sculpture, particularly in moments when they are under pressure to act impulsively, we are seeking to mediate peremptory drive discharge by interposing visual symbols between stimulus, need, wish, and action.

Art therapists can cite many instances of work with impulsive patients, where the promotion of symbol formation encourages a delayed response to stimulation. The common invitation to "put *it* [feeling, idea, impulse] on the paper" or to "express *it* with the clay"—*instead* of acting it out physically—is a way of taming impulsive drive discharge and promoting the development of higher ego functions.

Another area of psychic functioning in which symbolism plays an important role concerns the relationship of consciousness to the unconscious. Contemporary psychoanalysts are themselves somewhat divided on the subject. Beres states that "the individual who is using the symbol has the *capacity to know* that the symbol is not the original object" (1965, p. 7). This raises the question of consciousness. The symbol itself, which some psychologists call the *vehicle* or that which carries meaning, is understood by Beres and most psychoanalysts to be "a manifest production of which the person is conscious." On the other hand, that which is symbolized, sometimes called the *referent*, may be "conscious; easily available to consciousness that is, preconscious, or repressed and unconscious" (*Ibid.*, p. 8).

Here Beres parts company with earlier psychoanalytic writers, in particular Jones (1916) and Ferenczi (1912), who wrote the classic papers on the subject. For them, true symbolism in the psychoanalytic sense can only apply to symbols whose referents are unconscious. As soon as the symbolizer is aware of the thing being symbolized, it cannot be classed as true psychoanalytic symbolism. Jones's contention was "only what is repressed is symbolized, only what is repressed needs to by symbolized" (1920, p. 158).

For the general public today this idea has become commonplace. Likewise, most art therapists were long ago introduced to it through the writings of Margaret Naumburg, who wrote about it at length in *Schizophrenic Art: Its Meaning in Psychotherapy* (1950), and whose fundamental theories and practice were based on it (1953, 1966). Naumburg's work, and the work of those who follow her theory and method, are based on *making the unconscious conscious*, using the symbolic expression of artwork as a guide and an instrument in the process.

Let us now briefly scrutinize the various ways in which art making relates to this process. In our discussion of *mental representation* we found that, according to Beres, the symbol was the conscious derivative of the unconscious mental representation, and that symbolism therefore serves adaptation and communication by giving conscious expression to unconscious mental content. It is self-evident, then, that the symbolic vehicle—for art therapists, the artwork—must be conscious.

The *referent*—the idea or thing being symbolized—may, according to Beres, be conscious, preconscious, or unconscious. This, for art therapists, is the crux of the matter. First, how do we determine whether or what part of the symbolic imagery in the art derives from unconscious material? If we can decide that question, we are confronted by an even more perplexing set of questions: Is the person who made the symbol aware of the unconscious referent? Why is it appearing now? Should he be made aware of it? How should this awareness be brought about? The most important question for our theoretical understanding is: What will be the consequences of this awareness?

I cannot possibly answer all these questions here, but I would like to propose some preliminary responses to some of them by applying Beres' formulations on the psychic functions of symbolizers. It has long been accepted that visual images may reveal the unconscious wishes and conflicts of the individuals who make them. The numerous projective tests using drawings provide evidence of this, and the diagnostic value of this psychic function of symbolism seems indisputable. Through drawing, painting, and sculpture, wishes may be displaced from forbidden objects to their symbolic substitutes. Hence, we find numerous bloody battles on the artwork of young boys whose aggressive wishes press for expression.

We can say, at the least, that the inner mental representations may be objectified through becoming externalized in concrete visual form. The question remains whether or not this externalization changes the stage of the referent. Here we cannot hope for simple definitive answers. The history of art and an honest account of art therapy practice reveal numerous examples of artwork heavily laden with unconscious symbolism that does not change the awareness of the individuals who produced it. I am certain, for example, that Louise Nevelson was not conscious of her unresolved conflicts about sexuality and mourning, although she created sculpture that contains many references to these unconscious conflicts (Wilson, 1981).

Perhaps the effectiveness of art in such a case stems from the fact that the external symbolic representation allows distance to be created between the individual and his conflict. Although this does not lead to change, it may be serving a defensive purpose of considerable significance for the individual. There are many artists whom one feels would suffer great psychic pain if they were deprived of their artwork. Most art therapists, however, are more ambitious for their patients and seek ways to encourage or induce change in maladaptive functioning.

But, what if we suppose that—at least sometimes—the externalization accomplished by making a visual image changes the unconscious state of the referent—the idea being symbolized—to a preconscious state? This would explain a variety of phenomena seen regularly in the practice of art therapy. It has frequently been observed, for example, that making artwork frees patients who are otherwise blocked in verbal expression. To put an idea or feeling into words requires a conscious level of awareness—rather than a preconscious one—and it is a common occurrence in art therapy sessions for patients to readily speak about the story or meaning of their art production, after having maintained a stony silence when offered the opportunity simply to speak about themselves and their problems.

Another frequent phenomenon is seen with patients whose willingness to speak is not a problem, but whose capacity to organize their thoughts and perceptions is gravely impaired—as with schizophrenics. There are similar cases where a highly complex fantasy life may be presumed to exist, but conscious communication about it is unobtainable—as with schizoid patients. In all of the above cases, the production of artwork often seems to permit the expression, exploration, and organization of the underlying fantasies, once they are depicted consciously in concrete visual terms.

A clinical vignette may elucidate this point. Noah was an extremely intelligent and gifted schizoid, preadolescent boy in day treatment at a special school and treatment center. From early childhood he had been chronically unhappy, with frequent temper tantrums during which he broke furniture and hit his mother, and, in spite of his 160 IQ, he had always had difficulty in school, not doing homework, crying every day, and totally without friends.

Noah came to art therapy after several years of psychotherapy, during which fleeting and largely incoherent references had been made to his science fiction fantasy. In the year before he began art therapy, his psychotherapist found that when Noah entered sessions acutely upset and unable to speak; only through drawing was he able to regain internal controls and to reveal the nature of his distress. It was no surprise, then, that art therapy sessions allowed this extremely withdrawn boy to objectify his fantasy life. Gradually, a narrative tale unfolded through his artwork, depicting a never-ending battle between alien creatures and an intergalactic peace force.

An early work called "Imagination" by Noah portrayed a nameless planet in the year 7001 populated by odd creatures (Figure 4). This piece seemed to be a symbolic equivalent for Noah's defensive retreat into fantasy and the unhappy inner emptiness he was experiencing. During his first year in the art therapy Noah was able to identify and describe the characters in his fantasy, much as he had been able to tell of his daily dilemmas after drawing them for his psychotherapist. He seemed to be externalizing, exploring, and organizing his inner life—as he drew and modeled, depicting "Legrans" and "Lizardrons" battling for supremacy in their devastated milieu. He spoke about his invented creatures and their battles, and I remained within that metaphor in my verbal interventions with him.

By the end of the first year of art therapy, it seemed evident that his internal conflict over the management of his aggressive impulses was now appearing clearly in symbolic form in his art.

Figure 4

In the first two sessions of Noah's second year in treatment he made a new version of "Imagination" (Figure 5), the clay sculpture he had done the previous year (Figure 4). After working silently while finishing the details of this piece, Noah began to tell the story of its component parts. He explained that a thin, wedge-shaped missile aimed at earth would destroy the planet in 7103, a year following the date he had assigned to the sculpture. The missile had been sent by Lizardrons—mean bullies who had heard that earth was recovering from a nuclear blast and was becoming habitable again. Noah described the dome-shaped figure at the upper left of the scene as a "cloaked figure—an alien," a species of large beings from far away who could easily move forward and backward into different timeframes. He explained that when the aliens discover the cruelty and meanness of the Lizardrons, they fight them and drive them from the galaxy, with the warning that if the Lizardrons were to reappear and cause trouble the aliens would also return to protect the galaxy.

Several months after this session, at about the time he chose to paint the clay sculpture "Imagination II," Noah came to realize some of the meanings embedded in the science fiction fantasy he had depicted. After announcing that imagination comes from inside a person—to which I responded, "like your stories and pictures"—Noah proceeded to identify

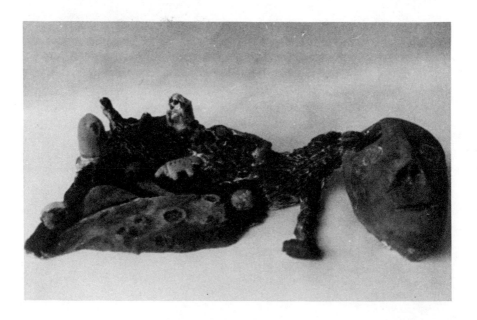

Figure 5

the Lizardrons as his bad feelings, and the battles he had been portraying as corresponding to an internal emotional struggle.

Though it was never made explicit, it seemed that the cloaked figure was the art therapist, an interpretation that became inescapable when he painted it the same color blue as the smock I wore during sessions. In retrospect, we can see that the idea of aliens as large beings who can move forward and backward at will seemed an excellent metaphor, since I came only once a week and had been away for a long time during the summer break. We can also see the rescuing function Noah had assigned to me in his science fiction fantasy, through the story of aliens driving out the mean Lizardrons.

The act of painting this sculpture several months after its original production seemed to serve a number of psychological purposes. First, it brought some of the fantasy material closer to the surface where it could be put into words, and second, it allowed Noah to modify his fantasy. This latter function was dramatically revealed when Noah covered the missile aimed at earth with black paint so that it seemed to disappear and announced that it was no longer going to destroy the earth.

What had earlier been inchoate, unconscious, and inexpressible had begun to take visible shape. It seems that an unconscious fantasy, through being given formal representation, was becoming more accessible to consciousness. In observing this process I experienced a feeling I have often encountered in art therapy. I felt that some deeply unconscious material had shifted upward and had reached a level of preconsciousness by virtue of taking form in the art.

For some patients this may be a sufficient goal, particularly since it may be accompanied by a cathartic experience. Yet there are other directions that this therapeutic progress through symbol formation can take. Two of them are well known to art therapists as the Naumburg (1966) and Kramer (1971) approaches. The former uses artwork initially to bring unconscious conflicts to the surface, and ultimately to lead patients to a conscious verbal awareness of these conflicts. The latter approach aims for a neutralization of the drive energy stimulating the symbolic expression, by guiding that expression toward sublimation in continued production of artwork. Since both of these approaches have been well described and documented elsewhere, I shall forego further discussion of them here.

Present-day psychoanalytic ego psychology with its developmental framework, can be most helpful to art therapists. Applying the theoretical formulations of David Beres on symbolism and mental representation, for example, we can better understand some of the ways in which art therapy seems to work. One lesson we can learn is that by making visual images, patients with defective ego functioning and impaired symbolization are helped to develop the capacity to symbolize, an ability fundamental to almost all civilized functioning. And, by understanding some of the roles played by symbolic expression in art, we may become more effective in our work and know better how to explain the results of our labors.

REFERENCES

Beres, D. Perception, imagination and reality. *International Journal of Psychoanalysis*, 1960, *41*, 327–334.

Beres, D. Symbol and object. *Bulletin of the Menninger Clinic*, 1965, *29*, 3–23.

Beres, D. The humanness of human beings: Psychoanalytic considerations. *Psychoanalytic Quarterly*, 1968, *37*, 487–522.

Beres, D., & Joseph, E. The concept of mental representation in psychoanalysis. *International Journal of Psychoanalysis*, 1970, *51*, 1–9.

Cassirer, E. *An essay on man*. New Haven, CT: Yale University Press, 1974.

Ferenczi, S. *Sex in psychoanalysis, Vol. 1* (1912). New York: Dover, 1956, pp. 214–237.

Fraiberg, S. Libidinal object constancy and mental representation. *Psychoanalytic Study of the Child*, Vol. 24. New York: International Universities Press, 1969, pp. 9–47.

Jones, E. The theory of symbolism (1916). In *Papers on Psychoanalysis*. London: Balliere, Tindall & Cox, 1920, pp. 129–186.

Kramer, E. *Art as therapy with children*. New York: Schoken, 1971.

Naumburg, M. *Schizophrenic art: Its meaning in psychotherapy*. New York: Grune & Stratton, 1950.

Naumburg, M. *Psychoneurotic art: Its function in psychotherapy*. New York: Grune & Stratton, 1953.

Naumburg, M. *Dynamically oriented art therapy: Its principles and practice*. New York: Grune & Stratton, 1966.

Piaget, J. *Play, dreams and imitation in childhood*. New York: Dutton, 1951.

Rubin, J. A. *Child art therapy*, rev. ed. New York: Van Nostrand Reinhold, 1984.

Sarno, M. T. Recovery and rehabilitation in aphasia. In M. T. Sarno (Ed.) *Acquired aphasia*. New York: Academic Press, 1981, pp. 485–529.

Werner, H., & Kaplan, B. *Symbol formation*. New York: Wiley & Sons, 1963.

Winnicott, D. W. Transitional objects and transitional phenomena. *International Journal of Psychoanalysis*, 1953, *34*, 89–97.

Wilson, L. Theory and practice of art therapy with the mentally retarded. *American Journal of Art Therapy*, 1977, *16*, 87–97.

Wilson, L. Louise Nevelson: Personal history and art. *American Journal of Art Therapy*, 1981, *20*, 79–97.

Wilson, L. Symbolism and art therapy: I. Symbolism's role in the development of ego functions. *American Journal of Art Therapy*, 1985a, *23*, 79–88.

Wilson, L. Symbolism and art therapy: II. Symbolism's relationship to basic psychic functioning. *American Journal of Art Therapy*, 1985b, *23*, 129–133.

4

An Object Relations Approach to Art Therapy

Arthur Robbins

A patient comes to my office. I immediately am aware of her eyes with their sad, liquid emptiness. Her face is expressionless, an occasional smile breaking through. At 47 she is unmarried and very tired. As her story unfolds, I learn that she does not need to work, for she has a small income from her parents' estate. This should allow her some ease, but she busily, even frantically, moves from one task to another. She feels her life rush by her, becoming increasingly aware that the span of one lifetime is not endless. Paradoxically, she feels younger than her age.

Life has been a series of short and long love affairs for this woman. Some dissolve before they begin, others are filled with pain and remorse. As she talks in a vague poetic way, I am interested and intrigued, but strangely disconnected. There's an ethereal quality about this patient that defies solidity or definition. The one thing that comes through loud and strong is the depth of her loneliness and sense of being lost. I feel the impulse to be warm and protective even as she eludes me, like sand slipping through my fingers. I'm reminded of an old movie, *Hiroshima Mon Amour*, the story of a young woman's personal disaster as mirrored in an atomic holocaust. Eroticism offers a desperate anchor in the midst of a chaotic world.

I ask this woman to draw a picture about herself, with the hope that I will get a more defined picture of the inner world in which she dwells. She protests: "I don't have enough time to do it in the session." To this,

Parts of this chapter appear in the recently published volume by Arthur Robbins, *The Artist as Therapist*, Human Sciences Press, 1987. Reproduced by permission of the publisher.

I ask if she would be willing to draw something about herself at home. She readily agrees.

Next session she brings me a set of pictures (Figure 1), all looking quickly drawn in a monochromatic blue. There is movement in her drawings, but a lack of dimension. Although particularly pleased with one picture that she says describes the sensual part of herself, the part that craves contact and needs to be touched, she has nothing else to say about this drawing. She does give some information about the other pictures, however. The hands reaching out represent the part of herself that needs to be a part of something bigger. In the fourth picture, which represents the Jewish community she loves, she expands further: "All those people around a big ark in a semicircle meet and are part of something bigger." Again, I am aware of eyes, as those in the picture stare out and search to be taken in. Her drawings are like soft, sensual fragments, reaching out to say, "Hold me."

The patient's representations of her body seem segmented rather than forming a flowing whole, leading me to wonder whether the holding she had received had been given by someone who was disengaged and unrelated. Putting these impressions together, I see the religious force giving her a feeling of aliveness and superficial cohesion and, along with her eroticism, acting as a compensatory mechanism for her lack of the most basic of connections, that of the mother and child's early resonance.

Although this patient has not spoken of her mother, I sense her presence in the room. She is a brisk, hurried person, easily overwhelming to her child. The child who still dwells within this patient is hungry for contact, while concurrently feeling frightened of being overwhelmed and controlled as she was by her mother. These dual pulls cause her to fragment and become diffuse when intimate contact is offered.

At the same time as images of the mother permeate the atmosphere, a sense of her father crowds into the room with us, in spite of his having gone unmentioned by the patient. I suspect that he is the one who supplied physical contact and warmth in a nonverbal way, offering her some semblance of definition.

In this brief description, I have attempted to hint at the complex interaction of objective and subjective realities that create a psychological space between two people from the beginning of therapy. Within this space, past and present merge to create a unique mood and atmosphere. I experience the patient's inner representations of her past expressed in the present. I sense, feel, and see the affects, moods, and attitudes originally connected to her past relationships as they are organized and represented in images and pictures that literally fill my office. These represen-

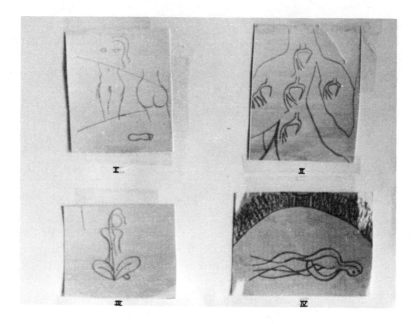

Figure 1

tations speak of the me and you inside each of us that create our individual perceptions of the world, and at the same time induce and shape the surrounding social world's response to each of us. The representations within any given patient make contact with the relationships I carry inside me. My internal mother, father, and child touch those of the patient at points of similar experience, perception, and feeling as we get to know one another. It becomes clear that in any single encounter between two people, there are multiple levels of consciousness entering into the engagement, as the relationships from each person's past make contact, become enmeshed, and occasionally lose sight of one another.

Art adds a dimension to this engagement. Sometimes the art mirrors or deepens what is already going on in the relationship. In other instances, the art form may offer something diametrically opposed to the verbal dialogue. This added dimension gives a new perspective on our internal relationships as it brings us to new levels of consciousness.

It is these early internalized relationships with their effect on one's current reality which form the core of object relations theory as I use it in my practice. I would like to digress for a moment, here, to make it clear that when I talk about object relations theory I am not referring to one unified theory which can be found in a single book or one which is espoused by a particular theoretician. My use of this term reflects my own distillation from a body of theory, itself derived from classical psycho-analytic theory.

Going back to its roots in psychoanalytic theory, the "object" in object theory refers to the who and what in which a person's libidinal energy is invested. By "libidinal energy," I mean that constitutional reservoir of energy and life that is part sexual, part aggressive, but is more than either. It is the fuel that motivates each of us to reach out and find relief and contact with the world. Within this framework, human behavior is con-ceptualized within a tripartite system of id, ego, and superego, which, when unbalanced, creates the conflicts manifesting themselves in the range of defenses and symptoms characteristic of the neuroses.

The id forces, which reflect primitive fantasies, wishes, etc., constantly try to make themselves felt and to find satisfaction. Derivatives of these forces are felt throughout life in such forms as dreams and fantasies and are the stuff of primary process thinking. With maturation, the ego and superego counter and modify the raw id forces: the ego, with its rational, logical secondary process thinking, working to integrate the demands of outer reality with the inner world; the superego, with its belief system consisting of such notions as the ideal, good, bad, and evil, influencing the ego's reactions to the id material. An imbalance among these forces is thought to arise when the Oedipal crisis is not successfully resolved.

Treatment, then, is directed at analyzing defenses, resistances, and the transference, as well as dealing with such issues as shame, guilt, and anxiety. There is a clear sense of an established internal me and you in the neurotic individual. Much emphasis is placed on making the uncon-scious conscious and on bringing primary process material within second-ary process organization. The ideal outcome of therapy involves modi-fying the defenses of the ego and prohibitions of the superego, to allow the patient's life space to expand and to tolerate a richer symbolic and imaginative existence.

The patient I described in the opening paragraph does not fall within the neurotic category. Like many patients in my practice, she roughly falls into the wide continuum of primitive mental states including: the psy-chotic, borderline, narcissistic personality, mood disorder, psychopath, and schizoid, all of whom suffer from deficits and problems in the early mother-child relationship. When I say "mother," I refer to the mothering agent, be it mother or any significant person in the child's life who offers nurturing and care. Treatment for this broad range of patients can no longer be seen in terms of making the unconscious conscious. Here, the disparate systems of mental structure lack integration and cohesiveness. The task, therefore, becomes one of building rather than uncovering, of completing lost dialogues connected to the early maternal matrix.

Resonance is important in this kind of therapeutic encounter. The therapist "mirrors," or offers emotional responsiveness, which facilitates the process of empathy, crucial in this treatment process. For instance, in the description of the patient I mentioned in the opening pages, a central theme of treatment would be object loss: the absence of a central figure to give cohesion to the patient's life. Here, the cognitive awareness of this issue by itself would be of little help. She would need a relationship in treatment that would both repair the damages of loss and give her courage to live through her feelings of pain and abandonment.

As in all treatment where the problems involve inadequate early object relations, there is a paradox. The therapist cannot actually be that which the patient lost, yet the therapist's presence and actual living with the patient's problems serve to repair the original damage and problem. In this treatment, we experience the patient's early losses and problems, contain and organize his/her experiences, and hope to give him/her a climate where trauma, disappointment, and confusion can be reorganized on a higher, more satisfying level. Other issues commonly encountered in dealing with more primitive mental states involve loss of boundaries and regression to fusion states, both of which will be tested out and experienced within the treatment relationship.

Art, in this context, can be a container or organizer that mirrors internal object relations and their associated defenses and developmental problems. The art therapy relationship offers a safe framework within which to investigate and experience the object world. The style and manner of the expressed art form will exhibit the various levels of definition the relationship creates. Thus, in the opening clinical example, the abstract, but self-contained quality of the art mirrors the quality of the therapeutic relationship.

Art therapy offers the possibility for psychological space, or that which is created through the interactions of two individuals, to be reorganized by mirroring or complementarity (offering opposites). This space has much in common with what Winnicott calls transitional space (1971). It is an intermediate area that is neither inside nor outside, but which bridges subjective and objective reality. By extension, dead or pathological space can also occur either in the art form or in the relationship, when expression is weighed down by oppressive defenses. Here, relationships are experienced and programmed to recreate sterile childhood interactions. Pathological space is one particular dimension of a transitional space and can be experienced on at least two different levels.

In the creative act, the various representations of the patient's world are shaped and reflected through artistic form. This likewise occurs within the interpersonal therapeutic relationship and can either mirror or complement what is going on in the art expression. The skill of the art therapist is brought to bear through his/her ability to maintain a positive, supportive relationship as a background, or structure, in order for the art therapy process to proceed. When pathological space takes over the interaction, it will take ingenuity and creativity on the part of the art therapist to ferret out the hidden object relations and find the appropriate art form to regenerate psychological space.

Implicit in these notions of transitional and pathological space is the idea that relationships are characterized by different energy systems which shape and form the space around us. Within each system, there are different levels of openness or closure, completeness or incompleteness. In primitive mental states, the art therapist offers a creative experience to help move the energy system from one level of differentiation to another. Another way of putting it is that we offer the missing link to complete the Gestalt through mirroring or complementarity.

Art therapy, then, strives to promote new levels of perceptual organization that involves shifts in energy patterns. The art form offers an added means for working with splits and polarities and integrating them into new wholes. The representations from our past are expressed through image and symbol and expand the boundaries of objective reality. Each of these images is shaped by energy, sensation, and color with its own rhythm, volume, and weight. Being nonverbal in nature, these symbols and images are often difficult to express clearly in verbal form and therefore lend themselves well to the medium of art.

This introduces the complex question of the use of words in art therapy. Secondary process thinking, with its foundation in words, must be evoked if the ego is to gain mastery and understanding of primitive material. Although there is secondary process thinking involved in the logic and judgment used in the process of giving artistic form to a personal image, words are more directly hooked to reality. Changing poetic metaphor into an art expression serves as a transition to the world of words and helps to make sense of the truism that although verbal material is strongly connected to reality, not all of reality is encompassed by words. From this perspective, different levels of reality can be experienced and understood within the context of nonverbal expression. The art form, then, organizes object relations and mirrors them back to the patient.

Inherent in the clinical use of object relations theory is a deep-seated understanding of and sensitivity to developmental lines and how they manifest themselves in adult normality and pathology. Although Freud and his direct theoretical heirs postulated a developmental schema that begins at birth, they believed that the Oedipal crisis was so overwhelming that it overrode all that went before. Margaret Mahler incorporates Freud's drive theory, but places greatest importance on the first three years of life and the vicissitudes of the mother-child interaction in shaping the personality (Mahler, Pine, & Bergman, 1975). It is here, Mahler says, that the foundations of an inside me and you are laid down.

Mahler's developmental levels begin with the stage of normal autism at birth, characterized by a blissful oneness with mother. At about three months of age the process of attachment begins with what Mahler calls symbiosis. Slowly, out of a nondifferentiated mass, the me and you inside of the child become defined. As we trace the crucial stages of symbiosis, where mother and child struggle with separateness and sameness, individuation and differentiation are born and the child proceeds through the subphases of hatching, practicing, and rapprochement. The child's growth from symbiosis to separation and individuation culminates in the achievement of an identity and object constancy. At this point, which occurs at about two and a half years of age, the child has a firm sense of self and differentiated other and is able to relate to people as wholes, rather than as need satisfiers. Significantly, the child now tolerates ambivalence, having mended the splits of good and bad, and can maintain a narcissistic equilibrium by a form of self-feeding and self-affirmation that is unique to him/herself.

Horner gives an excellent outline of some of the problems that are associated with each developmental period and connects pathology with issues stemming from faulty early object relations (1979). Problems in the normal autistic phase form the basis of primary infantile autism, which is characterized by a lack of attachment and organization. Proceeding along the very early stages of attachment of the first couple of months, psychopathic personalities are viewed as having had problems in making primitive attachments, although having had a satisfactory initial period of normal autism. Around the fourth and fifth months, when normal symbiosis starts, failures in differentiation create the problems of discrimination of inner and outer reality seen in psychotic states. Schizoid character formation is described as stemming from denial of the attachment started in the differentiating phase of symbiosis.

Finally, in the rapprochement stage, occurring somewhere between 12 and 18 months, there are failures in integration and self-cohesion. Problems here result in the borderline and narcissistic personalities. Both types retreat from autonomy, the task of the rapprochement crisis, but they characteristically do so in different ways. The borderline personality tends toward fusion states and a pervasive use of splitting good and bad in his search for the ideal, whereas the narcissistic personality takes refuge in a grandiose self. Although differing in form, there is in both an attempt to return to the perfection of an early state of oneness with mother. Also associated with failures in the rapprochement stage are the affective disorders. These individuals have not resolved the dilemma of good and bad existing side by side in one space. All that is good and nurturing remains on the outside, while their hunger and greed, which are bad, stay on the inside.

Each developmental problem generates a particular clinical picture with its own pain and anxiety and recreates it in the therapeutic relationship. The art therapist is faced with the challenge of differentiating sometimes similar pictures and reacting appropriately.

Put another way, each developmental problem requires a complex art frame to help transform pathological into therapeutic space. Where pathological space lies stagnant, therapeutic space promotes new solutions and new potentialities, with the accompanying sense of a self being reborn. By implication, there is room for new relationships and expanded levels of awareness. The challenge for the art therapist is to provide an art experience that makes this transition possible and keeps therapeutic space alive. Canned recipes that relate to each developmental level cannot hope to satisfactorily address issues of such manifold complexity. What is called upon is the art therapist's artistry in using his/her conscious symbolic awareness of the patient's art work and relationship to keep the therapeutic process moving.

Winnicott's conceptualization of creativity and play help tie together the threads of developmental theory, the use of art, and therapeutic technique. Winnicott approaches these relationships from the vantage point of how individuals handle inner and outer space. He begins at the start of life when the mother's anticipation of her baby's needs allows the infant to maintain the illusion that mother's breast is part of the infant. In his words:

> From birth, therefore, the human being is concerned with the problem of the relationship between what is objectively perceived and what is subjectively conceived of, and in the solution of this problem there is no help for the human being who has not been started off well enough by the mother. *The intermediate area to which I am referring is the area that is allowed to the infant between primary creativity and the objective perception based on reality-testing*. The transitional phenomena represent the early stages of the use of illusion, without which there is no meaning for the human being in the idea of relationship with an object as perceived by others as external to that being (1971, p. 11).

Creativity, then, is put within the context of human development. The origins of illusion provide the foundation for the creation of the transitional space of inner and outer reality. In this space, the child at first maintains the illusion that the world is his/hers and that he/she can maintain the blissful state of oneness. Only gradually is this illusion of oneness reorganized to take in the demands of outer reality. The goal of development is not one of giving up illusion, however, but one of developing the skills and techniques to make our illusions reality. Creativity within the context of human relationships permits one's inner imaginative world to become congruent with the outside so that each person shapes his/her destiny. One's ability to actually *be* the artist of his/her social world is contingent on having successfully met the developmental challenges of one's past. At times, because of the deficiencies and problems of one's past, artistic expression may be a means to rediscover creativity and innovation, although this creativity may not carry over into social relationships. We all know of artists for whom this is true. Art without a supportive therapeutic relationship will not repair developmental deficits.

In order to recover early creativity and recreate the transitional space so necessary to bridge inner and outer realities, both patient and therapist must be prepared to play, says Winnicott. In fact, Winnicott describes treatment as play or, in some cases, as helping the patient to move toward being able to play. If art therapists are to serve this role, they, likewise, must be ready to play. Play, as described by Winnicott, is not aimless activity or simply having fun, although fun may be one of the ingredients. The essence of play in therapy involves the capacity to relax intellectual controls, and to become non-goal-oriented and open-ended in experiencing and working with the psychological space of patients. Here, images and symbols move into consciousness with their own logic and organization regarding time and place. Through symbolic play patients are helped to organize psychological space, both within the art form and within the art relationship. Form and content become one through a synthesis of primary and secondary processes, also allowing the merging of bound and unbound energy and balancing between fusion and separateness, organization and loss of control. Therapeutic play, then, becomes the means by which to create a holding environment of relatedness and resonance within which deficits in early object relations can be repaired and the potential for creative living can be regenerated.

It should be noted that each developmental period requires a different form of holding. For instance, in patients who have suffered extreme deficiencies in the normal autistic phase resulting in autistic psychosis, the holding environment in the art form and relationship involves structure, sensory contact, and a capturing of the rhythm in disrhythmic patients. Patients who have been traumatized in the early stages of symbiosis, when self and other have not been clearly defined, require structure and boundaries as well as clarity and definition. Because their worlds are so chaotic and disorganized, the holding needs to be gentle, but firm, with verbalization to clarify and connect the worlds of image and outer reality.

For the psychopathic individual, whose capability for attachment has been severely impaired by deficits in the symbiotic phase, the world of power and games is the language that connects him/her to people. To be effective, the art therapist must enter the world of power and games and play within the rules of this patient's world. Demonstrating a degree of savvy and alertness to the psychopathic game plan seems very important, while "feeding" this kind of patient with materials or love with the hope of providing and promoting attachment is a misuse and abuse of the therapeutic relationship. Here, as in other instances, avoiding experiences that are out of sync with a patient's object life is the prime diagnostic and therapeutic issue, requiring skill and artistry as well as thought.

Much has been written about the borderline patient, and the author refers the reader to Masterson and Kernberg as important resources in this area. Here the patient is stuck in the rapprochement phase of separation-individuation. Think back to the "terrible twos" when a parent often feels he or she can do nothing right. The child, aware of his separateness and yet frightened of his aloneness, wants to go in two different directions at the same time. The dilemma for the child is to separate while maintaining connection. As he screams, yells, and objects "No," the child's cries for autonomy are enmeshed with the silent need to be held, a need often rejected when the parent tries to come near the child. In a two-year-old this is understandable. In an adult patient, the picture can be confusing and infuriating. Maintaining a cognitive understanding of these issues is of immeasurable help to the art therapist.

This patient literally consumes both art materials and patience. The task of the art therapist is to keep a very strong and clear perception of what the patient is regressing to when he or she becomes frightened and "disappears" beneath a cloud of hunger for succor and support. Furthermore, the art therapist must not be taken in by swings between devaluation and overevaluation and must be sensitive to the ever-present splits of good and bad. This patient is wonderfully adept at splitting a therapeutic team into warring camps. Also part of the picture are such defenses as projective identification (identifying with what we project outward), withdrawal, introjection, and denial. Manifestations of these must be attended to and confronted in the art therapeutic play. Needless to say, a passive approach is not the best holding environment for the borderline patient.

By contrast, the idealization a narcissistic patient offers an art therapist is usually not defensive in nature. Here, it is an important developmental step in the treatment process. This patient has not been adequately mirrored or affirmed by a consistent maternal object, so the art therapy interaction can provide a crucial reparative opportunity to the patient, offering the long-sought-after mirroring and definition missed in the early family matrix. The interplay of art and the interpersonal therapeutic relationship can vary. At times the patient may take in the mirroring of the art in a way that parallels the therapeutic relationship. At others, the patient's ability to deal with the much wanted and feared mirroring is tenuous enough that it will only be tolerated on a nonverbal level.

Depressive mood states offer another example of splitting, but one that differs in quality from that used by the borderline personality. Also arrested at the rapprochement level, patients with affective disorders have not been able to integrate the good and bad inside themselves and have held on to strong, hostile introjects while expelling all that is good. Art exercises are directed at helping the patient find strength and self-worth through the discovery of his or her own artistic expression. It is the nourishment found in the experience and mastery which promotes the discovery of a good me that had been lost and fused with an internal bad object.

The art therapist's assessment of developmental level and his/her ability to experience, organize, and reflect back the inner state of the patient provide the environment for the patient to reclaim a lost experience and find new levels of self-definition and integration. Again, I cannot emphasize too strongly that growth occurs from the process of going through the pain of an unmet stage of development rather than from the therapist's gratifying the patient in his/her hunger. I repeat the paradox of treatment: I am with you, but separate; I understand your need, but I cannot take away your pain. To rob a patient of his/her anger, pain, and despair, no matter how well intentioned, is to do a disservice. What art therapists can offer is a holding environment, which can make pain bearable and can allow progress and growth to proceed.

Implied in this approach is the notion of duality in our internal psychic structure, a duality that necessitates experiencing at one and the same time softness and hardness, structure and lack of it, distance and closeness, warmth and cold. The resonance art therapists offer patients complements these dualities, so that the aesthetic expression flowing between patient and therapist allows ample room for the complexity of authentic communication. There is a constant exhibition of the integration of opposites, as well as synthesis of primary and secondary process. Room also exists for progression and regression, fusion and separateness.

In summary, object relations theory as applied to art therapy is but a method to seek out and organize an array of different impressions coming from many levels of awareness. Together, they offer opportunities for the creative use of one's personal resources in responding to therapeutic communications. An art experience seems to be an ideal form in which to understand the complicated interconnections of creativity development, pathology, and treatment technique. The nonverbal image captures the inexplicable essences of our past relationships and gives them shape and meaning. As art therapists, our skills in integrating all this offer a special and powerful dimension to a therapeutic team. Our challenge will be one of utilizing these concepts from psychiatry and psychoanalysis, while maintaining the visions and perceptions we have as artists. Within this perspective, verbal and nonverbal behavior coalesce into a mind/body whole as we, as artists and therapists, give recognition to our respect for continuity and individuation.

REFERENCES

Bion, W. F. *Second thoughts*. New York: Jason Aronson, 1967.

Horner, A. *Object relations and the developing ego in therapy*. New York: Jason Aronson, 1979.

Kernberg, O. *Borderline conditions and pathological narcissism*. New York: Jason Aronson, 1975.

Mahler, M., Pine, F., & Bergman, A. *The psychological birth of the human infant: Symbiosis and individuation*. New York: Basic Books, 1975.

Masterson, J. *Psychotherapy of the borderline adult*. New York: Brunner/Mazel, 1976.

Winnicott, D. W. *Playing and reality*. New York: Basic Books, 1971.

SOURCE BOOKS

Greenberg, J., & Mitchell, S. *Object Relations in Psychanalytic Theory*. Cambridge, MA: Harvard University Press, 1983.

Robbins, A. *Expressive therapy: A creative arts approach to depth oriented treatment*. New York: Human Sciences Press, 1980.

Robbins, A., & Sibley, L. *Creative art therapy*. New York: Brunner/Mazel, 1976.

5

A Self Psychology Approach
to Art Therapy

Mildred Lachman-Chapin

Heinz Kohut was a psychoanalyst trained at the Chicago Institute of Psychoanalysis and active on their training staff. In 1959 he published a paper in which he examined the importance of introspection and empathy as the essential ingredients of psychoanalytic observation. Following this seminal paper, he developed a body of theory that has since come to be known as "Self Psychology." This was first formulated in his book *The Analysis of the Self*, published in 1971. In 1977 *The Restoration of the Self* expanded his ideas, making clear his departure from classical Freudian theory and practice. *The Psychology of the Self* (1978) offered case material, illustrating treatment approaches using this theoretical base. In *How Does Analysis Cure?* (1984) Kohut refines and adds to his theories.

Empathy, or vicarious introspection (knowing what the other person is feeling by acknowledging your own feelings which repeat or reflect his), became not only the key observational tool for Kohut, but also an essential treatment modality. He was interested in the kind of psychopathological manifestations that he later termed narcissistic personality disturbances. Essentially these kinds of clients suffer from feelings of inner emptiness, a deep lack of self-esteem, and difficulties in their social and sexual lives which had hitherto been unresponsive to psychoanalysis. He questioned these clients' primary relationship to their inner selves, formulating basic concepts of what he called self-cohesion, or consolidation of the self.

In Kohut's view, early failure in empathy on the part of parental figures is the primary genetic factor causing narcissistic personality disorders (and other pre-Oedipal problems). Failure of empathy in the earliest months of life has a causal role in the pathology of self-cohesion, as well as affecting the development of later libidinal and aggressive conflicts. And, for the most part, it is through empathic response in the therapeutic situation that cure is achieved.

NARCISSISTIC DEVELOPMENT

Kohut has not dealt much with the earliest stage of narcissistic development, primary narcissism, except to refer to it as a stage to which patients may regress in periods of psychotic fragmentation. I assume he means by primary narcissism what other authors (Mahler, Pine, & Bergman, 1975) have referred to as the stages of both normal autism and symbiotic dependency.

> The equilibrium of primary narcissism is disturbed by the unavoidable shortcomings of maternal care, but the child replaces the previous perfection (a) by establishing a grandiose and exhibitionistic image of the self: *the grandiose self*; and (b) by giving over the previous perfection to an admired, omnipotent (transitional) self-object: *the idealized parent imago* (Kohut, 1971, p. 25).

In other words, when the perfection of the original merger with the mother begins to fail, the child adopts an ''I-am-perfect'' view of the self (the archaic grandiose self) and, second, a ''you-are-perfect-and-I-am-part-of-you'' view of the parent (the idealized parent imago). These are the two basic narcissistic configurations with which Kohut's work is concerned.

> Under optimal developmental conditions, the exhibitionism and grandiosity of the archaic grandiose self are gradually tamed, and the whole structure ultimately becomes integrated into the adult personality and supplies the instinctual fuel for our ego-syntonic ambitions and purposes, for the enjoyment of our activities, and for important aspects of our self-esteem. And, under similarly favorable circumstances, the idealized parent imago, too, becomes integrated into the adult personality. Introjected as our idealized super-ego, it becomes an important component of our psychic organization by holding up to us the guiding leadership of its ideals. If the child, however, suffers severe narcissistic traumas, then the grandiose self does not merge into the relevant ego content but is retained in its unaltered form and strives for the fulfillment of its archaic aims. And if the child experiences traumatic disappointments in the admired adult, then the idealized parent imago, too, is retained in its unaltered form . . . (Kohut, 1971, pp. 27–28).

The above might be paraphrased by noting that when development proceeds optimally, the psychic energy that the infant invested in viewing him- or herself as omnipotent and perfect is gradually made available to the child for use in *doing things* to win attention and admiration. When the child fails to develop properly, he or she will not gain the capacity to satisfy narcissistic needs by taking age-appropriate actions. He or she will persist in expecting to gain attention and admiration while remaining passive or by engaging in forms of exhibitionism that never satisfy the infantile longings. With normal development, the idealized parent imago also undergoes a gradual transformation. Internalized, it takes the form of conscience and ideals that guide actions. When development is flawed, the child will continue to look to the "perfect" other for guidance and leadership.

The archaic grandiose self and the idealized parent imago represent the two poles of narcissism (Kohut refers to the bipolar self). Driven by ambition (from the grandiose self) and led by ideals (from the idealized parent imago) the self begins to form. During psychoanalysis special transferences relating to each of these develop. Clients suffering from deficiencies in the area of the grandiose self develop what Kohut calls "mirror transferences." In so doing they are seeking the confirmation of their grandiosity that they failed to receive as very young children from the primary or maternal figure. As an adult, a person cannot ask for such confirmation without feeling intense shame. And those clients whose need as young children to perceive perfection in a parent figure (often the father) was unmet develop "idealizing transferences."

Kohut places the "archaic grandiose self," the first stirrings to selfhood, around the end of the symbiotic phase and the beginning of the stage of individuation, or the rapprochement substage as defined by Mahler, Pine, and Bergman (1975), the toddler period in the middle of the second year.

Kohut's theories do not cover what happens in the development of the sense of self from birth until this period. I shall discuss a bit later how Winnicott's theories regarding transitional phenomena do provide a theoretical framework for the presymbiotic and symbiotic phases.

According to Kohut, during this period, at the end of the symbiotic stage, arise the core conflicts that may later result in the failure to develop a cohesive sense of self. If the child is to experience an age-appropriate grandiose self-image, he or she must feel that exhibitionistic display is safe and effective. The child is assured that this is so by the mother's mirroring, by "the gleam in the mother's eye" (Kohut, 1966). The child's efforts to exhibit him- or herself represent first attempts at individuation, at leaving the symbiotic ties with mother. To be successful, these feats of grandeur and omnipotence must be greeted by the mother with approval and admiration.

Kohut identifies two other kinds of mirror transferences that can be activated in dealing with the archaic grandiose self. One is a wish for merging, where the patient wants to share in the therapist's magic powers through identification, thereby furthering his or her grandiosity and sense of omnipotence. The other is twinship mirroring, where the patient feels somewhat separate but almost identical with the therapist. In his last book (1984), Kohut amplifies the twinship transference concept, making it a separate and more important kind of transference.

As the mirroring proceeds, the goal is to help the grandiose self become less archaic, more appropriate to the patient's age. When the client becomes invested in the product of his or her *own* action—that is, in his or her *own* artwork—this is progress. The sublimatory mechanism changes archaic responses into more ego-related psychic structures. It can be, as Kohut puts it, a "transmuting internalization," by which real ego building is accomplished. The longing for an empathic response from the maternal person who is still almost oneself is changed into a sense of self-pride in being watched over by "others," real others, as one produces. Real others, then, are objects separate from oneself. Narcissistic investment in an art product helps the client to individuate, to separate from the need to have his exhibitionistic yearnings confirmed in an archaic (infantile) fashion.

It is most important, however, that throughout the mirroring process therapists hold out the promise of ultimate approval for the *real* accomplishment, that is, for departure from symbiosis (or the infantile means of achieving satisfaction of narcissistic needs).

Mirroring is more technically described by Kohut as empathic responsiveness of the self-object. The term "self-object" also requires some definition.

Kohut's definition of self-object differs from the same term used earlier by Boyer and Giovacchini (1967, p. 260). These writers focus, as does Winnicott (1971), on the earlier infantile phases of the presymbiotic and symbiotic relationship to the mother (compared to Kohut's postsymbiotic reference point), giving quite a different meaning to the term self-object. They refer to the *mother* satisfying her own narcissistic needs by "projecting usually the devalued parts of herself, her bad introjects" (Giovacchini, 1984) onto the infant. This usually results in the infant's self-hatred and feeling of badness, and later self-destructiveness. Kohut's use of the term self-object, in contrast, here refers to the *child's* need for the mother to satisfy his own narcissistic development.

Kohut refers to the self-object as a person or thing valued for its function in enhancing oneself. This differs from a true object, a person who is valued and related to in his or her own right. In the early developmental stages of narcissism a self-object is needed by the child and used for the kind of mirroring we have been describing. Failure in the empathic response of a self-object can inflict damaging blows on the growing child's sense of self.

The analyst functions as a self-object in the psychoanalytic treatment of a patient with a narcissistic personality disorder. The mirror transferences described above invite the analyst to respond empathically with a specific kind of nurturing. Ideally, over time the patient will feel the response, recognize what he or she is asking of the analyst, reconstruct genetically some personal history, and, most important, profit by the reparative empathic experience in that he or she will begin to build ego structures less dependent on archaic primary self-objects. Put another way, the patient will develop more abstract and aim-inhibited self-objects.

An example of this process can be found in the case to follow, particularly in the therapeutic sequence represented in Figures 3, 4, and 5 (see pp. 86–88). In Figure 3, Mary sees herself as a devouring and destructive person, whose need for control and almost physical possession of the object is global, omnipotent; the object is seen as something or someone who can and *must* be globally possessable and devourable. I contributed Figure 4. She is led to understand her archaic self-object needs in the perspective of an adult looking at a newborn. She then, in producing Figure 5, seems to be seeing herself still "hungry," but within some kind of structured environment. This translated for her into an understanding that her hungers could now be looked at in terms of what they actually were in the present reality. She had been fearful of going on a trip with her new-found boyfriend, afraid she would become like the devouring fish in Figure 3 and ruin everything. She was able, after this interchange, to actually take the trip and enjoy it. She had modulated her initial response, as if needing an archaic self-object, to one in which the self-object, the boyfriend's company on a trip, was more concrete, limited, manageable in reality.

Kohut speaks of tension regulation as one of the goals of ego structuralization. In the earliest stage of infancy, the stage of primary narcissism when the child feels inner tension, he or she has no way of relieving it. Only by ministrations from outside the child, that is, from the mother, is the child soothed. Acceptance of soothing from the "good-enough mother" (Winnicott, 1971) relieves inner tension for the moment. Later the child's adoption of a transitional object whereby the absent mother is mentally invoked allows the child to relieve tension somewhat by him- or herself through partly psychic means (*Ibid.*). This means of regulating tension by oneself is a rudimentary step in ego structuring.

Kohut, like Winnicott before him, pointed out that artistic work functions as a means of dealing with pain and tension both by providing a way of expressing it (rather than keeping it operating *within* the body-mind) and by transforming the tension into some form of self-regulatory mechanism such as is operative with the transitional object. The mechanism can be described as recall or imaging of an object when it is not there—a crucial first step; the introjection of the object, taking it in but not yet identifying with it; and then identification with the object to the point where it becomes part of the person. This process Kohut calls *transmuting internalization*, or structure building. It means the person has achieved a more independent way of relieving his or her own tension. Thus, art and creativity are seen as a way not only to relieve tension but also to build ego strength.

As artists we are drawn to an empathic way of relating to the world. In our art we project our subjective state onto the work we create. The work objectifies and expresses our introspection in a form outside ourselves which other persons can grasp through their empathy. We, in turn, grasp empathically the artwork produced by others. Thus we, as artists, are attuned to the empathic response as a therapeutic element, especially as we help clients to produce expressive works of art and as we respond to their creations.

We are also very much involved as artists in expressing the self. When faced with troubled patients, whatever their pathological label, we artists may intuitively recognize that these people are troubled in their "selves." Here again, our qualities as artists equip us to function as therapists. It may also be that certain unresolved grandiose exhibitionist stirrings are part of our own makeup. Here we can not only mirror and accept empathically these archaic strivings in our clients, but can offer to them a solution we ourselves have found. Art can be used as a form of exhibition, as a way to create, to be magic, to be understood, admired, and affirmed.

I believe that the artwork itself can then become a self-object for the client. He is helped to shift from considering the therapist as sole self-object, to the creation of a self-object of his own. This effects a step toward individuation, and the art therapist is there to give the longed-for empathic response.

Another way I have found to provide a kind of mirroring empathic response is by doing art along with the client. At some point during the session, after we have dialogued with words for a while, we each set about doing a work of art, usually not looking at what the other is doing. I am intensely focused on the client and his concerns, but do not plan what I will do. When we both finish, we first consider the client's work; then we look at mine. After the client has responded to my work, I offer my own comments. This becomes a response to the client through my pre-conscious processes, formed by my artistic skills and informed by my clinical judgment. It is a daring procedure. All good therapists use their own unconscious responses, but here there is a *visible* product to be examined by both client and the therapist. It documents the therapist's response. The client becomes vividly aware of the reality of the person he is relating to. The therapist, on the other hand, cannot avoid looking at whatever countertransference issues or personal problems appear in his artwork and must deal with them in order to further the therapeutic relationship with the client.

The art therapist has used him/herself as an artist. The client has received a very concrete and vivid empathic response from a "real" person.

As noted earlier, Kohut's theories deal with the development of narcissism at the point of the infant's leaving the symbiotic bond with mother. His descriptions of the various kinds of narcissistic transferences refer to the client's unmet needs as he begins to individuate. That is, Kohut is concerned with the client who has had traumatic experiences with parental figures as he emerges from what would be presumed to be a successful symbiotic relationship. But what happens if the first year and a half or so have not provided the child with a healthy merging relationship with mother? As Giovacchini (1984, p. 89) points out in discussing narcissistically disturbed patients, "The impact of the traumatic environment is felt from the very beginning of life, and distortions of ego development and defects occur in both presymbiotic and symbiotic phases." Here is where Winnicott's (1971) theories about transitional phenomena are extremely useful.

The grandiosity that Kohut is talking about becomes, then, a continuation of what Winnicott describes as happening much earlier, during the first year of life, when the *child* takes a transitional object and learns thereby the magic of creating something psychically. Giovacchini (1984) adds to this some interesting ideas about the *mother's* grandiosity, i.e., treating her child as a transitional object, becoming unwilling to relinquish her omnipotent power over the child. This is another way to look at the failure in empathic response to the child's need to individuate, a subject upon which Kohut's theories are particularly focused.

In the case that follows, Mary has an unmet need for reciprocity, for an empathic response from the external world. I believe this stemmed from her very earliest attempts to bond with her mother. She had not been able to enjoy a healthy symbiosis with mother where she could learn to soothe herself with the kind of grandiose creativity that Winnicott describes. Although this case does not fit Kohut's formulations in terms of the patient needing first and foremost to individuate, it does point up the need of this kind of client for a response in terms of the development of self, *no matter at what stage*. My technique in art therapy, as decribed above, would be the same: an empathic art response to what the client's needs are *at the level of his needs*. Clinical judgment determines what that level is.

For example, Mary's implicit questions are: What is merging? Is it safe to merge? Will I destroy the person I merge with?

For patients whose need is to try to emerge from a fairly successful symbiosis, the question is: Can I use my omnipotent powers to destroy the bond with mother? Can I destroy mother's hold on me? Can I destroy the merged mother in my mind? Will she admire and encourage and approve my audacities of separation and accomplishment? Will she empathize with my exercised prowess? If I need at times to remerge, will she let me? If she fails me, will there be someone wise I can be like, separate yet the same?

So, although self-psychology has become associated with Kohut and his disciples, psychoanalysts and psychologists from many other theoretical frameworks are looking at the development of self, adding their own enriching perspectives.

For me, art is a way to provide nurturing, empathic responses for the developing self, with the therapist ever aware of the particular self-developmental step the client is ready and asking for.

CASE EXAMPLE

Mary was a young woman in her early twenties who had been taking drugs since early adolescence, and who was admitted to a psychiatric hospital after a suicide attempt. She had had a number of drug-related hospitalizations and been in treatment, usually briefly, with several therapists. Her family had given up on her; from their point of view, this was to be a final attempt to help her.

As part of a treatment team I did individual art therapy with her while she was hospitalized and continued to see her as an outpatient. She responded very well to the interactive technique which I have described; so this was the way we worked together most of the time. In the hospital, she would sit in bed, working on a lap board and insisting on having the room dimly lit. I sat beside the bed, using a lap board. When she was an outpatient, we sat at a card table, facing each other. I propped a board up so that she could not see me work, and I rarely looked at what she was doing until she was finished.

Following are two examples of such art interchanges, one done while she was in the hospital, and one as an outpatient.

Figure 1, "See Me Sometimes," was done in the hospital in anticipation of a visit by a former boyfriend, the first visitor since her admission two months earlier. I asked her to do a picture about what she expected, what her thoughts and feelings were about seeing him again. She refused. Instead, working from a scribble, she produced the head of a man "smoking a reefer." He had a stitched-up slit across the side of his face, two frontal eyes on a profile figure, the hair standing on end. The figure seemed to

Figure 1

have an expression of disorientation, possibly drug induced. I referred to her drug episodes with her boyfriend. She denied this interpretation, said she didn't like the picture, quickly turned it over, and produced Figure 1.

She said this was like Mae West who said, "Come up and see me sometime." It was "psychedelic," she said, and "fun." She referred to the brightly colored undulating form flowing out of the left side of the female figure as "psychedelic disco lights." She spoke with a kind of tough disdain, "cool," as if she didn't care. The female figure has red arms and shoulders. The border surrounding the figure is a dark and dull blue-black.

My impressions as I saw this image were that she was referring to what she felt was the sexy and exciting life she had had with her boyfriend, and to the compartmentalized nature of that distant life. It was a boxed-in memory, suggesting, by its distinct border, a kind of separation from her real self; just as the sexy-looking figure was self-absorbed, sending out "vibes," but not connected to anyone. It may also have referred to her pronounced feelings of confinement in the hospital, with no visitation or telephone privileges until this impending visit. The picture looks bleak, brassy, sad. My associations were to a little girl, dressing up in mother's outrageous finery, trying to be sexually grown up. I did not voice any of these ideas to her.

Instead I showed her my picture, Figure 2. I worked from a scribble, producing this figure which she said looked like a nun. She said it was funny to see a nun all naked and feeding a baby. Then she giggled and talked about stories she had heard about nuns having sexual intercourse. She seemed fascinated by this image. She titled it "The Naked Nun." We talked about babies and mothers and she repeated her complaints about her own mother which had been one primary theme of our work all along. She had spoken of her mother as being cold, demanding, expecting too much of her, demanding support from her child instead of the other way around, etc. She had been out of contact with her mother for some time before the hospitalization, dealing only with her father when any family contact was necessary. And in the picture the nun–mother is not looking

Figure 2

at the baby, not even making the visual connection between mother and child that is so elemental.

Mary was an adopted child. Her mother was a diabetic and couldn't have children of her own. Mary's pictures up to that point had many images and references to oral themes. And indeed her psychiatrist spoke of her as "never having found her mouth." He explained that she had not seemed to have been adequately bonded to mother, to have achieved the symbiotic bond that is the precursor to the development of self-soothing capacities. Drug taking, he theorized, was her attempt at a kind of self-soothing. She was fundamentally unattached, as suggested in her picture, Figure 1, not having formed the first essential bond with mother, unable to make later relationships and attachments to other people. The sexuality depicted in this picture is false, an imitation of adult activity, but without relationship to another person. It is frantic, narcissistic, and exhibitionistic.

My picture was, I believe, my preconscious sense of her strange relationship to mother and birth. I did not think of the mothering figure as a nun. That was *her* association. As a matter of fact, I don't remember having any conscious thoughts about this picture. But as she developed her associations, it became clear to me that what I had depicted in this picture *for her* was an unnatural mother, someone who wasn't supposed to be sexual and therefore to have a child. It condenses in one image the ideas of coldness, chastity, and mothering. The mother's body, as naked, warm flesh, is forbidden to her and felt as prohibited by the child. The sexual union that produced the child was also forbidden, illegal. This suggests thoughts about her natural mother who may have given Mary up for adoption because she was illegitimate. It also suggests that sexuality is a remote, illicit activity, magically creating a child but having nothing to do with a relationship, either to the sexual partner or to the child that is produced. Some of these ideas about sexuality are implicit in her own picture of herself, Figure 1. My picture presented her with the implications for her of her own thoughts about her birth and her fundamental early lack of connection with her mother.

None of this was verbalized between us as interpretations of our pictures. We simply talked about her anger at her mother (in the present) and references to lewd nun stories. But, just as my picture had come from my unconscious, mirroring for her what she was saying at a deep level about early, verbally inaccessible experiences, it was, through its image and her associations to it, able to convey to her some of the meaning that I could later articulate for myself.

I believe it was this kind of dialogue through our art which helped her to break out of her psychic cocoon in the hospital. She gradually became able to let herself be cared for by various members of the hospital team, to experience some self-soothing, to form some meager relationships, and eventually to leave the hospital.

She made a remarkably rapid adjustment to life outside the hospital, was able to get and to hold a part-time job, and to find a new boyfriend. When that relationship began to deepen, she became afraid. She drew Figure 3, "Devouring," after telling me that her boyfriend had invited her to take a trip to visit some of his friends, and that she was disturbed and fearful. This picture was a response to my asking her to try to depict her fear.

She said the large fish at the bottom was herself, that she was about to bite on the hook, and that once she got the hook in her mouth, she would pull down the whole boat with all the people on it and they would

Figure 3

Figure 4

all drown. Then she spoke about all the relationships in her life that she had ruined and said that she was afraid she would make a mess of this one too.

I showed her my picture, Figure 4, which I had not yet titled. She described what she saw—a mama bird and some eggs in a nest—but had no other thoughts or associations to this picture. I then explained that the eggs in the nest would hatch, and hungry little birds would emerge. I said that for newborn animals (and infants as well) eating was a matter of life and death, that they are blindly voracious, needing and wanting only to fill themselves with food. I explained that this thoughtless, all-consuming greed and need may feel to the infant frighteningly destructive. I said that perhaps her present wish to be close to her boyfriend may have that same quality of potentially destructive greed, that sometimes we reexperience in later life the frighteningly devouring nature of this hunger.

I suggested that perhaps her own mother bird hadn't brought the worms in a satisfying enough way. She immediately retorted, "So you take it." "Right," I said, "you reach out and devour." She called her picture, then, "Devouring"; I called mine "About to Devour."

In this interchange, I had seen her begin her picture before I began mine. What I had seen was the sharp, hungry mouth of the fish that she began with. I thought of a newborn chick, so that my picture of the eggs in the nest was a conscious response to her initial image.

Figure 5, "Wish to Survive," was done by her at the next session. She had clearly continued to think of her devouring hungers, but had begun to see them not so much as destructive and frightening as expressing her own vital needs. She had gotten in touch with a primitive sense of self which, in itself, began to give her some psychic structure. The geometrical network that forms the environment for this poignant, animallike figure suggests such structure.

In the first picture dialogue Mary was presenting herself as a sexual woman having "fun." Sexuality implies intimate physical contact with someone, yet her picture was lonely, self-absorbed, enclosed, sad. My picture was an empathic response to her essential loneliness and lack of truly satisfying physical intimate contact at a primary, infantile level. As

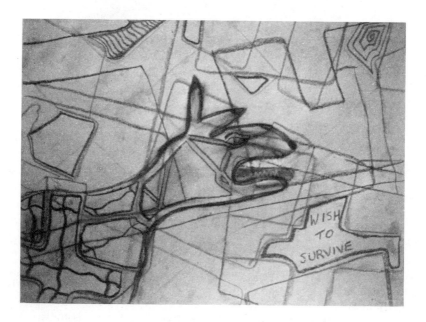

Figure 5

had been shown during her hospitalization, this indeed was the level of her pain.

In the second picture dialogue Mary was expressing her fear of the destructiveness of her own omnivorous needs. My picture in this case provided a context in which she could understand her needs. It was a way of reframing for her what she was at last getting in touch with but was unable to tolerate.

In both dialogues, through empathic response from my artwork, I could acknowledge her grandiosity (being looked at, Figure 1, and being powerfully destructive, Figure 3) as well as her feeling of disappointment at a failure of empathy in early maternal response (Figure 2.). I was responding to her very early experiences of the developing self, which often cannot be expressed in words, having occurred before the development of language. Also, I think that an empathic response in words may not be felt as immediately as is this kind of artistic imagery.

This does not mean that the dialogue, to be effective, must be in terms of representational imagery. These picture dialogues were chosen for ease of presentation and reproduction. There are just as many instances, in this case and others, of abstract or nonrepresentational drawings and sculptures by the client and myself. Formal elements of line, color, and shape can be the expressive language of visual/artistic communication and can be just as powerful as representational pictures or sculptures.

Mary had had a traumatic mothering experience, probably from the beginning of her life. She had not received the kind of maternal empathic responses that provide what Winnicott (1971) calls the "holding environment." Thus, vital steps in the development of a cohesive self were missing. For such people, working with an artist in this kind of pictorial dialogue can provide a way of experiencing a primal (pre-Oedipal) relationship, where the person can engage more successfully in a mutuality that allows him to contribute something—to make reparation, perhaps, for some of the primitive hostility and mortal fears engendered in the infantile dyad.

RELEVANCE TO DIAGNOSIS

These treatment approaches are especially indicated for clients with narcissistic personality disorders or borderline conditions. They are also useful, I have found, with higher-functioning clients whose presenting symptoms are more Oedipal in nature. These are people whose continuing difficulties in love and sexual relationships can be seen as stemming in part from a shaky sense of self. Pre-Oedipal relationships with mother, especially unresolved grandiosity and/or overidealization, may be important areas to examine in this connection. Behind the vague, unrewarding, uneven lives of these often worldly and well-functioning individuals is a need for a more cohesive sense of self and a real separation from early mother imagos. Attuned to signs of such early deficits, the art therapist can respond at some point in treatment with a self-psychology approach.

IMPLICATIONS FOR TREATMENT AND TRAINING

Clearly, art therapists must focus attention on pre-Oedipal development. Verbal psychoanalytic technique, developed largely with and for Oedipal conflicts, is not a sufficient model for us as art therapists.

We should question our use of confrontation and interpretation, determining more clearly to what sectors of an individual's personality we are responding, to make our techniques and responses more fitting and useful. More precisely, there is a need to study and train ourselves to recognize and respond to the narcissistic components of our patients' psyches, the better to promote healing through appropriate responses to idealizing and mirror transferences.

Kohut's ideas clarified for me some of what I have been doing all along in my work as an art therapist. He has helped me to better understand what there is in the universal nature of art that makes it work in therapy. My reading of Kohut has led me to concentrate on the earliest narcissistic elements of the creative drive and how best to respond to these. It has meant concentrating my efforts on maintaining an empathic, supportive role, using confrontation and interpretation as one option among many and then only when a particular situation seemed to justify such techniques.

Not all of our clients are dealing with narcissistic traumas, so that our responses to patients must be as varied and finely tuned as the state of our therapeutic skills allows. This means that with certain of our patients interpretation and confrontation focused on resolution of conflict will be called for.

Kohut (1984) postulates the need for self-objects throughout life for everyone. If Kohut is right, as I believe he is, then art in its various forms may be a means of satisfying a lifelong yearning. And art therapists can help people to meet this need.

I have found it gratifying that Kohut (1966) and his predecessors (primarily Winnicott), in emphasizing the importance of the development of the self during the earliest pre-Oedipal stages, have made a place for art and the artist in furthering such development.

The art therapist must serve an empathic, nurturing function for clients who lack a cohesive sense of self because of its failure to develop during the pre-Oedipal period. This is typical of a great many psychiatric clients, particularly those classified today as borderline or narcissistic personality disorders rather than neurotic. Art and the art therapist can be used by many clients in finding ways to express *without shame* those grandiose, exhibitionistic wishes which have not been integrated into the personality and sense of self. As artists, art therapists are particularly suited to performing this task because we share, to a greater extent than the average person, our clients' need to exhibit themselves and receive attention, or to meet grandiose expectations of parental figures. But also, as artists, we have achieved some success in channeling our narcissistic energy into the creation of age-appropriate (socially valuable), highly cathected products that strengthen the sense of self. Moreover, the nature of our artistic pursuits has sharpened our powers of empathy.

REFERENCES

Boyer, L. B., & Giovacchini, P. L. *Psychoanalytic treatment of schizophrenic, borderline and characterological disorders*. New York: Aronson, 1967.

Giovacchini, P. L. The psychoanalytic paradox. *Psychoanalytic Review*, 1984, *71*, 81–104.

Kohut, H. Introspection, empathy and psychoanalysis. *Journal of the American Psychoanalytic Association*, 1959, 7, 459–483.

Kohut, H. Forms and transformations of narcissism. *Journal of the American Psychoanalytic Association*, 1966, *14*, 243–272.

Kohut, H. *The analysis of the self*. New York: International Universities Press, 1971.

Kohut, II. *The restoration of the self*. New York: International Universities Press, 1977.

Kohut, H. *The psychology of the self*. New York: International Universities Press, 1978.

Kohut, H. *How does analysis cure?* Chicago: University of Chicago Press, 1984.

Lachman, M. Book review of *Therapeutic consultations in child psychiatry* and *Playing and reality* (both by D. W. Winnicott). *American Journal of Art Therapy*, 1972, *11*, 153–155.

Mahler, M., Pine, F., & Bergman, A. *The psychological birth of the human infant*. New York: Basic Books, 1975.

Winnicott, D. W. *Playing and reality*. New York: Basic Books, 1971.

6

Jungian Analytic Art Therapy

Michael Edwards

Theories of personality are open to abuse as well as to sensitive and imaginative implementation. Jungian theory is, of course, no exception. Although Jung proposed and elaborated a complex and essentially non-reductive model of the psyche, it is all too easy to miss the spirit of Jung's ideas while attempting to adhere to them in a rigid or overliteral way. If there is the possibility of being too narrow, there is an alternative possibility of trivializing concepts by failing to draw attention to the subjective and affective links by means of which they come alive in the therapeutic situation. I hope that both traps can be avoided in attempting to synthesize those aspects of Jungian and post-Jungian thought that have contributed to the practice of art therapy in general and to Jungian art therapy in particular.

Few art therapists would deny the importance of Freud in the development of art therapy concepts and practice. Jung's influence is also usually acknowledged but, except by Jungian therapists, briefly and with a sense of ambivalence. This would not be surprising if Jung's contribution had been negligible, but that is not the case. In his own life and in his approach to analytic treatment Jung seems to have anticipated ideas about the use of imagery in therapy to which most present-day art therapists would subscribe. Why, then, has he been all but ignored in the art therapy literature?

Although not a trained artist, Jung was evidently quite a talented amateur landscape painter. Two of his early paintings were made not long after he had qualified and accepted a position as assistant staff physician at the Burghölzi psychiatric hospital in Zürich. However, it was not with landscapes but with inner sources of imagery that Jung was preoccupied throughout his life (Jaffé, 1979).

In *Memories, Dreams, Reflections* (1963) Jung describes a boyhood of vivid dreams and eidetic fantasy images. In his tenth year, at a time of stress and personal alienation, he discovered relief in making a secret totemic figure:

> I had in those days a yellow, varnished pencil-case of the kind commonly used by primary-school pupils, with a little lock and the customary ruler. At the end of this ruler I now carved a little manikin, about two inches long, with frock coat, top hat, and shiny black boots. I coloured him black with ink, sawed him off the ruler, and put him in the pencil case, where I made him a little bed. I even made a coat for him out of a bit of wool. In the case I also placed a smooth, oblong blackish stone from the Rhine, which I had painted with water colours to look as though it was divided into an upper and lower half, and had long been carried around in my trouser pocket. This was his stone. All this was a great secret. Secretly I took the case to the forbidden attic at the top of the house . . . and hid it with great satisfaction on one of the beams under the roof. . . . I felt safe, and the tormenting sense of being at odds with myself was gone (p. 34).

Jung later describes how, in 1913, while he was still feeling disoriented by the trauma of his break with Freud, he found stability by building symbolic structures with stones from the Zürich lakeshore:

> I went on with the building game after the noon meal every day, whenever the weather permitted. As soon as I was through eating, I began playing, and continued to do so until the patients arrived; and if I was finished with my work early enough in the evening, I went back to building. In the course of this activity my thoughts clarified, and I was able to grasp the fantasies whose presence in myself I dimly felt (*Ibid.*, pp. 168–169).

Throughout the rest of his life, and particularly at times of personal crisis, Jung drew, painted, and sculpted representations of his inner experiences. He makes it clear that this was not a peripheral activity, but on the contrary was a vivid source of personal insight into his situation; this, in turn, informed the development of many of his psychological theories. No other major psychologist has attended to his own inner life through imagery in this way. In fact, Jung's theories can best be understood in the context of the value he attached to the subjective reality of spontaneously generated images.

Freud had, of course, led the way in giving recognition and importance to such imagery, especially in dreams, but there is an important distinction to be made. Freud treated the dream, the fantasy, or the unconscious factor in a picture as a puzzle to be solved and explained in terms of psychoanalytic theory, whereas Jung attempted to relate to the unconscious image as an entity in its own right. In doing so he examined images from a number of perspectives, cultural as well as psychological. It is an open, hermeneutic mode of interpretation, lacking the economy and elegance of Freud's method, but offering instead a psychological reevaluation of traditional ways of understanding inner experience.

From a realization of the psychological value that he personally discovered in exploring images from the unconscious, Jung began to encourage his patients to make visual representations of their dream and fantasy material. This began at least as early as 1917 and continued throughout Jung's analytic work. His closest followers worked in a similar way. The paintings and drawings were not generally made during the sessions, but were nevertheless considered as integral to the ongoing therapeutic process. Although the extent to which Jung's patients used pictorial imagery in their therapy is not widely known, he made a number of references to this aspect of his treatment methods, most notably in 1931 in "The Aims of Psychotherapy," a paper that appears in *The Practice of Psychotherapy* (*Collected Works, Vol. 16*, 1966):

> But why do I encourage patients to express themselves at a certain stage of development by means of brush, pencil or pen? My purpose is the same here as in my handling of dreams: I wish to produce an effect. In the childish conditions described above, the patient remains in a passive state; but now he begins to play an active part. At first he puts on paper what has come to him in fantasy, and thereby gives it the status of a deliberate act. He not only talks about it, but he is actually *doing* something about it. Psychologically speaking, it is one thing for a person to have an interesting conversation with his doctor once a week—the results of which hang somewhere or other in mid-air—and quite another thing to struggle for hours at a time with refractory brush and colours, and to produce in the end something which, at its face value, is perfectly senseless. Were his fantasy *really* senseless to him, the effort to paint it would be so irksome that he could scarcely be brought to perform this exercise a second time. But since his fantasy does not seem to him entirely senseless, his busying himself with it increases its effect upon him. Moreover, the effort to give visible form to the image enforces a study of it in all its parts, so that in this way its effects can be completely experienced.

It will be noted that Jung does not seem to be describing either catharsis or sublimation, but the idea that the patient enters into a relationship *with* an unconscious image. Jung continues:

It is true, I must add, that the mere execution of the pictures is not all that is required. It is necessary besides to have an intellectual and emotional understanding of them: they must be consciously integrated, made intelligible, and morally assimilated. We must subject them to a process of interpretation.

Although Jung also says a little later that he has not yet succeeded in making the technique clear, in a form suitable for publication, in essentials he has described some familiar aspects of art as therapy.

There is a further surprising dimension to the comparative neglect of Jung by most art therapists. The acknowledged pioneer art therapist Margaret Naumburg was more than sympathetic to Jungian ideas at the time she founded, in 1915, the school that was later called Walden (Cremin, 1961, p. 211). Beck, too, says that Naumburg "had the advantage of knowing Freudian teaching but happened to be more attracted to that of the Swiss psychiatrist and psychologist, Carl Gustav Jung" (1958, p. 201). Like her sister, Florence Cane, Naumburg undertook a Jungian analysis with Beatrice Hinckle between 1914 and 1917, a time when relations between Freudians and Jungians were at their most acrimonious. Hinckle was actually the first translator of Jung's *Wandlungen und Symbole der Libido* (1912), published as *Psychology of the Unconscious* (1916), which presented a view of symbolism significantly different from Freud's and which had a great deal to do with precipitating the break between the two men.

In her books, Naumburg gives most space to Jung in *Schizophrenic Art* (1950), although this is mostly confined to a discussion of *Mythology of the Soul* by Baynes (1940), which includes two long art psychotherapy case histories. Baynes, who had worked closely with Jung in the 1930s, was a major influence, through Irene Champernowne, on the establishment of art therapy in Britain.

After this time, possibly as a result of a swing toward Freudian psychoanalysis in North America, Naumburg's writing increasingly shows a preference for Freud's terminology and concepts. However, she retained a modest skepticism about classical psychoanalytic methods. Indeed, what remains of Jung in Naumburg's later writing seems to have been absorbed into her own theories of art therapy, which she steadfastly contrasts with more reductive approaches. Jung's early impact on art therapy, as on art education (Read, 1943; Robertson, 1963), was more inspirational than conceptual. His theories were not easily described, but they seemed to liberate the child-centered ideas of both Naumburg and Cane, which were implemented at Walden (Beck, 1959; Cremin, 1961).

Jung never published an extended account of his personal and professional experience with imagery, although he refers many times throughout his writings to the technique of "active imagination," in which the drawing and painting of images from the unconscious can play a crucial part. *The Archetypes and the Collective Unconscious* (*Collected Works*, Vol. 9, part 1, 1968) and *Alchemical Studies* (*Collected Works*, Vol. 13, 1968) both contain many illustrations of his patients' artwork. Jung first wrote about active imagination in a 1916 paper "The Transcendent Function," but he did not publish this until 1957 (*Collected Works*, Vol. 8, 1969). *Man and His Symbols* (1964) was a late attempt to make some of his theories more accessible, linking the therapeutic process with archetypal symbolism as found in mythology, alchemy, religion, fairy tales, and the arts. Despite Jung's own early experiences with unconscious imagery, he was inclined to the view that his methods were more suited to the second half of life, the age group from which most of his patients came. However, Jungian therapists now work with patients of all ages.

A further problem with Jung's presentation of his theories about the use of imagery is that, unlike Freud, he was not disposed to mention clinical material. There are virtually no case histories to be found in all but his earliest writings, and the artwork he shows is accompanied by only the briefest of explanations, which focus on archetypal aspects of the imagery, not on the patient's personal associations. It is wrong to infer from this, however, that he did not elicit such associations. Jung makes it clear that he was essentially patient-centered in his methods, and that successful interpretations of images can only be made through mutual understanding and insight between patient and therapist, bringing about a synthesis of personal and archetypal material (*Collected Works*, Vol. 8, 1969, pp. 116–121 and 477). However, as is the case with other psychodynamic therapies, it is difficult to imagine theory in practice unless one has experienced it personally or has had access to detailed clinical material.

Notwithstanding these possible causes, there is, I feel sure, another and more significant reason for the neglect of Jung by most art therapists. Once Freud and Jung began to go their separate ways after 1913, Jung's ideas were actively rejected by the majority of Freudians. With the spread and subsequent development of psychoanalysis, the initial attempt to preserve what was felt to be the integrity of Freud's theories turned into an outright condemnation of those who disagreed with him. The revisions of psychoanalytic theory by both Adler and Jung were felt to be betrayals. Such feelings were not one-sided, although Jung maintained that he continued to accept the majority of Freud's ideas and only disputed their claims to comprehensiveness and exclusivity. After Jung's departure, Freud rarely referred to Jung, and then only in scathing terms, but it was Edward Glover who, in *Freud or Jung?* (1950), set out to demolish credibility for

Jung's theories. Glover, who was a strong Freudian loyalist, is often cited as a psychoanalytic authority on Jung. Ernst Kris, for example, in *Psycho-analytic Explorations in Art* (1952), an influential book for early art therapists, seems to derive his limited understanding of Jung almost entirely from Glover. The Freud/Jung split is therefore historically important for art therapy and continues to affect present practice. I should like to explore this historical aspect a little further, with a view to setting Jungian art therapy in context.

Questions of loyalty figured strongly in the early days of psychoanalysis and tend to persist, not only in the literature, but also in the handling of knowledge and insight by successive generations of therapists. Since the quarrel between Freud and Jung was accompanied by such bitterness, it is not surprising that little attention should have been given to the insights of each school by the followers of the other. There are significant transference issues here. The founding fathers are still exerting emotional as well as intellectual power. All psychodynamic therapies are really oral traditions as well as bodies of knowledge, and art therapy is no exception. Much more is passed on during training than mere technical concepts, through interaction with therapists who themselves are closely linked by a generation or two to founding figures. Parental disapproval lurks constantly in the background, and challenges to this authority have to be carefully monitored. Thus, despite the scientific pretensions of psychodynamic theories, they are often heavily loaded with transference implications, because they have been learned in a transference context.

There were transference and countertransference issues between Freud and Jung too, although the manifest cause of their final disagreement was over theory. The most important way in which they differed theoretically was over conceptions of symbolism. As stated earlier, Jung attempted to understand symbolic images in their own terms, in a strongly empathic way, rather than simply as secondary process revisions, disguising primary process impulses.

This view originated in his researches, which convinced Jung that incest taboos in primitive societies were not, as Freud believed, the *result* of incestuous practices and desires, but rather were unconscious cultural structures of belief, of wide functional application, which depended on the *metaphor* of actual incest for their conceptual basis and potency. The totem, for example, can be seen to have blatant sexual connotations, but these serve to focus attention only on its literal rather than metaphoric meaning. Jung ascribed to symbolic events and images a collective origin, experienced individually, with an added dimension of profound spiritual significance or *numinosity* derived from their deeply unconscious source

(Storr, 1983, p. 16). Freud regarded such cultural symbols as products of universally experienced fantasies of childhood, attributing numinous experience solely to the transference.

For Jung, the collective unconscious expresses itself through the personal unconscious. As the personal unconscious is structured by the *complexes*, so the collective unconscious is structured by the archetypes. Thus Jung linked some of his earliest researches in word association, which led to the theory of complexes, with later researches and clinical findings, which led to the theory of archetypes. Although Jung maintained that he more or less accepted Freud's model of the personal unconscious, its context and function are greatly changed by the assumption that behind every complex lies an archetype. In Jungian theory the symbolic image is neither wholly archetypal nor wholly personal, but derives from and bridges both levels of the psyche. Consciousness, through the ego, may be brought to bear on the unconscious image, giving it visible *form* and, by interpretation, *meaning* which can be integrated into life (*Collected Works, Vol. 6*, 1971, pp. 442–447).

The symbolic image, for Jung, is its own best explanation; the unconscious does not lie, and it is only the ego which sometimes needs to defend itself against the truth. The image reveals its meaning when it is "accepted" as a projection which virtually speaks for itself, but in a way that is characteristic of its inherent nature. This acceptance of the unconscious image is not passive; it is treated neither as a symptom nor as a work of art. A relationship is encouraged between the image and its maker, by actively stimulating imaginative inquiry and dialogue, the essence of "active imagination."

Jung's insistence on a fundamental difference between a *symbol* and a *sign* is important here. For the most part, he regarded signs as images which can be shown to refer to discoverable and specific events or fantasies in an individual's past—the repressed material of psychoanalysis. He regarded images as symbolic when they induced strong affects, while also defying complete or precise verbal description. It can be seen, therefore, that Jung attributed symbolic status to images that Freud would have seen as resistant to interpretation, because of unconscious defense mechanisms. However, Freud confessed himself unable to offer an adequate explanation for the power of artistic imagery, and it seems to me that Jung gives absolute authenticity to the image, reaffirming connections between images in therapy and in art. The connections are archetypal, not aesthetic.

Jung believed that the deepest levels of the unconscious are already prestructured at birth by the archetypes, psychologically paralleling the biological instincts. Like the instincts, archetypes can remain dormant in an individual until activated by events in that person's experience. For example, a woman who becomes a mother for the first time discovers *in herself* an archetypal role of mothering, adequate or otherwise. The archetype gives a particular style to the basic instinct, rather in the same way that a particular species of bird will build a nest in a recognizable way. There are, naturally, many archetypal possibilities within the human species. The archetypal role is given substance and lived out, with and through the raw materials of everyday life, including genetic endowment and environmental conditioning. The archetype works through the complex, which is also unconscious, and through the living situation of the individual. The bird, too, builds its nest with whatever is available.

Archetypes unconsciously structure universal happenings in life, such as the symbiotic attachment to and eventual separation from the mother, making a relationship to the father, passing childhood and adolescent milestones, falling in love, dealing with birth and death issues. Behind the real parents stand the archetypal parent figures, just as other important people in life are also overshadowed by archetypal projections. These may manifest, in contemporary form, benign and destructive characteristics reminiscent of collective figures: the gods and goddesses and mythological and fairy tale archetypal images, which, according to Jung, personify states of affect in the unconscious (Campbell, 1949; Jung et al., 1964; Jung, *Collected Works, Vol. 13*, 1968; Von Franz, 1982).

THE PERSONIFIED IMAGE IN ART THERAPY

The therapeutic relationship is both simplified and complicated by the artwork. It is simplified because the relationship does not have to depend solely on confrontation, with the attendant transference issues in central focus. Instead, the relationship takes place partly through the artwork, which can variously be described as a buffer, filter, screen, or container. In this triangular situation, the artwork mediates between patient and therapist. Even when resistances are high and the patient produces nothing, the art therapist remains a representative of symbolic communication through art; he or she is "the art person" throughout. Every relationship with a patient in art therapy is somewhat oblique. However, if this allows more freedom to the therapist in terms of transference, simplifying the psychotherapeutic role, I believe also that the therapeutic alliance in art therapy is complicated by factors arising in the minds of both patient and therapist which are born of the marriage—if marriage it is—between art and psychotherapy. It may be helpful to look at some of these factors from a Jungian perspective.

THE EXPERIENCE OF IMAGE MAKING

There is a dynamic in the art therapy setting which is not often discussed. This is the patient's interaction with the medium and with whatever images emerge. It is a dialogue that takes place parallel to, and somewhat independently of, the relationship to the art therapist (see Figure 1).

Making a mark on paper, or twisting clay into the first shape that suggests itself, begins as an entirely private matter. This act may be preceded by doubt and anxiety about taking the initial step. For the nonartist, the prospect of image making is a heroic undertaking, and at this stage the skill of the art therapist is often directed at reassurance. After the initial shock of beginning, when the decision is taken to enter into a relationship with the medium, what follows can still be fraught with uncertainty. The correspondence between what is experienced inside and what is expressed outside rarely feels exact, even to a mature artist in good psy-

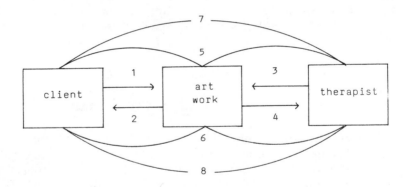

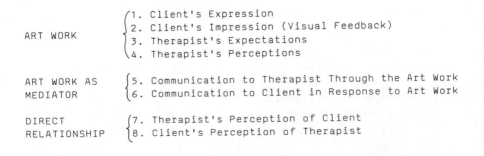

ART WORK
1. Client's Expression
2. Client's Impression (Visual Feedback)
3. Therapist's Expectations
4. Therapist's Perceptions

ART WORK AS MEDIATOR
5. Communication to Therapist Through the Art Work
6. Communication to Client in Response to Art Work

DIRECT RELATIONSHIP
7. Therapist's Perception of Client
8. Client's Perception of Therapist

Figure 1

chological health. For a patient, the connection between inner and outer reality may be bewilderingly absent. This can lead to increased anxiety or a defensive withdrawal of investment in the activity.

From the moment of the first expressive gesture, the subsequent stages of creating do not usually conform to will or expectation. Even a consciously planned and deliberately executed image has a way of seeming to speak back to its creator with a personality of its own. What is more, the personality of the image may not be immediately likable. It frequently, even usually, has an alien aspect, a quality of "otherness." And yet it has to be faced that the image, despite its alien characteristics, definitely belongs to the person who made it. The dialogue now begins between the person and the image the person has made. At the same time, the image itself is still in a process of transformation or resolution. It calls for attention.

The "otherness" of images can be disconcertingly unpredictable. Occasionally, the emerging shapes can be friendly, slipping easily and amazingly into configurations that far exceed intentions or imaginings. When this happens, one can only follow, somewhat fearfully, in case the spell is broken. This sometimes happens, and then suddenly the friendly image becomes a betrayer, or is betrayed, leading to immediate disappointment and, worse, the shame of defeat. This can be doubly distressing, because failure seems to belong to the image maker in a way that success rarely does. Sometimes, too, from the first expressive gesture, it is obvious that progress will be painfully won. The process does not flow; rather, each addition looks vulnerable, awkward, or ineffective. The image maker is reminded of all the previous occasions in which there was a sense of artistic inadequacy because, worst of all, it is not clear how to put the matter right or, to put this another way, *to know what the image is asking from its maker.* If there is persistence with a troublesome image in an attempt to bring it under control, or make it seem more authentic, this can feel like an act of reparation, in the Kleinian sense. If the attempt is abandoned, or the image destroyed, then there is a sense of lost opportunity, in fact a real loss. Acting out the literal destruction of an image is rarely a satisfying experience.

In Jungian terms, the above passage is written from the point of view of the patient's ego, based on my own ego recollections of similar struggles with images from the unconscious. All art therapists have techniques for trying to help another through this hazardous journey. Depending on who the person is, I will usually try to convey the idea that the image has a life of its own, and that therefore whatever happens is right. If this works, the individual becomes interested in the unpredictable, and the ego learns to watch and relate to the process, rather than seeking to gain absolute control over it. At a later stage, this can develop into recognition that a healing process is taking place by the constellation of a patient-therapist relationship with the patient. This requires, I believe, a parallel therapist-patient internal relationship within the therapist.

In *Revisioning Psychology* (1975) James Hillman writes about personification of emotions as an ancient psychological tradition:

> [It is a] necessary mode of understanding the world and of being in it. It began with the Greeks and Romans, who personified such psychic powers as Fame, Insolence, Night, Ugliness, Timing, Hope, to name but a few. . . . Personifying not only aids discrimination; it also offers another avenue of loving, of imagining things in a personal form so that we can find access to them with our hearts (pp. 13–14).

The idea of personifying our thoughts and feelings may seem curiously out of keeping with twentieth-century life, and yet, Hillman argues, it brings the imagination to bear on problems, conflicts, and aspirations. Personified images can be allowed to come to consciousness in the imagination and, better still, can be visually represented. What I referred to earlier as a sense of "otherness" about one's own visual images is also an experience of personification at its simplest. It is from this point that a sense of dialogue with the unconscious can begin.

For the patient, working with pictorial images in a spontaneous way almost always seems to call up another side of the personality. The otherness has to be recognized as one's own, and it can be truly astonishing to discover hidden aspects of the personality confronting the conscious ego. It is for this reason that to have a sense of dialogue with one's images can be so important; if the images are seen by the patient or therapist as nothing but the portrayal of a problem, then the possibility of a deeper and perhaps more complex meaning is lost. In my view, this is where diagnosis through art can be damaging to the healing possibilities in the image, because diagnosis often leads to value judgments and a "good" or "bad" prognosis; this tends to undermine the way in which imagery can carry several meanings at a time.

The image that becomes an actual object confronts its maker with a host of possibilities. If the originating impulse has arisen from the unconscious, then its expression will be a unique configuration of forms and associated affects. It is most important that the image be regarded by both patient and therapist in a variety of ways, from different perspectives, in different time settings, and in different contexts. The issue is not, or should not be, who does the interpreting, client or therapist, but rather, that a severely reductive stance by either party may (and probably will) miss subtle overtones and nuances of an image, which need to be responded to with nonjudgmental acceptance. It is the therapist's role, I believe, to establish a therapeutic frame in which the image can be allowed its own authority, without overwhelming the client with its message, but also without being stripped of its iconological power.

For the patient, as the image-making process comes to some kind of completion, the dialogue, which until now has been from a close perspective, at times seemingly entirely *within* the image, changes to a more distant perception. The image as separate object allows the maker to stare, step back, move across the room. This can be a wholly new experience of the artwork. If the situation permits, I like to be able to share with a patient the surprise that often comes with seeing the work at a distance. Its otherness has finally established itself. It is the moment at which the image becomes a part of the outer world; it inhabits the room and exerts its own influence on whoever happens to be there. The completed image, however incomplete, primitive, regressive, or alien, is a new factor in the situation; it is both a statement about and a personification of what was formerly inner experience. What is more, it reminds both patient and therapist that it has an existence that is independent of its maker. Properly looked after, it may last a lifetime or longer. It can be surveyed briefly—I will sometimes ask for the transitory first impression, before more developed perceptions begin to take over—casually, out of the corner of an eye, in detail, and at length. A picture can be turned on its side or upside down, discussed animatedly or regarded silently, and can be compared with other images. Associations may be elicited by both patient and therapist in a hermeneutic style of interpretation. This is very different from using a patient's associations in a reductive way, leading to pathologizing of the image by treating it as a symptom.

Once the first examination of the artwork is over, subsequent dialogues with the image may take place: tomorrow, in a month, a year, or even 10 years' time. On each occasion it is likely to have changed less in reality than it *seems* to have changed. Whenever we look at the same image, we see it a little differently.

As a personified object, the image may demand a particular way of being in the world, at least for a time. Certain images seem to need to be lived with, because, we might say, their otherness needs to be assimilated gradually. On the other hand, and as is so often the case in art therapy, the image possesses an element of *vulnerability*; in which case the assimilation needs to take place in a protected situation, where it will not be exposed to more public viewing than is appropriate for it. Equally, some images are too powerful or too frightening for assimilation. In this case the therapist is carrying an ego role for the patient by taking some responsibility for the image which threatens to overwhelm, by putting it away in a safe place (the symbolism will be apparent), or simply by agreeing to take care of it.

The image is related to by both patient and therapist as if it were an extended part of the person who made it, which, in a metaphoric sense, it is. However, the perception of the image as independent and semi-autonomous must also be preserved, to allow for its personified aspect and to permit imaginative dialogue with it. Transference feelings are less strongly projected onto the therapist because they are experienced more objectively through the artwork. The therapist is able to channel countertransference feelings into caring about, and bringing ideas to, the image. The notion of the image as, on one level, an extension of the personality and, on another, an independent entity is in keeping with Jung's view of the symbol as having both past and future aspects: It is linked to the past by actual events from the person's life, and to the present and future by the archetypal structure inherent in the situation. The therapist's associations and ideas can facilitate the bringing to consciousness of archetypal material, while also offering the client greater flexibility and choice within what seem to be the psychological determinants of the situation. It is important to emphasize that this has to be a mutually convincing synthesis of the real-world situation and of the imaginal world of metaphor and creative possibility. Archetypal factors are inescapable, but determine behavior negatively only when they remain completely unconscious. By allowing, through the imagination, a sense of participation and dialogue with archetypal (and personal) material in personified form, it is possible to integrate unacknowledged aspects of personality and, with increased consciousness, come to better terms with life. This might be described as the ability to live within one's personal myth rather than be lived by it.

I have stressed what I believe to be something of the nature of a healing role for image making from a Jungian point of view. There is much that I have had to set aside, including the relation of imagery to the four functions, intuition, sensation, feeling, and thinking; to extraversion and introversion; and to the archetypes themselves and how they might be present themselves in the course of therapy. I do not propose to describe either the functions or the attitude types, since they are fairly well known and in any case are easily to be found in the Jungian literature (for example, in *Jung's Psychological Types [Collected Works,* Vol. 6, 1971*]*). Nor is there space to enter into a discussion of the archetypes (*Collected Works*, Vol. 9, part 1, 1968) or the complexes (*Collected Works*, Vol. 7, 1966). These topics can be touched on only in very general terms.

Jung believed that individuals tend to develop a definite predisposition toward using one or more of the four functions in everyday life, while others remain, to a greater or lesser extent, unconscious. Some writers, such as Sir Herbert Read in *Education Through Art* (1943), have attempted to show that the function types can be recognized through the style of the artwork (pp. 143–145, 219–220). One problem with this approach is that it is rarely clear whether a person makes images from the conscious or the unconscious side of the personality. The unconscious aspects may predominate, and this is particularly the case with the kind of spontaneously generated artwork that is produced in therapy. What this implies is that a patient who may habitually function as, for example, an extraverted thinking/sensation type may experience a less developed and, hence, more primitive form of introverted feeling/intuition in the artwork. The "weak" or "inferior" function (Jung, *Collected Works, Vol. 6*, 1971, pp. 450–451) can take on a persecutory role or can emerge in a compulsive and even obsessive way. Thus, here too the unconscious factor determines the course of therapy. It is, therefore, extremely difficult to generalize, since the conscious personality, through the ego, is also at least partly involved.

In Jungian analytic therapy there is a tendency for certain archetypal themes to present themselves in an almost predictable sequence. How this happens will vary with every individual, but certainly quite often the early stages of therapy deal with the *shadow*, the denied and sometimes feared part of the personality that roughly corresponds, according to Jung, to the contents of the Freudian personal unconscious. Thus, the quality of otherness to which I have referred may be particularly associated with the shadow when the art activity, or the images that come from it, are feared or rejected. At a later stage, what Jung described as the contrasexual figures—the *animus* in the woman and the *anima* in the man—may appear as definite personifications. Whereas at first these may only be experienced by projection, it would be part of the therapist's task to help the patient recognize these figures as internal and psychic in origin, and ultimately to integrate them as far as is possible. However, archetypal contents, being collective rather than personal, can never be fully assimilated, and it would be more accurate to describe the therapeutic goal as learning to trust the inner figures, as sources of insight and creative development in the individuation process.

Although there were times when Jung would make a clinical comment about professional artwork, as in his 1932 paper on Picasso (*Collected Works, Vol. 15*, 1966), I personally do not find this consistent with what I understand of his psychology; it begs too many of the questions raised by the breadth and inclusiveness of Jung's researches. Jungian therapists will sometimes make a kind of diagnosis by drawing attention to what they perceive as the dominance of a particular archetypal figure, saying that, for example, a patient may have a "negative animus problem" or is in the grip of the "terrible mother." Since the language of such comments is highly metaphoric, it is difficult to convey the meaning intended. The archetypes contain both positive (creative) and negative (destructive) characteristics and, according to which seem to be surfacing in a patient's life, such archetypal dynamics might be noted diagnostically, as might imagery from the personal unconscious, in a more Freudian sense.

Although it would be foolish to suggest that any theory should be so open-ended as to undermine its own credibility, I think that a considerable virtue of Jungian theory is that it is hermeneutic in its approach to interpretation; it depends on the assumption that unconscious factors can be inferred from psychological clues, like those found in spontaneous imagery. Since Jung developed a multidimensional method of trying to comprehend symbolic images, and since symbols are, by his own definition, beyond full intellectual comprehension, any diagnostic or even interpretive comment is both tentative and relative. There are occasions, however, when a reductive interpretation may be used, when there is a need to bring particular issues into focus.

Another major issue that besets Jungian therapists and most art therapists is whether the emergence of particular material is favorable or unfavorable to the client. It is often difficult to know whether such material is being worked through or whether it is prognostic. Should the therapist be alarmed by, for example, self-destructive imagery or relieved that a previously unconscious impulse seems to be coming to consciousness, where it can be drawn into therapeutic work? The answer is probably that both should be taken into account. The appearance in therapy of potentially destructive material should not close the doors to other alternatives than acting out, although the latter possibility has to be constantly kept in mind, but so too does the need for a more empathic response, for greater sensitivity and depth, which might be precluded by focusing too narrowly on diagnostic implications in the artwork.

For me, Hillman, in writing about dreams, expresses almost better than anyone what can be lost in therapy by categorizing psychic material into the sick and the healthy. He takes an extreme position:

> For us the golden rule in touching any dream is keeping it alive. Dream-work is conservation. We have to set aside what we naturally and usually do: projecting the dream into the future, reducing the dream to the past, extracting from the dream a message. These moves lose the dream in exchange for what we get from it. Conservation implies holding onto what is and even assuming that what is is right, except for ego. Everything in the dream is doing what it must, following psychic necessity along the wandering course of its

purposes, except the ego. The river must be dry, the bridge so high, the tree uprooted, the dog run over, the party conceal a poisoner, the dentist demand complete extraction—only the ego's position comes under suspicion. It tends to do the wrong thing and makes the wrong appraisals, because it cannot see in the dark (*The Dream and the Underworld*, 1979, pp. 116–117).

Hillman's attempt to diminish the omnipotent authority of the ego is consistent with Jung's view that the unconscious has a compensatory function in relation to consciousness. The ego is not to be abandoned or denied, but its role in therapy is to act as mediator, not to try to control the process entirely from the point of view of consciousness.

THEORY INTO PRACTICE

My own practice of art therapy has recently included working with adolescents and families in a hospital day treatment program, seeing a small number of clients privately, and conducting various workshops with students, practicing therapists, and others. My role is naturally very different in each case, but there is some consistency in the way I attempt to facilitate individuals' interaction with their own images. In workshops I also sometimes use relaxation, dance movement, or voice improvisation exercises, leading toward, or working out from, the images themselves. Very often, I will get people to do writing, as a form of active imagination, in response to their images, with a view to amplifying meaning. The central focus remains with the artwork, unlike psychoanalytic free association, where the artwork may serve only as a point of departure. This writing can be in the form of a story or poem; occasionally I will ask an individual to write a letter to the image, telling it how it is experienced; this will often prompt a "reply" from the image, and there can follow an interchange of "correspondence."

Such an exercise has to be very carefully related to the situation and can never be prescriptive; when used successfully, it can facilitate the move from projection to personification. Once the personified affects are experienced as definite entities, a sense of working *with* the unconscious begins. This may be a far from comfortable sequence of events, possibly involving shadow personalities or negative aspects of parental archetypes. On the other hand, there may be figures or other symbolic images which convey a transcending sense of relating to new energies and depths of meaning. What is important is that such personified figures are related to as inner images, however relevantly they might also be linked with people in the artist's real-life situation.

With a child or more seriously disturbed adult, there is usually little direct interpretation, but rather a sense of mutual involvement in the imagery, a staying with the symbolism. The therapist's ego can act as a guide, while investment in and valuing of the art therapy process can be expressed through countertransference to the artwork, or, more accurately in Jungian terms, by the therapist trying to maintain contact with the Self (Schwartz-Salant, 1982, p. 14), Jung's term for the archetypal center of the conscious/unconscious psyche.

A therapist in training, or a patient with good ego strength and who has reached a sufficient stage of independence within the therapeutic relationship, may be encouraged to research the imagery as well as to make personal associations. This hermeneutic process involves searching for meaning, using the imagination, and noting what is experienced as authentic. The therapist's countertransference reactions need to be carefully monitored in this approach.

Two contrasting examples may help to illustrate something of the way a Jungian approach to art therapy can work in practice. In the first, an 18-year-old adolescent, who had been described as "borderline" following several bizarre self-destructive acts, had been in weekly art therapy for about eight months. His later pictures were almost entirely produced by squeezing copious amounts of acrylic paint onto the paper, which, after folding, opened into Rorschach-like configurations. My patience was feeling strained by the apparently defensive nature of this activity, as also perhaps by the quantity of expensive paint that was being consumed. This was no simple limit-testing situation, however, nor do I think that it could be adequately described as regression. He seemed very invested indeed in what was happening, and I derived some comfort from this, as also from the information that he was coping better than previously in other aspects of his life. The pictures were increasingly used by him as vehicles for projection, and he gave some of them names like "Confusion/Delusion" and "Prehistoric Crustacean." The final picture in this series marked a significant change in our relationship and in his progress (Figure 2). This time, *I* saw quite as clearly as he did the demon that emerged from the mess of paint, as also a tiny, doll-like figure at the bottom. We both sensed a new rapport and were able to talk about the picture from a similar viewpoint. It seemed as if the image was the one he had been "accidentally" trying for, and that the response from me—authenticating his own demon—was what he needed.

The second example is from the journal of a woman in a group. I think that these extracts give some idea of dialoguing with imagery in the way that I have described:

When I left this week's workshop, I was puzzled by the emptiness and "lack of connection" that I was experiencing. . . . My discom-

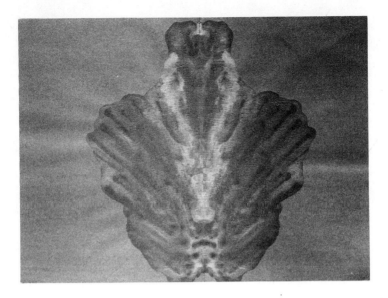

Figure 2

fort began during the session when I tried to engage my image in conversation—it was stilted, wouldn't flow and seemed extremely unnatural. My conversation with K.'s work, by contrast, flowed smoothly and easily. There was no *affect* stirred, felt, or expressed during almost the entire session. When I realized this, I tried to follow that feeling, or lack of it, to its source. I recalled that while lying relaxed on the floor I was very aware of my heartbeat and that I had fantasized a responding beat from the depths of the earth.

Someone got up from the floor and went to sit at the table—but it was not me. *I* stayed where I was. That someone very deliberately selected an image from the past and decided to paint a version of it. It was an "ego choice," but who was orchestrating things? With which complex did the ego align itself and which one was projected? The image produced was, in itself, split. It showed a woman's body apparently emerging from the earth, as far as just above waist level [Figure 3]. In yesterday's image, there is an oddly injured look about the woman's head—a kind of spreading bruise. . . . She has her eyes closed—going inward or shutting out? Neither. It struck me, at about 2:00 A.M., that the reason I had had difficulty in our conversation was that she was, in fact, *dead*.

Why did I choose a dead issue? Why was it not safe for me to be as I am today? There was a definite regression—not a complete denial—but a portrayal of an earlier version, perhaps, of myself. Why

Figure 3

did I choose specifically *that* stage to which to regress? What was
forbidden/acceptable then? There was not much play—that much
is for sure; everything was very serious. The barriers were up and
there were rigid boundaries. It was "safe" for me then, devoid of
emotion. Yesterday I reexperienced the affect of that time in terms
of no affect: a straightforward denial of feelings. No wonder her
head looks bruised. She is a self-battered woman who wouldn't laugh
and couldn't cry. She was also very boring—she probably bored herself to death. And yet, as Hillman (1979) says, "We easily lose touch
with the subtle kinds of death. . . . " When we have put our day
world notions to sleep "(d)eath is the most profoundly radical way
of expressing the shift in consciousness." (pp. 65–66)

To conclude . . . who is the woman? This is certainly no whimpering Persephone—this has the appearance, at least, of a woman of purpose, going down of her own free will. For this image to have presented itself in this particular form, at this particular time, even though consciously chosen and based on a previous image, it must live somewhere still. Somewhere in my own psyche there lives, paradoxically, a dead woman.

COMMENTS AND CONCLUSION

Later in the workshop series this woman experienced a vivid sense of reconnection to her lower body, especially the legs (Figure 4) With this

Figure 4

came a spontaneous release of affect, which she was able to integrate into her personal life. Thus, a tendency toward dissociative deadness of affect was related to, not simply as a problem, but as an archetypal factor in the psyche. In the case of the male patient, the archetypal possession, which, in Jungian terms, characterized his borderline life experience, was objectified in the imagery, perceived, and thereby weakened or loosened in its grip on the conscious personality. The ego of the individual, in both cases, was able to give up some of its unrealistic striving for autonomy by admitting to—and also relating to—alien figures in the unconscious.

It is the therapist's task to ensure that such a compromise by the ego is made with sensitivity, often putting the therapist into the temporary "holding" role with which most art therapists are familiar. In both examples, the therapeutic work consisted in affirming respect for and trust in the imagery—not as romanticized art for art's sake, nor, in these instances, as a source of clinical information, nor even as an interesting intellectual adventure into archetypal configurations—but as a symbolic and potentially insight-provoking synthesis of internal and external realities.

As Freud's major contribution to art therapy was in demonstrating the latent content in dreams and fantasies, so Jung's was to treat such images as communications from the psyche to be understood in their own terms and on many levels. Thus, from a Jungian perspective, the image can never be adequately described, however true certain interpretations may be in some sense. Jung, I believe, restored to the psychotherapeutic view of fantasy and dream images an acknowledgment of their complex and subtle affinity with artistic values and insights—which are, in turn, inevitably shaped by both personal and archetypal determinants in the unconscious.

REFERENCES

Baynes, H. G. *Mythology of the soul*. London: Balliere, Tindall & Cox, 1940.

Beck, R. H. Progressive education and American progressivism: Margaret Naumburg. *Teachers College Record*, 1958–1959, *LX*, 198–208.

Campbell, J. *The hero with a thousand faces*. New York: Bollingen, 1949.

Cremin, L. *The transformation of the school 1876–1957*. New York: Vintage Books, 1961.

Glover, E. *Freud or Jung?* New York: Meridian, 1950.

Hillman, J. *Revisioning psychology*. New York: Harper, 1975.

Hillman, J. *The dream and the underworld*. New York: Harper, 1979.

Jaffé, A. (Ed.). *C. G. Jung: Word and image*. Princeton, NJ: Princeton University Press, 1979.

Jung, C. G. (1912). *Wandlungen und symbole der libido, and (1916) Psychology of the unconscious*, Hinckle, B. (trans.). Revised (1956) as *Symbols of transformation, Collected Works, Vol. 5*. Princeton, NJ: Princeton University Press.

Jung, C. G. *Memories, dreams, reflections*. Jaffé, A. (Ed.). London: Collins and Routledge & Kegan Paul, 1963.

Jung, C. G., et al. *Man and his symbols*. London: Aldus, 1964.

Jung, C. G. The aims of psychotherapy. In *The practice of psychotherapy. Collected Works, Vol. 16*. Princeton, NJ: Princeton University Press, 1966.

Jung, C. G. On the psychology of the unconscious. In *Two essays on analytical psychology, Collected works, Vol. 7*. Princeton, NJ: Princeton University Press, 1966.

Jung, C. G. *The spirit in man, art and literature, Collected Works, Vol. 15*. Princeton, NJ: Princeton University Press, 1966.

Jung, C. G. *Alchemical studies, Collected works, Vol. 13*. Princeton, NJ: Princeton University Press, 1968.

Jung, C. G. *The archetypes and the collective unconscious. Collected works, Vol. 9, part 1*. Princeton, NJ: Princeton University Press, 1968.

Jung, C. G. General aspects of dream psychology, and The transcendent function. In *The structure and dynamics of the psyche Collected works, Vol. 8*, Princeton, NJ: Princeton University Press, 1969.

Jung, C. G. *Psychological types. Collected works, Vol. 6*. Princeton, NJ: Princeton University Press, 1971.

Kris, E. *Psychoanalytic explorations in art*. New York: International Universities Press, 1952.

Naumburg, M. *Schizophrenic art: Its meaning in psychotherapy*. New York: Grune & Stratton, 1950.

Read, H. *Education through art*. London: Faber & Faber, 1943.

Robertson, S. *Rosegarden and labyrinth*. London: Routledge & Kegan Pual, 1963.

Schwartz-Salant, N. *Narcissism and character transformation*. Toronto: Inner City Books, 1982.

Storr, A. *The essential Jung*. Princeton, NJ: Princeton University Press, 1983.

Von Franz, M.-L. *An introduction to the interpretation of fairy tales*. Dallas: Spring, 1982.

7

Healing Through the Visual Arts— A Jungian Approach

Edith Wallace

If you bring forth that which is within you, what you bring forth will save you. If you do not bring forth what is within you, what you do not bring forth will destroy you.

Gospel of St. Thomas

HISTORY AND DESCRIPTION OF ACTIVE IMAGINATION

To talk or write about the Jungian approach to therapy is a formidable task, and I consider it inadequate because Jung needs to be experienced; this is the reason I originally became involved in art therapy, and it made me realize the importance of Jung's view of the unconscious to art therapy.

I have chosen one method—that of active imagination-which deals with images and is based on the fact that we must trust such images, which arise from the depth of the psyche. This method presupposes that truth resides in the unconscious—not only on a personal, ego level, but as a profound historical truth—and is manifested in archetypal images arising from the collective unconscious. The central archetype which Jung called the "self" is of special importance as a healing factor. It has a regulating, stabilizing function, compensating for any imbalance that might arise. It could also be called one's inner wisdom and guide; I like to call it the "creative source."

We know today, thanks to the work of the great trailblazers in the field of depth psychology, that anything contained in the unconscious but not brought to light will have a life of its own and an influence on consciousness. According to Jung, this influence can be beneficent as well as noxious, and we are certainly far from knowing the total depth of the unconscious—as the word itself indicates. In other words, the mystery of life as well as the wish to penetrate it will be with us forever.

Since the image precedes the word, we can through images (as well as through body movement) evoke unknown aspects of the psyche and bring them to the light of consciousness; this results in understanding and often healing. For healing to take place, however, we must take the consequences of what we have understood and bring our understanding into the reality of lived life.

When we open ourselves to the unconscious—the irrational—there is danger as well as reward. Jung was well aware of this, as he describes in his memoirs:

> As a result of my experiments I learned how helpful it can be, from the therapeutic point of view, to find the particular images which lie behind emotions. . . . In order to grasp the fantasies which were stirring in me "underground," I knew that I had to let myself plummet down into them, as it were. I felt not only violent resistance to this, but a distinct fear. . . . It was during Advent of the year 1913—December 12, to be exact—that I resolved upon the decisive step. I was sitting at my desk once more, thinking over my fears. Then I let myself drop. Suddenly it was as though the ground literally gave way beneath my feet, and I plunged down into dark depths. I could not fend off a feeling of panic. But then, abruptly, at not too great a depth I landed on my feet. . . . (1961, pp. 177–179).

The irrational and that which is behind it manifests in emotionality, sometimes uncontrollably so. It is the first sign of a message from the depth, and if we can be detached enough, it can become a dialogue between conscious and unconscious. The progression can then be from (1) emotionality to (2) a specific emotion, which may find expression in (3) an image, which can reduce the violence of the emotion; the image may be explained in (4) words, which represent articulation necessary for conscious understanding—a message received.

Today we are much closer to accepting that other, irrational side—as in the studies of right and left brain functioning, and in modern science, especially physics (Capra, 1975)—much more so than was possible in Jung's time. While confronted with certain fantasies that had great emotional impact, Jung knew he would have to step right into them if he wished to bring understanding to this uncharted territory of the psyche. Before using the method (which he later called "*active imagination*") on others and publishing it, he experimented on himself, as related in the above quote from his autobiography. By his own request, these memoirs were not published until his death in 1961. Active imagination is first mentioned in "The Transcendent Function," an essay written in 1916 but not published until 1957 (*Collected Works, Vol. 9*). In 1935 Jung lectured at the Tavistock Clinic in London to a group of medical doctors. In the discussion he was asked about active imagination, to which he gave the following explanation:

> A fantasy is more or less your own invention, and remains on the surface of personal things and conscious expectations. But active imagination, as the term denotes, means that the images have a life of their own and that the symbolic events develop according to their own logic—that is, of course, if your conscious reason does not interfere. . . . For instance, if my unconscious should prefer not to give me ideas, I could not proceed with my lecture, because I could not invent the next step (*Collected Works, Vol. 18*, pp. 171–172).

In his commentary on *The Secret of the Golden Flower* (1931), Jung remarks:

> . . . in cases of a high degree of inflexibility in the conscious oftentimes the hands alone can fantasy; they model or draw figures that are quite foreign to the conscious (*Collected Works, Vol. 13*, p. 17).

In the collected correspondence, there is a letter of April 1931 to Count Hermann Keyserling, who had apparently consulted Jung about some experiences that his very rational mind could not fathom. Jung responds: "The unconscious has a different rhythm from consciousness and different goals." He advises Keyserling to subordinate his philosophical skill and descriptive powers to those unknown contents and ask, "Who or what has come alive . . . who or what has entered my psychic life and created disturbances and wants to be heard?" To this you should add:

> Let it speak. Then switch off your noisy consciousness and listen quietly inward and look at the images that appear before your inner eye, or hearken to the words which the muscles of your speech apparatus are trying to form. Write down what then comes without criticism. Images should be drawn or painted assiduously, no matter whether you can do it or not. Once you have got at least fragments of these contents, then you may meditate on them *afterwards*. Don't criticize anything away! If any questions arise, put them to the unconscious again the next day. Don't be content with your own explanations no matter how intelligent they are. Remember, your health is seriously at stake and that the unconscious has an unknown, far-reaching control over it.

Treat any drawings the same way. Meditate on them afterwards and everyday go on developing what is unsatisfactory about them. The important thing is to let the unconscious take the lead. You must always be convinced that you have mere afterknowledge and nothing else. In this case, the unconscious really does know better. (April 23, 1931) (See Adler & Jaffe, 1973, pp. 82–83)

Jung's simple definition of active imagination (from *Essays on a Science of Mythology*) follows: "A method, devised by myself, of introspection for observing the stream of interior images" (1949, p. 228). This, however, is not enough. In *Memories, Dreams, Reflections*, he writes expressly: "The images of the unconscious place in a great responsibility upon a man. Failure to understand them, or a shirking of ethical responsibility deprives him of his wholeness and imposes a painful fragmentariness on his life. Recognizing the world means creating it" (1961, p. 193).

An example of spontaneous active imagination may clarify. While working in a private mental hospital, a woman patient of mine who had suffered from involutional melancholia was at that time coming out of her depression. Had I told her that it was time for her to go home, I might have met with opposition. The hospital was a comfortable place with no obligations for her, whereas going home meant shouldering her usual responsibilities. Her unconscious came to our aid. Needless to say, she neither knew anything about active imagination nor about Jung and my close connection with him. One day she came to her session with this story: "You know, doctor," she said, "I had this image: I had been walking in the woods and I was coming out of them and there was the main highway. I told myself, 'Oh no, it cannot be,' and I tried to pull myself back in. But every time I did that I was in the same place again." She understood, she got the message, *and* she went home.

This fulfills all the requirements of active imagination. Marie-Louise von Franz has spelled it out in an essay recently republished as a supplement to Margaret Keyes' *The Inward Journey*. She breaks down active imagination into four different stages, with which I concur:

1. "First one must empty one's mind from the trains of thought of the ego" (1983, p. 125). She points out that this is difficult for some people and adds that it may then be easier to paint. She also points to both similarity to and difference from meditation: emptying the mind is similar; the welcoming and dealing with the images is, of course, very different.

2. Now we let the image enter our field of attention. This requires a special kind of inner focusing. It is necessary to catch the images without holding on with so much concentration that the very tension of the endeavor could arrest the process. Nor can we allow image after image

to pass by with too little focus on our part. If there is no observer, there cannot be any relating either; such people forget that there is a process going on that is happening to *them*.

3. Now is the time to write down what has been seen, to paint or sculpt or dance or write music that was heard, to give outer form to the experience. However, not everything can produce images, and active imagination can start with any of the metioned media. It is the step of materializing which usually means body involvement, and often a body impulse as well as a body understanding.

4. This is the phase when we must take the consequences of messages received, the ethical confrontation Jung speaks about. We must again remember that something is happening to us as we are and live in reality. What has been happening is not some kind of evasive fantasy dreamt by an imaginary ego—an attitude that prevents any kind of transformation, as if we were not touched by the whole process. In active imagination we start with picking up messages from the unconscious.

ART AND ACTIVE IMAGINATION

The difference between active imagination and the dream is that we are fully awake witnesses to what is happening while it is happening. It is one of Jung's ways of using and understanding spontaneously arising manifestations of contents from the unconscious: images, body movement, words, or music; in other words, the arts in psychotherapy. Although Jung made a very clear distinction between art and active imagination, I do not think that the lines can be so clearly drawn. Jung stressed that when and while we are involved in this process of active imagination through any of the arts, we must not call it "art"—our focus being on deep understanding and healing, not on the aesthetic aspect which could lead us astray. He describes it amusingly in his autobiography when, after having painted some exquisitely beautiful images, he heard a female voice in answer to his question: "What is this?" saying "This is art." He says that he had to reject that notion, because his aim was to know and understand the *meaning* of the images and to take the consequences. "If I had taken these fantasies of the unconscious as art, they would have carried no more conviction than visual perceptions, as if I were watching a movie. I would have felt no moral obligation towards them" (1961, p. 187).

It is my contention that the search of any real artist is the same as Jung's search for "the supreme presentiments of consciousness and the loftiest intuitions of the spirit." See Paul Klee's essays on modern art (1945) or Kandinsky's *Concerning the Spiritual in Art* (1947). Closer to our time, some of Morris Graves' paintings are witness to such a striving, as was Van Gogh's (1963) ardent search for the sun and light, which in the end killed him. One statement of his may be germane here: "There is something infinite in painting—there are hidden things of harmony or contrast in colours, things which are effective in themselves and which cannot be expressed through any other medium." For the artist, effectiveness may be different from what the psychologist is looking for; however, the two are closely related. Depth of psychological understanding is crucial for the artist and the work of art. On the other hand, if we have both the talent, which gives confidence, and the aim and devoted intent of the artist, we may dare more easily to look deeply into places of "greatest reward and greatest danger," as Jung has described it.

There is magic in both healing and creating. Creating comes and goes and we become the instrument for it. In *The Last Unicorn*, Peter Beagle describes such an experience: "Molly was not frightened. The magic lifted her as gently as though she were a note of music and it were singing her. She could feel that it was never far from being wild and dangerous, but she was sorry when it set her down" (1968, p. 231). Most of us have experienced something like that in certain encounters with the unconscious. We may experience what Molly felt whenever creation or healing takes place.

Yet, we also have to make our conscious contribution. As Jung said: "The unconscious functions satisfactorily only when the conscious mind fulfills its task to the very limit" (*Collected Works, Vol. 8*, p. 296, ¶568). But the most essential preparation is to let go, in order to allow the "magic" to come through. As the magician in *The Last Unicorn* says: "I did not know that I was so empty, to be so full" (p. 218). When first he sacrifices his minor gifts, he throws them to the winds and then whispers to the magic: "Do as you will. Do as you will" (p. 74).

If healing means—at least in part—recovery of potential, this "emptiness" is essential for the process to occur. The stage needs to be set for listening to that inner voice; to make it heard or visible requires stillness. Images imposed from the outside can be an intrusion and an interference to the arising of inner images. What we must "throw to the winds" to be "empty" in the process of creation (and healing) is that which we have learned, all aspects of conditioning. We must again become like a child who knows and trusts its own powers. There is no need to strive for the genuine, the original, the spontaneous; they are simply there, and often they will surprise us because we have moved so far away from them.

In retrospect, I think that one reason I prefer using brilliant, translucent-colored tissue papers, which often produce beautiful results, is that they encourage confidence—confidence to go on, to stay with the process, to go deeper, and through it to enhance development and growth. The emphasis is on *transformation*; however, there is no transformation without first healing. If the aim is to get to the cellar and the cellar stairs are cluttered, our first task is to take care of the clutter.

DIALOGUE

One aspect of active imagination that needs to be emphasized is *dialogue*. The aim is that the conscious and the unconscious talk to each other. The dialogue starts with oneself and the many people of one's inner household. As they appear, they can be confronted, we can come to terms with them, and they can turn from opposers to helpers. All this is part of growth, development, and healing; it is a lifetime's work, an ongoing process. *Dialogue* means confrontation, which is possible only when there is a vis-à-vis. This vis-à-vis may start with: (1) emotionality; if we can step back—not identify—emotionality becomes (2) a specific emotion which can be expressed, first (3) in images, and then (4) in words. This is the inner process, and it goes from more to less irrational. The *process* in a series of dreams, visions, or pictures is a story, the unfolding of a message or messages needed for growth and development. It can dissolve a complex and integrate those pieces that could be integrated only after the dissolution of the complex. This is the healing process. In the growth process it is more a balancing of opposites to make them live peacefully together—"mysterium conjunctionis"—a coming to terms, often through dialogue.

Continuing use of any art medium can foster this kind of process. In active imagination the initial material is that which arises from the unconscious, from inside. This does not mean that it cannot be stimulated or even started by an outer image, especially if there is a strong emotional response to something on the outside. This usually indicates some corresponding image on the inside that can and wants to be pursued and brought to the light of day.

I had my first experience with art therapy when I used active imagination in a most unorthodox way. I started work with a group and invited members to use translucent–colored tissue papers for collaging. This medium seemed helpful for the purpose of opening up to contexts from the unconscious. Working with tissue paper, glue, and brush brought forth freer shapes, which seemed to emerge from a greater depth of the psyche: it acted as an opener and channel builder. Eventually, shapes would emerge that had great impact and meaning. But this could happen only if the work was done playfully, unselfconsciously, as a child would do it, without preconceived ideas or notions, without manipulation. It meant just very seriously enjoying the process of playing while enjoying the colors, sometimes taking pleasure in what emerged, sometimes being surprised, pleasantly or unpleasantly, but always eventually finding meaning in what had emerged. In addition, it set the stage for allowing what Ehrenzweig (1965) has called "the unconscious form-sense" to become manifest.

Images come in a series. Often a story unfolds that wants to be written down. Discoveries happen sometimes only after the story. However, something has been touched, the person is moved to write a story after having seen the images—the meaning is there. Most of the time, the person has been touched deeply enough to bring about transformation. It is exciting and absorbing work, often continued for years. The absorption is reminiscent of both child and artist. This is also valuable work at those moments in life when nothing seems to want to move, outwardly or inwardly, when one is stuck. One of the values of this work consists in opening new channels, in furthering process. The doing is the first step, the first part of the dialogue. The first injunction is: Forget all you know, all preconceived ideas, all known forms or images that have appeared before. Play!

Once this process has unfolded, in all its spontaneity, we then take a very close look at what has appeared. We let it speak to us, and we need to "listen" as we did before, when something wanted to become manifest. Now we need to know *what* has manifested, to catch the message. This is also a dialogue, the injunction being: Let it speak back to you; what does it say to you? This *looking*, to which a good deal of time is given, is a three-step process:

First: "Looking" in the ordinary sense—just simply looking at the object and realizing that something has been produced.

Second: "Noticing" that one can see more things than appeared to be there at first—a different kind of perceiving, but still connected with actual appearance.

Third: "Seeing." This is a true recognition, a revelation: there is more to it than meets the eye. This hits me, it has meaning, it tells me something that I did not know before. I receive a message. I see the world anew, my world; I perceive a truth. Only this third step is a step into depth. It is another way of making contact with the deep, which is the aim. The whole process is a far cry from analyzing and diagnosing; these are only surface procedures compared to this third-stage process, which leads to understanding in the true sense. It requires patient but relentless observation, while awakening a kind of perception different from a deliberate procedure of analysis. Such manifestations from the unconscious need constant circumambulation to be understood, and I say "constant" advisedly. We may have only gotten hold of the dog's tail, when it is his face we need to see. That means: Don't let go of the tail, work your way up to the face. If we let go, the dog is likely to run away. All this takes time.

The liberating effect is apparent in every workshop; however, it happens only when there is a true letting go. Those who cling to the known cannot reach it, and there are always some who cling ardently because the other mode has been their security. The method is simple, but there are pitfalls. The ego is ever ready to step in and take over, leading back to conditioned responses rather than spontaneous emergence of the contents of the unconscious. The tissue paper lends itself to simple play with form and color. Often amazingly recognizable forms appear. If at the moment of recognition, while still in the process of composing, we step in and outline the recognized shape or help it along in other ways, the whole loses its genuineness and lacks the revelation of that which is new; the dialogue is lost. The temptation is great because the known is the safer ground; it is easier to be in control than to allow events to happen. Such "events" come from a source of greater truth and wisdom, but we are foolish enough not to want to hear the message. It is the jealous ego which wants to be ruler in the house and is always extremely alert to maintain this position.

We are surrounded by "notions" and it is difficult to disregard them. Though early conditioning is often mentioned and considered, the fact that conditioning goes on all the time is usually forgotten. Every bit of reading we do is a form of conditioning. There is often very little left that comes from our own depths, spontaneously and genuinely, unless we deliberately open channels and are keenly aware of the possibility of interferences before we get to the core. Of course, the path to the unconscious often presents itself in an unordered and chaotic form, which is hard for most people to accept. To give an example: a middle-aged man in one of my workshops, a building contractor by trade, made a collage with the mood and feeling of nature in an abstract way, which was not "reasonable" order. At the last minute, and quite deliberately, he put a sun in one corner. It was just too unbearable for him otherwise. But another person in the group detected it as a last-minute addition and confronted him with the question: hadn't he stuck the sun on as an afterthought? He had to admit this was true. Only "when man is capable of being in uncertainties, mysteries, doubts without any irritable reaching after fact and reason" is he capable of creation in the arts.

The creative process requires that we not be in control, but that we be confronted with laws which are unknown and possibly unknowable to us. Such an openness must also determine how we look at what we have produced, and how we look into and then verbalize what we see,

"Art cannot be reasoned out, it must be seen into" (Eliot, 1959, p. 131). The verbalization itself requires a careful use of words, economically and to the point, like the use of words in poetry. At times I use *haiku* writing in the workshops, as a training for saying much with few words. The inner story can unfold only through receptivity to what wishes to be said, and this applies to verbalization as well as to image making. In verbalizing there is the added danger that we use words in the superficial cliché way that we are used to, unless we *listen*. Haiku writing must happen—like Athene from the head of Zeus. This does not mean that we can indiscriminately allow raw contents to be thrown up. There may be a moment of readiness, but to *allow* contents from the unconscious to arise, sometimes accompanied by great emotionality, is not the same as "acting out." Letting be, allowing, can best be achieved in a playful way, and the joy of a playful way is usually felt. We can go by the motto: "All art is meditation." With all the excitement, once one takes brush in hand a calm descends, a concentration ensues, which makes the "listening" possible.

Play has been described as a "non-purposive state" (Winnicott, 1971, p. 55). By adulthood we are so conditioned that we have to trick ourselves into being open. One trick is to play, and that means: play seriously and work playfully. We must step aside to allow the depth, the unconditioned, to speak. For Jung, play was a necessity. He states (1923) "It is serious play. . . . it is play from inner necessity. The creative mind plays with the object it loves" (*Collected Works, Vol. 6*, pp. 154–155).

Fantasy is that which *we* spin; real depth, as it can be expressed in myth or fairy tale, for instance, spins *us*. Hans Christian Andersen is a good example for both fantasy tale and true fairy tale, one on a human level and the other on a deeper one. Sometimes he strikes both in one story, as in "The Little Mermaid," his most popular tale in Denmark. On one level, the romantic tale, one kind of striving to become human is foiled, no matter how great the suffering and the sacrifice. However, the effort is not unrewarded, the reward being the chance for an immortal soul, the lonely road to greater depth or height.

Such comparisons to myth or fairy tale or any other age-old manifestation that originated from the depth of the psyche are called "amplifications." They help us to understand the symbolic meaning of a present-day image that comes from the same depth. A true "symbol" creates a connection between conscious and unconscious. Its form expresses something that cannot be said more clearly, because it is not yet clearly understood. It is, however, a help to understanding what goes on in the depth of the psyche, which leads to self-understanding and self-knowledge—always a healing and growth factor. Once understood, the symbol has done its job; its function fulfilled, it often loses power and meaning.

As far as diagnosis is concerned, labels are for the safety of the therapist to the detriment of the patient. We are presented with an individual with his/her specific mixture of problems. The pieces to the puzzle are all askew. They need to be put together to make the picture which then represents this particular person. For therapeutic pruposes we need to see—and that acts as "diagnosis"—where the pieces are askew and how they might be put together. When we see the picture, we see the real person who may find his/her individual story, which characterizes that person—the "individual myth," as Jung has named it. That could be the end result, perhaps the ideal result.

What we can do is to point to what has been produced by the unconscious of the person who has come to consult with us. There is an inbuilt regulating factor in the psyche as there is physiologically, as many have pointed out. We can and must rely on that. The healing factor comes from the life force of the patient. We may need to know whether that life force is strong enough, and how much and what kind of assistance is needed to get it on its way. There are instances where the life force is damaged, as in psychosis. The emphasis in therapy is on the *healing* factor of the *psyche*—not what we as therapists *know*—even though we need to know much. We work with our being, more than with our knowledge.

Art therapy, active imagination, and meditation are *methods* and, I believe, precious ones. They are means of making the psyche speak, bringing to light that which was hidden in the dark, either doing damage or left unused-and that in itself can do damage. Too much unused potential leads to sickness. Lived potential means health, at least psychic health (even though many an artist has ruined his/her physical health through sheer neglect of the body). Art can be an obsession. But it is that driving force which can be our ally in art therapy, and we must engage that ally.

The difference between art therapy and active imagination on the one side and meditation on the other is that the first two focus on what arise as images and make full use of them for understanding. In true meditation, any arising content is to be disregarded as only a manifestation of the mind, since the aim is to get beyond mental manifestations. It can be considered a more advanced stage of development, to be used when we are ready for a different kind of revelation. Such revelations can also have a healing effect, for which we have to empty the mind first. However, the task of the therapist is to take care of the clutter on the cellar stairs—as I said—before we can get to the cellar of our being, our own depth. Once we have cleared the way, the time may have come for meditation. Only a strong ego can take the back seat, so our first task is to strengthen the ego. Even in active imagination, as we have been warned, there is danger if we are confronted with a situation where the ego is weak or absent, as in pyschosis. This is a contraindication to using the method. But when the situation and the time are right, all three methods can be used.

At times, we may invite images but find ourselves confronted with emptiness, which is the aim of meditation. This can be frustrating, even frightening; it should not be done without a guide. When we hope for manifestations from the unconscious, whether in dreams or through artwork, there comes a moment for a new dimension to break through. It seems that we often need to go through a moment of emptiness. This is the time for the "leap in the dark"—the jump—which is a quantum jump. It is necessary for the "guide," the therapist, to know about the workings of the psyche. Jung speaks of an "individuation process" and "integration of the personality" and the fact that there is a regulating factor in the psyche, a guiding wisdom: the Self. For this reason, guided imagery, unless used simply as a stimulus, makes little sense. Rather, we need to learn to trust our inner wisdom, to know that in the unconscious the truth resides—the truth both in a superficial, very personal sense and in the deepest, transpersonal sense.

It is sometimes difficult for people to take images that arise from the unconscious seriously, and we must take them absolutely seriously, but not as absolutes. This is the place where all the resistances and objections arise: "It is only play; I should be doing something more serious, more important!" However, there is nothing more important. I have suggested that we play seriously and work playfully. Any manifestation from the unconscious speaks a symbolic language, says something which—being not yet understood—cannot find a clearer language.

AN EXAMPLE OF ACTIVE IMAGINATION

Having emphasized the need to listen so much, I might sound as if I were advocating passivity at all costs. This is, of course, not so. Setting the stage for transformation can be a very active pursuit and quite hard work. We have in the following an interesting illustration of the balance and timing between activity—what we can and must do—and standing still or taking a "leap in the dark," not knowing where it will land us.

It is the story of a young woman—in her late twenties—who, as the first two pictures show (Figures 1 and 2), was struggling to get out of the protective womb of the mother. She then had some visual images that—characteristically—moved, so there was a process going, a story which she wrote down and later illustrated. Before giving her story, I must emphasize the fact that this young woman had been working with me for

Figure 1   *Figure 2*

some time, and she was now ready for such a process. Although active imagination per se can and often needs to be done by the analysand on his/her own, there must be some supervision, and there must be readiness.

Christina's Story

December 29th. I can see only darkness; then I see that there is a lake with faint reflections of light on it. The water leads into a tunnel. I am in a green boat on the lake; I have a pole to push the boat forward. I go into the tunnel (Figure 3). The only source of light is a small white light in the distance. It illumines the walls of the tunnel. They are wet and shiny. It is very quiet, the water is motionless. Only the boat makes ripples on the surface as it moves forward. I push the boat until the passage becomes too narrow and I leave the boat and dig. I had expected rock, but there is crumbly earth. I break through and find that I am looking out on a huge vault, like the inside of a huge bowl. I am on the side, about two-thirds up. There are lights in the crevices above, like a firmament, but I know it is all deep under the earth. I must get down to the bottom. I find that I have a sturdy white nylon rope, and I fasten it to something securely and let myself down. The bottom of the vault is pitch dark, and swampy. I manage to move on by stepping on tufts of grass. Then I feel

Figure 3

rather than see a huge snake. She is not threatening, but very powerful. I get up on her back and she carries me. We come to a place where I see a blue glow, like an iridescent blue glass bowl. Around it dance flames; they are blue like the inside of candle flames. Around the blue flame sits a circle of dwarflike little men, guarding it. In the middle of the blue is something gleaming white-yellowish; I can't see what it is.

December 30th. Then suddenly I am inside the blue bubble, which now seems as high as a room. It has a round hole in the middle of the bottom; out of the hole shoots up a jet of water, and it balances a luminous white large pearl—the white thing I saw from afar. As I look at the shimmering pearl dancing on the water, I know that I shall fall into the hole if I take it. I hesitate, stretch out my hand, withdraw it. Then I take heart and take it. I fall, and am on a meadow with spring flowers (Figure 4). I look at the pearl in my hand. It feels soft, gelatinous. It is now a small object of the form of a child, but all covered with the gelatinous substance, so that I can't see its limbs or its features. I know I must protect it from drying out. I find some huge green leaves, and I pluck some and carefully wrap the child into them.

January 1st. I take my leaf-wrapped bundle and go into the forest. It is a spruce forest, no undergrowth, all dark and quiet. An animal comes

Figure 4

toward me on the path, a wolf with yellow eyes. He quietly tugs on the bundle; I understand he wants me to come along. We go to the left into the forest, off the path, and go until we reach a freer space and a brook. We follow it back up to its source. It comes out of a little pool, very clear, but so deep that one can't see to the bottom. On the water is a big strong leaf, shaped like a receptacle for my bundle. I put my bundle into this leaflike bowl and am just about to take my hands off when I see the edges curl together and the water begins to move, in a churning and downward-sucking motion. I snatch the bundle back. I have it safely, but now the water recedes when I try to catch some in my hands to moisten the bundle. The wolf has watched all this; now he looks at me inscrutably, turns and vanishes into the forest. I begin to worry; where shall I get water so that the bundle doesn't dry out? Then it starts to rain gently; I go back down alongside the brook until I come to the edge of the forest. Night has fallen. There is a moon, and some misty clouds.

I have come to a pasture. I see a cow and walk toward her (Figure 5). I see that the leaves of my bundle have wilted and take the top leaf off to look at the child. The cow starts licking it, and slowly there emerges a boy–child with black hair and blue eyes.

Figure 5

January 5th. I need milk for it. I am thinking about milking the cow, and then I see she has vanished. In front of me stands a young woman. She has bared breasts, she is beautiful. I know she is a whore; I also know that she is the one who has abundant milk for the baby.

This process represents a transformation story, a new birth, a change from daughter to mother, from being carried and protected to being responsible for carrying and protecting a precious child that was behind the luminous pearl which she acquired through her own effort and trust. At first she has to be active: (1) she pushes the boat with a pole; when she gets stuck (2) she digs; (3) after finding a rope, she fastens and lets herself down on it; (4) she moves on by carefully stepping on tufts of grass to avoid the swamp; (5) she climbs on the back of a huge snake who carries her; and all along she knows she wants to get to the bottom of it, although she is already deep down under the earth. The encounter with the snake is an important moment in the story (Figure 6). The huge snake is an ele- mental creature who now carries her, and it is female according to her own statement—she knows that it is. Her wish to be carried is also a need, not to be expected from her own mother or any substitute, but from an elemental archetypal force in nature, also in her nature.

Then comes the "leap" for the pearl and after that decisive step there is a change. The light quality, the very atmosphere of the place—as the

Figure 6

illustration shows—has changed. This is reminiscent of the events in the Grimm story of "Mother Holle." A girl who has lost her spindle while spinning by a well is sent back by her wicked stepmother to bring back the spindle, and in despair she jumps into the well where the spindle was lost and finds herself on the same kind of sunlit, flower-strewn meadow as in Christina's picture (Figure 4). She also shows the same courage and fortitude. Tasks to be done also await her, as well as a reward. Christina is now concerned for a child in need of her care—she becomes the caring, carrying, protecting mother looking for nourishment as well.

In the gnostic "Hymn of the Pearl," in which a young man is sent by his father to retrieve a lost pearl, the pearl represents the soul. The young hero at first forgets all about his mission and gets into bad company, but finally, in real distress, he remembers and returns home with the pearl, the soul regained. The dwarflike figures in Christina's vision are the guardians of the pearl, those underground helpers we all have, the "cabiroi" of whom Goethe in *Faust* (Part 2) says: "Small in length, mighty in strength."

There is one more crucial moment in Christina's story. Guided and challenged by a wolf, she comes to a source of water where she can wet her bundle which needs to be kept moist (= given life). She is ready to take her hands off the bundle when she notices that the water recedes "in a churning, downward-sucking motion." Now, and this is the crucial moment, she is alert and aware enough to snatch the bundle, to prevent this newborn child from disappearing into the unconscious, when all the work would have been lost. At this moment the wolf leaves, as if he had been sent to test her. Now help comes in the form of rain—which comes from above—contrasted with the pool of water, which had come out of the earth. The cow, who has appeared in the moonlit landscape, is not the one to provide milk to nourish this new-found spirit, represented by the boy–child. Nourishment must now come from a human being, a young woman who knows how to relate to men, even though, as a whore, she is not the best representative of a fulfilling, intimate relationship. The transformation that has taken place is from a child, protected and carried by the mother, to an adult, who knows how to care for her own soul and knows how to protect and find nourishment for her new-found spirit.

The consequence she had to take was to move away from the mother world; for one thing, it was now time for her to work in analysis with a man. All this also made it possible for her to withdraw projections such as all of her expectations accompanied by negative feelings for her own mother. The Great Mother—earth, snake—had come to her aid and had made her courageous actions possible. Such archetypal forces reside in all of us, often as strong, driving forces.

> . . . what counts . . . is not how explicitly an archetype can be formulated but how much I am gripped by it. . . . The "living idea" is always perfect and always numinous. Human formulation adds nothing and takes away nothing, for the archetype is autonomous and the only question is whether a man is gripped by it or not. If he can formulate it more or less, then he can more easily integrate it with consciousness, talk about it more reasonably and explain its meaning a bit more rationally. But he does not possess it more or in a more perfect way than the man who cannot formulate his "possession." Intellectual formulation becomes important only when the memory of the original experience threatens to disappear, or when its irrationality seems inapprehensible by consciousness. It is an auxiliary only, not an essential (Jung, *Collected Works, Vol. 14*, p. 524).

This quote from Jung sounds like a rationale for art therapy. Though he may not have used that term, "images," their use and understanding are of utmost importance in Jungian therapy. The aim is not to produce art, but to use that which comes from hidden sources—which can be brought to light through art media—to promote understanding, consciousness, growth, and transformation. It is always a process, whether for the artist, the "patient," or the healer. Let us not be satisfied with reductive, analyzing, diagnosing ego psychology. We might learn from artists in search of soul, spirit, or a deeper meaning in life. What is this obsession with sunlight that drove Van Gogh to paint in the bright sunshine of summer looking at yellow cornfields in Provence? What was Kandinsky looking for when he wrote *Concerning the Spiritual in Art?* (1947)

Through highlighting and illustrating what Jung meant by active imagination, I hope to have clarified what may be of use in art therapy, a process that accelerates both healing and a chance to bring out creative potential—the two are synonymous in my mind. If we do not live our potential—or at least part thereof—we become sick. Living our potential means health and wholeness. Sometimes we have to descend into the depth to find the "treasure hard to attain." And then, as Jung said, "The centering process is, in my experience, the never-to-be surpassed climax of the whole development, and is characterized as such by the fact that it brings with it the greatest possible therapeutic effect (*Collected Works, Vol. 14*, p. 203).

REFERENCES

Adler, G., & Jaffe, A. (Eds.). *C. G. Jung letters*. Vol. I. Princeton, NJ: Princeton University Press, 1973.
Beagle, P. S. *The last unicorn*. New York: Viking, 1968.
Capra, F. *The tao of physics*. Boulder, CO: Shambala, 1975.
Ehrenzweig, A. *The psycho-analysis of artistic vision and hearing*. New York: George Braziller, 1965.
Eliot, A. *Sight and insight*. New York: McDowell, Oblensky, 1959.
Jung, C. G. *Essays on a science of mythology, Collected Works, Vol. 9*. Princeton, NJ: Princeton University Press, 1969.
Jung, C. G. *Memories, dreams, reflections*. New York: Vintage Books, 1961.
Jung, C. G. (1931) Commentary on *The secret of the golden flower, Collected Works, Vol. 13*. Princeton, NJ: Princeton University Press, 1967.
Jung, C. G. (1923) *Psychological types, Collected Works, Vol. 6*, Princeton, NJ: Princeton University Press, 1971.
Jung, C. G. *On the nature of dreams, Collected Works, Vol. 8*. Princeton, NJ: Princeton University Press, 1972.
Jung, C. G. (1935). *The Tavistock lectures. Analytical psychology: Its theory and practice. Collected Works, Vol. 18*. Princeton, NJ: Princeton University Press, 1976.
Kandinsky, W. *Concerning the spiritual in art*. New York: Wittenborn, 1947.
Klee, P. *On modern art*. London: Faber and Faber, 1945.
Van Gogh, V. (Roskill, M., Ed.) *The letters of Vincent Van Gogh*. New York: Atheneum, 1963.
von Franz, M.-L. Introduction. In M. F. Keyes, *The inward journey*. La Salle, IL: Open Court, 1983.
Winnicott, D. W. *Playing and reality*. New York: Basic Books, 1971.

RECOMMENDED READINGS

Edinger, E. F. *Ego and archetype*. Baltimore, MD: Pelican Books, 1973.

Hannah, B. *Encounters with the soul: Active imagination as developed by C. G. Jung*. Santa Monica, CA: Sigo Press, 1981.

Harding, M. E. What makes the symbol effective as a healing agent in analytical psychology? *International Record of Medicine*, 1958, *171*(12), 732–736.

Hull, C. F. Bibliographical notes on active imagination in the works of C. G. Jung. *Spring* (a yearly publication), 1971, pp. 115–120.

Jacobi, J. Pictures from the unconscious. *Journal of Projective Techniques*, 1955, *19*(3).

Jacobi, J. *Vom Bilderreich der Seele: Wege and Umwege zu sich selbst*. Freiburg: Walter-Verlag, 1969.

Jung, C. G. *Analytical psychology: Its theory and practice*. New York: Pantheon, 1968.

Jung, C. G. *Man and his symbols*. New York: Doubleday, 1964.

Jung, C. G. *The spirit in man, art and literature, Collected Works, Vol. 15*. Princeton, NJ: Princeton University Press, 1966.

Kalff, D. M. *Sandplay*. Santa Monica, CA: Sigo Press, 1980.

Keyes, M. F. *The inward journey: Art as therapy for you*. La Salle, IL: Open Court, 1983.

Neumann, E. *Art and the creative unconscious*. New York: Pantheon, 1959.

Neumann, E. *Creative man*. Princeton, NJ: Princeton University Press, 1979.

Perry, J. W. *The self in the psychotic process*. (Foreword by C. G. Jung.) Berkeley, CA: University of California Press, 1953.

Perry. J. W. *The far side of madness*. Englewood Cliffs, NJ: Prentice-Hall, 1974.

Sandplay studies: Origins, theory and practice. San Francisco: C. G. Jung Institute, 1981.

Wallace, E. Creativity and Jungian thought. *Art Psychotherapy*, 1975, *2*, 181–187.

Wallace, E. Establishing connections between two worlds. In I. Baker (Ed.), *Treatment in analytical psychology*. Felbach: Adolph Bonz, 1980.

Weaver, R. *The old wise woman: A study of active imagination*. London: Vincent Stuart, 1964.

Weinrib, E. *Images of the self: The sandplay theory*. Boston, MA: Sigo Press, 1983.

SECTION II

HUMANISTIC APPROACHES

The chapters in this section do not derive from a shared theoretical framework, as do those in the first, where all acknowledge a debt to either Freud or Jung. What they do have in common is an optimistic view of human nature and of the human condition, seeing people in a process of growth and development, with the potential to take responsibility for their fate. Many of those initiating these "third-force" movements in psychology did so themselves in reaction to the Freudian idea of "psychic determinism," the concept that human beings are largely at the mercy of unconscious dynamics, which are difficult both to know and to master. Adler and Perls (Gestalt), in fact, were both trained as psychoanalysts, only later rejecting classical theory and technique as inadequate. This was also true of Binswanger, a psychiatrist involved in the development of existential or phenomenological psychotherapy.

In regard to art therapy, Freud's (1928) admitted difficulty in explaining the artist and the creative process led to what many have seen as narrowly reductionistic theories about the source and functions of creative work. A number of psychoanalysts have struggled to go beyond the founder in this area, some with striking success (Deri, 1984; Erikson, 1977; Gedo, 1983; Kris, 1952; Pruyser, 1983; Rose, 1980; Winnicott, 1971). Nevertheless, many art therapists remain highly critical and cite the shortcomings of Freudian theory about art and creativity as one of their reasons for turning to other frameworks. This is true for both Josef Garai, author of Chapter 11 on humanistic/holistic approaches, and Mala Betensky, author of Chapter 9 on a phenomenological approach to art therapy.

Both Garai and Betensky have written and presented on their respective topics before, as you will see in the references for each chapter. This is also true of Janie Rhyne, who has published her ideas about a Gestalt approach to art therapy in various forms, including a widely used book. Rose Garlock, on the other hand, has not been active as a writer, but is typical of the vast majority of art therapists, devoting her energies primarily to doing clinical work. Like many in our field, she "found" a theoretical framework when she found a "home" at the Alfred Adler Clinic, a place where she could work with groups of people in art and other creative therapies. Since her story seemed like that of most art therapists, who are not theoreticians but clinicians at heart, it seemed to me that it might well be included. Although Adler's theories are not, like the others in this book, widely influential in our field, he stands as an example of those many well-known renegades from Freud's early ranks.* In another way, Garlock stands as an example of those art therapists who have (understandably) adopted the theoretical stance of the institutions where they and their work have been supported.

The only major humanistic approach which is probably used by many art therapists but which was not included separately is that known as "person-centered" (formerly "client-centered"), developed originally by Carl Rogers, a psychologist (briefly noted by Garai in his chapter). Although many art therapists, especially students in training, utilize a "nondirective" approach, none has specifically embraced Rogers' theory as a primary framework for his or her work. Perhaps that is in part because it emphasizes the necessary conditions for good therapeutic work (e.g., a psychologically safe environment, empathy and positive regard on the part of the therapist) that alone—like *art* alone—are not always enough. Even Rogers himself has become interested in more active techniques in recent years, incorporating confrontation into his latest work with encounter groups, for example.

One further word about the grouping in this section: each of these approaches tends to be assertively open-minded and antidoctrinaire.** There is no "classical" technique for example, in Gestalt, humanistic, or phenomenological therapy, and indeed, such a notion is quite out of synchrony with the individualistic thrust of both the founders and the followers of these orientations. As noted in the Introduction to the book, each chapter represents the individual author's selection of ideas from a particular theory as a basis for his or her clinical work. Read in that light,

---

*Although Adler is sometimes grouped with psychodynamic theorists, it seemed to me that, with his view of humans as both striving and social, he belonged more appropriately in this section of the book.

**One outcome of this relative openness in "third-force" orientations is that their followers freely adopt those elements of psychodynamic theories which seem to fit, such as Garai's inclusion of Jung in Chapter 11 on humanistic/holistic approaches to art therapy.

they should prove interesting and stimulating to the reader. Although psychodynamic approaches dominated art therapy in the past, many feel that humanistic ones will be dominant in the future.

REFERENCES

Deri, S. *Symbolization and creativity*. New York: International Universities Press, 1984.

Erikson, E. H. *Toys and reasons*. New York: W. W. Norton, 1977.

Freud, S. (1928) Dostoevsky and parricide. *Stand. Ed.*, Vol. 21. London: Hogarth Press, 1961, pp. 177–198.

Gedo, J. E. *Portraits of the artist*. New York: Guilford Press, 1983.

Kris, E. *Psychoanalytic explorations in art*. New York: Schocken Books, 1952.

Pruyser, P. W. *The play of the imagination*. New York: International Universities Press, 1983.

Rose, G. *The power of form*. New York: International Universities Press, 1980.

Winnicott, D. W. *Playing and reality*. New York: Basic Books, 1971.

8

A Program of Creative Arts Therapies Based on the Theories of Alfred Adler

Rose Garlock

Alfred Adler can be considered the father of modern forms of social and group therapy. The core of his teaching deals with man as a social animal rather than as a creature with an exclusively individual destiny. Believing that the individual is faced largely with problems that can be solved only through sufficient social interest, he felt that socialization was the only rational and optimistic approach to the future of mankind. He felt that man was not alone in this world, but a part of a cosmic experience. He believed that man could, in a sense, achieve salvation only by immersing himself in social rather than personal goals. He stressed the importance of having a set of moral principles based on social feeling, if one was to have a sense of freedom of choice based on mental health.

> . . . only in togetherness and interdependence can the individual accomplish his self-realization; the value-creating function of the single entity within the community of man lifts the person from the purely biological plane of self-preservation and existentiality to the level of essentiality (Adler & Deutsch, 1959, p. 20).

At the same time, Adler believed in free will rather than determinism. He believed that man has a hand in his own destiny, and that his emotions are "the nervous energy that sparks us" (*Ibid.*, p. 59). Altogether, he placed great emphasis on the unity of the personality. "All actions are interactions" (*Ibid.*, p. 76); whatever is called a character trait or personal quality is actually "a way of movement, a way of dealing with others"

139

(*Ibid.*, p. 77). To understand man one must understand his motivation, the role he plays in life, his conflicts, and his awareness of the social world around him. In this sense, "the community alone can make a human being out of an organism" (*Ibid.*, p. 142).

> . . . the healthy, developing individual must constantly balance the anxious tension of separateness from consensual beliefs with the joys of new discovery about the world in a dialectic of growth (*Ibid.*, p. 96).

The belief that neuroses limit one's life forces and restrict one's activities within a social community led Alfred Adler to the practice of group therapy, and from there to the creative force of art and play therapy. He believed that because a play situation was not real, it was therefore a safer world in which the disturbed individual could relax. There, he could be encouraged to develop normal relationships, free from anxiety and distortions, and at the same time reveal tendencies and patterns that underlay his neuroses by analyzing his life-styles and goals. The therapist would function as a guide toward freedom of expression and social adjustment. Although Adler called this theory "individual psychology," it was an approach which evolved into a cooperative harmony between the individual and society. He assumed the underlying importance of the individual's subjective phenomenological world and believed (1) that there is an organismic unity of the individual, (2) that there is a striving for success, (3) that each individual is unique in his life-style, (4) that the individual's self-determination is a creative force, and finally, (5) that the individual seeks a positive social orientation.

In the course of developing his theories, Adler broke away from the opposing assumptions of Freud that instincts, drives, and the unconscious were the forces that led to irrationality. In his attempts to lead disturbed, conflicted individuals to a healthy, satisfying, and socially constructive life, Adler turned to the idea of the "therapeutic social club." The therapeutic social club was an experiment that had been created by Dr. Joshua Bierer in 1938 in London, England (Bierer, n.d.). It was first devised for acutely neurotic and psychotic patients in mental hospitals. However, the usefulness of the clubs soon became apparent, and very quickly, from a small beginning, the idea spread to many hospital and outpatient departments in England as well as in other countries.

> Examination of the characteristic traits for the growing existentialist movement in literature, art, philosophy, psychology, and psychoanalysis would lead us to infer that we are witnessing here another swing of the historical pendulum, away from chains of the dominant

rationalistic orientation toward another era of individual freedom. The greatness of Alfred Adler lies in the fact that he clearly anticipated this future development (*Ibid.*, p. 166).

In a therapeutic social club there exists the possibility of developing and expanding one's creative potential, whether it is in the area of the arts or relating to others as individuals, or in regard to the functioning of the group. According to Adler, social interest represents the strongest and closest emotional relationship that can exist between two human beings, and the possibility of fulfilling such goals does not depend on the individual alone or on the intellect. It depends on social interest, which is expressed objectively, and on having something in common with other persons.

In 1954, having been assistant director of a recreation and community program in a public-school system near New York City, I had considerable experience in what might be called "lay-group therapy." At the same time, I was studying art and psychology at Columbia University. That year I was granted a sabbatical leave for study and went to Europe. While in Paris, I was introduced to Mme. and M. Berenson, Jungian analysts. In addition to being a lay analyst, M. Berenson was also an art therapist. We developed a positive relationship, and I was invited to observe him working with two children in art therapy. I was impressed with his work and made arrangements to study art therapy with him.

One day, Mme. Berenson asked if I was planning to attend the Third International Congress of Psychotherapy in Zurich. I replied, "No, I am only a student and probably not qualified." "If you had a letter from Dr. Lagache, head of the psychoanalytic association in Paris, you would be able to attend," she countered. I therefore spoke with another friend who had some contact with the doctor and received a letter of invitation to the meeting. With 17 American dollars and the letter, I attended my first psychoanalytic conference. It was an exciting introduction to the field of psychotherapy. At the conference there were several joint meetings with the Adlerians, who were meeting in Zurich at the same time. At one of these meetings I met an Adlerian who had attended a session on the therapeutic social clubs of London, England. Her descriptions of these clubs made a deep impression on me.

When I returned to the United States in September, we met again. Since I had an M.A. and was a graduate of the National Recreation School, as well as my other qualifications, I was invited to participate in the creation of the first therapeutic social club in the United States at the Alfred Adler Mental Hygiene Clinic in New York City. One year after its inception, I became the director.

When patients first came to the club, they lacked the social feeling of belonging. In the warm, accepting atmosphere they found opportunities to relax, to relate, and to feel part of the group. Perhaps for the first time in their lives, they were more comfortable with themselves. Most had had few experiences in childhood of positive relationships with people and had therefore failed to develop social and emotional capacities. At the same time, many of these patients lacked the potential needed for developing true social feeling.

In order to create a functioning program it was necessary to develop cooperation among members. I devised committees on which the patients participated, such as program, refreshment, and clean-up committees, and anything else that would promote interaction. Developing an awareness of other members' weaknesses, strengths, and needs helped to create the social interest which had been neglected in their early development. Caring for the more distressed members, and learning to be of assistance to them at the club, and often on the outside; enabled many patients to respond to the needs of those with problems greater than their own, which helped some to become more social, healthier human beings.

The program was designed to function in a cooperative, social fashion. Members cared for one another. They visited those members who returned to the hospital and helped each other to readjust to living in the outside world. Opportunities to develop self-esteem were also available. A member could work on one of the many committees, prepare refreshments, chair a meeting, plan weekend projects, as well as week-day programs for those who were not working. Helping those who returned from the hospital to reestablish their living quarters, whether in a walk-up on the Lower East Side or a single room in one of the many hotels in the center of the city, was of great value in developing an interrelationship with and responsiveness to others. Most important to the members was the feeling of belonging to a group, where they were accepted for themselves and were supported in many ways akin to a surrogate family.

When the program was first organized, it was limited to clients of the Adler Clinic. Several years later, Dr. Bierer, who had created the program in London, visited the Alfred Adler Clinic in New York City. A special meeting was held to honor him, at which I was invited to give a report on the therapeutic social club. When Dr. Bierer learned that the social club was limited to clients of the Clinic he was surprised and suggested that the program should be open to all who wished to participate. The program was then made available to all throughout the city and its environs, and patients came from all boroughs of New York and from all the hospitals and clinics.

Shortly after this period, new medications became available for the mentally ill in hospitals, clinics, and private physicians' offices. As a result, many came to the club reacting to the medication—sometimes dulled, occasionally hallucinating or angry, and at times suicidal. They often came when allowed out of the hospital on a day or a weekend pass.

The program was held in an apartment, one of two that constituted the facilities of the clinic. For many years, it met every Saturday from 2:00 until 5:00 P.M. Later, when the need for expansion became evident and more funds were available, the program was expanded to include a session from 6:00 to 9:00 P.M. on Friday evenings. In most cases, a person visiting the club for the first time brought a report from the social worker or doctor, although sometimes the report was sent later. Sometimes members brought friends or acquaintances to the club. Often, we had visitors from other clinics or other cities and, occasionally, from other countries.

The program at the therapeutic social club consisted of both individual and group activities, as well as a regular meeting during the last hour of the session at which refreshments were served. The program was subject to change for special events, such as holidays and birthdays. Upon arrival at the club, members signed up for individual activities such as art therapy, dance therapy, music therapy, or vocational guidance. The group activities were art, poetry, dance, music, and psychodrama.

The staff consisted of a dance therapist, a music therapist, and a poetry therapist. I conducted the individual and group art therapy and, occasionally, the art and poetry therapy. As I had also studied psychodrama with the Morenos at their Institute in Beacon, New York, I also led the psychodrama group. Often we had volunteers, who were always welcome. There were also students of the Alfred Adler Training Institute, who were able to lead and study some of the activities. One led the poetry group for a year and then wrote his thesis based on his findings. Another continued to work in the program at the social club after he was graduated from the Adler Institute. Throughout the 19 years of my directorship, as many varieties of programs as could be devised were developed. As noted previously, the last hour of the afternoon was devoted to the meeting of all members present that day. It was led by those members who were able to assume such leadership. At the meetings, plans were made for future programs so that members had a feeling of continuity. They learned to carry through such projects, feeling fulfilled and emotionally enriched when they saw concrete realization of their plans.

Early in the development of the club, the dues were set at 50 cents. Those who did not have the funds paid as much as they could afford. Although refreshments were served at each meeting, eating dinner together afterward at one of the nearby restaurants was a further extension of the club's efforts to encourage relationships. The social club became, for many, a substitute home. It was a place where a person could be accepted for himself, a place in which he could participate in activities of his own choice and, most important, where he might see a familiar face and could make new friends. It was a place where an individual could be accepted, whether he was withdrawn or sociable, or even if he was somewhat hysterical. It was a place where members became friends, and many would visit with each other during the week outside of the club. It was a place where a person could receive sympathy for his emotional needs, and which provided a "family," so that anyone could count on being visited if he or she had to return to the hospital. The club created the only sense of family and community that many of the members had ever experienced.

I still recall some of the comments of the members, which speak eloquently of the importance of the club in their lives. Jean, for example, said: "I feel good when I leave the social club. I feel somebody needs me. I come, I play Ping-Pong. I draw and dance. I offer to buy refreshments for next week." John painted and played Ping-Pong. He also went out with the other men to eat and to bowl. His paintings were very successful, and he felt deep satisfaction whenever he was complimented by the group. The ego building involved in such interactions was vital to the members' mental health.

The club also took many weekend trips—several to my cabin in Woodstock, New York. There they hiked and rode horseback, after they had planned the program for the weekend. They also did the chores, such as shopping for food, cooking, and planning the meals. The spirit of good will and cooperation created a new warmth and understanding among the members. Holiday celebrations, such as Thanksgiving and Christmas, were also planned and enjoyed by the members.

CASE STUDY

Diane, age 30, was quiet, soft-spoken, and attractive, with curly black hair; she was well liked by most of the others. She was one of the most regular members, always participating in dance and art, and occasionally in other activities. She also participated in the club meetings and in the after-club and weekend projects. Diane seldom spoke of her family. We did learn that because of family problems in her early childhood, she had been placed in Catholic and Jewish children's homes. When she was nine years old, she was united with her family for two years. It was not until she was in her early teens that she was reunited permanently with part of her family. For two years after this, she was treated as a retarded child, which she was not. She played the piano, even copying music scores.

Eventually, she was trained in a professional area. However, during the 14 years she was at the social club, she was unable to work.

During her many years of participation in the program, Diane often had to return to one of the hospitals in the city. Her need for love and attention was so great that she readily attached herself to anyone who gave the least sign of accepting her, whether it was a psychiatrist, one of the therapists at the club, or another member. When something distressing occurred, such as the death of her psychiatrist in an accident or the transfer of a physician to a different facility, Diane would often return to the hospital. She was frequently suicidal and tried many times to injure herself. If, during a meeting, I heard a crash of broken glass, I would dash into the kitchen and sometimes find Diane standing among the shattered pieces with one sharp fragment in her hand.

I have saved some of the drawings which the members did. These drawings reveal the anger and frustration, the despair and hopelessness that some of the members of the club experienced. Going back over Diane's drawings, I find that many of them (as well as many by other members) are drawings of fences, being fenced in, or fencing oneself in (Figure 1). The patient seems to be walling herself in for protection.

Figure 1

There's a sign on the fence that says "keep out!" When I asked Diane who put it there, she replied, "Me." When I wondered if she knew why, Diane said: "'Cause they get hurt. That is to keep people from getting hurt." When I asked what was behind the fence, she answered, "A graveyard. They want the people to sleep untroubled without anyone getting into the graveyard and cracking up." As if to further express the intensity of her depression, she finished her discussion of the black crayon drawing by pointing to the circle in the upper-right hand corner and saying, "That's the black moon."

Diane also did a drawing depicting cacti in an arid desert. About this picture she said, "I lived in Arizona for seven months after I graduated from high school. I kept losing jobs. They said I was dreaming. I was depressed and afraid. I thought if I moved I wouldn't be depressed. When I looked at this drawing, it seems to be saying, 'Keep out, you may hurt me again.'"

Diane lived alone in a walk-up in one of the impoverished areas of the city. She drank coffee and ate chocolates incessantly. She was left unsupervised. Only when it became evident that she had cancer was better housing and care given to her. Finally, she was confined to a wheelchair, and for the first time in her life she received the tender, loving care for which she had been longing. Although she had been in and out of hospitals for many years, her mother came to visit her only once. Diane seldom spoke of her brothers and sisters, and when she did, it was only to say that when they fought, she was the one who was hit. Her mother called her "bad" and "retarded." At one time she told me, "It was rough going in school. I was afraid that I was mentally retarded."

One day she drew a picture of "an unhappy girl" (Figure 2), which another member said must be a self-portrait. The group let her know that, as one woman said, "I'd like to see that girl laughing and happy." Diane replied: "A person cannot seek help 'cause they feel they are bad. I mean feel no good—all bad, evil." Another club member responded supportively: "Even murderers are given help." And yet another addressed Diane: "Since you feel you are so bad, there must be a reason for it. Are you doing anything that makes you feel bad?" Diane's reply was simple, direct, and stark: "When I get angry, I'm evil and I feel bad."

Diane was aware of her anger. She said, "I just can't find positive things; I'm demanding. I don't have many friends." One of her goals was to "keep out of the hospital." She wanted to be independent: "I'd like that more than anything!" One time, after being committed to the hospital and kept under constant supervision after one of her suicidal attempts, Diane ran away. From the period during which she attended the club, a period of 14 years (1960–1974), I have saved 123 drawings. Although it

Figure 2

was during those years that she was often missing, having been returned to one of the many hospitals in the city and environs, I believe that were it not for the club, she would not have survived.

Diane was only one of many desperate cases who came to the Therapeutic Social Club. Despite the fact that they were unable to take complete charge of their lives and were in and out of hospital, these people—when they were out—found that there was a place for them to go that was sympathetic and comforting. The therapeutic social club was a place to meet others who were in the same situation and a place where they had the opportunity to learn to cooperate. There, they discovered new ways to master life situations outside of a hospital environment. There, they could learn or relearn the art of being social human beings. They could develop the capacity to give and to take, in the out-of-hospital realities of life. The club was a place to reevaluate their early childhood attitudes and personality traits, and through the group therapy situation, there was an opportunity for them to develop more positive goals in life.

Several years after I had organized the therapeutic social club and was convinced of its value in a clinic, I approached a group therapist at one of the largest mental health clinics in the city and shortly thereafter organized and conducted a similar program. Today, that social rehabilitation program uses the facilities of an entire building.

My hope was that by this time there would have been many such facilities available throughout the nation. My regret is that there are not enough group social opportunities in our cities, especially for patients who leave the hospitals without adequate follow-up, housing, and care. In the large cities of our country, the majority of the helpless and, by this time, hopeless, street people are the mentally ill. They are the ones who would benefit deeply from a program like the therapeutic social club built, as it was, around group arts therapy. The many creative activities that could be made available would promote better attitudes toward work and healthier relationships in general. Some of the people who were involved in my program eventually became leaders in helping organizations. Perhaps because of the emphasis on the arts, they also became more creative individuals, who participated in activities within their own communities. The therapeutic social club at the Alfred Adler Clinic at present meets all day, five days a week.

REFERENCES

Adler, K. A., & Deutsch, D. (Eds.). *Essays in individual psychology*. New York & London: Grove Press, 1959.

Ansbacher, H. L., & Ansbacher, R. R. *The individual psychology of Alfred Adler*. New York: Basic Books, 1956.

Ansbacher, H. L., & Ansbacher, R. R. (Eds.). *Alfred Adler: Superiority and social interest. A collection of later writings*. Evanston, IL: Northwestern University Press, 1964.

Bierer, Joshua. *Therapeutic Social Clubs*. London: H. K. Lewis & Co., Ltd., n.d.

9

Phenomenology of Therapeutic Art Expression and Art Therapy

Mala G. Betensky

The term phenomenology has been known in philosophy since the middle of the 18th century and was subsequently elaborated on by a number of philosophers into a variety of divergent themes. In the beginning of the 20th century, Edmund Husserl, founder of modern phenomenology, gave it a new meaning which gained significance as his Science of Consciousness, a study of phenomena (things, objects) as they present themselves in consciousness as immediate experiences (Husserl, 1913). A phenomenon (a verbal noun, from the Greek verb "to appear") can be perceived and observed with our senses and with our minds. Phenomena include visible, touchable, and audible things in the world around us, as well as thoughts, feelings, dreams, fantasies, and all that stems from the human mind and spirit and belongs in the realm of mental experience. By means of the study of consciousness, Husserl tried to reduce the perception of phenomena to their essence.

Phenomenology grew into a movement in Western Europe, reached the United States in the middle of the 20th century, and was introduced to university courses in philosophy and phenomenological psychology. Phenomenology influenced psychotherapies, particularly those of humanistic origins, with a call to turn "to the things themselves," and to an investigation of the fullness of subjective experiencing of "things," away from preconceived or inferred theories about them.

I became acquainted with philosophical phenomenology in my student years. Its strong interest in the qualitative exploration of the human experience appealed to me. Its opposition to the restriction of psychology to behavior and behavior control, and to mechanistic, associationistic views as well as to reductionist tendencies in the study of man, was what I was looking for. I had already arrived at a synthesis of my background and interest among psychology, psychotherapy, the history of ideas, and art. But I was searching for an appropriate method that I could use experientially, and some aspects of phenomenology seemed quite naturally to answer my quest. By then, art had become central in my psychotherapeutic work, and phenomenological theory, as well as some aspects of phenomenological method, appeared appropriate in art therapy. The following discussion of phenomenological art expression and art therapy is the result of many years of practicing this synthesis and studying other approaches (Betensky, 1976, 1977; Betensky & Nucho, 1979).

Since theoretical considerations are essential to art therapy, which is empirically oriented, the first part of this chapter will be devoted to a basic concept of Husserlian phenomenology: intentionality (Husserl, 1913).

MAN IN THE WORLD, THE SUBJECT OF INTENTIONALITY

Art has to do with man and his very being, man who is deeply moved and often burdened with being in his own world and in that of the people around him. In art therapy, we often meet overburdened man, preoccupied with his own world and its stresses. At times he is compelled to flee from the burden—into pathology. His art-therapeutic work may become a source not only of immediate release, but also a preintentional record of his experience of stress and flight. Guided by the therapist into the intentional perception and study of his art, truly seeing his own painting or sculpture may open new possibilities for him.

The act of *seeing* is of vital importance. Perhaps this is one of art therapy's most important contributions to general therapy and to phenomenology itself, because art therapy pays attention to authentic experience in a twofold way. First, clients in art therapy produce an art projection that is a direct experience. Then, they experience its appearance in their eyes and in their immediate consciousness, and this is a second direct experience. In the second experience, however, they need some help, for they must learn how to look in order to see all that can be seen in the art production.

When I succeeded in suspending all my *a priori* judgments and all acquired notions about what I was supposed to see, when I trained my eyes to look with openness and with intention at the art object, I began to see things in that object that I had not seen before. Slowly I began to understand the truth in Merleau-Ponty's statement that "to look at an object is to inhabit it and from this habitation to grasp all things'' (1962, p. 168). This is a phenomenologist's way of looking in order to see, seeing with intentionality.

Intentionality and Meaning

Intentionality means that I am intent on the thing that I am looking at. By means of my intent look, I make that thing appear to my consciousness more clearly than before I was intent on looking at it. The object of my attention begins to exist for me more than it did before. It is becoming important to me. Now it *means* something to me. At times, a meaning becomes vital to my existence, to my being. Indeed, man is an intentional being with an intentional consciousness that makes the world actual to him. Intentionality may even help to invent new worlds and to make the invisible visible, as in the arts and sciences.

Intentionality as Relatedness

Intentionality also means that our consciousness always relates to somebody or to something. This, in turn, means that it is always directed to reality, i.e., to the world. Thus, intentionality has direction built into it. A client of mine, overburdened and withdrawn, persisted for some time in drawing tables, stools, airplanes on the ground, and other still objects. Cautious about making contact with the world, he was trying to direct his intentionality—sensory, rational, and emotional—first to inanimate objects. He was not simply hiding his feelings. On the contrary, he was turning toward everyday objects and was trying to get to know them in the *lebenswelt*, the everyday life (Husserl relates the immediate experience of phenomena to the world of everyday life). Hence, his production of a variety of stools and tables in various positions. His was the beginning of a return from an escape from being in the world.

Intentionality and Body

Intentionality of consciousness resides in the body, and that explains man's orientation to the world. That the body is intentional is an obvious fact. We are born into a world that is already there; thus, our body meets the world. With our senses developing in and along with the body and with our growing consciousness, we discern things in the world. Nor do we go about it in a piecemeal manner, appropriating each activity to its own sense organ alone. When our eyes see and our ears hear, it is not a function of the eyes or ears alone; it is the whole body that is conscious of what the eye discerns in the visible world and what the ear hears in the sonorous world.

The famous art teacher Nicolaides (1941) expressed it well when he taught his students how to look at a model. He said that "what the eye sees; i.e., the various parts of the body, actions and directions, is but the result of the inner impulse, and to understand that one must use something more than the eyes." And when we run or rush, our whole body is in motion along with our legs, quite consciously intent on the purpose and destination of our running. Thus, our body is permeated with intentionality within the wider unity of the body.

Unity of Body

The wider unity of the body includes sexuality in a phenomenological way. Merleau-Ponty (1962) studied the phenomenological nature and role of sexuality, in contrast to the psychosexual view of orthodox psychoanalysis about artistic symbols, based on the emotional and bodily priority of sex (cf. Arnheim, 1972a). He perceives sexuality as a generality that finds its expression in many behavioral ways—rational, emotional, bodily—that are not explicitly sexual. Phenomenologically seen, sexuality is not a force of itself and by itself. It transcends itself, along with other forces in human existence, and merges with those other forces, so that we cannot pinpoint exactly which force makes us do what. Together, these forces characterize our body in a subjectively unique unity.

Unity of Emotion and Unity of Expression

The same intentionality permeates emotion, in contrast to the dualistic view of emotions as separate forces capable of influencing the body. In Strasser's (1977) philosophy of feeling, man's emotion is a "determinate mode of man's gradually accustoming himself to the world," this gradual accommodation being characterized by *motus*, movement. This explains the general animation or state of excitement of the whole person in anticipation of an emotional experience. *Motus* is also evident in many manifestations of expressivity characterized by the unity of body-consciousness-feeling. The experience of *motus* is known to artists and inventors in all arts and sciences. Art therapists, too, notice the rising *motus* in the subtle, but observable transition in their clients' art processes from pleasurable play with art materials to the more serious art expression.

Established by Klages (1936) as the principle of the unity of expression, this important principle seemed to have been submerged in American psychology by the extraordinary impact of Freudian psychology and the popular wave of behaviorism. It has reappeared, however, in more elaborate form, in Strasser's work, and in the recent phenomenological writings of Remy C. Kwant (1978), who studies expression as a creative disclosure of being. Strasser clearly places emotion within intentionality and discerns three phases of emotion accompanying expression: the preintentional, the intentional, and the metaintentional. This, too, is a helpful classification for the art therapist's observation and guidance of a client's visual perception of the completed art expression. The preintentional phase of emotion is a vague state experienced as some pressure generated from an impression, ever so slight, of an unidentified object in the field of vision. The vagueness becomes intentional in the second phase, where it connects with the identified object. It turns metaintentional in the third phase, when the object is fully perceived and felt as part of the person's existence.

Meaning

The important thing about this crescendo of intentionality of emotion in relation to the object, particularly in the case of the client's art expression, is that in the process an additional factor emerges: meaning (Frankl, 1969). Meaning appears early in life when the baby, as soon as it is physically ready, busies its eyes with a visual area in an effort to structure a bit of the surrounding reality. This is the child's movement toward the world. It is also a first expressive activity, and it is on a preconscious and preintentional level. In the process of growth, it becomes conscious, emotion-laden, and meaningful, when the child is physically ready to interact with the world. In that interaction, the child organizes his visual field so that a certain object in that field becomes visible to his eyes and thereby begins to exist for him more than other things in that field of vision. It then takes on some importance for him, and thus becomes meaningful. I often observe a similar structuring and emergence of meaning in my clients' discoveries as they look at their art expressions. I also find that the emergence of meanings, even small subjective ones, when a line or a color suddenly becomes visible, enables the client to see unrealized possibilities or untapped potencies. This may have some bearing on the question of the unconscious in phenomenological thinking about art therapy.

Phenomenology of the Unconscious

The vagueness of stirrings toward an object yet to be identified in a visual field, classified in phenomenology as preconscious and preintentional, is probably the closest meeting point between the unconsciousness-minded psychoanalysis and consciousness-minded phenomenology. Historically, the study of consciousness was not well known at the time that Freud formulated his brilliant conceptions, nor were the founders of phenomenology interested in psychoanalysis then. Much the same could also be said about Gestalt psychology at the time of its beginnings. The lack of mutual interest and contact among these orientations can easily be understood as a result of each school's total focusing on the challenge of its own early endeavors.

Somewhat later, however, phenomenologists did write about the unconscious. Husserl stated that the unconscious "is anything but a phenomenological nothing, but itself is a marginal mode (*Grenzmodus*) of consciousness" (Spiegelberg, 1972, p. 236). And Martin Heidegger (1960), one of the founders of phenomenology, comes somewhat closer to the unconscious through his concept of *Dasein* (being-in-the-world). He presents the concept of two dimensions of being: the dimension that does not show itself (ontological) is intimately interwoven with the one that does show itself (ontic). He thinks that phenomenology can reveal the concealed dimension of being. Thus, the unconscious processes are hidden in the ontological dimension of *Dasein* which phenomenology can reveal (Richardson, 1965). And yet, Heidegger is also convinced that beyond the phenomena of phenomenology there is "nothing else" (Mook, n.d.).

It seems to me that art therapy comes closest to the fulfillment of the task that Heidegger assigned to phenomenology: revealing the hidden aspects of man's being as phenomena accessible to consciousness and to conscious investigation. Art therapy can best achieve this aim phenomenologically by means of a free expressive process, with art materials freely chosen by the client, along with a method in which the client views his art production as a phenomenon within a structured field of vision.

SPECIAL FEATURES OF THE APPROACH

Since the essential component in art therapy is art, many of the same structural components present in an artist's work also appear in the products of art therapy at a client's level of ability. From research and studies in the psychology of art (Kreitler & Kreitler, 1972), we learn that the structural components of art carry and convey expressive qualities. In studies of this subject, round and oval lines in pastel colors have been found to convey warm emotions; strong reds and some other basic colors indicated strong, aggressive, but also loving feelings; zigzag lines with pointed angles related to violence; and upward or downward lines expressed corresponding moods and modes of being (Betensky, n.d.). While more refined in the fine arts, and touching on universal meanings, in art therapy, these components convey mostly subjective meanings about the overburdened self, though occasionally they approach universal truths in their untrained simplicity.

The Gestalt psychology of art contributes much to art therapy, with its concepts of a Gestalt—its inner relationships and "whole" qualities—and the importance of seeing (Arnheim, 1969, 1972b). Gestalt psychology also contributes its theory of isomorphism, which gains more clarity in the light of the phenomenological unity and intentionality of body.

Clinical psychology (particularly the Rorschach examination and some drawing tests) is capable of enriching art therapy, if we know how to use such aspects as color, form, and movement and can skillfully combine them with the appropriate elements of clients' art expressions. On the Rorschach, *form* is the shape of a blot visually perceived as fixed in its outline; *color* responses are determined by color as well as by form, and by color alone; and *movement* responses are influenced by subjects' visual memories of movement observed, experienced, or imagined in relation to form or to parts of it. From experience and observation in art therapy we know that areas, even daubs, of color can define form; that in some productions areas of color merge in ways that defy form; that in others form dominates color; and that in still others color is omitted in parts or details of an otherwise-chromatic painting. We also see movement in patient art and stillness in the absence of movement; and we can distinguish inward and outward kinds of movement.

The following example indicates concurrences and contradictions between a client's Rorschach responses, formally structured on the perceptive process, and her spontaneous art expression, informally based on the creative process. The client and therapist benefited from the possibility of working with comparative areas of expression within the same set of concepts.

The Rorschach and Mrs. N.

On her Rorschach examination, Mrs. N. scored outstanding sharpness of form visualization in many tiny areas of the blots. She gave no color responses, even on the most colorful cards, and had only one response with color as a second determinant. Good, original, and miniscule form was her dominant response. Her Rorschach protocol presented an intelligent person in stabilized depression. Reluctant about using art materials, she agreed to "play" with paint and pastels. In all of her seven productions on large (18″ × 24″) paper, the entire surface was covered with light grays, dark grays, blue-grays, and gray-browns, which spread over a few daubs of red and yellow crowded together in the bottom right corner.

No form was directly visible, nor did the colors define form. Yet her involvement was visibly growing and intriguing to me. When the productions were mounted for the "What do you see?" procedure, I was amazed to see—among the light and dark shadings of the flowing colors—tiny clear figures and faces with large eyes, as I followed her finger tracing the outlines of the now-visible forms.

Her art productions, springing from the creative process, concurred with the precise, statistically calculated Rorschach diagnosis of depression. On the Rorschach she perceived and reported depression. In her artwork she painted the depression spreading over her emotions. Sharpness of minute form perception, along with a scarcity of color responses, is, indeed, a symptom of profound depression. Thus, an art therapist may notice indications of depression in a client's use of color and form even before a Rorschach is administered. The concurrence of my client's painting with her Rorschach responses and diagnosis helped me not only to better understand her difficulties, but also to decide about the direction of art therapy with her.

The House-Tree-Person Drawing Test

The H-T-P test (Buck, 1948; Hammer, 1958) is popularly, but often inappropriately, used by art therapists as an art therapy "technique." It can be very beneficial to clients when properly used, not as a "technique" taken out of its intended context, but as a diagnostic and therapeutic method. During my internship in child psychotherapy at a mental health clinic in the late fifties, I asked youngsters to use color for the H-T-P test, first as an experiment, then routinely as a sequel to the original pencil-and-paper version—for diagnostic purposes. For therapeutic purposes, I mount the two series of achromatic and chromatic productions vertically side by side. There are then two parallel columns of pictures that can be examined silently, horizontally as well as vertically, by the clients. This viewing is followed by description and unfolding, according to the phenomenological method. This therapeutic application of the H-T-P test has proved to be most fruitful as a source of clients' self-discovery, particularly in regard to how they feel about themselves in the present, how they felt about themselves in the past, and how they feel about the world they live in.

Art Materials

Another essential feature is art materials. Several sizes and textures of paper, other surfaces for painting or drawing, pastels, poster paints, water colors, collage materials, soft wood, earth clay, and the appropriate tools should all be available to the client. These materials are active participants in the client's artwork. They challenge his sight and touch. They stimulate emotional arousal and consciousness all at once. Being themselves bits of the world, these materials contribute to the client's getting back in touch with the world. Thus, there is an ongoing dynamic process between material and art maker. It is of special interest for the art therapist to notice which of the materials evokes the most expressiveness from the client (Betensky, 1982).

Before the Artwork Process

Informal experimentation with art materials is most helpful to children, adolescents, and adults—like mixing paints, or dropping a drop of one color into another to watch how the color spreads and then reversing the sequence. Both "experiments" serve not just as a "warmup," but also as an important, yet pleasurable way of creating new possibilities and taking small, safe risks.

Words

Yes, the phenomenological approach does use speech, because words are expression, just as art is; because consciousness, thought, and speech are one; and because in phenomenology we intend to articulate, and that is the job of words. In this method, however, words have a special role at an appropriate time, as specified in the following discussion.

The Art Therapist

The therapist's task is to watch the client at work, in addition to giving active guidance or participating in other ways. It is largely a silent task, but the therapist as participant–observer is far from being passive. He or she is busy unobtrusively observing the client's facial and bodily expressions of moods and his modes of choosing and using art materials during the creative process. Sensing to what extent the client needs the art therapist's physical closeness or other support is another aspect of the task, and noticing one's own visceral and emotional reactions to what the client does is yet another (Geller, 1980).

THE PHENOMENOLOGICAL METHOD OF ART THERAPY

The following is a general outline indicating the structure of the method. It is applicable to individual sessions as well as to the overall process of therapy. Of its four sequences, the first two were briefly dealt with

earlier in the chapter. The major contribution of the method lies in sequences 3 and 4, which will be discussed below.

> *Sequence 1:* Pre-art play with art materials
> Direct experiencing
> *Sequence 2:* The process of artwork—Creating a phenomenon
> *Sequence 3:* Phenomenological intuiting
> *Phase 1:* Perceiving
> 1. Visual display
> 2. Distancing
> 3. Intentional looking
> *Phase 2:* What-do-you-see procedure
> 1. Phenomenological description
> 2. Phenomenological unfolding
> *Sequence 4:* Phenomenological integration

Sequence 3, phenomenological intuiting, deals with the client's direct
experience of his production, in two phases. Phase 1 facilitates its perception. The first step in that phase is *visual display* of the art expression.
When the client indicates that the artwork is completed, both he and the
therapist place the sculpture or tape the picture where it can be con-
veniently viewed.

The next step is *distancing*: the therapist suggests that they both step
back or move their chairs back to gain perspective. The art product is now
a phenomenon with an existence of its own. It is now a part of the world,
separate from its maker, with its own properties. It can now be examined
objectively, from a distance, and without preconceived notions. The
powerful emotions contained in the visual product can now be viewed
with a certain measure of detachment.

The third step is the process of *intentional looking* at the art expression. The therapist now asks the client to take a long look at the picture,
sculpture, or collage. She may say something like this: ''Now take a good
look at it. First study it and see what you can observe. When the picture
is right in front of your eyes, you don't always notice things that you can
see later when you have gained some distance from your picture. So, take
a long look and try to see everything that can be seen in your art.'' The
client now concentrates and looks. Distractions are avoided. He is in
communication with the phenomenon he has produced. The art maker
becomes the receiver of messages that he had deposited, half-knowingly,
in his artwork. Now, as beholder, he receives the messages embedded in
the art expression, which has become his phenomenal field. His awareness

is now deepened and enriched by new observations which strike him as discoveries. It is important for the therapist to realize that a great deal of this activity may be taking place in silence. It is therefore essential that the client be given sufficient time to examine the artwork and, most important, that the therapist learn the importance of silence, develop the ease to bear it, and guard against casual comments that might distract the client.

Now follows the therapist's invitation to the client to share the results of the three earlier steps: that is, visual display, distancing, and intentional looking at the artwork. The therapist will simply ask the client, "What do you see?"

This question is very simple and naive on the surface. It contains, however, two fundamental aspects of the phenomenological approach. One is the emphasis on the importance of individual perception and meaning—what do *YOU* see? You, the maker of the picture, do not need to see it the way others do. YOUR way of seeing is essential and that is what we are now interested in. Through this question the value and the rightness of subjective reality are underscored. According to the phenomenological view, each person's inner reality is a fact of paramount importance.

The other notion contained in the question "What do you see?" deals with phenomenological evidence. What we are now concerned with is that all that can be SEEN is seen in the art expression itself, not just surmised or thought out from a preestablished theory. This is achieved by guiding the client to notice specific structural components in his art expression and the feelings those convey to him; how certain components relate to one or more other components; whether they complement, clash, or coexist; what the organization of the art production is; whether the components of content may be grouped in any way, and what the groupings share in common, and whether that is seen in the art expression. Gradually, vague feelings reach awareness, and a new ability to identify and name feelings appears.

Phenomenological Description

Phenomenological seeing is really getting the self in touch with the art expression in a very precise way. This is possible by virtue of a kinship and an ongoing interaction between the self and the outer world, the art expression serving as the center. In answer to the question "What do you see?" the client-turned-beholder gives a *description*, as precisely as he can, of what *is* in the picture. The art therapist's guidance may be needed with the naming of the elements of the art.

Phenomenological Unfolding

The phenomenological discussion of the art expression constitutes the second phase of the phenomenological method. The therapist helps the client to unfold, as it were, the private meanings contained on various levels in the visual product. In this, as well as in the previous phase, the therapist merely indicates points for discussion, addressing those points to components and objects *in the art*.

The following excerpt from a 12-year-old girl's *description* of her picture (Figure 1) indicates that the art therapist's initiatives are limited

Figure 1

to some guidance in the naming of elements, and to addressing points for discussion to components and objects in the art.

T: What do you see, J?

J: I see a girl playing with her ball in the park.

T: Playing with her ball.

J: Can I say something else I just saw?

T: Of course, just say it.

J: Well, now I see that she doesn't really care to play with the ball.

T: Mmm . . . I was wondering about that. What else do you see?

J: Nothing, really. Oh, over there is her dad, in the back, kind of behind.

T: Mm hmm. Her dad.

J: Yeah. And he doesn't care to walk. [sounds angry]

T: What else can you see on your picture?

J: [pointing far up] Oh, oh, see that house? That's our house, and see my mom? She goes back into the house? See, she told my dad to take me to the park and . . . and now I don't see anything else. [abruptly] [cries, then quiet]

T: [handing a tissue to J] Well, I remember, when I had tears in my eyes I couldn't see well at all, so I will see for you right now. And what I see on your picture has lots of bright colors and is very pleasant to look at.

J: You mean the sun and the trees? The sun, I made it setting. It makes everything in the park so pretty.

T: Yes, that is what I see, and you put it all in the picture. Now, what would you call all these things at sunset on your picture—things that are not people, but that make people feel what you just described? Find a word for it, can you?

J: You mean, the whole park and the sky and the sun? Something like what's around? Or background?

T: That's it, you just said it, background. Now let's go back to the people in the foreground.

J: The girl and her dad.

T: Mmm hmmm. What on the picture shows us that she doesn't really care to play with the ball, and that Dad doesn't really care to walk? Can you take another look and tell us?

J: Well, see, the ball is rolling away, almost to the end of the paper, and she doesn't run after it. She just walks, and her face is, kind of, worried? The mouth . . . oh, I don't know how to draw what a mouth . . . looks like. [grimaces]

T: What about the mouth on the picture?

J: It's just a straight line, looks like mad or something.

T: And the father?

J: Oh, he looks like he wasn't there. See, he didn't want to go. He was mad with me. And, oh look, I forgot to fill in his blazer. And I didn't hardly make him a face.

Answers to the question "What do you see?" frequently act as catalysts, drawing out from the client the essence of his existential dilemma as simply as he is able to state it. A withdrawn adolescent boy who produced a picture of a fish in a net responded to this question with a reality-oriented description: "I see a fish . . . caught in a net." He went on to say, with growing tension in his voice, that the fish "feels sad and mad." In a subsequent session the *description* continued, when the boy was able to point to the lines in the picture that conveyed the "stiffness" of the fish, its immobility, and, in contrast to that, the brilliant colors "decorating" the fish. In reply to the therapist's wonderment about this contrast, the boy said that the fish was "mad . . . because *he* couldn't show his colors to all the other fishes in the water." The pronoun *he* served as a transition to the boy's subsequent ability to refer directly to himself. This is an example of a process of self-discovery in *becoming*: the preintentional level of identifying himself with the fish was becoming intentional.

An adolescent girl responded to the question about her picture (Figure 2): "Well, I see a group of people. They are sort of standing around and they look sort of distressed, and everything."* These first statements are then discussed and further specified, and the girl's often used "and everything," for which she had no clear concept (though it meant something to her), is gradually clarified and understood by both client and therapist as the discussion of the visual product proceeds. The therapist must be a good listener to pick up vague clues from a client's slow and laborious verbal reflections about his art expressions.

The unfolding of the ideas and feelings contained in the visual product usually proceeds along one of two lines. One line of treatment will start with the client and deal with the content of the picture or sculpture. The other will emphasize the structural properties of the visual product and the relationships between these properties. The therapist will usually go along with the client's description of content and will then turn to structure. With the adolescent girl, the therapist tried to find out: Who might the people be? Why are they all huddled together? Are they trying to

---

*The following dialogue excerpts and picture are part of the author's videotaped art therapy session with "An Adolescent Girl" produced by Aina Nucho, Ph.D., ATR, The Media Center, School of Social Work and Community Planning, University of Maryland, Baltimore, Maryland.

Figure 2

protect themselves from the cold or, perhaps, from something else? What is happening to them right now? What might happen in a moment? Much as this approach yields in the client's interesting observations about subject matter, it is not all.

From a phenomenological perspective, discussions of the content are somewhat less fruitful than are the possibilities offered by the structural components of the artwork. With their property of conveying emotional meanings, they represent the inner reality of the client more accurately and more acutely than the content, which is on a somewhat more disguised level of symbolization.

T: Now let's take a look at the placement of the figures. Which figures are placed where on the sheet of paper?

Cl: Well, the people are all sorta huddled together, and um . . . they seem like they are all sorta huddled together in little groups. . . .

T: Which groups are huddled together? Can you make some groupings there?

Cl: This group right here and these three figures . . . and these three right here and those two . . . and that one up there. . . .

In a later session, "that one up there" became the center of self-discovery: the girl recognized herself.

Sequence 4—Phenomenological Integration

The last sequence in the phenomenological method is phenomenological integration. Three aspects of self-discovery can be discerned in this phase. The first consists of the client's reflections back to the development of his artwork. He may comment on his original intentions and on the actual outcomes of those intentions as he sees them in the completed work. Although some components of the completed product may have been decided upon and executed deliberately, others may have arisen perchance or as if on their own, without a deliberate decision or even with no awareness on the part of the art maker. Here is an example of this taken from a videotape:

Cl: It looks like this person right here . . . ummm . . . is not worried as
      all the others. . . .
T: Which one?
Cl: This one right here.
T: The one in yellow?
Cl: Uh huh.
T: Is not worried as the others? Uh, huh, uh huh. [long pause] Were you
      aware of that while you were drawing it? Or do you see it now?
Cl: No, I see it now.

The second aspect of phenomenological integration is the search for similarities and differences in the same client's artwork over time. By looking at the current art expression together with previous work, the client discovers certain recurrent components or themes in his work (Betensky, 1973). The adolescent girl, for instance, noticed how the sense of "heaviness" present in two pictures she selected was handled differently in each. This intraseries comparison leads to a discernment of patterns, first in one's art and then in one's responses to situations in life. The development of an ability to discern patterns in the art expressions leads the client to a further recognition of patterns in his behavior. A questioning of such patterns by the client himself then follows, and that eventually leads to change.

The third aspect of phenomenological integration flows naturally from the foregoing. It is the search for the parallels between the client's struggles with the process of art expression and his efforts to cope with real-life experiences. From a discussion of the changes she had made "here on the paper'' in a videotaped art therapy session, the adolescent girl proceeded to comment on how she was now more able to choose and to make friends, and also to schedule her classes at school—two of her major difficulties in life situations of the recent past.

CONCLUSION

Through the act of looking at their own art expressions, new facets of themselves become apparent to the art makers, and new communication takes place between the art expression and the subjective experience of the client-turned-beholder. Clients learn to perceive more clearly and more articulately the phenomena of the formal components and their interaction in the artwork. They connect those with their inner psychological forces and apply the newly acquired art of looking to phenomena outside and around themselves, in their own world and in that of others.

As they discover facets of themselves in their interactions with others, yet another interesting occurrence takes place: they transcend their self-centeredness and become a member of the world—literally—in their everyday life. They assume responsibility for their artwork from the start and actively participate in the intellectual and artistic process of working through the difficulties that have arisen in interactions between themselves and others. This is the particular contribution of the phenomenological approach to art expression in therapy—arrived at through artwork and the subsequent treatment of the organization of the art expression—from preintentional functioning to fully intentional living.

REFERENCES

Arnheim, R. *Visual thinking*. Berkeley: University of California Press, 1969.

Arnheim, R. Artistic symbols—Freudian and otherwise. In *Toward a psychology of art*. Berkeley: University of California Press, 1972a.

Arnheim, R. *Toward a psychology of art*. Berkeley: University of California Press, 1972b.

Betensky, M. Patterns of visual expression in art psychotherapy. *Art Psychotherapy*, 1973, *1*, 121–129.

Betensky, M. The phenomenological approach to art expression and art therapy. *Art Psychotherapy*, 1976, *4*, 173–179.

Betensky, M. Phenomenology of self-expression in theory and practice. *Confinia Psychiatrica*, 1978, *21*, 31–36.

Betensky, M., & Nucho, A. O. The phenomenological approach to art therapy. *Proceedings, 10th Annual Conference*. Baltimore, MD: American Art Therapy Association, 1979.

Betensky, M. Media potential: Its use and misuse in art therapy. *Proceedings, 13th Annual Conference*. Baltimore, MD: American Art Therapy Association, 1982, pp. 111–113.

Betensky, M. *Structural patterns in spontaneously expressed affect with an art medium*. Unpublished paper, 1984.

Buck, J. N. The H-T-P test. *Journal of Clinical Psychology*, 1948, *4*, 151–159.

Frankl, V. E. *Man's search for meaning*. Boston: Beacon Press, 1969.

Geller, S. *The unique dynamics of an art therapist and her client*. Unpublished paper, April 1980.

Hammer, E. F. (Ed.). *The clinical application of projective drawings*. Springfield, IL: Charles C Thomas, 1958.

Heidegger, M. *Sein und Zeit*. Tubingen, Federal Republic of Germany: Neimeyer, 1960.

Husserl, E. *Ideas* (1913) reprinted in 1976 by Humanities Press (New Jersey). (Cf. also *Husserliana*, microfilm, New School for Social Research, New York.)

Klages, L. *Grundlege der Wissenschaft vom Ausdruck*. Leipzig: Foundation for the Science of Expression, 1936.

Kreitler, H., & Kreitler, S. *Psychology of the arts*. Durham, NC: Duke University Press, 1972.

Kwant, R. C. *Phenomenology of expression*. Atlantic Highlands, NJ: Humanities Press, 1978.

Merleau-Ponty, M. *Phenomenology of perception*. London: Routledge & Kegan Paul, 1962, pp. 154–173.

Mook, B. *A phenomenological approach to the process of psychotherapy*. Unpublished paper, no date.

Nicolaides, K. *The natural way to draw*. Boston: Houghton Mifflin Co., 1941.

Richardson, W. J. The place of the unconscious in Heidegger. *Review of Existential Psychology and Psychiatry*, 1965, *5*, 265–290.

Spiegelberg, H. *Phenomenology in psychology and psychiatry*. Evanston, IL: Northwestern University Press, 1972.

Strasser, S. *Phenomenology of feeling*. Pittsburgh, PA: Duquesne University Press, 1977.

10

Gestalt Art Therapy

Janie Rhyne

INTRODUCTION

Like other approaches in our field, Gestalt art therapy has developed
in alignment with theories and practices underlying broader-based disciplines in psychology and psychotherapy. Gestalt art therapy grew out of
two very different movements. The first, Gestalt psychology, developed
from laboratory research in perception and learning; the second, Gestalt
therapy, evolved from applications in psychotherapeutic practice. Gestalt
psychologists have earned respected places in academia, but do not extend their concepts to clinical applications. Gestalt therapists base much
of their practice on some theories of Gestalt psychology, but have adapted
those concepts to support therapeutic interventions. Gestalt art experience has incorporated ideas from both areas and aims for their integration in a Gestalt approach to art therapy.

In this chapter, I delineate briefly a history of how Gestalt psychology,
Gestalt therapy, and Gestalt art experience are ideologically related; I
outline Gestalt tenets that I consider most relevant to the practice of
Gestalt art therapy; I briefly introduce several other clinicians who incorporate art experience, creative process, and visual language into their
work as Gestalt therapists. I then fill in my outline of Gestalt theories in
general, with more specific directives that I find useful in my own way
of doing art therapy. To illustrate how a flexibly structured approach is
applied in therapeutic process, I describe the way in which one of my
clients represented her thoughts and feelings as she experienced transi-
tions in therapeutic process and in her pursuit of self-directed changes
in her life-style. The graphic representations created by the client include
not only her drawings, but also the words she used to describe and inter-
pret her own messages. In communicating with me, this client was en-

couraged to translate intrapersonal insights into interpersonal relationships. Such self-awareness fosters active autonomy in choice making, in the larger environment of "the world out there."

FROM GESTALT PSYCHOLOGY TO GESTALT THERAPY

People are likely to think, speak, and write of Gestalt therapy as a revolutionary way of doing therapy, practiced and preached by Fritz Perls in California during the 1960s. Fritz was a charismatic character, and it was through his personal vividness that Gestalt therapy was publicized; he still stands out as the dramatic figure in the development of a psychotherapeutic approach called "Gestalt." But Gestalt theories and practices, viewed from a historical perspective, cannot be understood as a sudden phenomenal event springing from one man's practice originating in one time and place. The beginnings of the Gestalt movement can be traced back to the early 1900s. From these generative ideas it has been further expanded, integrated, and supported during the quarter-century since the audacious Fritz was in center stage.

Gestalt perception and its implications were investigated by three German psychologists in the early 1900s. In laboratory experiments, they were interested in the phenomena of how organisms, both animal and human, make sense of what they perceive in the world around them. In a book by Nordby and Hall, *A Guide to Psychologists and Their Concepts* (1974), the theoretical views of Gestalt psychology are succinctly outlined, as they were formulated by Wertheimer, Kohler, and Koffka. Fleeing from Nazi Germany, these men brought Gestalt psychology to the United States. Two other German psychologists, Lewin and Goldstein, also immigrating from Germany in the 1930s, were strongly influenced by Gestalt principles, which they incorporated into their own theories and applied in their professional practice. Lewin, a social psychologist who had been associated with the Gestalt psychologists in Berlin, was known for his "field theories," especially as he and his students investigated and applied them in group dynamics. His formulations have had "wide applications in the areas of personality, social psychology, child psychology, and industrial psychology" (Nordby & Hall, 1974, p. 110). Goldstein, a neuropsychiatrist, also strongly influenced by Gestalt psychology while still in Germany, was the leading exponent of "'organismic theory,' which emphasizes . . . the unity, integration, consistency, and coherence of the normal person. Disorganization is pathological, and is usually produced by the impact of an oppressive or threatening environment" (*Ibid.*, p. 66). These eminent scientists, engaged in research, teaching, and practice, influenced many other professionals in psychology and in psychotherapy in the United States.

Fritz Perls came to New York in 1947, also in flight from Nazi Germany, but with an in-between decade of living in South Africa, where both he and his wife Laura practiced psychoanalysis. By that time, ideas from Gestalt psychology had already been recognized, questioned, valued, and assimilated into approaches in many areas—philosophy, the arts, training and growth groups, organizational development, etc. In the forties, Fritz Perls had published *Ego, Hunger and Aggression* (1947), which he dedicated to Gestalt psychologist Max Wertheimer; in a 1969 reprint it is subtitled "The Beginning of Gestalt Therapy." However, it is not really a book about Gestalt therapy; it is a book about the Perls' revisions of Freud's psychoanalytic theories. At least two of its chapters were written by Laura Perls, who had studied Gestalt psychology during her training as a psychologist before she met and married Fritz. In a 1978 interview, Laura said, "I was first a Gestaltist and then became an analyst. Fritz was an analyst first and then came to Gestalt and never quite got into it" (Rosenfeld, 1978, p. 11). In New York Laura and Fritz met Paul Goodman, a controversial but prolific writer. From an incomplete manuscript, worked on by both Fritz and Laura, Paul Goodman developed, elaborated, and made comprehensible the theoretical base of Gestalt therapy in a book published in 1951. *Gestalt Therapy: Growth and Excitement in the Human Personality* (Perls, Hefferline, & Goodman, 1951) had a mixed reception. Gestalt psychologists saw it as an unfounded claim to associations with their domain and rejected any connection with Gestalt therapy. However, other psychotherapists recognized its value. The New York Institute for Gestalt Therapy was established in 1952, and the Cleveland Institute was founded soon afterward by a group of people who had studied with the New York Institute staff.

Laura Perls stayed in New York and Fritz wandered. He eventually found his time and place in 1963 at Esalen Institute in California. From that time he was hailed as the founder of Gestalt therapy; he was then 70 years old. From a lifetime of wandering, both geographically and ideologically, Fritz brought to his way of being and working at Esalen a rich mixture of personal and theoretical ideas which he applied during the last six years of his life. In his role as practitioner he demonstrated his rebelliousness, his early fascination with theater, his education as a psychoanalyst, his training analysis with Wilhelm Reich, his pragmatic use of some findings by Gestalt psychologists, and his courage in challenging "phoniness"—in himself as well as in others. As practitioner, he also acted as a director of improvisational theater with patients, with the group members and himself enacting personal dramas in the interest of an awareness of human complexity.

Fritz invented therapeutic techniques, too; he experimented with them, continuously exploring how he could use them in becoming a more effective psychotherapist. Unfortunately, many of Fritz's "techniques" have been popularized as "rules and games" that some may use as a substitute for personal effectiveness as a therapist. Fritz decried this reduction of his creative methods to mere "gimmickry." Though he basked in the image of himself as a great performer and often played the clown, he took his therapeutic task quite seriously and was dedicated to authenticity as a psychotherapist.

As a theoretician Fritz was not so serious; he was interested in theories when he could connect them with his ideas. He talked theory when he wanted to, but he admitted—even bragged—that he never really studied the texts of Gestalt psychologists. In his books, which are mostly transcribed conversations, he commented on theoretical systems in an off-handed manner, dismissing concepts with generalizations. He downplayed his own role as theoretician, too. In 1969, using his own inimitable vocabulary, he wrote:

> I have often been called the founder of Gestalt Therapy. That's crap. If you call me the finder or re-finder of Gestalt Therapy, Okeh. Gestalt is as ancient and old as the world itself. The world, and especially every organism, maintains itself, and the only law which is constant is the forming of Gestalt—wholes, completeness. A Gestalt is an organic function (Perls, 1969, p. 15).

He was right, of course; Gestalt formation was discovered, not invented. Though Gestalt therapy does focus on "organismic" functioning, both in theory and in practice, other therapies also assume "wholeness," and some explicitly emphasize a "holistic" approach.

Humanistic psychology, developed as a "third force" in the field previously dominated in the first half of our century by the two branches of psychology—psychoanalysis and behaviorism—also assumes the implications of organismic theory. It is taken for granted as

> more of an attitude or orientation or frame of reference than it is a systematic behavior theory. It says, in effect, that since everything is related to the whole, true understanding results from the correct placing of a phenomenon within the context of the total system . . . since the normal healthy human being, or any other organism for that matter, always functions as an organized whole (Hall & Lindzey, 1978, p. 271).

Which approaches are defined as "humanistic" depends on the context. Since the sixties, "new" psychotherapies have sprung up like plants in the rainfall after a dry season. In the midst of this proliferation, roots and branches get intertwined; it is not easy to see what they sprouted from, or what directions they are growing in, or which ones will thrive. Gestalt therapy is presently flourishing; it can no longer be dismissed as a fad. There are approximately 50 institutes training Gestalt therapists internationally. The leading edge is toward wider applications in counseling, family therapy, preventive psychiatry, community relations, and other publicly beneficial areas. Other Gestalt therapists have gone more private, turning toward meditation, zen, and other spiritual disciplines, seeking an integration of inner conflicts.

Gestalt art experience is humanistically oriented; from the rich soil of California in the 1960s, it sprouted and grew like a weed, natural and indigenous. Workshops with Fritz Perls and training at the Gestalt Institute of San Francisco fostered its growth, and so did dialogue with other humanistic psychologists. Innovative therapeutic approaches were growing rampant there and then; Gestalt art experience was one of these. I brought to my training as a Gestalt therapist, education and experience as a professional artist. Also, for some years I had worked with various populations using art as an expressive language; and I had been intrigued by the way implications from Gestalt psychology supported my own understanding of art as communication. So I brought with me some seedlings that I had gathered in other times and places.

GESTALT ASSUMPTIONS AND APPLICATIONS

Underlying a Gestalt approach are some assumptions about human nature that are commonly applied in a Gestalt therapeutic process. In this section, I outline those that seem relevant and important to me.

In a recently revised text, *Theory and Practice of Counseling and Psychotherapy*, Corey has defined the basic assumption and the key concepts of Gestalt therapy,

> The basic assumption of Gestalt therapy is that individuals can themselves deal effectively with their life problems. The central task of the therapist is to help clients fully experience their being in the here and now by becoming aware of how they prevent themselves from feeling and experiencing in the present. Therefore, the approach is basically non-interpretive, and clients carry out their own therapy as much as possible. They make their own interpretations, create their own direct statements, and find their own meanings. Finally, clients are encouraged to experience directly in the present their struggles of "unfinished business" from their past. By experiencing their conflicts instead of merely talking about them, they gradually expand their own level of awareness and integrate the fragmented and unknown part of their personality (Corey, 1982, p. 98).

Rooted in existential philosophy and phenomenology, Gestalt stresses assumptions of personal responsibility for the course of one's life; Gestalt therapists challenge clients toward growth and the development of their innate potential. In keeping with other existential psychotherapies, the therapist maintains genuine contact with the client. Believing that no human being can be other than subjective in any relationship, existential-minded Gestaltists aim for authenticity rather than for objectivity. This means that the therapist enters into the relationship mutually with the client, accepting that the therapeutic process will foster changes in both of them. Transference is not encouraged; it is seen as an avoidance of the present-centered, person-to-person relationship.

In writing of therapeutic processes and goals, Corey describes therapist functions and a number of techniques that have been popularized and adapted for use by therapists and leaders of groups loosely labeled as "Gestalt." Many of these "rules and games" were a part of the wider repertoire of Fritz Perls; they are too often used by people who lack Fritz's perceptiveness and depth of understanding. They can be incorporated into group art therapy, but are not necessarily appropriate.

Gestalt work with dreams is similar to the way a Gestalt art therapist evokes clients' awareness of meanings expressed spontaneously in their visual imagery. Dreams are assumed to represent existential messages that reflect current ways of being in the world. Clients recognize that the dream configuration is their own creation; they are asked to "work through" their self-created images by "taking the part" of each person and thing in the dream. For Gestalt art therapists, this is an effective way to elicit more awareness of personal meanings made graphic through art media.

ART AND GESTALT APPROACHES

Several years ago I wrote about how the linkage between Gestalt psychology and Gestalt therapy was easily observable in the activity of Art therapy (Rhyne, 1980). I wrote that theories which are difficult to explain in the abstract can be immediately comprehended as they are applied to understanding concrete referents in the forms of art. In an art therapy process, the concepts are transposed into vivid percepts as we engage in expressive art experience.

In my work as an art therapist, patients, clients, students and I communicate verbally, of course, but we do so mostly in reference to some representations they have created in non-verbal media. So we have the concrete artifact present among us; its presence allows us to experience and express immediate perceptions and awareness. We do not have to talk *about* configurations, figure/ground relationships, dynamic movement, contact/boundaries, coherence and fragmentation in the abstract; rather we speak *of* these phenomena in the very act of perceiving and becoming aware of what is obviously there. Though we can't be too sure of how directly the figurative content of the expressive forms portray the ideas and actions of the image-maker, we presume surely that humanly created forms show similarity in structure with human behavior. So instead of talking about isomorphism we are observing the sense of the theory as we apply it (Rhyne, 1980, p. 77).

I further described how we contact each other through the presence of the drawing, seeing the interplay of lines, shapes, and forms within the wholeness of it as a Gestalt. I told how enactment of the forms, through sounds, gestures, and movements, brings into play kinesthetic and other sensory-based immediate perceptions. Without pushing for interpretations, we explore the dimensions of the drawing and elaborate its impact through active present experiencing. Personal meanings may or may not emerge in the course of discovering; the client's expressive process is directed toward an expanded awareness of what makes sense to her in her own life. I concluded that

no matter what direction we take we will still be relating what we do to premises gathered from Gestalt psychologists: though we need not ever mention their theories nor use their vocabularies, my client and I have applied their tenets in a kind of Gestalt therapy that I like to do (*Ibid.*, p. 78).

Other Gestalt therapists incorporate art, in keeping with their own ways of working with clients; among these Joseph Zinker stands out as a beautifully articulate proponent of *Creative Process in Gestalt Therapy* (1977). In the chapter "Art in Gestalt Therapy," Zinker writes:

The reason drawing or painting may be "therapeutic" is that, when experienced as a process, it allows the artist to know himself as a whole person within a relatively short period of time. He not only becomes aware of internal movement toward experiential wholeness, but he also receives visual confirmation of such movement from the drawings he produces. (p. 236)

Zinker is a painter as well as a practicing psychotherapist, and he believes that "all creative activity begins with movement." He designs "Gestalt art workshops" so that the participants begin literally moving their physical bodies in space, responding to the rhythms of accompanying music. They start drawing only after they have been enabled to "ground their bodies and locate their energy."

> Participants are asked to get into their mobility by concentrating their energy on moving from inner activity outward. Music facilitates this process. They are encouraged to move at their own pace and in their own idiosyncratic way. All movement is good. All spontaneous activity is nurtured and supported. (p. 242)

Celia Thompson-Taupin, a registered art therapist active with the Gestalt Institute of San Francisco, also leads Gestalt art groups. In an article "Where Do Your Lines Lead?" she tells how she involves groups in making and in enacting their own experiences in "the line game."

> The line game is played by tacking a large sheet of paper on the wall and having on hand a basket of crayons or pieces of chalk of various colors. One person at a time is "it." That person comes up to the paper and is told, "Select a color and draw a line or a shape." That being done, he is told, "Now another, with a different color." I usually ask the person to make the sound and movement of each line or shape. Other group members are encouraged to mimic and get into the spirit of how each line feels to the person who is "it." At this point, many choices are open. One possibility is the "gestalting" of the two lines or shapes by "it." Another, used in the episodes below, is to say to "it," "Now use people in the group to be your lines and dramatize what is going on. You are the director of the play for the next few minutes—and you can also be one of the characters. It's your show." What happens from this moment on is rarely dull and often involving for the whole group (1976, p. 113).

Violet Oaklander, in her book *Windows to Our Children* (1978), tells of her Gestalt work with children and adolescents. She encourages them to express their feelings with art media, dream work, role playing, storytelling, creative dramatics, and other kinds of enactment. She writes that her "goal" is to help the child "become aware of herself and her existence in the world." Ms. Oaklander is a certified member of the Los Angeles Gestalt Therapy Institute and uses Gestalt in her practice of marriage, family, and child counseling. Increasingly, other therapists and counselors are including Gestalt art experience in their repertoire of therapeutic modalities, synthesizing ideas from many sources as they apply them in ways that are appropriate to their own specializations.

For many years I have led Gestalt art experience groups—sometimes in weekend or five-day workshops, and sometimes ongoing, continuing for weeks or months. I found group art experience invigorating for me and for those who joined in. They were lively and exciting; participants, whether clients or trainees, stimulated, supported, and challenged each other—and me. There were slow times, too, and desperate struggles to break through deadening layers of "unfinished business" that got in the way of savoring present awareness and contacts. In many ways the groups were therapeutic and were directed toward encouraging people to shed neurotic patterns and get on with living fuller, more constructive lives. I still lead such groups and still find them exhilarating.

During the years, I have also worked with clients in one-to-one sessions, in longer-term, quieter, and more individualized ways. With some clients, I find that a Gestalt approach which is supportive as well as challenging can strengthen them, as they seek to take charge of and change the course of their troubled lives. I will describe and illustrate one way in which a client and I are currently working through her present problems.

STRUCTURED GESTALT APPROACH WITH
A PRIVATE CLIENT: WENDY

This way of working through visual/verbal perceptions illustrates visual thinking in action; it demonstrates how "thinking with the senses" can be part of a therapeutic process. Rudolf Arnheim (1969) has insisted that physical and psychological phenomena are isomorphic—their forms are similarly structured. In this kind of Gestalt art therapy I assume that the clients' created images are isomorphic with their behavioral patterns. Thus, the dynamics of perceived structures in drawings can be transposed into a recognition of behavioral patterns, and then into an expansion of clients' awareness of how they can bring about changes in their existence.

Clients are asked to make sequential abstract drawings representing their own responses to a series of words naming emotionally laden experiences. The whole series is regarded as a Gestalt—a configuration created by the clients. Each drawing is a part of the whole sequence; each drawing is also a Gestalt in itself. So when a client and I discuss the drawings, we arrange them so that we can see them all at once and, at the same time, so that we can pick up any one of them for selective study.

In observing the drawings, we focus on structure and form as content; we pay attention to implied directional movements in the lines and shapes; we are interested in interrelationships among forms and in perceiving how these imply dynamic tensions. We are especially observant of how figure/ground relationships are organized; we identify those forms that seem to demand attention. We ask how these visual figures may be related to present concerns in the client's actual living. We scan all the drawings together, looking for visual patternings that make sense in terms of the client's actual behaviors. We pool our resources in recognizing how our perceptions can aid understanding, in order to foster the client's healthy growth and integration.

A client, whom I call Wendy, is making her way through troubled times; she has been in therapy with me for almost a year. She is a very attractive, 25-year-old woman. Only recently has she discovered that she is also very perceptive and intelligent. Now she wants to actively develop her capabilities in real life. This is not easy for her. As her history shows, Wendy has rebelled against what she doesn't want, but has not yet found out what sort of life she does want and can create responsibly.

Wendy was born and bred in a town big enough to have a country club, a gathering showplace for upper-middle-class success, solidarity, and taken-for-granted privileges. Wendy's family "belongs"; in their immaculate home the prime values are godliness, cleanliness, propriety, orderliness, goal setting, rationality, and conformity. Within this value system, the family has prospered. Wendy has defied their values and has no sense of belonging anywhere.

Wendy has three brothers and no sisters. She remembers that even as a small child, "running away" from her brothers and her parents was her way of finding her "spot." Sometimes she literally ran into the woods, refusing to be found; other times she climbed a favorite tree and hid in its branches, or she nested herself in the vines covering an old stile crossing a fence that bounded the family space. Wendy also has vivid memories of her intense excitement in discovering how brightly she could cover things with color; she loved leaves and grasses and bits of bark collected on "little walks in the woods." She felt an affinity for small things and enjoyed "getting lost" in fantasies where she felt free to "be air" or "a leaf floating in a breeze." Wendy still has fearful dreams of being very little, trying to get away from being "choked" or "belted" by large parental figures who attempt to curb her wanderings.

During high school, Wendy went even more into her inner world of fantasizing and questioning. Later, after two years away at art school, she found friends who also questioned, but she didn't accept their answers. Back in her hometown, she fell in love with an artistic young man who seemed to know what he wanted; Wendy came with him to the university to go on with her art. The young man soon left her; Wendy became pregnant in a rebound affair with another young man she barely knew. She gave birth to a daughter, but refused to marry the baby's father. Wendy's family, frustrated and angry, "disowned" her. On Aid for Dependent Children for the last three years, Wendy has lived alone in a trailer park with her little girl as her companion in fairy-tale fantasies that the "world out there" was not worth confronting.

But, as time passed, Wendy began going to bars at night, meeting and getting involved with men, wanting relationships. Her dependency needs led her into too-close, too-fast sexual affairs; her needs for independence kept her out of any relationship that might lead to marriage. Wendy's family wanted to "reown" her while dictating the terms—get married or get a job. They knew nothing of what Wendy calls her "sleazy" life at a local bar for "derelicts." She visited her parents' home, agreed to accompany them to the country club, but her mother had hysterics when Wendy donned a "sweatshirt" dress for the occasion. Furious at her family's demands, she still longed for their acceptance. Alternately defiant and ashamed, Wendy doubted the existence of God but felt she was surely going to hell.

Wendy came into therapy with me, paying my reduced fee with money she earned as a "cleaning lady." She described her life as being like that of a rabbit, scuttling around in underground burrows, connected by long, dark tunnels. She poked her head out in the light of reality with real fear that she would be destroyed. Now she is venturing out more. Her old conflicts with her mother are now out in the open, and there are fierce confrontations. Her mother still slams doors in her anger, and Wendy is left alone, but now she no longer runs away and hides. At night, in the security of her trailer, she sometimes paints large, sloppy pictures of her frustration, and other times she writes in an ongoing journal, questioning and wondering about religious beliefs broader than those of her parents. She does battle with men, too, not wanting to settle for "sex for sex's sake."

Wendy's drawings and paintings are full of activity. They reflect her determination to take an active rather than a passive role in directing her movements in her own life space—sometimes underground in her introspective times, and sometimes out in the open, fighting to make a place for herself and her daughter. Her life-style is rather "schizzy": figure/ground relations quickly shift, polarities and conflicts are evident, and ambiguities appear often. Wendy is aware of what she is experiencing; she is frightened and concerned. And she is also showing her courage in dealing with the choices and decisions she must make. She says with sadness and fortitude, "Nobody else can do it for me; it's all up to me." Wendy's present concerns are with the transition from childhood dependency to adult independence. Her difficulties in maturation, however, involve problems that were not dealt with in her past. As a child, Wendy's natural development was thwarted by her family's imposition of a rearing that ignored her individuality.

In working with Wendy, as with other clients, I am guided by my own beliefs about human nature and my personal constructs of how individuals can maximize their fullest maturation. I believe that, from their psychoevolutionary history, human organisms are naturally endowed with innate urges for survival, and for the actualization of inherent potentials. These are the prime motivations for all behavior. Human beings strive toward growth, selecting from their environments whatever resources are available for assimilation. Human beings try to change incompatible circumstances; what they cannot change they adapt to and come to terms with environmental realities. Thus innate "urges" toward self-realization and existential "musts" toward autonomy are allied in directing all of us toward a sense of unity within ourselves and of appreciation of differences in contact with others.

Wendy expressed her natural creativity early in her life, but it was neither appreciated nor even recognized by her family or by the nuns charged with her education. They tried to force her into a mold where she didn't fit; Wendy responded by creating a private environment wherein she felt at home. Her innate urge for actualization of her own potentials was, and still is, healthy and intact. What she has not developed is a realization that she must also come to terms with what she cannot change in her environment. Her existential struggle is with her conflicting directions in moving out into more contact with outer actualities and, at the same time, staying with the further exploration of inner resources available to her as she makes her own choices.

The drawings shown here are taken from a series of those done by Wendy during the last few months. As I do with other clients, I initially asked her to make simple abstract drawings of her experience of eight primary emotions: (1) fear, (2) anger, (3) joy, (4) sadness, (5) disgust, (6) acceptance, (7) anticipation, and (8) surprise. Sometimes, I also ask for drawings of "being sane" and "going crazy." Generally, we spend at least one session looking at the drawings together and tape-recording the clients' descriptions, associations, and sometimes personal interpretations of their own visual messages. I ask the clients to compare the drawings in terms of similarities and differences and to verbalize any recognitions of figures that emerge and of patterns of which they are aware. The clients do most of the talking; they express in words whatever the experience evokes in response to their creations. After the recorded session I suggest that they do drawings of other experiences that seem important to them—to develop and elaborate the themes that pattern their lives. We continue this process of letting one drawing lead to the making of another; sometimes I suggest the topics and sometimes the clients do so. Between us, we keep ourselves up to date, using drawings made between sessions to enhance our awareness of current happenings in the clients' lives.

I will use some of Wendy's drawings and some of her words, to demonstrate in part how clients and I work together, how we use these graphic representations as guidelines to direct the therapeutic process in times of transition. I have chosen six drawings from a fuller series made initially by Wendy and kept up to date with others created by her from time to time. I have chosen to illustrate how Wendy expresses (1) anger and fear; (2) anticipation and surprise; (3) acceptance; and (4) present state. I based my choice on my observation that how people express these emotions reflects their openness to initiate changes. I perceive *anger* and *fear* as being emotionally loaded with past-oriented, deeply enmeshed habitual "fight-or-flight" reactive behavior. *Anticipation* and *surprise* are more future-oriented; self-fulfilling prophecies show up in the guise of *anticipation*; willingness to open up to novel experience is suggested in *surprise*. *Acceptance* is present oriented, indicating readiness to "come to terms" with others and the environment; *present states* are expressions of what is figural in the person's here-and-now experience.

To our first five sessions Wendy brought paintings she had made during the past few years, as well as those she was presently working on in the privacy of her trailer home. We used these as references, while she described the events and processes occurring in her life. For her sixth session, I assigned the "homework" of doing drawings of commonly experienced states of mind. Wendy made the drawings of *anger, fear, anticipation*, and *surprise*, and we explored what they meant to her during the following three sessions. Wendy's words, as I quote them here, were taken from tape recordings made while she was describing the drawings of emotions I had assigned to her as "homework" during the months of June, November, and the following January.

Anger (Figure 1) "is coming down from the top . . . those white pointed shapes are coming down into the gray . . . the anger eats the gray . . . I mean it overpowers that and it cuts through . . . [the black squares and rectangles] come out from the side . . . they are rational . . . they are over the white shapes [anger]. The squares [rationality] move around the triangles [anger] . . . the crosshatching is whatever I am angry at . . . another person, outside world . . . noises that happen.

Fear (Figure 2) "is a vertical rectangle on the left side . . . two thick vertical lines . . . a nose is coming out and this is what it's looking at . . . all this white space . . . and there's absolutely nothing in that white space 'cause there's nothing to fear. Inside the rectangle there are all the things . . . thinking to fear about . . . a strong black line is a kind of block that keeps fear in check . . . just like the square black line keeps surprise in check."

Anticipation (Figure 3) "is a nice thing to feel . . . an exciting thing. When I anticipate something, that takes up my total thought so that's why the background is black. This white shape coming down from the top is almost like a fish jumping into a pond and he hasn't touched the pond

Figure 1

yet. He's just about there. A fish knows that he wants water but he doesn't know what the next hole is going to be like.''

Surprise (Figure 4): ''inside the square is an organismic shape . . . and inside the organism is a little-bitty black square . . . that's the point of surprise . . . and the squiggling lines that are spreading out . . . that's my reaction to surprise . . . it's a shock, sometimes . . . but the outer square, done with the heavy black lines, sort of keeps the surprise in check.''

Our weekly sessions continued for three months. Then, Wendy began cancelling and postponing sessions, calling on the phone saying, ''Something came up and I can't come.'' Her voice would trail off when I asked for reasons. After six weeks of no sessions at all, Wendy called for an appointment; though she kept it, she spent the time avoiding contact with me or with her own problems. I then asked her to make drawings of some emotions named by me; *Acceptance* (Figure 5) was made at that time. Wendy spoke of it in rather impersonal terms: Acceptance ''was the hardest to draw . . . another person is on the top . . . shapes like black teeth . . . and I'm the white teeth on the bottom . . . the part in between is the outside world . . . all those black dots . . . thoughts and different people, everything else . . . the up-and-down lines are the interactions between two people . . . they're roots . . . mine are going up to the other person . . . the horizontal lines are the uniqueness of each person . . . I'm the black line at the bottom . . . with wavy distrust lines between me and my teeth. I'm rejecting two thin black lines from the other person that come down in the center . . . but I am accepting one that has come down through my teeth and my distrust line and other obstacles to get into the heart of mores and values."

For the next session, a week later, I suggested that Wendy do drawings of emotions that she was experiencing and to name the ones she considered important. She did a series of figurative drawings, depicting herself as a child. Then, after another week's absence, she brought in a drawing

Figure 2

Figure 3

that she named *Contempt* (Figure 6). "My face toward me . . . eyes and a striped beak, a large and a powerful being looking down on a small embryonic being that can't help itself . . . at first I identified with that little being and then I saw myself turning into the monster. . . . " While describing it, she confessed that in the last few months she had "fallen in love," gotten pregnant, had an abortion, and was desperately confused about her own "evil and sin."

We stopped tape-recording at this point; Wendy was sad and crying for the "little embryonic being," but she was also ready to begin working through her conflicting perceptions and directions in moving into the world. In *Anger* she had dramatized coming down into the "outside noisiness" of "whatever"; the force of her "white anger" is interrupted by "rational squares" that move across, getting in the way of her movement. She uses heavy black lines as boundaries around her sharp angry thrusts. She keeps *Fear* and *Surprise* "in check" with heavy black lines, but there is a lot of activity going on inside and between the boundaries. Wendy *Anticipates* with pleasure and excitement and considers *Acceptance* with distrust but also with willingness to let someone reach into the heart of her private space. Wendy's labeling of the present as *Contempt* allowed her to face both her helplessness and her power. In the months following, Wendy always kept her weekly appointments, bringing with her drawings and paintings that emerged from her deepening sense of her own values and goals.

Working through these polarities has not been easy for her. She has become more aware of how her message relates to feeling helpless in her family of origin; having an abortion, thus using her power to take away life; and being a mother, who is now responsible for making a way for herself and her child in the "outside" world. Wendy's visual language,

Figure 4

Figure 5

in many other drawings not shown here, includes a heavy black line as
a boundary between inner and outer realities. She also frequently uses ir-
regularly shaped dots to describe the outside world. In *Anticipation*, no
boundaries or outsiders are involved. In *Contempt*, Wendy does not include either "outer world" or any boundaries between the two related
figures. She now knows that both of these are aspects of her personality,
and that she must own and integrate them into her awareness if she is to
function effectively.

Though the kind of structured activity I have described in working with
Wendy is quite different from the spontaneous enactments used in Gestalt
art therapy, either in groups or with individuals, the same principles apply
here as in the freer approach. The simple abstract drawings are considered
as a part of a larger whole; qualities and properties are interactive within
the field; the client describes and interprets her own drawings in visual/

verbal language; I keep in contact with the client through the presence of her drawings; and, important to me, we are working together with an existential aim of facilitating the client's awareness that she is responsible for choicemaking and for self-direction in living her own life.

SUMMARY

Gestalt art therapy deals with the whole configuration of personal expressiveness in visual messages, in voice tone, in body language, and in verbal content as well. Gestalt art therapy is aimed toward encouraging—even insisting on—responsible, honest, direct communication between client and therapist. Contact between client and therapist can be in the mutual exploration of visually portrayed statements and is often extended to enactment in movement, vocalization, and other active manipula-

Figure 6

tion of persons and materials in space and time. This is done in such a way that the therapist can observe—and sometimes enter into—the art drama being created by the client.

Theoretical backing for this sometimes rowdy kind of behavior comes from the Gestalt concept that our human activity, like any other organic activity, is that of an organism contacting and interacting within the configuration that is our environment. Through our senses we become aware, we perceive in action, we gain insight about the nature of the world and of our place in it by contacting what's "out there" directly with our basic, innate organismic perceptual system. Thus, Gestaltists encourage experimentation and exploration through sensorimotor activation, believing that this often facilitates recognition and clarification of problems.

In a therapy session the therapist is also a part of the configuration—another organism who naturally perceives and actively responds. A Gestalt art therapist is also likely to focus on the active movement in the art done by clients; he/she interests clients in the forms and patterns of their visual message; he/she encourages clients to actively perceive what is going on in lines, shapes, textures, colors, and movements. He/she wants clients to experience their created forms, and to make this experience a part of their organismic awareness. He/she aims to evoke in clients a sensing of how their forms can express personally involving meanings.

Gestalt art therapists are more likely to give workshops than to present papers. Like other practitioners, we have our bags of tricks and even games and gimmicks we can write about, demonstrate, and sometimes teach to others. But the theoretical background of both academic Gestalt psychology and applied Gestalt therapy still requires eliciting from intelligent, human organisms their own awareness and insight.

Gestalt art therapy is not for everybody, neither for all art therapists nor for all clients. It is surely not the only kind of good therapy. It doesn't always work; some patients are not able to mobilize themselves, much less manipulate their environments. Insight seems to be unavailable to some patients; holding them responsible for their perceptions is too much to ask.

Though many of us have advocated "lose your mind and come to your senses," we know that "use your senses and come to your mind" is what we really aim for. Gestalt art therapy demands of clients that they must "do the work," not only of creating the visible representations, but also of recognizing their own self-configurations. In spite of all the emphasis on the experiential in Gestalt art therapy, the theoretical background and actual practice involve therapist and client in a highly cognitive activity. Rudolf Arnheim says that those who practice the arts are "thinking with their senses" (1969, p. v.). That's a premise underlying the work of all Gestalt art therapists; the theories of Gestalt psychology are based on this respect for human nature's ability to recognize the forms that balance and satisfy. Gestalt art therapists work toward activating in all clients their best potential for perceiving in their own visual messages their needs and their resources. Like other Gestalt therapists, we work very hard not to get in the clients' way when they gain the true insight that they, on some level of awareness, can sense and use their own resources for activating growth and excitement in their unique human personalities.

REFERENCES

Arnheim, R. *Visual thinking.* Berkeley: University of California Press, 1969.

Corey, G. *Theory and practice of counseling and psychotherapy.* Rev. Ed. Monterey, CA: Brooks/Cole Publishing Co., 1982.

Hall, C. S., & Lindzey, G. L. *Theories of personality*, 3rd ed. New York: John Wiley & Sons, 1978.

Nordby, V. J., & Hall, S. H. *A guide to psychologists and their concepts.* San Francisco: W. H. Freeman and Company, 1974.

Oaklander, V. *Windows to our children.* Lafayette, CA: Real People Press, 1978.

Perls, F. S. *Ego, hunger and aggression* (1947). New York: Vintage Books: 1969 reprint.

Perls, F. S. *Gestalt therapy verbatim.* Lafayette, CA: Real People Press, 1969.

Perls, F., Hefferline, R. F., & Goodman, P. *Gestalt therapy: Growth and excitement in the human personality.* New York: Dell Publishing Co., 1951.

Rhyne, J. Gestalt psychology/Gestalt therapy: Forms/contexts. In *A Festschrift for Laura Perls—The Gestalt Journal*, 1980, *8*(1), 77–78.

Rosenfeld, E. An oral history of gestalt therapy, Part 1: A conversation with Laura Perls. *The Gestalt Journal*, 1978, *1*(1), 8–31.

Thompson-Taupin, C. Where do your lines lead? Gestalt art groups. In J. Downing (Ed.). *Gestalt awareness.* New York: Harper and Row, 1976.

Zinker, J. *Creative process in Gestalt therapy.* New York: Brunner/Mazel, 1977.

RECOMMENDED READINGS

The best of Fritz Perls' writings are listed in the references.

For an enjoyable experience, which is also truly informative: *Gestalt Therapy Integrated* by Erving and Miriam Polster. New York: Vintage Books, 1973.

For a number of varied approaches used in Gestalt therapy: *Gestalt Therapy Now* edited by Joen Fagan and Irma Lee Shepherd, New York: Harper/Colophon Books, 1970.

Another collection of articles is: *The Handbook of Gestalt Therapy* edited by Chris Hatcher and Philip Himelstein, New York: Jacob Aronson, 1976.

The *Gestalt Journal*, published semiannually (Box 990, Highland Park, NY 12528) includes new ideas and arguments from Gestalt therapists and has given Laura Perls the attention she deserves.

And, of course, there is *Gestalt Art Experience* by Janie Rhyne, newly reprinted by Magnolia Street Publishers, 1250 W. Victoria, Chicago, IL 60660.

11

A Humanistic Approach
to Art Therapy

Josef E. Garai

A humanistic approach to art therapy requires the postulation of hypotheses that are in accordance with the basic philosophical tenets and established practices of humanism. These were clearly outlined by Charlotte Bühler (1971) as follows: (1) A person must be studied as a whole. (2) A person's life must be studied as a whole, i.e., on a developmental basis interrelating all the stages from birth to death. (3) Self-realization and fulfillment, rather than adjustment and absence of tension, are the basic goals of human beings that provide meaning and identity. (4) There are three basic life tendencies: the need for pleasure, characterized by personal satisfaction in sex, love and ego recognition; the need to belong and find security through self-limiting adaptation to society; and the need for creative accomplishments. (5) Each individual has a deep need to integrate these three basic needs in a pattern that is characteristic of his or her identity. (6) Each individual faces the need to balance conflicting tendencies or polarities within his or her own psyche. (7) Guilt and anxiety are not the exclusive result of superego prohibitions, but are caused equally often by the failure to utilize one's own inherent creative potential or failure to create a meaningful life-style. (8) Identity is fluid and yet stable throughout a person's life requiring continued attempts to reintegrate and to reconcile polar tendencies and different needs.

In my own work, I have developed the humanistic approach to art therapy as a broad framework permitting the integration of a variety of

Parts of this chapter have already been published in the *American Journal of Art Therapy*, 1974, *13*(2): 151–164.

recently emerging theoretical models in an effort to broaden and deepen the scope of interaction between inner experience and outer reality. This approach is based on three assumptions: First, the humanistic therapist does not regard people as "mentally ill" but rather as encountering specific problems in their efforts to cope with life as a result of intrapsychically or environmentally caused conflicts. Treatment must be directed toward reinforcement of the will to live and development of the ability to find meaning and identity in as fully creative a life-style as possible.

The second assumption implies that the inability to cope successfully with the vicissitudes of life or to find satisfactory avenues toward self-actualization, meaning, and identity is a common phenomenon affecting most people to a greater or lesser extent at different stages of their lives. The so-called identity crisis is not a one-stage phenomenon the adolescent goes through to reach "maturity"; identity crises may occur at each stage of life when a transition toward some new kind of life-style is required. The assumption that life is an ongoing process with the need for continuous growth, change, and development forms the essence of such a psychodynamic humanistic approach. Instead of waiting to "cure" people when periods of tension and "identity crises" occur, the humanistic art therapist attempts to assist the client in his or her attempts to integrate the various "identity crises" into creative-expressive life-styles and to prepare movement toward further experiences of change. This preventive mental health care is based on promotion of those types of life experiences that enhance curiosity, excitement, self-expression, and intimacy.

The third assumption implies that self-actualization resulting from the adoption of life-styles of genuine self-disclosure and honesty remains basically sterile unless the self-actualizing person is able to formulate a *self-transcendent* goal that makes life more meaningful by adding a "spiritual" dimension to it, as suggested by Frankl (1963, 1973). This requires a conscious commitment to relate one's own self-actualizing needs to those of the community at large, both through the attainment of genuine interpersonal intimacy and through increasing openness and honesty in relations with others in efforts to improve and expand the opportunities in the life space of the community. My three principles can be summarized as follows: (1) emphasis on life-problem solving, (2) encouragement of self-actualization through creative expression, and (3) emphasis on relating self-actualization to intimacy and trust in interpersonal relations and the search for self-transcendent life goals.

In accordance with these basic philosophical considerations, patient and therapist embark together on a journey of exploration of inner images, fantasies, dreams, and archetypes. This adventure into the depths of the psyche enables both to crystallize blocked or unexplored facets of the inner experience to bring about increased awareness of deep feelings, anxieties, and hopes. Humanistic art therapy can become the royal road to the emergence of *creative man* who is no longer alienated from the inexhaustible wellsprings of his vital inner energies revealed in his dreams, myths, fantasies, and intuitive imagery. It appears paradoxical that man has been able and willing to extend his most intensive exploration into the outer spaces of planets and the solar system, but he has been unable or unwilling to explore the vast uncharted territories of his own "inner space."

My theory is greatly influenced by Otto Rank, whose book *Art and Artist* (1932) takes the reader on a journey of discovery through the realms of creation and encourages a person to become an "artist in life" shaping his or her own existence. Rank believes that it is the depth of inner experiences that needs to be tapped to assist the individual to integrate their meanings into his or her whole life history so as to become the true "artist in life."

The goal of humanistic art therapy consists in the development of the rhythmically balanced personality who can establish a rhythmical flow between the polarities of love and anger, weakness and strength, privacy and intimacy, cooperation and competition, dependency and independence, dominance and submission, hope and despair, and so on. The atmosphere the humanistic art therapist attempts to create reflects the total absence of moralistic judgmental attitudes suggesting that man must be either good or bad, strong or weak, loving or hating, and dependent or independent. It confirms the conviction that man can be both good and bad, strong and weak, loving and angry, and dependent and independent. Once man is aware of these conflicting polarities, he can give up perfectionistic standards of performance and behavior to proceed toward self-actualizing choices and commitments rather than self-destructive ones.

The application of these principles in the methodology and practice of art therapy was first described a decade ago (Garai, 1975). They were brought up to date four years later in another article entitled "New Horizons of the Humanistic Approach to Expressive Therapies and Creativity Development" (Garai, 1979). The emphasis on holistic personality integration suggested by Buhler was reformulated as follows: (1) Holistic integration aims at a harmonious cooperation between body and mind, body and spirit, and mind and spirit; (2) the holistically integrated person must seek to achieve such integration not only within himself, but also with the ecological environment (Frankl, 1963, 1973; Jung, 1971; Maslow, 1975; Rank, 1932; Roszak, 1979).

Another important development relates to the recognition that the different modalities of creative-expressive therapies represented by art, dance and movement, music, poetry, and drama therapies have common objectives. They are all meant to replace the traditional emphasis in the healing process on ''illness,'' stress, anxiety, and psychoneurotic or psychotic symptoms, with a concentration on the individual's unfulfilled creative potential in the search for meaningful life-styles, physical, mental, and spiritual wholeness, and increased expressiveness of feeling, thoughts, and ideas in the creative process. The goal of therapy is not getting rid of fear, unhappiness, and anxiety. It is to transform these feelings into honest expressions in some creative modality, in order to experience the joy and exhilaration flowing from the accomplishment of such authentic expression. Instead of seeking to avoid sickness, the individual is seen to seek the exceptional psychological and physical well-being described by many (Houston, 1982; Jacobi, 1965; Jourard, 1971; Moustakas, 1977; Muller, 1982; Peters & Waterman, 1982).

The author has recently described the seven areas that reflect new horizons of the humanistic-holistic approach as follows: (1) promotion of the holistic approach to health care; (2) achievement of genuine individuation; (3) movement from autonomy to intimacy reflected in satisfactory interpersonal relationships; (4) formulation of meaningful life goals; (5) adoption of a holistic perspective of the life-cycle; (6) awareness of the fluidity and stability of individual identity throughout the changes and crises of the life-span; and (7) the use of empathy and intuition in the development of deeper levels of symbolic communication (Garai, 1976). How these seven basic principles of the humanistic-holistic approach can be applied in the practice of art therapy is described in detail in ''Holistic Healing Through Creative Expression: A Training Manual in Holistic Healing for Creative-Expressive Arts Therapists'' (Garai, 1984).

As an example of how one of these principles can be applied in the practice of art therapy, I will describe an exercise designed to achieve an awareness of individuation. Individuation can best be described as the attainment of authenticity, autonomy, and the actualization of the self through creative expression. The most important step leading to individuation is accomplishment of the developmental task of learning to be a separate person able to take charge of one's own life. It requires completion of the process of separation from significant others, especially mother and father. This separation leads to genuine individuation, providing the basis for autonomy. The autonomous person is able to take full charge of his or her own life. He can enjoy the state of aloneness without experiencing feelings of loneliness and despair. He has the courage to stand alone without feeling lost or abandoned.

The art exercise that helps a person to move toward genuine individuation initially requires the participant to depict—in crayon drawings and with plasticine clay modelings—feelings of intolerable loneliness caused by the absence or unavailability of a close and cherished person. In a subsequent drawing or modeling, the individual describes the type of aloneness that permits separate space, freedom from intrusion, and the ability to select any activity without concern about the judgment or criticism of others. A comparison of the symbolic meanings of the crayon drawings and the plasticine clay modelings from both stages provides insights into the way each individual handles problems of loss, and how each attempts to move toward constructive aloneness. Indeed, every creative person knows how important it is to preserve one's own individual space and freedom of choice, and how these basic needs require the temporary exclusion of even the closest friends and lovers, as when one is engaged in the process of creation.

Another art exercise is designed to achieve an awareness of holistic personality integration. Each subject is given two pieces of colored plasticine modeling clay, two sheets of sketching paper, and an assortment of crayons. The following instructions are then given: "Take a piece of clay, close your eyes, and model the clay with your eyes closed while listening to the instructions. Imagine that you are fragmenting and splitting yourself, that you engage in activities or thoughts that cut off your body from your mind, your mind from your spirit, and yourself from your natural environment. Try to impart these splitting tendencies to the piece of clay you are modeling." After 12 minutes, the following instructions are given: "Now wait until I count from 1 to 3. When you hear the number 3 called out, open your eyes and place the clay figure of your self-fragmentation next to the first sheet of paper. Then mark this sheet with the number 1 in the upper-left-hand corner and proceed to draw the experience of your self-splitting, in any way you desire." Then participants draw their pictures.

The second art exercise is initiated with the following instructions: "Now take another piece of clay, close your eyes, and model it with your eyes closed, while listening to the instructions. Let images come to your mind, depicting how you attempt to integrate your body, mind, and spirit harmoniously, so as to satisfy your basic needs and feel whole within yourself and within your environment." After 12 minutes, the following instructions are added: "Wait until I count from 1 to 3. When you hear the number 3 called out, open your eyes, place the clay figure of your self-integration next to the second sheet of paper, mark this sheet with the number 3 in the upper-left-hand corner, and proceed to draw the experience of your harmonious self-integration in any way you wish."

A comparison of drawings and clay models between the fragmentation and the integration conditions is then made by the participants, first in dyads, then in groups of four, and finally by the whole group with the assistance of the leader. The goal is to clarify the movements of individuals from fragmentation to self-integration, as reflected by their interpretations of the symbolic meanings of their clay models and crayon drawings. It is a simple, yet powerful method of helping people achieve an awareness of holistic integration.

HUMANISTIC DEFINITIONS OF CREATIVITY

Humanistic definitions of creativity differ from the definitions postulated by other schools of psychological thought. These other models define creativity as a secondary phenomenon rather than as an innate human drive. These theories may be called "deficiency compensation theories." They include traditional psychoanalytic theory, which postulates that creativity results from the sublimation of libido, i.e., the channeling of sexual energy (libido) into substitute forms of socially acceptable behavior. Freud (1925, 1958) believed that the great achievements of civilization arose from the sublimation of libido, or the innate human sexual drive. The idea that Leonardo da Vinci created his sublime paintings, Michelangelo his immortal sculptures, Shakespeare his plays and sonnets, and Beethoven his great symphonies because of some frustration of their sexual drive seems untenable to humanistic psychologists.

Other theories that deny the primacy of creativity as an innate human striving independent of the sexual drive or libido are also unsatisfactory. These include modifications of the Freudian position, such as Kubie's theory (1958), as well as Kris's suggestion that creativity requires a "regression in the service of the ego" (1952). Adler theorized that creativity stems from man's need to achieve superiority and perfection, in order to overcome basic feelings of inferiority, and Rank (1932, 1973) suggested that creativity is the result of man's struggle between the life fear and the death fear, that it represents an attempt to overcome the death fear by gaining immortality through the act of creating something that outlasts its creator (cf. Meerloo, 1968). All of these theories are "deficiency compensation theories" and are unacceptable to humanistic psychologists, because they reject the assumption of creativity as an independent and innate human drive.

Humanistic psychologists and therapists are drawn to dynamic-holistic theories of creativity. These include Jung's theory, which assumes the presence of a "collective unconscious" that encompasses the experiences and memories of the human race throughout its history, even including prehistoric and prehuman periods. This *collective unconscious* evokes *archetypes* and *symbols*, which constitute the reservoir of creative ideas possessed by both the artist and every person. Jung postulates an innate creative drive as common to all human beings (Jacobi, 1965). He contrasts such archetypes as the *persona*, i.e., the social role we play, with the *shadow*, which reveals the unconscious counterpart of the persona. The "good mother" archetype is contrasted with the shadow archetype of the "evil witch," when the mother's behavior as the nurturant, comforting, and dependable source of support alternates with her imposition of restrictions and prohibitions on the child's freedom of choice (Jung, 1960, 1969, 1971).

Neumann has deepened our perception of the archetypes and the creative unconscious following Jung's theory (1955, 1959). Another archetype is the *anima*, which represents the "feminine" characteristics such as emotionality, tenderness, and sensitivity in the male psyche, whereas the *animus* expresses the "masculine" tendencies in the female psyche, which include assertiveness, aggression, and sharp logic. The animus and anima are similar to the yin and yang of the Eastern philosophies. Other pairs of archetypes and shadow archetypes are those of the fool and the wise man, death and rebirth, God and the devil (Jung, 1959). Jung also postulates a dichotomy between introversion and extroversion, which contributes to our understanding of different types of creative persons and processes (1960).

May's theory (1953, 1976) states that authentic creativity is the process of bringing something new into being. Creative persons, such as artists, poets, scientists, and composers, are the ones who, according to Plato, express *being itself*. They are the ones who enlarge human consciousness. The symbols these creators use require as a response a basic change in life of the observer. The creative process is an encounter between the creator and the environment: The painter encounters the landscape. The intensity of the encounter, the absorption of the creator in the creative act, and his/her transformation of the environment and of his/her own self determine the quality of the creative process. Genuine creativity is characterized by an intensity of awareness, a heightened state of consciousness, and joy at the moment of execution. Creativity involves the whole person, with the unconscious acting in unity with consciousness. It is, therefore, not irrational but rather suprarational. It is a mystical experience in which the individual merges with the cosmos and in which total unity alternates with vast diversity.

Moustakas (1977) has developed a theory that creativity involves personal growth, self-renewal, and self-actualization. He shows that significant gains in awareness and self-knowledge are kindled from within, rather than from external sources. Moustakas claims that each human being has the innate ability to be creative and to relate authentically to other human beings, while maintaining his/her unique individuality. This potential is, however, threatened by pressures toward conformity exerted by society and by movements toward material gain, superficial communication, and safe, conventional relationships. He emphasizes the significance of honesty and freedom in human relationships within a framework of ethical responsibility and high moral standards.

Moustakas believes that crises precipitate periods of self-doubt that move the person toward new awareness, resolution, and changes in the self. He clarifies the difference between neurotic and healthy anger and shows how the honest expression of feelings can be used for growth when it releases tension and paves the way for deeper ties and greater honesty between the persons involved in communication. Moustakas uses vivid sensory images and stresses the importance and meaningfulness of silence, self-dialogue, and meditation in creative discovery. He states that creativity, which is inherent in each human being from birth, requires the expression of each person's uniqueness, individuality, and particular ways of expressing authentic feelings as a matter of life and death. Each individual has his or her unique style of creative expression, which resembles a fingerprint, characteristic only of that person.

Langer (1967, 1970) proceeds from the assumption that the concept of symbolism is the characteristically *human* element in cognition, and that *symbolic* expression and understanding have brought about the great departure from animal mentality. She defines art as the symbolic expression of an artist's knowledge of feeling, which is quite different from symptomatic expressions of currently felt emotions. Like Jung, May, and Moustakas, she stresses the importance of individuation and identity formation resulting from involvement in the creative process. Langer's theory is closely related to the need to express symbolic meaning as proposed by others (Garai, 1977/78; Jung, 1971; Singer & Pope, 1978).

In line with this emphasis on symbolization, humanistic art therapists have been influenced by the recent findings of brain research. Some have devised specific techniques to reinforce intuition, empathy, and spatial discrimination, the dominant characteristics of the right hemisphere, in order to achieve harmonious coordination between these traits and the dominant characteristics of the left hemisphere, logical reasoning and rational thinking. In our society, the emphasis on logical thinking, reasoning, and rationality in the educational system has led to diminished training in empathy, intuition, and imagination, which are indispensable for problem solving and innovative decision making.

FURTHER APPLICATIONS OF HUMANISTIC THEORIES

Humanistic art therapists also utilize dream interpretation, to help their clients to get in touch with important messages from the personal and the collective unconscious, which can become incentives for creative innovation and problem solving. Examples of dream interpretations using art have been described by several workers (Ahsen, 1973, 1977; Garai, 1976, 1984; Von Franz, 1972). Whereas Freud believed that dreams can be interpreted as symbolic expressions of infantile childhood wishes revealing repressed libidinal strivings, humanistic therapists tend to regard dreams, like Jung, as symbolic messages from the deepest layers of the unconscious. These messages may relate to certain unfulfilled creative aspirations, and to aspects of autonomy and identity that require further conscious attention to find some resolution. Dreams can actually lead to the resolution of problems.

Creative problem solving is evident in the dreams of Niels Bohr, the Swedish physicist, who won the Nobel Prize for his solution of the mystery of the composition of the atom (Garai, 1976). In his dream, Bohr saw a huge sun with fiery flames radiating in rays away from the center. Then he saw little suns radiating similar flames arranged in an elliptical orbit intersecting with the large sun. Then he saw another elliptical orbit with little suns and flares intersecting the first two orbits and finally a third elliptical orbit with little flares also intersecting with all other orbits. After he awoke from this dream, he wrote it down and began to meditate on its meaning. After a period of two more days, he postulated his theory: The atom is composed of a nuclear core, which is intersected by three elliptical orbits of protons, electrons, and neutrons. The large sun symbolized the core, the first elliptical orbit the protons, the second the electrons, and the third the "neutrons," i.e., those particles which were neither protons nor electrons. Of course, Bohr had been totally preoccupied during his waking hours with his explorations of the atom, but his dream enabled him to find the imagery that made it possible to put the various strands of the theory together.

Humanistic art therapists can utilize dream interpretation in a variety of ways. I have found it most beneficial to use mental imagery to assist workshop participants in remembering a recent or recurrent dream. They are then asked to draw the dream with crayons or to model it with plasticine clay. With the assistance of the leader, the dreams are then interpreted as messages from the collective unconscious, and their specific significance for the dreamer at this particular juncture in time is explored. The dreamer is then encouraged to define his/her unfulfilled desires for growth, self-actualization, and individuation, through archetypes (Jung. 1959) and eidetic imagery (Ahsen, 1973, 1977).

Humanistic art therapists have recently become aware of the importance of mental imagery in the healing process. Simonton (1980) describes how he uses imagery to reinforce his laser beam therapy with patients who suffer from advanced stages of cancer. He asks the patient during laser beam therapy to imagine that the laser beam is attacking the cancer cells by being directed to the actual site of the cancer. Then he asks the patient to imagine that his own healthy cancer-fighting cells are forming a power-ful rear guard joining the frontal attack of the laser beam to conquer the cancer together. Simonton found that the addition of the patient's own immunological defenses, through imagining this scenario, accelerated the cure significantly. Imagery is frequently employed in holistic healing. I have sometimes encouraged my clients—instead of taking pain-killing drugs—to imagine their pain, how heavy it feels, and how it affects specific parts or organs of their body. Then, they are asked to draw with crayons a picture of the pain. Next, they are asked to imagine that the pain is gradually leaving their body, that their muscles begin to relax, and that they feel that it is no longer bothering them. When invited to draw the pain leaving the body, they sometimes experience a similar, but longer-lasting effect than that derived from drugs.

Another effective method utilizing guided imagery requires a client who is unable to solve an important intrapsychic or interpersonal problem to imagine that he is relaxing on a quiet beach or near a mountain pond and thinking about ways to solve this particular dilemma. If this appears to be very difficult and the client feels "stuck with it," he can call on his "inner adviser" and tell him about the problem, and by holding a dialogue with him move toward a solution of this problem. The art therapist may ask the client to draw the dialogue with the "inner adviser," in order to ascertain the symbolic meanings of the messages received. A variety of methods that can be adopted for self-healing, or healing under the guid-ance of an experienced art therapist, are described by King in his fasci-nating book *Imagineering for Health: Self-Healing Through the Use of Your Mind* (1981). The authors of such books tend to emphasize their belief that healing and transformation are determined mainly by the in-dividual's ability to listen to the messages emanating from his/her own mind (Feldenkrais, 1973; Naisbitt, 1982; Walsh & Shapiro, 1983).

CASE MATERIAL

How the humanistic art therapist approaches the diagnosis and treat-ment of clients is described in the case histories and drawings in the article "Reflections of the Struggle for Identity in Art Therapy" (Garai, 1973).

The comprehension of symbolic meaning, the sharing of prelogical, paralogical, mythological, magical, and allegoric symbols, images, and thought processes, can circumvent the treacherous duplicity of verbal communication. It may create an immediate emotional bond between therapist and client. In order to succeed in the establishment of such a relationship, the art therapist must constantly check back with his client to see if he is attuned to that person's symbolic messages. And he must never jump to premature conclusions about the meaning of certain symbolic messages, derived from the "universal" symbolism of well-known psychoanalytic or mythological theories. He must always keep in mind the specific symbolic meaning of the message for the client at this particular stage of his life, and in the context of his whole life history and experience.

Thus, for instance, a young business executive who drew a picture of himself trying to climb up a very *high* flagpole and falling off just below the summit at first accepted the art therapist's interpretation that he seemed to fear the loss of his sexual potency. When further questioning resulted in the finding that his sex drive had become stronger and been satisfied more frequently than ever before, the traditional psychoanalytic explanation seemed to be disproved. The flagpole was really a symbol of his desire to reach the top of the ladder of success in his company, and his fear of being unable to reach the top position had been aroused by the remark of one of his competitors made on the previous day to the effect that he had better try to go more slowly in his efforts to reach the top in order not to attract the envy and retribution of his competitors.

Therapeutic Process*

The following excerpt from a case history of a client in art therapy further illustrates the humanistic approach. Ken, a student of fine arts, entered psychotherapy at the age of 21 because he went into a psychotic episode as a result of the use of marijuana. He was a tall, well-built young man whose deep-seated, penetrating eyes usually had a suspicious expression. At the beginning of therapy, he was unable to complete his artwork for graduation, had broken up with his girlfriend, had quarreled with his mother, and was afraid of "going crazy." He was the only child of parents who divorced when he was five years old. He was still greatly attached to his overprotective, seductive, rejecting mother, whose love he had sought to gain in his childhood by playing the "cute clown" and by intellectual precocity. He harbored deep feelings of resentment against his father who had remarried since and who had never acknowledged him as an artist. Ken suffered from severe depressive reactions combined with

---

*A more complete account of this case study appeared as an article: "The Use of Painting to Resolve an Artist's Identity Conflicts," *American Journal of Art Therapy*, 1974, *13*, 151–164.

feelings of guilt and repressed anger. There were paranoid projections, hysterical symptoms, and various psychosomatic complaints. He vacillated between impulsive acting out and withdrawal into dreamlike states. He was diagnosed as an inadequate personality with passive-aggressive dependency strivings and sexual confusion.

In a series of paintings of self-portraits and the dreams he experienced, Ken was able to resolve his identity conflicts and move toward increasing self-actualization in individual and then group art therapy. The first painting that he brought before the group (Figure 1) shows him with an expression of defiance. Ken said, "This is me as the 'monkey' performing to please my mother   I act like a helpless clown. . . ."

Figure 1

In Figure 2, he depicts himself as framed by a playing card. His feelings about this painting fluctuated between depression and elation. When asked to express his feelings in words, he said: "Life is a game of chance. My game is that of the king on the throne clad in a sailor's jacket. The throne gives me power and authority. Yet the sailor's jacket promises me free-roaming self-direction in a kind of happy-go-lucky frame of mind. . . . I guess it's the conflict between the father and the child in me. . . . I have the wings of the bumblebee, which permit me to gather the honey of life in free flight . . . yet my hands and feet feel like heavy solid stones holding me down. . . . I feel that I am always held back by some pool of water from flying into the open air. . . . "

At this specific moment of his life, Ken was simultaneously experiencing the novelty of success and the familiarity of fear of failure. He had

Figure 2

found a warm and responsive woman who had moved into his apartment, and he had also sold one of his paintings for an unexpectedly high price. These new experiences of success led to exhilaration, on the one hand, and to the reawakening of his old fears of failure and insignificance. The conflict between his desire to move out into the world and enjoy life and the desire to cling to his familiar pattern of immobility, withdrawal, and helplessness is poignantly expressed in this painting. The therapist was able to assist Ken in relating this conflict to his past overdependency on maternal guidance and his still uncharted future. This led to a reinforcement of Ken's tendency to move away from excessive dependency on his mother and helped him to begin to work through his excessive guilt about self-actualization.

His dependency was expressed in a series of paintings. Figure 3 had been created shortly before the onset of Ken's therapy—it depicts a dream scene, which he described as follows: "I am the black man in a crowd in the city. . . . I am the gorilla in the red shirt. . . . I'm really a 'dumb fuck' taking care of the queen. She is my mother with a crown on her head and an anxious look on her face . . . worried about being raped by the brute. On my head is a figure, half bird and half woman . . . the bird is clawing my head. It's a symbol of my mother not letting go of me." This painting contains the three archetypal maternal figures—the queen mother, the witch mother, and the prostitute mother—with the latter lying prone at the right of the "gorilla" who has turned away from her toward the mother queen. Ken sees women as being simultaneously alluring seductresses, devouring and oppressive witches, and demanding queens. His black face, white arm, and red shirt reflect inner conflict between purity and sin, "goodness" and "badness," pleasure and pain, virginity and promiscuity, and depression and joy—themes that emerge in various guises in the work of many creative artists.

Several months later, Ken brought in a painting of another dream, from which he remembered awakening in a state of joyful relief (Figure 4). He explained it as follows: "My mother is finally dead . . . buried in the rocktomb. Her head is cut off and she breathes her last gasp. . . . The monkeys are glad and dancing around the grave. The green guy [bottom left] is me getting rid of my anger and laughing. The blue fellow [bottom right] represents my more serious self that grieves about her death and wants to contemplate the newly won freedom." Two members of the group pointed to a yellowish penis on the "serious self," which showed a strong erection. Ken eventually acknowledged it and then explained that imagining his mother's symbolic death permitted him to enjoy his sexuality and potency without further guilt feelings.

Polar conflicts constitute a rich source of productivity in the creative

Figure 3

expression of many artists. I believe that such conflicts are not in them-selves neurotic but are rather the very essence of human existence. Ken's paintings are not merely a weapon in his struggle to deal with his neurotic problems. They also demonstrate the artist's ability to probe into the depths of the primary process and to emerge with ever-new perspectives.

CONCLUSION

The humanistic art therapist is also deeply concerned about the future of the world and the challenges mankind will face, while we move into the third millennium. Theodor Roszak, the social philosopher, explained in his book *Person/Planet: The Creative Disintegration of Industrial*

Society (1979) that we are entering the *age of the person*. This means that for the first time in the history of mankind, the assertion of each individual's right to the fullest development of his/her unique personhood and identity becomes the sacred trust and shared goal of society. This new principle is bound to profoundly change the role of all our institutions and agencies, whether they relate to government, education, the professions, science, industry, business, etc. All these organizational frameworks will henceforth be evaluated in terms of their ability to respond effectively to and provide opportunities for the personal growth, self-fulfillment, and life enrichment of their individual members. They can no longer claim that their members must pay allegiance to their norms, values, and organi-

Figure 4

zational structure rather than seek self-actualization, growth, and new challenges (Roszak, 1979).

In her ground-breaking book *The Aquarian Conspiracy: Personal and Social Transformation in the 1980's* (1980) Marilyn Ferguson presents a vivid description of this new movement, which seeks to establish the *age of the person*. An informal network of people from all walks of life, all income levels, and all status categories, from the humblest to the highest, forms the "Aquarian conspiracy," which seeks to bring about profound transformations in the lives of people in order to create the conditions that accelerate the developments characteristic of the *age of the person*. Ferguson claims that the Aquarian conspiracy consists of a leaderless but powerful network, which is working to bring about a radical change in the United States. Its members have broken with certain key elements of Western thought, and they have even broken continuity with history.

It is a conspiracy without a political doctrine, without a manifesto, with conspirators who seek power only to disperse it, and whose strategies are pragmatic, even scientific, but whose perspective sounds so mystical that they hesitate to discuss it. They are activists asking different kinds of questions who challenge the establishment from within. The conspirators include all levels of society. They are linked and made kindred by their *inner* discoveries and earthquakes. You can break through old limits, past inertia and fear, to levels of fulfillment that once seemed impossible . . . to richness of choice, freedom, and human closeness. You can be more productive, confident, comfortable with insecurity. Problems can be experienced as challenges, a chance for renewal rather than stress. Habitual defensiveness and worry can fall away. It can all be otherwise.

For the first time, people are relying on the authenticity of their own *inner changes* in their attempts to change society as a whole. In the past, we believed that fundamental changes in the structure or system of society would bring about changes in personality and life-styles. The socialistic society was supposed to produce the idealized "socialistic man," and the democratic society the idealized "democrat." The Aquarian conspirators believe that only profound personal inner transformations in the lives of many people can lead to a fundamental societal transformation.

The ideas of Ferguson (1980) and Roszak (1979) were summarized by Garai (1984) to formulate the following basic principles all humanistic-holistic approaches have in common. These are: (1) Each individual has the right to the fullest development of his or her unique identity, personhood, and life-style. (2) Each individual has the right to expect respect for his or her unique personhood, identity, and integrity or wholeness from all other people. (3) Each individual is encouraged to associate himself or herself with any other individuals on the basis of sharing common goals, interests, ideas, handicaps, life-styles as he or she sees fit. (4) Each individual has the right to challenge any authority or institution to respond positively to his or her need for recognition of his or her unique personhood and identity. (5) Each individual is encouraged to seek both internal wholeness, i.e., a harmonious balance between body, mind, and spirit, and external wholeness, i.e., a wholesome connectedness with other people in the microcosmic and the macrocosmic environment. It is interesting to note the fact that these five principles have always been espoused by humanistic psychologists and therapists (Houston, 1982; Hubbard, 1982).

Summarizing the basic position of humanistic-holistic approaches to art therapy, we may state that the ancient principle *mens sana in corpore sano in spiritu sano in mundo sano* parallels this approach, whose ideal is *a healthy mind in a healthy body in a healthy spirit in a healthy world.* The person who genuinely experiences his wholeness respects the integrity, identity, individuation, and idealism (the four I's) of both himself and every other human being. Such a holistic philosophy leads to a way of life of care, compassion, and concern (the three C's), which flows organically from the integration of authenticity, autonomy, and actualization of self (the three A's).

The humanistic-holistic art therapist believes that the attainment of this way of living constitutes a goal that is within the reach of every single human being. Therefore, he is engaged in a lifelong journey, together with his clients. This basic credo will inspire him or her with the "courage to create," which Rollo May has so eloquently described (1976). It will also inspire him or her with the "courage to heal," since the original meaning of the word "healing" conveys the sense of "making whole." The truly dedicated healer is a healed or whole individual, who heals or makes whole those whose sacred trust rests in him as the healer who, in healing himself, is healing others.

REFERENCES

Ahsen, A. *Basic Concepts of eidetic psychotherapy.* New York: Brandon House, 1973.

Ahsen, A. *Psycheye: Self-analytic consciousness.* New York: Brandon House, 1977.

Bühler, C. Basic theoretical concepts of humanistic psychology. *American Psychologist,* 1971, *24,* 378–386.

Feldenkrais, M. *Body and mature behavior.* New York: International Universities Press, 1973.

Ferguson, M. *The aquarian conspiracy: Personal and social transformation in the 1980's.* Los Angeles: J. P. Tarcher, 1980.

Frankl, V. E. *Man's search for meaning*. New York: Pocket Books, 1963.

Frankl, V. E. *The doctor and the soul*. New York: Random House, 1973.

Freud, S. *Collected papers*. London: Institute for Psychoanalysis and Hogarth Press, 1925.

Freud, S. *On dreams*. New York: Norton, 1952.

Freud, S. *On creativity and the unconscious*. New York: Harper & Row, 1958.

Garai, J. E. Reflections on the struggle for identity in art therapy. *Art Psychotherapy*, 1973, *1*, 261–275.

Garai, J. E. The humanistic approach to art therapy and creativity development. *New-ways*, 1975, *1*(2), 2, 8, 19.

Garai, J. E. New vistas in the exploration of inner and outer space through art therapy. *Art Psychotherapy*, 1976, *3*, 157–167.

Garai, J. E. The will and empathy in art therapy. *Journal of the Otto Rank Association*, Winter 1977/78, *12*(2), 32–53.

Garai, J. E. Death, birth, and rebirth through art therapy. *Behavior Today*, May 1978, 2–4.

Garai, J. E. New horizons of the humanistic approach to expressive therapies and creativity development, 1979, *6*, 177–183.

Garai, J. E. Holistic healing through creative expression: A training manual in holistic healing for creative-expressive arts therapists. *Art Therapy*, 1984, *1*(2), 76–82.

Houston, J. *The possible human: A course in enhancing your physical, mental, and creative abilities*. Los Angeles: J. P. Tarcher, 1982.

Hubbard, B. M. *The evolutionary journey: A personal guide to a positive future*. San Francisco: Evolutionary Press, 1982.

Jacobi, J. *The way of individuation*. London: Hodder & Stoughton, 1965.

Jourard, S. M. *The transparent self*. New York: Van Nostrand, 1971.

Jung, C. G. *Collected works*. Princeton, NJ: Princeton University Press, 1960.

Jung, G. C. *Four archetypes: Mother/rebirth/spirit/trickster*. Princeton, NJ: Princeton University Press, 1959, 1969.

Jung, C. G. *The spirit in man, art, and literature*. Princeton, NJ: Princeton University Press, 1971.

King, G. *Imagineering for health: Self-healing through the use of your mind*. Wheaton, IL: Theosophical Publishing House, 1981.

Kris, E. *Psychoanalytic explorations in art*. New York: Schocken, 1952.

Kubie, L. S. *Neurotic distortion of the creative process*. New York: Noonday Press, 1958.

Langer, S. K. *Mind: An essay on human feeling*. Baltimore, MD: Johns Hopkins University Press, 1967 (Vol. I), 1970 (Vol. II).

Maslow, A. H. *The farther reaches of human nature*. New York: Viking, 1975.

May, R. *Man's search for himself*. New York: Delta Dell, 1953.

May, R. *The courage to create*. New York: Bantam, 1976.

Meerloo, J. A. M. *Creativity and eternization*. New York: Humanities Press, 1968.

Moustakas, C. E. *Creative life*. New York: Van Nostrand Reinhold, 1977.

Muller, R. *New genesis: Shaping a global spirituality*. Garden City, NY: Doubleday, 1982.

Naisbitt, J. *Megatrends: Ten new directions transforming our lives*. New York: Warner, 1982.

Neumann, E. *The great mother: An analysis of the archetype*. Princeton, NJ: Princeton University Press, 1955.

Neumann, E. *Art and the creative unconscious: Four essays*. Princeton, NJ: Princeton University Press, 1959.

Peters, T. J., & Waterman, R. H. *In search of excellence: Lessons from America's best-run companies*. New York: Harper & Row, 1982.

Rank, O. *Art and artist: Creative urge and personality development*. New York: Knopf, 1932.

Rank, O. *The trauma of birth*. New York: Harper & Row, 1973.

Roszak, T. *Person/planet: The creative disintegration of industrial society*. Garden City, NY: Doubleday, 1979.

Simonton, C. *Getting well again*. New York: Bantam, 1980.

Singer, J. L., & Pope, K. S. *The power of human imagination: New methods in psychotherapy*. New York: Plenum Press, 1978.

Von Franz, M-L. *Creation myths: Patterns of creativity in creation myths*. New York: Spring Publishers, 1972.

Walsh, R., & Shapiro, D. H. *Beyond health and normality: Explorations of exceptional psychological well-being*. New York: Van Nostrand Reinhold, 1983.

SECTION III

BEHAVIORAL/COGNITIVE/ DEVELOPMENTAL APPROACHES

The approaches in this section share an emphasis on learning and sometimes manipulate the therapeutic situation to facilitate the patient's acquisition of a new skill or behavior. None of them, however, are identical to those techniques with similar names currently in vogue. In Ellen Roth's chapter on the application of behavioral techniques to the practice of art therapy, she describes approaches she has used as models as well as her own invention, "reality shaping." Her sensitive implementation of what could otherwise be quite mechanistic should help to allay the anxieties of many in our field about the dangers of what at first seems an intrinsically anticreative approach to treatment.

Similarly, what is currently known as "cognitive therapy" (Reda & Mahoney, 1984) is considerably more intellectual and self-conscious than Rawley Silver's approach to teaching cognitive skills through art experiences. From philosophers' explanations of what man expresses in art (Langer, 1957), to psychologists' studies of creative thinking (Arnheim, 1969; Barron, 1972; Gardner, 1982), the use of art activities as a way of promoting cognitive growth has had a natural evolution. Indeed, one hopes that Silver's own extensions of her work, from the hearing-impaired to the learning-disabled and brain-damaged, will inspire others to explore the potential of facilitating mentation through art with yet other cognitively damaged populations.

In the chapter on developmental approaches, Susan Aach and Carole Kunkle-Miller describe a way of working that uses various theories of social, emotional, and cognitive development as the primary frame of reference. The authors draw from theoreticians as diverse as Mahler and

209

Piaget in order to construct an art therapy that facilitates growth for individuals in whom it has been somehow impaired. Since there are so many different theories of development, it would be impossible to have a single form of art therapy based on growth. Nevertheless, the model of thinking employed by these two authors should serve as an inspiration for other art therapists who wish to ground their work in a developmental matrix.

Although it would be possible to think of employing a behavioral, a cognitive, or a developmental approach with patients whose only problems are emotional, it is probably not accidental that each of the authors in this section developed her theory and technique in the course of work with handicapped populations. In the case of Roth, Aach, and Kunkle-Miller, the children they served had fairly severe intellectual or sensory deficits, as well as social and emotional problems. More will be said in the Conclusion (Chapter 17) about the relevance of the population to the approach employed, but the reader would do well to pay close attention to those aspects of each orientation which may be related to the fact that the clients for whom they were developed were seriously disabled.

As is true for most chapters in this book, each author in this section has presented and published previously on her topic, one in book form (Silver, 1978). As has also been true in regard to other orientations, each has selected from available theory what seemed most relevant for her own clinical work. The reader should therefore remember that there are many other possible applications of each of these three approaches to art therapy, some of which have already been detailed by others—as in the behaviorally oriented "implosive" art therapy described by DeFrancisco (1983), the developmental art therapy detailed by Williams and Wood (1977), or the cognitive theory of art therapy outlined by Carnes (1979). The potential applications of behavioral, cognitive, and developmental approaches to art therapy are multiple, and I believe that most have not yet been explored or articulated. It is hoped that the reader will be inspired to think of yet additional ways of utilizing the kind of thinking reflected in this section.

REFERENCES

Arnheim, R. *Visual thinking*. Berkeley: University of California Press, 1969.
Barron, F. *Artists in the making*. New York: Seminar Press, 1972.
Carnes, J. J. Toward a cognitive theory of art therapy. *Art Psychotherapy*, 1979, 6, 69–75.
DeFrancisco, J. Implosive art therapy: A learning-theory based, psychodynamic approach. In L. Gantt & S. Whitman (Eds.). *The fine art of therapy*. Alexandria, VA: American Art Therapy Association, 1983, pp. 74–79.

Gardner, H. *Art, mind and brain: A cognitive approach to creativity.* New York: Basic Books, 1982.

Langer, S. *Problems of art.* New York: Charles Scribner & Sons, 1957.

Reda, M. A., & Mahoney, M. J. *Cognitive psychotherapies: Recent developments in theory, research, and practice.* Cambridge, MA: Ballinger Publishing Co., 1984.

Silver, R. A. *Developing cognitive and creative skills in art.* Baltimore, MD: University Park Press, 1978.

Williams, G. H., & Wood, M. M. *Developmental art therapy.* Baltimore, MD: University Park Press, 1977.

12

A Behavioral Approach
to Art Therapy

Ellen A. Roth

Behavior therapy is a technique designed to treat undesirable behavior which is directly observed, i.e., behavior which psychodynamic therapy refers to as symptoms. The psychodynamic model of treatment is to first assess and then deal with the underlying psychological disorders that give rise to pathological symptoms. Behavior therapy rejects the notion that problematic behavior is a symptom of underlying conflicts maintained by unconscious dynamic processes. Rather, behaviorists view aberrant behavior as a learned phenomenon which is maintained by environmental and situational determinants. Their model of treatment is to first assess behavior, and then to alter it through procedures that modify old behavior or that teach new behaviors (e.g., conditioning techniques, systematic desensitization, modeling, etc.). Desired changes in behavior are defined and demonstrated empirically, and they are constantly evaluated throughout treatment.

Goldstein provides a useful introduction to the conceptual evolution of behavior therapy and its practical applications.

Behavioral influence in therapy has evolved in two directions, one based on Pavlovian concepts of learning which has as its major focus emotional learning, and Skinnerian methodology with its emphasis on observable behavior and change through contingent reinforcement. The former has developed in the outpatient setting, is usually a one-to-one therapy regimen, and is applicable to neurotic problems, while the latter has developed in inpatient settings, such as state hospitals and institutions for the mentally retarded. . . . the former . . . has come to be identified as "behavior therapy" while the Skinnerian applications are most often referred to as "behavior modification" (1973, p. 207).

213

Although the roots of behavior therapy may be traced to Pavlov, the Russian physiologist, behavioral psychology has emerged over the past 40 years as a predominantly American theory (Hall & Lindzey, 1975). The principle of *classical conditioning* investigated by Pavlov (1927) with the use of dogs is that when an unconditioned stimulus (food) is repeatedly paired with a neutral stimulus (the sound of a metronome), the neutral stimulus will eventually elicit the unconditioned reflex response (salivation) in the absence of the unconditioned stimulus (food). In this case, the sound of the metronome becomes a conditioned stimulus, and salivating to the sound a conditioned response.

An early application of classical conditioning is found in the work of Watson and Raynor (1920), who demonstrated that fears are learned by using classical conditioning techniques to induce fear reactions to rats, rabbits, and other furry objects in an infant. Wolpe (1958), who originated *systematic desensitization*, treated patients with maladaptive anxiety and phobias by pairing learned deep-muscle relaxation and hypnosis with a hierarchy of anxiety-evoking stimuli. The individual overcomes his anxiety by imagining anxiety-provoking scenes gradually, from the least to the most disturbing, in a "psychophysiological state that inhibits anxiety" (Brady, 1975, p. 1825). The effect is achieved through *counterconditioning*.

Skinner (1953) advanced the principles of *operant conditioning* first studied by Thorndike (1911). In operant conditioning, behaviors are controlled (strengthened or weakened) by the events that follow them. Positive *reinforcement* with primary reinforcers (e.g., food), social reinforcers (e.g., praise), or generalized reinforcers (e.g., money) increases the likelihood of a particular behavior recurring; *punishment* (e.g., disapproval) is likely to decrease its recurrence; and cessation of reinforcement (e.g., ignoring) leads to *extinction*.

Operant conditioning techniques include *shaping*. Shaping involves bringing a subject closer to a desired behavior by reinforcing small steps that gradually lead to the terminal behavior. This is done by reinforcing *successive approximations*, which include responses that either "resemble the final response or which include components of that response" (Kazdin, 1975, p. 37). Similar to shaping, *chaining* involves developing a sequence of behaviors.

In shaping behavior, there are two major classifications of *schedules* of reinforcement. These are identified as *interval* reinforcements and *ratio* reinforcements. *Continuous* reinforcement means that a behavior is reinforced each time it occurs. Once a behavior occurs consistently it can be maintained on an intermittent reinforcement schedule. Lutzker,

McGimsey-McRae, and McGimsey (1983) note that " . . . behaviors that are reinforced on an intermittent schedule are more resistant to extinction (i.e., they continue to be performed in the absence of reinforcement) because the individual performing the behavior has become accustomed to not having each performance of the behavior reinforced" (p. 33).

Shaping and chaining behavior are facilitated by *prompts*. Prompts include "cues, instructions, gestures, directions, examples, and models to initiate a response" (Kazdin, 1975, p. 41). The gradual removal of a prompt is referred to as *fading*.

Another important component of the operant paradigm is the concept of *generalization*. Learned behavior may be generalized or transferred to other settings (stimulus generalization), or changes in a behavior may be associated with changes in related behaviors (response generalization).

Some have investigated learning theories developed in the laboratory and have demonstrated their applicability to the study of personality and social behavior. Dollard and Miller's stimulus response theory of personality embraces psychoanalytic theory by translating psychoanalytic formulations into principles of learning. They postulate that all behavior, including neurotic behavior, is learned. Learned behavior is acquired as a function of four fundamental principals: drive, cue, response, and reinforcement.

> If neurotic behavior is learned, it should be unlearned by some combination of the same principles by which it was taught. We believe this to be the case. Psychotherapy establishes a set of conditions by which neurotic habits may be unlearned and non-neurotic habits learned. Therefore, we view the therapist as a kind of teacher and the patient as a learner (Dollard & Miller, 1950, pp. 7–8).

Bandura and Walters' social learning theory is concerned with observational learning and imitation, e.g., "the tendency for a person to reproduce the actions, attitudes, or emotional responses exhibited by real-life or symbolized models" (1963, p. 89). New behavioral responses are learned, or existing behaviors are modified, by observing the behavior of others. Exposure to models, therefore, can influence behavior negatively or positively. Additional behavioral *strategies* discussed by Goldstein (1973) include role playing, assertiveness training, flooding, and aversive techniques (e.g., electric shock). Questionnaires may also be helpful in assessing the client's problem(s).

Behaviorists define *neurosis* as "persistent unadaptive behaviors which have developed through learning or the deficit of adaptive behaviors due to insufficient learning" (Goldstein, 1973, p. 217). The goal of behav-

ioral approaches in treatment is "to reverse unadaptive learning and fur-
nish learning experiences where appropriate responses have not been
learned" (*Ibid.*, p. 220).

The behavioral approach to treatment begins by identifying a specific
complaint (*target behavior*) that requires modification. A *history* is taken
to learn what are the cause-and-effect relationships of the problem behavior. The therapist and client develop a trusting working relationship in
which the goal of therapy is mutually agreed upon. *Treatment goals* are
clearly stated, and the target behavior is carefully described. As noted by
Kazdin, "the target behaviors have to be defined explicitly so that they
can actually be observed, measured and agreed upon . . . " (1975, p. 66).
In strict behavior modification programs, the frequency of occurrence of
the target behavior is also first objectively assessed, which establishes a
baseline rate of performance. Appropriate techniques are administered
that will change behavior to the desired goal. Behavior is continuously
monitored to evaluate change and the efficacy of the treatment regimen.

RELEVANCE OF BEHAVIOR THEORY
TO ART THERAPY: COMMON GROUND

The behavioral approach to art therapy presented in this chapter involves the application of behavior modification techniques (operant conditioning and modeling procedures) to the practice of art therapy (with
emotionally disturbed, mentally retarded children). At first, the idea of
a behavioral approach to art therapy may appear antithetical. Art therapy,
with its roots in Freudian psychoanalysis, has traditionally approached
treatment from a psychodynamic perspective. Behavior therapy and behavior modification techniques are not concerned with the unconscious
as expressed through dreams, fantasies, or pictorial representations. Behavioral approaches reject ambiguous intrapsychic conflicts, the meaning of which can only be inferred, in favor of concentrating on overt behavior that can be assessed objectively.

Behavioral techniques, however, are used by psychodynamically oriented art therapists, usually without being labeled as such. For example,
an art therapist who encourages a blocked or inhibited patient to make
a scribble in order to involve the patient with media, and then praises the
individual for his/her participation, is using a behavioral approach (e.g.,
reinforcement).

Similarly, psychotherapy—including psychodynamically oriented art
therapy—and behavior therapy—including behaviorally oriented art therapy—do share other areas of common ground. All forms of psychotherapy
and behavior therapy, with or without art, share fundamental commonal-

ities, to the extent that they all are attempts to help human beings who have problems.

Sloane (1969) discusses several instances wherein psychotherapists utilize behaviorist techniques and vice versa, whether they recognize them as such or not. First, in both cases, a *relationship* between the therapist and the patient based on trust, acceptance, and tolerance is important. Second, both therapies use *reinforcements*. The behaviorist may encourage desirable behavior through praise or other social reinforcements. In a more subtle fashion, the psychotherapist may encourage an insightful train of thought by cues of approval (e.g., change of expression) or by an elaborate interpretation. The therapist, then, "not only transmits desired verbal behavior, but also some of his own expectations" (Sloane, 1969, p. 495). Third, both therapies rely on the phenomenon of *transference*, to the extent that both capitalize on the patient's desire to behave in a way that will please the therapist. Fourth, both incorporate benefits of *imitative* behavior. For example, a behaviorist technique to change behavior is to expose the individual to a *model* whom the individual holds in high regard. In psychotherapy, the therapist is usually held in high regard, and his attitudes and values may subtly influence the patient, even though he has not attempted to transmit them directly. Fifth, the concept of *insight* is applicable to both therapies. "Psychotherapeutic insight occurs when the patient comes to recognize some of the previously unconscious roots of his attitudes, beliefs, feelings, conflicts or behavior" (*Ibid.*, p. 498). In a comparable sense, "behavioral insight" occurs when a patient becomes aware of and is able to discriminate among the environmental stimuli that elicit inappropriate behavior on his part.

Additional similarities in the two approaches are cited by Marks and Gelder (1966). They include: (1) giving of advice and encouragement by the therapist; (2) conveying to the patient an expectation of improvement; (3) encouraging the patient "to recognize current sources of stress and repetitive patterns of behaviour" (p. 18); (4) manipulating the environment; (5) decreasing anxiety gradually: "Psychotherapists emphasize correct timing of graduated interpretations to prevent patients experiencing excessive anxiety; this is very similar to behaviour therapists gradually presenting anxiety-laden stimuli during desensitization" (pp. 18–19).

Other professionals today share the view that dynamic psychotherapy, which emphasizes the role of internal processes, and behavior therapy, which focuses on the functional adaptation of behavior, need not be dichotomized to an extreme. As Marmor states, " . . . all psychotherapy, regardless of the techniques used, is a learning process" (1971, p. 26). Similarly, London concludes, " . . . all learning theory formulations are, in fact, dynamic ones" (1973, p. 170).

Approaching art therapy from a behavioral model is not common practice, but it has been done and has been shown to be effective (DeFrancisco, 1983; Roth, 1978; van Sickle & Acker, 1975). I have found behavioral techniques to be especially useful in working with emotionally disturbed, mentally retarded children in art therapy (Roth, 1979, 1983; Roth & Barrett, 1980). This is a population with whom it has been empirically shown that behavior therapy is helpful in improving adaptive behavior (Keogh & Whitman, 1983; Thompson & Grabowski, 1972; Whitman, Sciback, & Reid, 1983). The application of behavioral techniques to art therapy treatment not only helps disturbed retarded children with their behavior, but addresses their emotional needs as well. A behavioral approach to art therapy has also been demonstrated to be effective with other populations, including severely anxious children (DeFrancisco, 1983) and aggressive adults (van Sickle & Acker, 1975). Others who might benefit from this approach are those who are neither highly verbal nor intellectually sophisticated.

REALITY SHAPING: A BEHAVIORAL APPROACH

An art therapy approach of special utility for emotionally disturbed, mentally retarded children is "reality shaping."* It combines traditional art therapy techniques with behavior modification principles; it involves education during the process of therapy. Reality shaping begins by identifying a concept that is poorly conveyed in the child's productions during art therapy sessions. This concept is then developed into representational form through the construction—first by the art therapist and then by the child—of increasingly complex two- and three-dimensional models. This structured technique gives concrete form to vague concepts that may underlie a child's pathology.

CASE ILLUSTRATIONS

Following are three cases illustrating the technique of *reality shaping* with disturbed retarded children. The children in these case studies were hospitalized in the John Merck Program for Emotionally Disturbed–Men-

---

*This technique was developed by the author while working in the John Merck Program, Western Psychiatric Institute and Clinic. It was previously published as follows: Roth, E. A. Art Therapy with Emotionally Disturbed–Mentally Retarded Children: A Technique of Reality Shaping. In B. K. Mandel et al. (Eds.). *The Dynamics of Creativity, The Proceedings of the Eighth Annual Conference of the American Art Therapy Association*. Baltimore: AATA, 1978.

tally Retarded Children (presently known as the JMP for Multiply Disabled Children), which provides a multidisciplinary approach to treatment and education in a therapeutic milieu.

The Case of Larry

This case concerns a six-year-old, mildly retarded boy named Larry.* Larry exhibited a severe speech delay and hyperactivity. He also had a history of destructive behavior. Repeated dangerous acts performed by this child included playing with knives, gas jets, and the kitchen stove. He had swallowed pills (for which he was hospitalized three times to have his stomach pumped), and he showed constant disruptive attention seeking. The event precipitating hospitalization was setting fire to his family's home. The fire was started by a cigarette lighter that Larry found in his mother's purse. He ignited a lampshade, and then stood outside the house watching it burn, while laughing and hysterically screaming, "Burn house, burn house." No one was hurt during the fire, but Larry's bedroom was badly damaged. Serious injury to family members could have occurred had not the father awakened and ushered everyone out of the house.

Larry's art therapy evaluation occurred soon after his admission to inpatient psychiatric hospitalization. During the session, he was free to choose whatever materials he wished to use. His first works of art were a series of paintings in which all the colors were smeared together, suggesting a high degree of anxiety, expressed through regression. No verbal comments accompanied these paintings. One month after admission to the unit, he began to participate in regular weekly half-hour art therapy sessions. His paintings, by this time, consisted of separate and distinct areas of color distributed around the paper; i.e., the colors were no longer smeared together.

Larry took an interest in small wooden craft sticks that were available for the children to use. He began by gluing the pieces of wood to a sheet of paper and then painting over them. For six weeks, his art products consisted mainly of groups of sticks glued vertically to the paper and then painted. Each of these wood formations was identified as "a house." It

---

*The child described in this case was referred to as "Mary" in an earlier publication. The pseudonym of "Larry" is being used at this time because the patient was really a boy. In an attempt to disguise the case, the sex of the child was changed. This, however, has resulted in some confusion because female firesetters are uncommon. Similarly, in cases 2 and 3, the sex of the child has also been changed from being overdisguised in an earlier publication (see footnote, p. 218).

was interesting to observe that in painting these formations, the color red, which is reminiscent of fire, was used selectively. For example, one red stick would appear in the center of the paper, surrounded by sticks that were blue, green, and black.

It was clear from Larry's art products that he had difficulty conceptualizing a house. At this point in therapy, I switched from using a nondirective approach to employing the technique of *reality shaping*, which incorporates behavior modification principles. The *goal* or *target behavior* was for Larry to represent a recognizable house on a two-dimensional surface. To help him to properly conceptualize a house, I prepared in advance of the next session a simple outline of a house made out of pieces of wood and glued the wooden sticks to a sheet of paper (Figure 1). The

Figure 1

same materials with which he had been working and with which he felt comfortable were therefore used to create the house schema. This *model* was the first step in *shaping* his understanding of how to represent a house. We talked about the various parts of the house. Larry could identify the roof and the windows, for which he was *positively reinforced* with praise. When he was not able to label the walls, chimney, or door, I identified these parts for him. Larry became physically involved with the model by painting over each section of the house as we talked about it. This also reinforced his understanding of how the parts were connected. Once again, the color red was used selectively, on one upstairs window and the door.

The second step in shaping Larry's ability to conceptualize and represent a house took place in the next art therapy session. Larry was invited to construct the outline of a house with sticks on paper, while referring to the model that we had made the previous week. He was encouraged to *imitate* the model. He was able to do this with *prompts* in the form of verbal instructions and physical guidance. Each time that he put a craft stick in an appropriate placement, he was praised (*continuous reinforcement*).

After he successfully made an outline of a house on a two-dimensional surface, the third step in shaping Larry's behavior was the construction of a three-dimensional house (Figure 2). This house ($10'' \times 10'' \times 10''$), which took 16 sessions to complete, was made out of the same wooden sticks with which he had accumulated a series of successful two-dimensional experiences. I facilitated his constructing the foundation of the house with verbal and physical *prompts*, as well as positive reinforcement. Once the foundation, which established the basic shape of the house, was laid, however, the prompts were *faded* out, and continuous reinforcement was replaced by *intermittent reinforcement*.

Larry was very protective of this house, always wanting reassurance that no one else would touch it. When the house was completed, he took it home. Shortly thereafter, reports from his mother revealed that he had slowly and deliberately taken the house apart, and that he kept the pieces in a drawer in his room. First, Larry had damaged his family's home. Now, by destroying his miniature house, he had perhaps symbolically mastered the situation.

Two months after the three-dimensional house was built, Larry spontaneously began to make x-ray paintings of a house. These paintings were very different from his earlier paintings, which had consisted of random shapes of color. They were characterized by a large rectangular shape (house), derived from an understanding of "houseness," based on the construction of his earlier houses. Various forms within the house were iden-

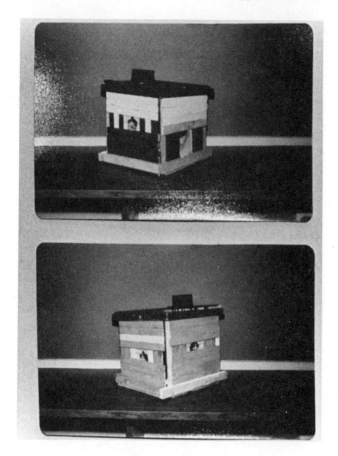

Figure 2

tified as household items, such as a couch, a window, etc. His paintings now possessed a sense of geometry and order, indicating that his ability to represent a house was beginning to *generalize* or transfer to another medium.

Larry's next major project was another three-dimensional house which he spontaneously chose to make. It was prefabricated out of cardboard and hence put together much more quickly than the first house. It was also painted. This house represented a synthesis of his previous work. It combined the exterior of the first three-dimensional house with the interior of his recent two-dimensional paintings. The interior of the cardboard house was divided in half. The partitioned area represented Larry's bedroom, to which he had previously set fire. It contained a red window.

The bedroom was the first concrete reference to the scene of the fire, although the subject of fire had been referred to by Larry in numerous therapy sessions.

Three weeks later, Larry created another house. It was a primitive structure made out of clay. It too was composed of an exterior and an interior. The interior contained a partitioned area with two beds. He stated that one bed was his, and that the other one was for me. I inferred from our relationship and the context of the session that my presence in the bedroom meant that the bedroom would be a safe place to be in, if I was there. Larry took this house home.

A few weeks later, Larry made a clearly recognizable drawing of a house, consisting of a rectangular base with a triangular roof. There was also a door and two windows. It was very similar to the first model of a house that he had made by gluing peices of wood to paper. It was clear that the *target behavior* of representing a recognizable house on a two-dimensional surface had been successfully achieved. Simultaneously, symbolic material associated with houses continued to emerge at an accelerated pace. For example, this recognizable house, which had generalized from three to two dimensions, was also enclosed within a red and orange border identified as a road. This border reflected ambivalent feelings concerning the house. It seemed to be a protective line, intended to shield the house from destruction. But the use of red also suggested a house surrounded by the threat of fire.

The following week, Larry began to make another three-dimensional house out of small matched pieces of wood. It consisted only of an exterior. While adding the chimney, he commented that his own home did not have a fireplace. Larry worked on this house intermittently for six weeks. During this time, he also used other art media.

Two paintings from this period were of special interest. One was an x-ray painting of a house. Next to the house was a figure identified as "Ellen," who was "coming to visit." This was the first human figure that Larry had represented in a year of art therapy. The second painting was of a "fire truck" going to a fire, also the first image of its kind.

During the next three months, Larry's art products focused on objects in his environment that were clearly identifiable, such as stoplights and parking garages, in addition to occasional houses. That he could at any time return to drawing the image of a house was evidence that the learned behavior was *maintained* over time.

In contrast to his carefully delineated paintings of objects, a painting emerged one day in which the colors were smeared together. The painting was identified as "Fire." I commented that it was "a picture of fire." Larry immediately responded, "I saw a real fire!" He recounted in detail the scene of the fire in his bedroom, although he did not make any reference as to how the fire had begun. From this time, Larry was able to deal more directly and openly with the subject of the fire in his home. He also made gains behaviorally and conceptually, as well as in his ability to graphically represent objects in the visual world.

Discussion. Behavior modification techniques were successful in teaching Larry how to represent a recognizable house. The construction of houses was meaningful to him on three different levels. First, developing the concept of a house into representational form was an achievement through which he experienced pleasure and the pride of accomplishment, serving to raise his self-esteem. Second, through the construction of three-dimensional houses, he was able to represent in concrete form the main structural aspects of a house. These miniature houses served to clarify and organize his concept of a house, which initially was extremely vague. Third, making two- and three-dimensional creations that actually resembled houses enabled Larry to bring into focus the reality of the firesetting incident that had been so traumatic. The houses facilitated his eventual ability to talk about fires, houses being burned, and other related, anxiety-provoking subjects. It was an opportunity for Larry to work through his conflicts within a supportive environment. By building miniature houses, he was also able to symbolically undo the harm he had caused by burning his own home, and thereby assuage his guilt.

The Case of Paul

The second case is of an eight-year-old, moderately retarded boy named Paul. Paul was admitted to inpatient psychiatric hospitalization with the parents' complaint that he was unmanageable at home. His behavior was described as stubborn, defiant, irritable, and he was destructive of property. He exhibited temper tantrums, was unresponsive to the environment, and was difficult to comfort. At times, he appeared disoriented; he was afraid to be alone. He tormented his siblings. He demonstrated both active and passive aggression toward his parents. He was aggressive toward peers. In unfamiliar situations, he was withdrawn.

During his diagnostic art evaluation, Paul made eight paintings. Each consisted of a large mass of smeared colors and dribbles, which were not identified. For the first two months of weekly art therapy, Paul's preferred medium was paint. His paintings consisted of large masses of smeared colors and dribbles, similar to the paintings he had made in his evaluation session. These paintings, however, were consistently identified as "trees." After two months of Paul identifying masses of smeared colors as "trees," I decided to use the technique of *reality shaping* to help him to properly conceptualize a tree. The *goal* of this procedure was for Paul to be able to represent a recognizable image of a tree on a two-dimensional surface.

To *shape* his understanding of what a tree looked like on paper, as opposed to in a natural outdoor environment, I prepared a three-dimensional model of a tree by taking a small branch with leaves and attaching it to a piece of wood. I taped the construction to a sheet of paper and then painted over the wooden trunk. Paul and I talked about the parts of a tree, initially differentiating in a general manner the tree-top and the tree-trunk. After reviewing the parts of the tree, I gave Paul the same three-dimensional materials that I had used. Together we made a similar model of a tree.

The next step involved transferring the three-dimensional form to a two-dimensional surface. The following week, Paul and I talked about the various parts of a tree while referring to the three-dimensional models. With verbal guidance (*prompts*) he was able to paint a recognizable tree, differentiating the tree-top (i.e., green mass of color) from the tree-trunk (i.e., linear brown brushstrokes extending downward from the tree-top). During this activity, he was *continuously reinforced* with praise for his appropriate mastery of the task.

Having successfully represented the general form of a tree, the next step in shaping the image involved further *differentiating* the tree-top by making forms suggestive of branches. With verbal cues and manual assistance, Paul was shown how to paint individual lines at the top of the trunk, which represented branches. Subsequently, he painted a similar model on his own. At this point, I had some concern that I had guided Paul into a very narrow and sterile conception of a tree. My fears, however, were soon relieved.

Two weeks later, he painted a series of trees, incorporating the forms that we had been developing, but adding his own personal color scheme. The trees that he painted were not green and brown. Rather they appeared in the full array of autumn tones (red, yellow, orange, purple). The target behavior of representing a tree on a two-dimensional surface was achieved. The development just described evolved over a period of five weeks. Once Paul had mastered the schema, his art work no longer focused exclusively on trees.

During the following year of art therapy, Paul occasionally spontaneously painted a tree or a group of trees. These trees incorporated the general form that differentiated the tree-top from the tree-trunk. This was evidence that Paul had internalized the schema of a tree, and that his learned behavior was maintained over time.

Discussion. The use of reality shaping was an effective means of teaching Paul how to paint a recognizable tree. Initially, his art work focused on smeared forms identified as "trees." His concept of a tree was given an appropriate schema through the use of three-dimensional and two-dimensional models. Although it is unclear exactly what trees meant to this child, it is clear that the image was an important one. Once he had mastered the tree, he was very pleased with himself. The activity served to raise his self-esteem, bolster his confidence, and expand his cognitive capacity by creating a visual link between an object in the real world and his concept of that object. When he could make a fairly accurate representational image of a tree, his art work no longer focused exclusively on trees. He began to incorporate other themes into his artwork as well (e.g., faces).

The Case of Kelly

The third case concerns a seven-year-old, mentally retarded girl named Kelly. Kelly suffered from a general developmental delay in motor, language, perceptual, and conceptual functioning. Her performance in these areas was uneven. Psychological testing revealed that her mental ability and social skills were not commensurate; these ranged from two to four years. At the time of her admission to inpatient psychiatric hospitalization, Kelly exhibited numerous inappropriate behaviors. She displayed frequent temper tantrums, a low frustration tolerance, poor ability to interact with peers, and her speech was largely echolalic.

At the time of her diagnostic evaluation, Kelly exhibited very dependent behavior. She required assistance in the form of physical contact to maintain graphic control. For example, when she placed my hand on hers, she could draw a circle. At such time, I did not control her drawing, but simply let her sweep my hand along with her own. As long as our hands were touching, her marks were linear and controlled. When I withdrew my hand, she resorted to random scribbling, the product of rhythmical motor activity.

Kelly began to participate in art therapy sessions on a regular basis four months after her initial diagnostic session. By this time, she no longer sought physical assistance when drawing or painting. Her response to my request to draw a person was a web of circular scribbles and random lines (Figure 3). As she made this drawing, she named numerous body parts and pointed to these parts on her own body. Nevertheless, they appear only as named scribbles.

In addition to drawing and painting, another art material that Kelly used often was plasticine. Her performance with this three-dimensional medium was more advanced than with two-dimensional materials. She often made numerous types of foods, and we pretended to eat them. This

Figure 3

suggested that a more deliberate use of three-dimensional media might promote developmental gains.

The *goal* of *reality shaping* was for Kelly to be able to draw a person, an image that had previously been a failure. I began by helping her to properly conceptualize a face. First, I made a model of a face by applying plasticine features on a plastic egg, thus creating a kind of Humpty-Dumpty. Second, we made a similar model using the first as a reference. Without prompting, Kelly's first face was a lump of plasticine stuck onto an egg. But with verbal prompts, physical *guidance*, and *continuous positive reinforcement*, she learned where to accurately place facial features. In making these Humpty-Dumpty faces (Figure 4), she acknowledged as physical references her facial features and mine too. She was encouraged to comment, with the placement of each feature, that they did not touch one another. Thus, separation of parts was learned.

Once Kelly had mastered the three-dimensional Humpty-Dumpty egg face, I drew the shape of an egg on a piece of paper. I suggested that she place pieces of plasticine within the shape where facial features belonged

Figure 4

and then trace around them (Figure 5). With guidance, she was able to do this. In helping her to conceptualize a facial schema on paper, I used the same materials with which she had been regularly interacting. The three-dimensional use of the plasticine was transferred to a two-dimensional surface.

Four weeks later, Kelly spontaneously drew a face on a sheet of paper, accurately placing facial features (Figure 6). She had internalized a facial schema, and she was able to represent it two-dimensionally. During the same session, she also made a finger painting of a face, which indicated that she was able to *generalize* the schema to other media.

After Kelly had demonstrated that she could accurately draw a face, I went back to the three-dimensional model and used the plastic eggs and plasticine to help her to conceptualize a more complete figure. Humpty-Dumpty was expanded to include a body, arms, and legs.

The same process for teaching Kelly to draw a face was applied to drawing a human figure. Plasticine features and appendages were added to a sheet of paper already containing the outline of a head and body. Kelly traced around the appendages to get a sense of their forms as well as where they existed in relationship to other body parts. The next step involved my drawing circular forms representing a head and a body and letting Kelly draw the arms and legs. Four months later, she was able to draw, by herself, a human figure incorporating all the body parts we had focused on. The target behavior of learning to draw a person was achieved.

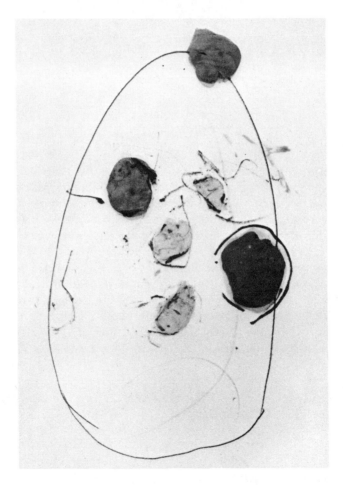

Figure 5

Figure 6

Discussion. During her 15½ months of art therapy, Kelly's artwork underwent significant changes. She developed the ability to make controlled marks without external support. By means of reality shaping, this ability was channeled into making a human figure through the use of three-dimensional and two-dimensional models. In addition, we talked about and pointed to her own facial features and body parts. Eventually, she was able to internalize a facial schema and to represent it on paper without reference to a physical model. The representation of additional body parts followed. Reality shaping focused on developing Kelly's drawing skills, teaching new behavior, and expanding her cognitive ability. It served as a means of orienting her to reality in terms of her body image. Kelly became aware of her individual body parts and the interrelatedness of her physical structure.

CONCLUDING COMMENTS

Reality shaping involves the use of behavior modification techniques and models to systematically teach new behavior and to develop concepts initially not fully understood by the child. By means of operant conditioning (prompting, shaping, and positive reinforcement) and modeling procedures, the child learns new behavior which is maintained over time. The technique provides a consistent approach that allows the child to build on preceding learned behavior. Two- and three-dimensional models serve as conceptual references and promote modeling behavior.

Reality shaping is not directed at assessing internal psychological variables or biological conditions. It is primarily concerned with teaching new behavior. While the child is learning new behavior and acquiring new behavioral skills, other gains may also occur. For example, this technique may facilitate the child's ability to express images that are disturbing, like Larry's house on fire. Disturbing ideas or fantasies that may underlie the child's pathology can then be explored, using more traditional art therapy approaches. Concepts that are not disturbing, but which are important to the child's sense of reality, can be developed and increase the child's ability to think abstractly. A diminished capacity to abstract is a notable feature of retardation (Cytryn & Lourie, 1975). Through the sequential use of simple concrete models, an increased level of abstraction for the child can be attained. Thus, a behavioral approach can be an effective means of treating through art therapy both the emotional disturbance and some cognitive effects of retardation.

REFERENCES

Bandura, A., & Walters, R. H. *Social learning and personality development*. New York: Holt, Rinehart, & Winston, 1963.

Brady, J. P. Behavior therapy. In A. Freedman, H. Kaplan, & B. Sadock (Eds.). *Comprehensive textbook of psychiatry/II* (Vol. 2). Baltimore: Williams & Wilkins, 1975, pp. 1824–1831.

Cytryn, L., & Lourie, R. Mental retardation. In A. Freedman, H. Kaplan, & B. Sadock (Eds.). *Comprehensive textbook of psychiatry/II* (Vol. 1). Baltimore: Williams & Wilkins, 1975, pp. 1158–1197.

DeFrancisco, J. Implosive art therapy: A learning-theory-based, psychodynamic approach. In L. Gantt & S. Whitman (Eds.). *The fine art of therapy*. Alexandria, VA: American Art Therapy Association, 1983, pp. 74–79.

Dollard, J., & Miller, N. E. *Personality and psychotherapy*. New York: McGraw-Hill, 1950.

Goldstein, A. Behavior therapy. In R. Corsini (Ed.). *Current psychotherapies*. Itasca, IL: F. E. Peacock, 1973, pp. 207–249.

Hall, C. S., & Lindzey, G. *Theories of personality*, 2nd ed. New York: John Wiley and Sons, 1975.

Kazdin, A. E. *Behavior modification in applied settings*. Homewood, IL: The Dorsey Press, 1975.

Keogh, D., & Whitman, T. Mental retardation in children. In M. Hersen, V. B. Van Hasselt, & J. L. Matson (Eds.). *Behavior therapy for the developmentally and physically disabled*. New York: Academic Press, 1983, pp. 205–246.

London, P. The end of ideology in behavior modification. *International Journal of Psychiatry*, 1973, *11*, 167–182.

Lutzker, J. R., McGimsey-McRae, S., & McGimsey, J. F. General description of behavioral approaches. In M. Hersen, V. B. Van Hasselt, and J. L. Matson (Eds.). *Behavior therapy for the developmentally and physically disabled.* New York: Academic Press, 1983, pp. 25–56.

Marks, I. M., & Gelder, M. G. Common ground between behaviour therapy and psychodynamic methods. *British Journal of Medical Psychology,* 1966, *39,* 11–23.

Marmor, J. Dynamic psychotherapy and behavior therapy. *Archives of General Psychiatry,* 1971, *24,* 22–28.

Pavlov, I. P. *Conditioned reflexes.* Trans. and Ed. by G. V. Anrep. London: Oxford University Press, 1927.

Roth, E. A. Art therapy with emotionally disturbed–mentally retarded children: A technique of reality shaping. In B. K. Mandel et al. (Eds.). *The dynamics of creativity.* Baltimore: American Art Therapy Association, 1978, pp. 168–172.

Roth, E. A. Choosing an appropriate candidate for art therapy among emotionally disturbed–mentally retarded children. In L. Gantt et al. (Eds.). *Art therapy: Expanding horizons.* Baltimore: American Art Therapy Association, 1979, pp. 48–55.

Roth, E. A. Art therapy to promote ego development in disturbed retarded children. In L. Gantt & S. Whitman (Eds.) *The fine art of therapy.* Alexandria, VA: American Art Therapy Association, 1983, pp. 13–19.

Roth, E., & Barrett, R. Parallels in art and play therapy with a disturbed retarded child. *The Arts in Psychotherapy,* 1980, *7,* 19–26.

Skinner, B. F. *Science and human behavior.* New York: The Free Press, 1953.

Sloane, R. B. The converging paths of behavior therapy and psychotherapy. *International Journal of Psychiatry,* 1969, *8,* 493–503.

Thompson, T., & Grabowski, J. (Eds.). *Behavior modification of the mentally retarded.* London: Oxford University Press, 1972.

Thorndike, E. L. *Animal intelligence* (1911). New York: Hafner Publishing Co. Reprinted 1965.

van Sickle, K. G., & Acker, L. E. Modification of an adult's problem behavior in an art therapy setting. *American Journal of Art Therapy,* 1975, *14,* 117–120.

Watson, J. B., & Raynor, R. Conditioned emotional reactions. *Journal of Experimental Psychology,* 1920, *3* (1), 1–14.

Whitman, T. L., Sciback, J. W., & Reid, D. H. (Eds.). *Behavior modification with the severely and profoundly retarded.* New York: Academic Press, 1983.

Wolpe, J. *Psychotherapy by reciprocal inhibition.* Stanford, CA: Stanford University Press, 1958.

13

A Cognitive Approach
to Art Therapy

Rawley A. Silver

Cognition is the process of knowing. The study of cognitive development is an attempt to explain how knowledge is acquired. In art therapy, the cognitive approach to be described may be defined as exploring the role of art in identifying, evaluating, and developing cognitive skills. It is based on the premise that art can be a language of cognition paralleling the spoken word. Cognitive skills can be evident in visual as well as verbal conventions. These skills, traditionally assessed and developed through language, can also be assessed and developed through certain art activities.

A cognitive approach to art therapy is also concerned with the diagnosis and treatment of emotional disorders. Emotions and cognition interact. Children who cannot keep up with their classmates tend to develop feelings of inadequacy. Adults who lose the ability to speak following a stroke tend to feel frustrated and depressed. The cognitive approach explores emotions as well as thoughts, seeks to ease tensions and to build self-confidence. It is particularly appropriate for children and adults who have difficulty articulating thoughts and feelings in words.

BACKGROUND LITERATURE

Cognition

Jerome Bruner (1966) described cognition as a means of organizing the barrage of stimuli from the outside world. We reduce the barrage by constructing models—imaginary representations. We match a few milliseconds of new experience to a remembered model, then anticipate what will happen next, responding to the model we happen to match. Thus,

233

thought is carried out by representing reality vicariously as well as economically. As Bruner points out, we represent with the aid of "intellectual prosthetic devices" such as language, but there are pictorial devices as well: "It is still true that a thousand words scarcely exhaust the richness of a single image" (Bruner, 1966).

Children's drawings are pictorial devices that can represent reality vicariously and economically and thus reflect their thinking. Children with inadequate language are deprived of opportunities to represent their experiences because they lack a major device for constructing models of reality. This alone could account for any cognitive deficiency they might have. If their visual-spatial abilities are intact, however, they may be able to construct visual models of reality and can then represent their experiences nonverbally by drawing them.

The Role of Language in Cognition

Language is obviously related to cognition; whether it is essential to cognition is the subject of debate. Some evidence suggests that language and thought develop independently, that language follows rather than precedes logical thinking, and that even though language expands and facilitates thought, high-level thinking can and does proceed without it (Arnheim, 1969; Furth, 1966; Piaget, 1970; Torrance, 1962).

A recurrent theme in the writing of Piaget is that logical thinking exists before the appearance of language, which occurs around the middle of the second year. By the beginning of the second year, most children are capable of repeating and generalizing their actions. If they have learned to pull a blanket to reach for a toy on top of it, they are capable of pulling the blanket to reach anything else on top. They can also generalize this causal action by using a stick to move a distant object or by pulling a string to reach what is attached.

In the thinking of normal children, language functions primarily to pin down their perceptions, organize their experiences, and understand and control their environments (Strauss & Kephart, 1955). By labeling perceptions with words, children can make their perceptions usable again and again. In addition, language opens up the whole area of vicarious experience. When children cannot obtain a desired result, they can substitute words for the unsuccessful activity and, by symbolizing, obtain it in imagination. By hearing about the experiences of others, children can obtain information that they would otherwise have to obtain themselves. Thus, they can use the experience of others and compare themselves to others, without having to have the experiences themselves.

Art symbols can serve these functions of language, not only for normal children, but especially for children and adults who have auditory or language impairments. Like linguistic symbols, art symbols can label perceptions and experiences. They can represent particular subjects or classes of subjects. For example, the painting of a man can represent the painter's father, authority figures in general, man in the abstract, or all three, just as the word "man" can represent each of all of these ideas, depending on the verbal context. People with inadequate language are handicapped in representing their thoughts effectively, but even though their capacity for language may be impaired, their capacity for symbolization may be intact. If so, they may be able to represent their thoughts nonverbally by drawing them.

Left- and Right-Hemisphere Thinking

A brief consideration of the different modes of thinking characteristic of the left and right hemispheres of the brain is relevant to this discussion. Left-brain thinking (verbal-analytical-sequential) predominates in our educational system, but this dominance may handicap students (and teachers) whose preferred mode of thinking is visual-spatial-simultaneous (right-brain thinking).

Studies have shown that people tend to favor either left- or right-brain thinking. Preferences are established early in life, and for some, visual thinking is the preferred mode (Witkin, 1962). Such individuals tend to solve problems through predominantly right-hemisphere activity. To illustrate, imagine that it is now 3:40 P.M. What time will it be in half an hour? One person solves the problem in mathematical and verbal terms; another arrives at the same solution by visualizing the hands and face of a clock (Arnheim, 1969).

Although our society values more highly the verbal and analytical skills of left-hemisphere thinking, we need and use both hemispheres. The hemispheres share information across connecting nerve fibers. In this manner, patterns and incoming information are relayed widely throughout the brain. For individuals who have difficulty putting thoughts into words or understanding what is said, right-hemisphere thinking could be more than a matter of preference in solving problems and processing information. Such individuals need tests that are independent of language skills and channels of communication that can bypass verbal impediments.

To illustrate, in the 1960s and 1970s, when manual communication was forbidden in schools for the deaf, the school day revolved around learning language. Some children (those whose handicaps were caused by damage to the brain rather than the ear) had virtually no language at all, but learned quickly nonetheless. One such child could read a map upside down and showed remarkable talent in art, but was believed to be retarded. I was unable to interest any psychologist in trying to test his intelligence until E. Paul Torrance volunteered to send his nonverbal test of creative thinking (1966) and score the results. He found that this child scored in the 99th percentile when compared with normal children his age (11). No one in his school was interested, however, because "language comes first," and this child remained in the school's special class for slow learners until he "graduated" at age 14.

Cognition cannot be separated from creativity. There is evidence that visual thinking is a crucial and central part of the creative process, according to Lutz in a review of statements by highly creative scientists (1978): Michael Faraday visualized the electric and magnetic lines of force; Einstein reported his reliance on mental imagery rather than language; Kekulé discovered the benzene ring through a vision of a series of atoms linked in a chain and biting its tail like a snake, etc. Lutz also cites a study by Martindale (1975) in which brain wave activity provides evidence that creativity is related to activity in the two brain hemispheres. When people classified as "low creative" were presented with creative tasks, they showed very little brain wave activity in either hemisphere. People classified as "creative" responded with both hemispheres when presented with creative tasks, producing large amounts of alpha waves, balanced nearly equally between the two hemispheres, suggesting that creative persons use both modes of hemispheric thinking.

Assessing and Developing Cognitive Skills Through Art

The above considerations have led the author to an approach to teaching and testing that uses art as the principal medium for expressing and receiving ideas. The reasoning is that this approach could be especially valuable to those who rely more on visual-spatial modes of thinking than on verbal-analytical modes; that certain concepts traditionally developed through language can also be developed nonverbally through art forms; and that the understanding of these concepts can be inferred from art forms such as drawing, painting, and sculpture.

The concepts under consideration are the three concepts said to be fundamental in mathematics and possibly in reading: space, sequential order, and class inclusion. The Bourbaki group of mathematicians have identified three independent structures (i.e., not reducible to one another) from which all mathematical structures can be generated (Piaget, 1970, pp. 3, 23). The first structure is based on the idea of a group and applies to numbers and classifications. The second structure is based on ideas of space and applies to neighborhoods, borders, points of view, and frames of reference. The third structure is based on ideas of sequential order and applies to relationships. Although these concepts of class, space, and order are usually developed through language, they can also be interpreted visually. Although they may seem highly abstract, they are observed in a primitive form in the thinking of normal children as young as six or seven years of age (Piaget, 1970).

Investigators in another field—reading disabilities—have arrived at similar conclusions. The same three concepts appear, in slightly different form, in reports by Alexander Bannatyne (1971), who found that dyslexic children obtain higher scores in certain subtests of the Wechsler Intelligence Scale for Children (WISC) than on other subtests. He regrouped the subtests into three categories: spatial, conceptual, and sequential, and found that dyslexic children, as a group, possessed higher visual-spatial skills (his spatial category), moderate conceptual skills (his conceptual category), and lower sequencing skills (his sequential category). Subsequent studies by other investigators confirmed his findings (Rugel, 1974; Smith et al., 1977). As Bannatyne observed, learning-disabled children often have intellectual abilities of a visual-spatial nature that are seldom recognized, allowed for, or trained, as a result of the current emphasis on linguistic, rather than visual-spatial, approaches to education.

A Drawing Test of Cognitive and Creative Skills (Silver, 1983)

The preceding considerations led to the construction of a test consisting of three drawing tasks based on the three concepts: *Predictive drawing* assesses the ability to sequence and to deal with hypothetical situations. *Drawing from observation* assesses the ability to represent spatial relationships of height, width, and depth. *Drawing from imagination* assesses the ability to deal with abstract concepts, creativity, and the projection of feelings.

Scoring is based, in part, on experiments by Piaget and Inhelder (1967), and by various other investigators who have traced the development of cognition through successive stages by presenting children with various tasks. Although their tasks were dependent on language skills, their observations about stages of development can serve as a paradigm for assessing responses in the form of drawings.

Predictive Drawing. As Piaget and Inhelder observe, adults are so used to thinking in terms of horizontals and verticals that the concepts may seem self-evident. The child of four or five, however, when asked to draw trees on the outline of a mountain, may draw them inside the outline. The child of five or six draws trees perpendicular to the incline. Not until the age of eight or nine do children tend to draw them upright. As for horizontal concepts, a four-year-old may scribble round shapes when asked to draw water in the outline of a bottle. Later, the child draws lines parallel to the base of the bottle even when the bottle is tilted. An older child may draw an oblique line in the tilted bottle. These lines become less oblique and more horizontal until, around the age of nine, the child draws horizontal lines immediately (Piaget & Inhelder, 1967, pp. 375–418). In the drawing test, the ability to represent concepts of horizontality and verticality is scored 0 to 5 points. The ability to order sequentially is also scored 0 to 5 points.

Drawing from Observation. In tracing the development of the concept of space, Piaget and Inhelder observe that young children begin by regarding single objects in isolation. Eventually, they develop a coordinated system, perceiving objects in three directions: left-right, before-behind, and above-below. (One of the characteristics of dyslexia is the confusion of similar letters such as p and q, or d and b, which may be caused by perceptual disorders.)

In the test, individuals are asked to draw an arrangement of three cylinders differing in size and a large stone. Responses indicate whether they know that the widest cylinder is the farthest to the left, the tallest to the right, and so on. Responses are scored for the ability to represent horizontal, vertical, and depth relationships. Like the other test drawings, these are scored on a scale of 0 to 5 points.

Drawing from Imagination. The ability to form concepts, particularly the concept of class inclusion, involves making selections, associating them with past experiences, and combining them into a context, such as selecting words and combining them into sentences. Selecting and combining are the two fundamental operations underlying verbal behavior, according to the linguist Roman Jakobson (1964, p. 25). In his view, the two fundamental kinds of language disorder are linked with verbal selection and combination. He describes receptive disorders as a disturbance in the ability to make selections and expressive disorders as a disturbance in the ability to combine parts into wholes.

Selecting and combining are no less fundamental in art activities. The painter, for example, selects and combines colors and shapes, and if his work is figurative, he selects and combines images as well. Selecting and combining are also fundamental in creative thinking. The creative person is often characterized as one who makes unusual leaps in associating experiences and in combining them innovatively. The creative person has an unusual ability to select and combine, regardless of whether his or her expression is through language, art, or another medium.

Finally, selecting and combining are fundamental to emotional adjustment. The impairment of concept formation is one of the main ways in which neurological damage impinges on thinking. The effects of mental disorder can often be discovered earlier in concept formation than in other thought processes, according to David Rapaport (1972). Impairment may escape detection in verbal expression, he notes, because verbal conventions often survive as "empty shells" even when the ability to form concepts has become disorganized.

To determine ability in this drawing task, subjects are asked to select two stimulus drawings, one from each group, and to combine them into a drawing that tells a story. They are encouraged to change the stimulus drawings and to add other images. Drawing responses are scored on a 5-point scale for the ability to select (content), the ability to combine (form), and the ability to represent (creativity). There are also two optional test items: language and projection.

Ability to Select. There are three recognized levels of this ability. The lowest level is perceptual, the intermediate level is functional, and the highest level is abstract. Joan Rigney Hornsby (in Bruner, 1966, pp. 79–85) found that normal children progress from grouping objects on the basis of perceptible attributes such as color or shape, to grouping based on function—what the selected subjects do, or what can be done to them. Adolescents develop true conceptual groupings on the basis of class— abstract, invisible attributes. In Hornsby's study, groupings based on perceptual attributes declined steadily from 47% at age six to 20% at age 11. At the same time, functional grouping increased from 30% at age six to 47% at age 11 (pp. 80–81).

Hornsby's experiments called for verbal responses. In these experiments, children were presented with pictures, asked to select objects that were alike in some way, and then asked to explain why they were alike. In the drawing test, similar information is elicited nonverbally, in order to determine whether an individual selects pictorial elements at the perceptual, functional, or conceptual level.

Ability to Combine. This ability is based on observations by Piaget and Inhelder (1967), who found that the most rudimentary spatial relationship is that of proximity. Before the age of seven, children typically regard objects in isolation. Gradually, they begin to consider objects in relation to neighboring objects and to external frames of reference, drawing a line parallel to the bottom of the paper to represent the ground and relating objects to one another along this line. Eventually, drawings become more coordinated as children take into account distances and proportions (pp. 430–436). In the test, a drawing receives the lowest score (1 point) if subjects seem related simply on the basis of proximity; 3 points are given for the presence of a baseline, and 5 points for overall coordination. A score of 2 or 4 is given for intermediate levels.

Ability to Represent. The scoring for this ability is based on observations by E. P. Torrance (1980), Piaget and Inhelder (1967), and others who have studied creativity and characterize the creative person as being highly original. Torrance cautions against separating creativity from intelligence, observing that these two entities are interacting or overlapping variables. In the test, the lowest score is given for drawings that are imitative, intermediate scores for drawings that restructure the stimulus drawings, and the highest score for drawings that are original or expressive.

Projection. The scoring for projection of emotions ranges from negative associations, such as life-threatening events, to positive associations, such as wish-fulfilling events. Ambivalent or unclear associations receive intermediate scores. An individual's score for projection is not included in his total score, because this range of scores does not indicate a progression from mental illness to mental health. Nevertheless, this score provides useful information about the person's adjustment.

Language. The scoring for language that is expressed in titles or explanations ranges from concrete to abstract. This score is also omitted from the total score because it is inapplicable to some individuals, such as deaf children who are likely to score low in language regardless of their cognitive skills. Considering language scores separately from cognitive scores also provides an opportunity to quantify any changes following programs designed to improve language skills.

To determine whether these test items were related to age and cognitive maturity, with scores increasing as children grow older, the test was administered to 513 children representing entire classes in nine schools in low-, middle-, and high-income areas in different parts of the United States, as well as to adults. To ascertain validity, scores were correlated with scores on a variety of recognized measures of intelligence and achievement. Reliability was determined through studies of interscorer and test-retest reliability.

The drawing test has served to identify children and adults with cognitive skills that escape detection on language-oriented tests of intelligence or achievement. It has also served as a pre-post intervention measure for assessing progress, as in the case study of Joey, reported later in this chapter.

Developing Cognitive and Creative Skills

For children like Joey, whose scores were below the norms for children their age, remedial procedures were designed in an attempt to improve levels of ability. The art materials and techniques found useful in developing cognitive skills include those which readily serve as a channel for representing ideas: drawing from imagination and from observation, painting using a palette and palette knife, and modeling with clay. The objectives are to widen the range of communication, to invite exploratory learning, to provide tasks that are self-rewarding, and to reinforce emotional balance. Emphasis is on demonstration rather than discussion (Silver, 1978).

Developing Concepts of Sequential Order Through Painting. The therapist demonstrates mixing a series of blue tints by placing a dab of blue poster paint on the upper-left-hand corner of a sheet of paper and a dab of white on the upper right. With a palette knife, she/he mixes a series of tints between the dabs by adding more and more white to tints of blue. The therapist then asks the children to find out how many tints they can mix on their own papers, and to use their tints in painting on the paper below. Later, red and yellow are added to their palettes and the children are encouraged to invent colors of their own. Each time one color is added to another, or to tints of white, a sequence has been produced. This kind of learning through doing can be reinforced by cutting up discarded paintings into squares of colors that can be placed in sequence, such as red, red-orange, orange, orange-yellow, and yellow. Children are asked to put the squares in order from red to yellow, from large to small, from light to dark, and so forth.

Developing Concepts of Space Through Drawing From Observation. To focus attention on spatial relationships, the therapist asks the children to sketch an orange and a cylinder made by rolling and taping a sheet of green construction paper. The arrangement is presented below eye level, in the center of the room. When the children have finished sketching, the therapist asks them to change seats with classmates on other sides of the arrangement, and to sketch it again. To reinforce thinking, the therapist may call attention to spatial relationships, such as pointing out that the orange is on the left when seen from one point of view, and on the right from another. Later, children draw and paint other subjects from observation, including one another.

Developing Concepts of Class Inclusion Through Stimulus Drawings (Silver, 1982). Stimulus drawings are used to stimulate associative thinking and to develop ability to form concepts. These drawings consist of 50 line drawings of people, animals, places, and things. The basic technique is to present the drawings in groups according to category, to ask individuals to select subjects from different groups, to imagine something happening between the subjects selected, and then to show what is happening in drawings of their own. When the drawings are finished, they are discussed. To reinforce the ability to select and associate on the basis of class or function, the therapist scrambles the stimulus drawings and presents tasks, such as "Find the ones that belong together" or "This drawing goes with this one. Can you find one that goes with this?"

Developing Concepts of Space, Order, and Class Through Modeling with Clay. The "brick" technique—forming clay into small blocks and pressing them together—is used to build human, animal, and other forms that can be associated with one another. The "slab" technique—placing lumps of clay between parallel sticks and rolling them flat—is used to build boxes or houses. The "coil" technique—rolling clay into "snakes" or balls of different size—is used to develop the ability to sequence. With all the above art activities, the therapist keeps daily logs, and by dating, numbering, and scoring key drawings, paintings, or sculptures, he is able to note changes in the ability to select, combine, and represent ideas; to perceive and represent spatial relationships and sequences; as well as in attitude toward self and others.

Studies Which have Used the Drawing Test and Art Techniques. These procedures have been used in a number of studies involving normal children (Hayes, 1978), learning-disabled adolescents (Moser, 1980), language- and hearing-impaired children (Silver, 1973, 1978), learning-disabled children (Silver & Lavin, 1977), and normal and handicapped children (Silver et al., 1980). The stimulus drawing technique has been used also with emotionally disturbed adolescents, schizophrenic adults, adult stroke patients (Sanburg, Silver, & Vilstrup, 1984), and gifted, handicapped children (Silver, 1983b).

JOEY, A CASE EXAMPLE

Joey, age eight, in the second grade, had been identified as a learning-disabled child with particular difficulty in learning to read. His IQ score was 91, below average, as measured by the Canadian Cognitive Abilities Test (CCAT). Only 2 of the 24 children in his class had lower scores.

As measured by the drawing test, however, Joey was far above average in one subtest and far below average in another subtest. In *drawing from imagination*, his score placed him in the 99th percentile, based on 103 second graders in our normative sample. It was also the highest in his class. On the other hand, his score in *drawing from observation* was in the 14th percentile and was the lowest in his class.

These findings raised several questions: Did Joey have cognitive strengths and weaknesses that had escaped detection on the CCAT? Would art experiences lead to improvement in cognitive skills, as measured by improvement in scores in the drawing test? If so, would improvement carry over to other school situations? Did Joey's responses to the stimulus drawings provide useful clues to attitudes toward himself and others that might influence his cognitive behavior, and if so, would a therapeutic atmosphere lead to improvement?

Joey's remediation teacher was interested in our art techniques. She worked with him individually, once a week for 12 weeks, supervised via correspondence and telephone.

While the art program with Joey was in progress, the CCAT was again administered, as was done once a year in his school. Joey's score increased 8 points, from 91 to 99, whereas the mean score of the 24 children in his class decreased from 113 to 108. When the art program ended, the drawing test was again administered. Joey's score on the *drawing from observation* subtest rose to the 85th percentile, from 4 to 10 points. His score on the *drawing from imagination* subtest declined from 14 to 11 points placing him in the 83rd percentile. How can these changes be explained? Was art experience responsible for Joey's gains and losses? Was it the individual attention of his teacher? There are few answers, unfortunately; Joey's teacher died suddenly, and no one else was available to work with him. When the CCAT was administered the following year, his score had dropped back to 90.

Joey's Drawings from Observation

Joey's pretest drawing is shown in Figure 1. Only one of the four objects is represented in the correct position—the tallest cylinder on the right. Joey had confused all the left-right and above-below relationships and failed to show any depth in his drawing although two objects in the arrangement were, in fact, in the foreground. Most eight-year-olds can perceive and represent accurately these left-right (horizontal) and above-below (vertical) relationships although they often miss the front-back (depth) relationships, drawing all objects in a row. Consequently, Joey's score, in the 14th percentile, suggests deficits in visual memory or per-

Figure 1

ception. Joey's posttest drawing is shown in Figure 2. All four objects are in the correct left-right position. Although Joey's discriminations of the vertical and depth relationships are rather crude, all four objects are relatively correct in their height and front-back relationships.

Joey's Drawings from Imagination

Joey's pretest drawing is shown in Figure 3. It goes beyond showing what his subjects do, the functional level typical of eight-year-olds. It indicates that he selected his subjects on the basis of an imaginative idea, implying more than is visible—the conceptual level. This drawing also shows that his ability to combine subjects pictorially goes beyond the baseline level typical of children his age (someone is upstairs). Furthermore, it also shows that his ability to represent goes beyond imitating or restructuring the stimulus drawings of the test booklet. This drawing is original and expressive of traits that are generally regarded as characteristic of highly creative individuals.

Perhaps the most revealing aspect of this drawing is its projection of emotions. Titled "The Killier" (sic), it seems to represent a doctor operating on a patient who calls out for help even though anesthetized. Upstairs, someone lies in bed, snoring, possibly another patient, possibly someone indifferent to what is going on downstairs. Even though Joey's teacher did not ask him to explain, his drawings nevertheless provide useful information about his sense of well-being. In his pretest drawing, the theme has to do with killing and suffering. Although we do not know whether Joey identified himself with the killer, the victim, or both, the world reflected in his drawing is a painful world.

Joey's posttest *drawing from imagination* is shown in Figure 4, titled "The Dog Chasing the Cat." There are several noteworthy differences from his pretest drawing. First, the world it reflects is no longer painful. Although the cat is being chased, it does not seem to be suffering. Thus one change was noted in Joey's projection score, no longer the expression of intense feelings of distress.

Another change is in the form of Figure 4: a house is in the background, a wall in front of the house, a tree in front of the wall, and the chase in front of the tree—spatial concepts that are unusual in drawings by eight-year-olds. Thus, there was a gain in score in *ability to combine*.

This gain was offset by lower scores in *ability to select* and *ability to represent*. Joey seems to have selected the dog and cat on the functional level, simply showing what they do. Furthermore, they seem static and

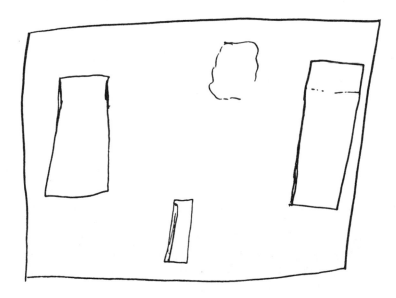

Figure 2

Figure 3

emotionally flat compared to what is going on in his pretest drawing. Was this decrease in expressiveness and creativity the price paid for Joey's gain in spatial skills?

Answers may lie in the drawing Joey produced in his last art session, the week before the posttest was administered. It is shown in Figure 5, "Seeing an Elephant in the Woods." For this drawing, a response to the stimulus drawings, Joey selected the elephant, the woods, and the mountain climber. The climber in the stimulus drawing is young, but in Joey's drawing he is elderly, wears dark glasses, and climbs a tree, looking in the wrong direction for the elephant, which is behind the climber.

Joey's drawing contradicts his title: the man could not see the elephant, nor could the elephant be seen from the airplane. The trees would hide it from view even if Joey had provided the plane with windows. Like his pretest *drawing from imagination*, this drawing scored in the 99th percentile, suggesting that Joey's expressiveness was still intact, but that he was still burdened by feelings of frustration and isolation.

Concluding Observations

Joey seems to have had cognitive strengths and weaknesses that escaped detection on the CCAT but were evident on the drawing test. Although his scores on the CCAT were below average; his scores on the drawing test were far above average in creativity and in the ability to associate and form concepts, as measured by the drawing-from-imagination subtest. On the other hand, his scores were far below average in the drawing-from-observation subtest, indicating that he had deficits in spatial thinking.

Figure 4

Seeing an Elephant in the Woods!

Figure 5

These results suggest that the drawing test can be useful in assessing cognitive skills which are fundamental in mathematics and reading, and which consequently can affect a child's self-image and self-esteem.

Joey improved in the ability to perceive and to represent spatial relationships, apparently as a result of the remedial art program. Although his gains were evident in his posttest scores, and suggested by the gains in his second CCAT scores, there was no evidence of carryover to other school learning. The art program consisted of 12 weekly sessions, not much time to expect transfer of learning from one situation to another. Perhaps a year-long program with pre- and posttests in reading and mathematics would clarify the usefulness of the cognitively based art procedures.

Evaluated for projection of emotions, Joey's drawings provide clues to feelings about himself and others in his world. Suffering and frustration are the themes which began with his pretest and recurred in his post-program responses to the stimulus drawings. Unfortunately, the teacher who worked with him had no training in art therapy, and it was never possible for us to meet, since we lived far apart. Consequently, her supervision was restricted to correspondence and long-distance phone calls; therefore, no psychotherapy could be attempted.

What if an art therapist had been able to work with Joey throughout the school year?—a rhetorical question without an answer, offered as a basis for and encouragement of further research, both with the drawing test and with art techniques based on cognitive development.

REFERENCES

Arnheim, R. *Visual thinking*. Berkeley: University of California Press, 1969.

Bannatyne, A. *Language, reading and learning disabilities*. Springfield, IL: Charles C Thomas, 1971.

Bruner, J. S. *Studies in cognitive growth*. New York: John Wiley and Sons, 1966.

Furth, H. Research with the deaf. *Volta Review*, 1966, *68*, 34–56.

Hayes, K. The relationships between drawing ability and reading scores. Unpublished master's thesis, College of New Rochelle, 1978.

Jakobson, R. Linguistic typology of aphasic impairment. In A. de Reuck & M. O'Connor (Eds.). *Disorders of language*. Boston: Little, Brown, 1964.

Lutz, K. *The implications of brain research for learning strategies and educational practice*. ERIC ED 163 068, 1978.

Martindale, C. What makes creative people different. *Psychology Today*, 1975, *9*, 44–50.

Moser, J. Drawing and painting and learning disabilities. Unpublished doctoral dissertation, New York University, 1980.

Piaget, J. *Genetic epistemology*. New York: Columbia University Press, 1970.

Piaget, J., & Inhelder, B. *The child's conception of space*. New York: W. W. Norton, 1967.

Rapaport, D. *Diagnostic psychological testing*. New York: International Universities Press, 1972.

Rugel, R. P. WISC subtest scores of disabled readers. *Journal of Learning Disabilities*, 1974, *7*(1), 48–52.

Sandburg, L., Silver, R. A., & Vilstrup, K. The stimulus drawing technique with adult psychiatric patients, stroke patients, and in adolescent art therapy. *Art Therapy*, 1984, *1*(3), 132–140.

Silver, R. A. *Cognitive skill development through art activities*. New York State Urban Education Project Report no. 147232101. ERIC ED 084 745, 1973.

Silver, R. A. Using art to evaluate and develop cognitive skills. *American Journal of Art Therapy*, 1976, *16*(1), 11–19.

Silver, R. A. *Developing cognitive and creative skills through art*. Baltimore: University Park Press, 1978. (Reprinted 1986). (Available from the American Art Therapy Association.)

Silver, R. A. *Stimulus drawings and techniques in therapy, development, and assessment*, Mamaroneck, NY: Trillium Books, 1982. (Available from American Art Therapy Association.) (3rd ed., 1986, Harrison, NY: Trillium Books [P.O. Box 984])

Silver, R. A. *Silver drawing test of cognitive and creative skills*. Seattle: Special Child Publications, 1983a.

Silver, R. A. Identifying gifted handicapped children through their drawings, *Art Therapy*, 1983b, *1*(1), 40–49.

Silver, R. A., & Lavin, C. The role of art in developing and evaluating cognitive skills. *Journal of Learning Disabilities*, 1977, *10*(7), 27–35.

Silver, R. A., Lavin, C., Boeve, E., Hayes, K., Itzler, J., O'Brien, J., Terner, N., & Wohlberg, P. *Assessing and developing cognitive skills in handicapped children through art*. NIE Project no. G79 0081. ERIC ED 209 878, 1980.

Smith, M. D., Coleman, J. M., Dokecki, P. R., & Davis, E. E. Intellectual characteristics of school-labeled learning disabled children. *Exceptional Children*, 1977, *43*, 352–357.

Strauss, A. A., & Kephart, N. C. *Psychopathology and education of the brain-injured child*, Vol 2. New York: Grune & Stratton, 1955.

Torrance, E. P. *Guiding creative talent*. Englewood Cliffs, NJ: Prentice-Hall, 1962.

Torrance, E. P. Creative intelligence and an agenda for the 80's. Viktor Lowenfeld Memorial Lecture, presented before the 1980 Convention of the National Art Education Association, Atlanta, GA (4 pp.).

Witkin, H. A. *Psychological differentiation*. New York: John Wiley and Sons, 1962.

14

A Developmental Approach
to Art Therapy

Susan Aach-Feldman and

Carole Kunkle-Miller

INTRODUCTION

The developmental approach to art therapy described in this chapter is based on information from a variety of perspectives. These include psychoanalytic notions of psychosexual (Freud, 1905) and psychosocial (Erikson, 1950) development, especially recent observations of the separation-individuation process (Mahler, Pine, & Bergman, 1975). They also include studies of cognitive growth (Bruner, 1964), especially those of Piaget (1951, 1954). An additional and critical frame of reference is provided by what is known about normal child development in art (DiLeo, 1977; Golomb, 1974; Goodnow, 1977; Harris, 1963; Kellogg, 1969; Lowenfeld, 1957; Rubin, 1978). Our developmental approach to art therapy focuses on normal development as the framework for understanding and intervening with clients whose development is not proceeding according to "normal" expectations. (See Table 1.)

Although it can be applied to any population, an art therapy approach based on developmental principles is of particular relevance to work with the disabled. Such an orientation is reflected in the early "art education therapy" of Victor Lowenfeld (1947) and in work with the handicapped by many art therapists (Anderson, 1978; Barlow, 1980; Gonick-Barris, 1976; Henley, 1986; Horovitz, 1980; Itzler, 1983; Kläger, 1977; Kramer, 1971; Kunkle-Miller & Aach, 1981; Livingston-Dunn, 1982; Lonker, 1982; Lyons, 1981; Minar, 1981; Roth, 1978; Silver, 1976; Uhlin, 1979; Wilson, 1977). It is especially critical to think developmentally when working with those functioning at the earliest, presymbolic stages of

251

Table 1. Summarization of Major Theories in Developmental Art Therapy

Theorists	Age of Expected Attainment of Skill			
	0–2 Years	2–4 Years	4–7 Years	
Erikson	Trust vs. mistrust consistency of experience separation	Autonomy vs. sharing (2–3) learning to control and let go	Initiative vs. guilt (3–5) develops right and wrong internalizes prohibitions from parents	
Piaget	Sensorimotor exploration through body trial-and-error process object permanence	Preoperational (2–7) egocentric learns to use symbolic substitutes learns to classify		
Lowenfeld		Manipulative random scribble controlled manipulation named manipulation early shapes	Preschematic representation of a person cephalopod houses/trees/animals no particular schema	
Hartley, Frank, & Goldenson	Exploration and experimentation Manipulation water play, block play	Product-process phase process of manipulation without intention creation of accidental form product itself important, not the representation	Representation of image with intention beginning of fantasy	

Golomb	Delight in action interest in how material moves and feels	Romancing stage use of media as if it had form Reading off stage looks for forms, names parts	Experimenting exploring different ways of doing
Rubin	Manipulation mouthing materials Forming more conscious control	Naming associating to the form Representing representing qualities of object Containing creation of boundaries	
Williams & Wood	Stage 1—Responding to the environment with pleasure sensory arousing art media as a means of motivation learning to trust	Stage 2—Learning skills that bring success able to use basic art tools and supplies shapes beginning to emerge	

artistic expression—a time when neither insight nor sublimation (the two most common goals in art therapy) is likely to be possible.

In order to meet the needs of such developmentally delayed clients, it is necessary to consider not only traditional art media, but also "pre-art" materials (Lonker, 1982). It is also helpful to analyze art behaviors according to levels of functioning, as is done in the "expressive therapies continuum" proposed by Kagin and Lusebrink (1978). A notable feature of the expressive therapies continuum model is the description of interaction with materials characteristic of each level in terms of "media dimensions variables," as well as the provision of criteria for assessing and selecting media, which are applicable to both traditional and pre-art materials. Another useful resource on which we have drawn are the observations of preschool children using all kinds of materials by Hartley, Frank, and Goldenson (1952), especially their discussion of the functions of "process" and "play" with expressive media.

An approach to art therapy assessment and treatment has evolved, which is appropriate to clients functioning at the earliest levels of expressive development. Using a Piagetian model, the focus will be on the "sensorimotor" and "preoperational" phases, spanning birth to age seven in the normally developing child. We focus on these early phases, since, when working with children with severe cognitive and physical as well as emotional impairments, we find that a more detailed conceptualization of this segment of the developmental art therapy continuum is required. Others, particularly Williams and Woods (1977), who first coined the phrase "developmental art therapy," worked primarily with emotionally disturbed children who possessed, however, more intact cognitive and motor abilities.

ASSESSMENT

The assessment of clients who are appropriate for art therapy treatment is determined by the therapist's style, the population characteristics, and the treatment setting. It may be nondirective (Naumburg, 1966, 1973; Rubin, 1973) or may require completion of a series of defined tasks (Kwiatkowska, 1978; Ulman, 1965). For the presymbolic client, the ability to make choices, to express affect through symbolization and/or verbal commentary, and even to use traditional art media appropriately may be limited. Recognizing these limitations, the therapist might conclude that the client would profit more from a structured than a nondirective interview. To ensure against bias, however, we recommend that the assessment of each presymbolic client follow a progression from nondirective to structured. Specifically, we suggest an assessment interview that combines, if indicated, two or three of the following components: (1) nondirective work with traditional and pre-art media, (2) structured work with traditional art media, and (3) structured work with pre-art media. With some clients, the total assessment can be conducted within an hour or two; some may require an assessment process that extends over a number of sessions. At the end of treatment, readministration of the entire assessment interview is recommended in order to evaluate client progress.

1. During the *nondirective segment*, the therapist offers a wide selection of materials, including both art and pre-art media (i.e., water, shaving cream, beans, rice). During this phase, the art therapist allows the client to select the media and to determine activity, theme, and content, if at all possible (Rubin, 1973). The amount of time assigned to this phase may vary and will be determined by the initiative and responses of the client.

2. In the *directive segment*, the therapist presents traditional art media, along with specific instructions. Standardized assessment measures may be administered, like the drawing of a person, house, or tree (Buck, 1948; Koppitz, 1968). Although standardized procedures provide increased objectivity and reliability, the dilemma with the presymbolic client is that such measures may have limited applicability because of the client's poor capacity for symbolization. The therapist may therefore choose to present less advanced assessment tasks, separately and in combination. In designing such tasks, the therapist should be mindful of the purpose—to identify the client's place in the hierarchy of skill development with traditional art media. Activities presented with clay, for example, might range from requesting a variety of physical manipulations (i.e., pressing, pounding, pinching), to forming shapes, to modeling a person. Separate activities can also examine the variation in client response (i.e., dexterity, pleasure) to specific media.

3. Another possible component of an art interview involves a *structured assessment of the use of pre-art media*. The therapist's observations focus on the client's involvement with the medium, in terms of orientation, manipulation, and organization. To evaluate orientation, the therapist can present a variety of qualitatively different (i.e., fluid, solid) types of media and note the response (i.e., aversive, positive). Structured informal assessment tasks can examine a variety of manipulative (i.e., scooping, pouring, banging) and organizational skills (i.e., combining, containing) relevant to the selected material.

Throughout the diagnostic assessment, whatever the task(s), the therapist gathers information about the client's level of skill and organization in the use of materials; response to media properties; use of structured versus nonstructured formats; and his capacity to express affect.

Level of Skill and Organization with Material

In a developmental art therapy assessment, one must evaluate the "complexity of operation" (Kagin, 1969). If a product results, evaluation can be conducted according to relevant knowledge in the area, whether graphic (Kellogg, 1969; Lowenfeld, 1957) or plastic (Golomb, 1974). To gain information about a presymbolic client's skill level with pre-art media, "process" observation is likely to be vital, since efforts at creating a product may be poorly articulated or even impossible.

Response to Media Properties

Kagin (1969), noting that particular "properties" of media elicit specific responses, suggests that evaluations use a continuum of media ranging from fluid (paint) to resistive (clay). A classification of media according to common sensory attributes (Aach, 1981) may also assist in the assessment process. Four categories for classifying media are suggested: "particle," "fluid," "moldable," and "graphic." Each category encompasses both pre-art and traditional art media. For example, the classification of fluid media includes both water and tempera paints, while seed play and collage are both considered activities with particle media. Such categories are useful in developing a framework for charting information about level of skill and organization with all materials.

Use of Structured and Nonstructured Formats

To evaluate the degree of structure or organization required for optimal creative activity, the client's responses to both unstructured and structured formats must be assessed. The therapist can compare the individual's efforts during "high" and "low project structure" phases of the assessment with both traditional and pre-art media (Kagin, 1969). The therapist will look at differences in response to the two formats in regard to: regression versus organization, dependency versus initiative, and attention span. The therapist can also assess motivation to work with the materials in the two kinds of formats. Based on such evaluations, a determination can be made of an appropriate "project structure" for the initial treatment phase.

Capacity for Expression of Affect

Assessing individual levels of affective expression depends on both verbal and nonverbal behaviors. Clients who are capable of being verbal can provide explicit information about the meaning of their artwork. Even with individuals functioning at a presymbolic level, it is useful to inquire about what a "scribble" might be, or what it "looks like," or what manipulating the material reminded them of. Mentally retarded adults have demonstrated the ability to produce "named associations" related to age-appropriate issues, such as sexual fantasies (Kunkle-Miller, 1978). This same potential may be presumed to exist in other developmentally disabled individuals as well.

The nonverbal responses of the client also provide significant data regarding affective expression. With a presymbolic client, nonverbal behaviors may be the *only* source of information. The closeness or distance the client chooses to place between himself and the art therapist, facial expressions, gestures, and the position and muscle tone of the body are uncensored affective responses which reveal much about any client. With individuals who do not speak, an observation of nonverbal behaviors provides useful information regarding both positive and negative reactions to the environment. Nonverbal behaviors can be reduced to their most basic elements by categorizing them according to sensory modality. In order to assess a client's preferred mode, visual, auditory, tactile, kinesthetic, olfactory, and gustatory experiences can be presented, and responses noted.

Assessment of a client's responsiveness to various stimuli is essential, since the ultimate concern is development of treatment strategies that will attract the client's attention and continue to stimulate interest. For instance, a client who is observed to exhibit an auditory form of self-stimulation (i.e., making inarticulate sounds, talking to himself) may respond positively to auditory stimuli presented by the art therapist (i.e., pounding clay, tapping markers on paper, or clapping hands). With disabled individuals, one or more sensory avenues may be impaired, so that it is necessary to identify which are "open" and therefore amenable to therapeutic intervention. The therapist may observe, for example, that the client demonstrates a more positive orientation to a particular modality (i.e., touch versus sight) or to particular variations in a modality (i.e., wet versus dry substances).

TREATMENT: THE SENSORIMOTOR PHASE

Sensorimotor is the first phase of development identified by Piaget, normally spanning the time between birth and age two. This early phase includes the essentials of motor, cognitive, and emotional growth upon which subsequent development is based. During this phase, the normally developing infant evolves from a totally undifferentiated state to one with greater clarity of sensations and perceptions, as well as a refinement of reflexes and movements. By the end of the phase, the individual acquires a variety of simple schemes, differentiates between self and other, and derives a basic understanding of cause and effect. The differentiation of self and other emerges through establishment of a close attachment and a trusting relationship. Knowledge of cause-and-effect relationships emerges from repeated interactions with the primary caretaker and with objects like toys and materials. The understanding of cause and effect and an active involvement in investigation of the environment signal the completion of the sensorimotor phase. When each aspect of development in this phase is realized, the child acquires what Williams and Wood (1977) call a "positive orientation to the environment."

Clients of various chronological ages may demonstrate characteristics of this phase, indicating that they are functioning in some areas at a developmental age of 0–2. However, the normal sense of curiosity leading to investigation of the environment, as well as the pleasure derived from that exploration, are often lacking in the developmentally delayed client. Motivation of clients at this stage of development is a difficult task, one which must take into account functioning level, interests, and chronological issues.

Materials

In the beginning of the sensorimotor phase, the child's primary interest is in his own body, followed by mother's body. This perspective was developed by the Freudian theorists, who described the body as the first toy. These early body experiences enable the child to learn differentiation of various kinesthetic and sensory inputs, as well as a basic definition of self—"me vs. not me" (Winnicott, 1971). Somatic experiences may provide a necessary conduit to establishing a basic tolerance, comfort, and familiarity with various sensations and movements, for clients of all ages. Movements that are first practiced without materials (opening and closing hands, squeezing) can subsequently become appropriate actions for manipulating materials.

Development of play on a kinesthetic level can be a catalyst for the exploration and manipulation of materials. This process may need to begin with the introduction of pre-art media. (See Figure 1.) The primary objective of interactions with pre-art media is to "expand sensory, perceptual and motor horizons" (Wilson, 1977, p. 87). Such materials are often essential, since many clients at a sensorimotor level of development demonstrate "resistance to external stimuli" and need simpler steps "to more complex stimuli" (Wilson, 1977, p. 89). Lonker (1982) believes that such materials help to decrease resistance by providing successive approxima-

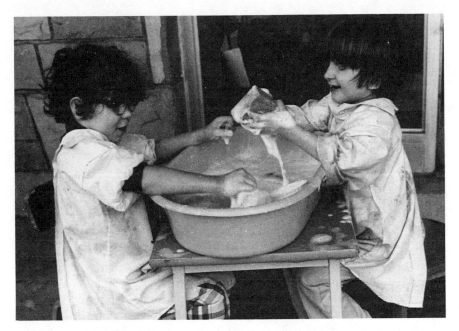

Photo by Susan Aach-Feldman

Figure 1

tions to the properties of traditional art media. Available pre-art materials include safe (digestible) and manipulable items like: "flour, cornstarch, salt, scent extracts, cornmeal, oatmeal, pudding, jello, shaving cream, crazy foam, sand paper, fur, feathers, beans, noodles, spaghetti, sand, water, etc." (Lonker, 1982, p. 14). For individuals with severe deficits in cognitive or ego functioning, the use of pre-art materials may need to be restricted. For example, a severely retarded individual may not be able to understand why smearing pudding is permissible during the treatment session, but not at mealtime.

Interest in traditional art media usually begins near the end of the sensorimotor phase. The focus on sensation and movement noted in earlier efforts with materials is replicated in initial efforts with crayons and paints. Since some clients may demonstrate a tendency to mouth and ingest media, evaluation of their safety is essential. Materials should be introduced in limited quantities, as some clients may not be able to tolerate too many novel stimuli at one time. The therapist may consider the full range of simple two- and three-dimensional art materials in selecting appropriate media.

To Foster Attachment and Differentiation of Self, Other, and Object

The client at a sensorimotor phase of emotional development demonstrates many characteristics of a young infant. Owing to a variety of factors, the client's resolution of the developmental tasks of infancy may be limited. Specifically, the capacity for attachment and the differentiation of a sense of self, other, and object may be impaired. Among behaviors indicating a poor sense of differentiation are: (1) poor awareness of people (i.e., severely limited responsiveness and initiative, verbally and nonverbally), and (2) poor awareness of objects (i.e., not setting or recognizing boundaries in use of materials).

In order to develop appropriate therapeutic interventions, even with clients at chronologically older ages, reference to the literature on emotional development during infancy provides useful and relevant guidelines. According to Mahler et al. (1975), development through three stages involves progression from a time of complete dependence (normal autism) to parallel functioning (normal symbiosis) to relative independence (separation-individuation). The sense of differentiation is facilitated through the caretaker's structuring of interpersonal and environmental interaction, which is distinct at each phase of the process. For the client at a sensorimotor level of development, the therapist needs to recapitulate the mother's relationship to the infant. Based on Mahler's three phases, we have identified three phases of work with art materials, ranging from extreme dependency to autonomous functioning, each requiring different interventions by the therapist.

With the client who demonstrates extreme dependency and disorientation, the therapist provides the impetus and functions as the agent for the play process with materials. For example, the therapist might physically direct and prompt the client through simple exploration with a natural material (i.e., beans, leaves). Exploratory movements would include touching, smelling, listening, observing, and perhaps even tasting the material.

With the client who has begun to respond to interpersonal cues, the therapist fosters reciprocity (i.e., mirroring, imitation) in the play process—engaging the client to anticipate and repeat demonstrated behaviors. To establish reciprocal play, use of each sensory modality is relevant and should be prompted. For example, the therapist might "mirror" the direction (i.e., forward, backward, sideways) of the client's hand movements, or of his rhythm while pounding clay.

With the client who demonstrates initiative and reciprocity in the play process, the therapist alternates between directive and reflective roles, functioning minimally as agent and model, while continuing to be facilitating. For example, with a client using a crayon, the therapist could facilitate attention to the mark-making process, could reinforce initiative, or could promote the selection of colors.

The client at the sensorimotor phase requires intensive and ongoing intervention to facilitate involvement with materials. Even though he is realistically very impaired, he can still explore and learn about the world, but it is essential that the art therapist "join into the play" (Rubin, 1984, p. 237) and "be more than usually active in helping the client learn to use . . . materials" (Wilson, 1977, p. 87).

The therapist needs to modify many elements of media presentation, in order to promote exploration in such a client. For example, to increase the range of movement of a cerebral palsied individual, the art therapist might present shaving cream or finger paint in a tray. The fluidity of the medium would increase the client's potential range of stroking movements, while the tray provides a safe form of containment. Aspects of structure to consider include motivation, prompts, practice steps, and reinforcement. Lonker's (1982) discussion of motivation and practice through use of "inherent structure" is useful in facilitating investigation at a sensorimotor level. Elements of media presentation to consider include proximity, containment, adaptation, and positioning. If a client has poor grasp, for example, providing broad-handled implements will be useful. Or, if clay is offered, the most pliable densities should be selected.

To Acquire a Positive Sensory Orientation and Simple Motor Schemes

The integration of basic sensory information and the refinement of a variety of simple motor schemes, typically occurring during the sensorimotor phase of development, is often inhibited with presymbolic clients. Lonker (1982) suggests that the therapist operate as a "guide of the senses," "introducing materials which are less obtrusive to his/her touch . . . [and being] aware of the [client's] sensory limitations in order to develop a trusting relationship." She also recommends the "gradual introduction of each texture or material along with 'talking through,' adding affect to the voice, and gestures" (1982, p. 13). Through this approach, the therapist begins the process of "emotionally desensitizing" the client to initially aversive tactile experiences. The eventual goal is to help the client to establish a positive orientation to a variety of qualitatively different types of combinations of media.

To promote independent manipulation and the refinement of a variety of simple motor schemes, the therapist may first need to evaluate various aspects of motor functioning, using toys and natural substances. Motor schemes typically demonstrated at a sensorimotor level include batting, shaking, banging, mouthing, pushing, turning, etc.

To Discover Cause-and-Effect Relationships

As awareness and coordination of sensation and movement develop through repeated practice with actions and objects, an interest in cause and effect emerges in art activity, as elsewhere. With disabled clients, impaired sensory systems may not provide enough information, or physical impairments may inhibit exploratory movement. The art therapist therefore needs to provide art experiences with "sequence" and "order" (Silver, 1973), where the client can "discover" relationships between cause and effect, like mixing colors of paint.

Case Study: Sensorimotor Phase

Matthew was a totally blind, developmentally delayed four year old, attending individual art therapy sessions. He was "tactile defensive" (aversion to touching and being touched) and had problems in language development (elective mutism), as well as cognitive impairments (severe mental retardation) and motor delays (semiindependent ambulation). His mental age was estimated to be between 20 and 35 months on the Stanford Binet Scale of Intelligence. His emotional development was characteristic of the earliest phase, with poor individuation of self and other and lack of independence or initiative in self-care and exploration of the environment. Higher functioning was believed possible, since Matthew's extensive delays appeared to reflect not only organic impairments, but also emotional difficulties.

Matthew's behavior during the initial art therapy sessions reflected his emotional problems. He engaged in a variety of self-stimulating behaviors (hand flapping), and there was no verbal or nonverbal interaction. Upon presentation of both preart and traditional art media, Matthew screeched, cried, and withdrew his hands. Since self-directed activity was minimal, the art therapist used a structured approach for treatment intervention. Temporal boundaries of the session were indicated through songs at the outset, such as "This is Art Time," and at the end, such as "Goodbye Art Time." Also using song, each individual present—Matthew and the therapist—was indicated physically and named. The rationale for such song activities was to foster identification and differentiation of the event (i.e., art) and the individual (therapist). Over a nine-month period, Matthew progressed from responding with screeches and hand flapping, to rocking in rhythm to the songs, to verbalization of segments of the "temporal" songs. For example, the therapist would say, "This is . . . " and Matthew would respond, "art time."

Following the initial greeting, the therapist focused on playful activities that would stimulate the expression of positive affect and encourage the development of trust. Such games included hugging, stroking, tickling, knee bouncing, touching, etc. Sometimes music was used here too, such as singing "Eentsy, Weentsy Spider" while making gentle tickling movements on Matthew's leg, trunk, and arm (cf. Figure 2). These activities focused on touch and movement involving Matthew's and the therapist's body, rather than materials. Though the therapist functioned as agent in the process, Matthew's initiative was invited by waiting for a response after each play trial. After about three months, Matthew began to indicate enjoyment when playing a variety of games. Subsequently, during the "pause period" following each play trial, he began to make movements or sounds that the therapist interpreted as a request for the activity to be repeated. The therapist then began to wait for Matthew's "request" before repeating a game. The emergence of this "requesting behavior" was seen as a major step toward beginning reciprocal play and comprehending cause-effect relationships.

Efforts to reduce Matthew's tactile defensiveness utilized pre-art media. The therapist introduced a variety of qualitatively different materials over time, including water (fluid), shaving cream (moldable), and seeds (par-

Photo by Lynn Johnson

Figure 2

ticle). Through hand-over-hand direction and the use of song, a variety
of exploratory movements were encouraged, such as batting, stroking,
and patting. Over a period of nine months, Matthew began to engage in
self-directed exploration of fluid media, such as water. Matthew also began
to tolerate structured exploration of other types of media. A decrease in
screeching and crying behavior was noted, though resistance continued
in efforts to withdraw his hands when the therapist was not directing his
efforts.

For Matthew, it was necessary to provide a structured approach in
order to increase an awareness of self and other, to develop an understanding of cause-effect relationships, and to promote self-directed sensory and motor exploration. Through growth being promoted in each of
these areas, Matthew could gradually assume some of the role as "agent"
for the play. As reciprocal play and directed exploration of materials
increased, the incidence of self-stimulating behaviors decreased.

TREATMENT: THE PREOPERATIONAL PHASE

The client at the preoperational phase functions between the developmental ages of two and seven years. The onset of the preoperational
period signals a transformation in the approach to materials, characterized
by discrimination and organization of basic sensory and motor responses.
During this phase, "thinking is not yet part of an organized structure"
(Levick, 1983, p. 32), yet progression toward representation and symbolism is observed. This symbolism is egocentric, focusing on representation of the individual's subjective reality. During this phase, language
is developing, allowing the labeling of thoughts and feelings, thereby
facilitating the therapeutic process. As all of these skills develop, the
individual is both capable and desirous of more autonomous functioning.

Materials

A wider variety of materials can now be introduced, owing to differentiation of self and object, refinements in the coordination of sensory and
motor responses, and a greater interest in exploring and manipulating the
environment. Sand and water continue to provide important opportunities for exploration. Their use as outlets for the expression and release
of tensions is of primary importance. Also, the individual's fascination
with devising routines for organizing and controlling his world generally,
and materials specifically, can be successfully initiated on such pliable
media as sand and water. Activities with these pre-art materials can serve

as precursors for organization and composition with traditional art media. Use of a broad range of media (crayons, paint, clay) now becomes appropriate, though at times redirection of inappropriate responses (e.g., mouthing), modeling, or directed practice may be necessary to facilitate stage-appropriate efforts at investigation. The transition from sensorimotor to preoperational is facilitated by imitation and the emergence of dramatic play, so that art materials can first be investigated through play, before they assume importance for their representational potential.

To Promote Autonomy

The physical maturation that generally occurs between the sensorimotor and preoperational stages provides individuals with the ability and the desire to perform tasks of increasing complexity with increasing autonomy. "Muscular maturation sets the stage for experimentation with two simultaneous social modalities: holding on and letting go" (Erikson, 1950, p. 251). Hartley, Frank, and Goldenson (1952) note that children's play reflects a fascination with such sequences as pouring water or sand in and out of cups, a culturally appropriate manner of exploring curiosity about body products and the elimination process. Emotionally, the individual at this stage is attempting to work through separation from mother, with such behaviors as crying and clinging (i.e., holding on) and negativism and pushing away (letting go). The preoperational individual who is chronologically older may not be so concerned with toileting, but control and separation issues remain important.

Lonker (1982) notes that even severely and profoundly impaired individuals desire some level of independent functioning. Therefore, promotion of independence and autonomy are important objectives for the art therapist. Whereas the therapist previously acted more as an agent for the play process, now she encourages the client to choose alternatives and reinforces initiative. Specific adaptation of the tools themselves may be needed for the disabled client to use them independently, such as attaching a broad piece of foam rubber to the handle of a paintbrush. Similarly, a carefully devised project can result in a successful art experience, building confidence rather than frustration and negativism. To facilitate the client's ability to find and select materials with maximum independence, the storage and presentation of supplies must be consonant with sensory and motor skills. Issues to consider include the proximity of work surfaces and storage areas, the accessibility of supplies (in open or closed containers, on high or low shelves), and the quantity of materials made available.

To Promote the Expression and Differentiation of Feelings

As the individual moves through the preoperational phase, he or she becomes more cognizant of feeling states, differentiating between various affects and their antecedents. Such feelings as anger, sadness, and fear, which were previously generalized as "painful" or "bad," now become separated and clarified. Since differentiation of feelings is not a simple task, the therapist often needs to promote awareness of specific feeling states. This means developing a sensitivity to and an understanding of various modes of affective expression, from a joyful shriek to an angry punch, so that the therapist can name the affect that is being exhibited. For example, the client aggressively punches the clay and the therapist comments, "You are really mad at that clay today." Language-impaired clients may require very specific and concrete examples of the various feeling states. Photographs, especially of the client, showing different kinds of feelings (anger, sad, happy, afraid, lonely) may be useful in the labeling and differentiation process. The therapist can then say, "Point to the picture that shows me how you are feeling today."

The Development of Sensory Discrimination

At a preoperational level, sensory investigation focuses on discrimination and the formation of percepts. To promote sensory discrimination and percept formation, activities with both pre-art and traditional art media are recommended. The client can be guided to observe and identify characteristics like "full" and "empty," using such materials as water or seeds and containers. Using clay or flour and water mixtures, characteristics such as "wet" and "dry" can be examined. The client can be encouraged to perform actions that promote a change in properties. By describing and labeling the client's efforts, the therapist reinforces identification of these concepts. Providing such feedback in a playful manner can enhance attention and motivation. For example, the therapist could improvise songs with lyrics that reflect and accompany the client's efforts. Skills at observation, interpretation, and identification are developed through such an empirical approach to sensory discrimination, as the client plays an active role in the discovery process.

To foster the client's efforts at learning specific manipulative actions, the therapist needs to identify motor skills necessary for the use of various media and then plan appropriate activities. To foster efforts at grouping manipulative efforts into sequences, the therapist needs to analyze the series of actions required for specific activities. Having identified skill sequences to be learned, the therapist can then help clients to practice by providing verbal cues. For example, to glue blocks on cardboard, the client must reach for the glue, spread it on each block, turn the block over, and press it down. The therapist might make directive statements such as "touch the glue, spread it on the block, etc." To teach a sequence of motor schemes, the therapist might also present verbal cues in a rhythmical and musical structure, by suggesting a "Gluing Song." The lyrics, sung to the tune of the "Hokey Pokey," could be as follows:

> You put your finger in.
> You take your finger out
> You put your finger on the block,
> And you rub it all about.
> You turn the block over,
> And you press it down.
> And that's how you make it stick!

Planned arrangements of media and tools on the work surface can also help the client who is learning to sequence actions. If each item is assigned a consistent location, the spatial order can guide the client in correct performance of the sequence.

To Develop the Capacity for Symbolization

For the presymbolic client, the development of symbolization is dependent on the promotion of imitation, association, and approximation. *Imitation* requires the perception of physical or behavioral characteristics and the invention of simple forms of equivalence through enactment (discovery of similarities). These perceptions must be "linked up" or *associated* with the medium or art process, in order to transform them into graphic or plastic symbolic expressions. *Approximation* of the features of people and objects becomes possible, once an association of feelings and ideas with created forms has occurred. The presymbolic client frequently has difficulty with abstract thinking processes like imitation and association. Producing symbolic forms and articulating features is often complex, frustrating, and confusing, because of deficits in motor coordination, ego development, or intellect.

To develop skills in *imitation*, the therapist can promote simulation of life experiences in the manipulation and use of materials. For example, using dramatic play, the therapist may assist the client to imitate events (eating), objects (car), or people (mother) (cf. Golomb, 1974, pp. 5–7; Rubin, 1978, p. 38). Through imitative play using gesture and sound, the client can practice simulating ideas, events, and objects. In this way, the client can relate a "form" with an experience or idea and begin to understand the process of representation and abstraction. The process of imitation, therefore, provides a mechanism for relating form and idea, the first step toward symbolization.

The presymbolic client may also require direction and support from the therapist to *associate* known feelings, objects, and events with art media, process, or product. To facilitate the development of associations, the therapist can focus on visual, tactile, and kinesthetic aspects of the art experience. For example, crayon taps may remind the client of raindrops, or the colors brown and red may be associated with peanut butter and jelly or autumn leaves. A focus on lines or shapes can also elicit associations, like faces, objects, or animals.

Finally, it is necessary to foster skills at *approximation* in order to promote symbolic art production. Underlying such approximation is the discrimination of qualitative and quantitative characteristics of significant items. To assist emotionally disturbed, mentally retarded clients, Roth (1978) provided three-dimensional models as "conceptual references." She used models to define specific attributes of objects the client showed an interest in representing.

Approximation is also dependent on knowledge of manipulative techniques. The presymbolic client is often inexperienced in creating particular shapes and forms. To encourage the representation of features and properties, directive teaching of specific manipulative techniques may be required. For example, when a totally blind child wanted to make a puppet, he needed to learn simple techniques for construction using papier-mâché. When skills at symbol formation are limited owing to motor impairments, the therapist should evaluate media selected and modify project structure. For example, if modeling a figure of Plasticene clay is too difficult, the therapist could present a way of assembling a figure with Baker's clay. The wedge of clay could be sliced into six segments and distinct body parts identified by the client. Then, using even gross movements, the connections and placement of parts could be attempted.

Case Study: Preoperational Phase

This is the story of Henry, a case study demonstrating the emergence of symbolism. Typically, case studies focus on the progression of client improvement, without specific examination of the therapeutic strategies employed. The following case example demonstrates therapeutic interventions appropriate for a preoperational child, while tracing the client's transition from presymbolic play to symbolic expression.

Henry was a five-year-old child who was developmentally delayed. He was admitted as an inpatient to a psychiatric hospital, with the following presenting problems: failure to develop speech (delayed language), delayed self-help skills (encopresis), and a high level of anxiety in unfamiliar situations and with unfamiliar adults. Although his mental age was three years, 11 months, he presented emotional issues common to a younger child, such as separation anxiety, negativism, and battles for control. Henry demonstrated potential, yet his language and emotional disabilities were preventing development.

Henry's behaviors during the initial art therapy sessions were indicative of his emotional difficulties. He ran away from the art therapist, avoided eye contact, refused to look at the art materials, and lay on the floor, covering his face with his hands. Although the first step in any therapeutic relationship is the establishment of trust, with this particular child this basic goal was even more significant. Respecting his need for distance, the art therapist backed away and began painting at the easel herself. The rationale behind this strategy was to act as a role model and to assess the child's ability to imitate and reciprocate nonverbal responses from the therapist. Henry nonverbally gestured toward the easel and then initiated painting. He smeared brown paint and then experimented by overlapping additional colors in shapeless forms (Figure 3). His motor schemes were

Figure 3

those of controlled scribbling, and there was also evidence of emotional issues related to the encopresis (smearing the brown paint).

Once Henry felt comfortable enough to have eye contact, the therapist communicated with him using a "total communications" approach—voice, gestures, and sign language—and sometimes by singing. Sign language was used in order to communicate at his level through a nonverbal mode, thereby facilitating the development of a trusting relationship. Singing was employed as a minimally threatening way of getting his attention and giving direction.

In addition, the context of the communications was aimed at reinforcing language and the concept of associating or "naming." The therapist verbally and nonverbally reinforced whatever Henry was "doing" and "making." For example, "You are making circles. What else could you add to the circle?" The intention was to reinforce creative behavior as well as to promote the development of the next level of manipulative or graphic skill. The ultimate goal was Henry's expression of emotional difficulties, which would presumably be facilitated by the development of symbolic schemas. Because of Henry's difficulty in establishing relationships with others, the ability to represent a human face schema seemed critical. One method of promoting this idea was the creation by the therapist of a primitive mask, which was then used in "peek-a-boo" games. The focus throughout therapy was on the development of skills that would permit the expression and resolution of emotional conflicts. An emphasis on manipulative and cognitive skills, as well as affective expression, was necessary in order for progress to occur.

After three months of weekly art therapy treatment, Henry began to make paintings composed of more distinguishable forms and cleaner colors. He articulated graphic shapes, ranging from a circle to the letter "H" (which he identified with his name), to a house, to a human face (Figure 4). During one of his last sessions, Henry painted the outline of a face with a large black mouth, which he then pounded aggressively with markers. For a child who cannot speak, the mouth is a reminder of his frustration in verbal communication. The pounding was probably Henry's way of symbolically expressing his feelings about his disability. Henry's interactions with the therapist also changed dramatically over the course of treatment, from extreme avoidance to reciprocal interaction. The number of "signs" and verbal communications increased, and Henry's ability to express basic concepts through art improved. His graphic skills progressed from controlled scribbles to preschematic representations (Lowenfeld, 1957).

Henry used art as a language for expressing himself. Developmental art therapy enabled him to make the transition—from exploring without any intent to create a form—to creating basic representational images, which

Figure 4

he associated with himself and his environment, to symbolic imagery, which represented significant affective concerns. Such gains were made through treatment strategies which led to the attainment of the developmental objectives outlined in this chapter. By differentiating feelings, developing motor schemes, and learning to create a basic symbol, Henry was able to improve his ways of handling feelings and of interacting with others.

CONCLUSION

A developmental approach to art therapy, based on understandings of cognitive, emotional, and artistic maturation, has been found especially useful with clients at a presymbolic level of expression in art. The case studies illustrate applications of this approach with two children—one operating at a sensorimotor level and the other functioning in the preoperational phase of development.

REFERENCES

Aach, S. Art and the IEP. In L. Kearns, M. Ditson, & B. Roehner (Eds.), *Readings: Developing arts programs for handicapped students*: Harrisburg, PA: Arts in Special Education Project of Pennsylvania, 1981.

272 *Approaches to Art Therapy*

Anderson, F. *Art for all the children*. Springfield, IL: Charles C Thomas, 1978.
Barlow, G. Editorial—Art therapy and art education: A special issue. *Art Education*, 1980, *33*(4).
Bruner, J. The course of cognitive growth. *American Psychologist*, 1964, *19*, 1–15.
Buck, J. N. The H.T.P. test. *Journal of Clinical Psychology*, 1948, *4*, 151–159.
DiLeo, J. *Child development: Analysis and synthesis*. New York: Brunner/Mazel, 1977.
Erikson, E. *Childhood and society*. New York: Norton, 1950.
Freud, S. Three essays on the theory of sexuality (1905). In *Standard Edition, Vol. 7*. London: Hogarth, 1962.
Golomb, C. *Young children's sculpture and drawing*. Cambridge, MA: Harvard University Press, 1974.
Gonick-Barris, S. E. Art for children with minimal brain dysfunction. *American Journal of Art Therapy*, 1976, *15*, 67–73.
Goodnow, J. *Children drawing*. Cambridge, MA: Harvard University Press, 1977.
Harris, D. B. *Children's drawings as measures of intellectual maturity: A revision of the Goodenough Draw-a-Man test*. New York: Harcourt, Brace & World, 1963.
Hartley, R., Frank, L., & Goldenson, R. *Understanding children's play*. New York: Columbia University Press, 1952.
Henley, D. K. Approaching artistic sublimation in low-functioning individuals. *Art Therapy*, July 1986, *3* (2).
Horovitz, E. G. Case study: Developing the body image of a visually handicapped child. *American Journal of Art Therapy*, October 1980, *20* (1).
Itzler, J. Body image: A developmental, approach for learning disabled children. In DiMaria, A., Kramer, E., & Roth, E. (Eds.), *Art therapy: Still growing*. Alexandria, VA: American Art Therapy Association, 1983.
Kagin, S. *The effects of structure on the painting of retarded youth*. Unpublished master's thesis, University of Tulsa, OK, 1969.
Kagin, S., & Lusebrink, V. The expressive therapies continuum. *Journal of Art Psychotherapy*, 1978, *5*, 171–179.
Kellogg, R. *Analyzing children's art*. Palo Alto, CA: National Press Books, 1969.
Kläger, M. A retarded woman's graphic and verbal expression. *American Journal of Art Therapy*, July 1977, *16*(4).
Koppitz, E. *Psychological evaluation of children's human figure drawings*. New York: Grune & Stratton, 1968.
Kramer, E. *Art as therapy with children*. New York: Schocken Books, 1971.
Kunkle-Miller, C. Art therapy with mentally retarded adults. *Art Psychotherapy*, 1978, *5*, 123–133.
Kunkle-Miller, C., & Aach, S. Pre-symbolic levels of expression: Their relation to the theory and practice of art therapy. In Gantt, L., & Whitman, S. (Eds.), *The fine art of therapy*. Alexandria, VA: American Art Therapy Association, 1981.
Kwiatkowska, H. *Family therapy and evaluation through art*. Springfield, IL: Charles C Thomas, 1978.
Levick, M. F. *They could not talk and so they drew*. Springfield, IL: Charles C Thomas, 1983.
Livingston-Dunn, C. *Functional art therapy for the severely handicapped*. De Kalb, IL: Northern Illinois University Press, 1982.
Lonker, S. *A sensorial approach to art: Pre-art discovery with severely and profoundly impaired children*. Harrisburg, PA: Arts in Special Education Project of Pennsylvania, 1982.

Lowenfeld, V. *Creative and mental growth.* New York: Macmillan, 1947 (3rd ed., 1957).

Lyons, S. Art in special education. In L. Kearns, M. Ditson, & B. Roehner (Eds.). *Readings: Developing arts programs for handicapped students.* Harrisburg, PA: Arts in Special Education Project of Pennsylvania, 1981.

Mahler, M., Pine, F., & Bergman, A. *The psychological birth of the human infant.* New York: Basic Books, 1975.

Minar, V. The use of geometric shapes in developing cognitive and perceptual skills. *Prism*, 1981, *1*(4), 12–15.

Naumburg, M. *Dynamically oriented art therapy: Its principles and practices.* New York: Grune & Stratton, 1966.

Naumburg, M. *An introduction to art therapy: Studies of the "tree" art expression of behavioral problem children and adolescents as a means of diagnosis and therapy.* New York: Teachers College Press, Columbia University, 1973.

Piaget, J. *Play, dreams and imitation in childhood.* New York: W. W. Norton, 1951.

Piaget, J. *The construction of reality in the child.* New York: Basic Books, 1954.

Roth, E. A. Art therapy with emotionally disturbed-mentally retarded children: A technique of reality shaping. In B. K. Mandel, et al. (Eds.), *The dynamics of creativity.* Baltimore: American Art Therapy Association, 1978.

Rubin, J. A. A diagnostic art interview. *Art Psychotherapy*, 1973, *1*, 31–43.

Rubin, J. A. *Child art therapy: Understanding and helping children grow through art.* New York: Van Nostrand Reinhold, 1978 (2nd ed., 1984).

Schaefer-Simmern, H. *The unfolding of artistic activity.* Berkeley: University of California Press, 1961.

Silver, R. *A study of cognitive skills development through art experiences: An educational program for language and hearing impaired and aphasic children.* (ERIC Document Reproduction Service No. ED 084 745), 1973.

Silver, R. Using art to evaluate and develop cognitive skills. *American Journal of Art Therapy*, 1976, *16*, 11–19.

Uhlin, D. *Art for exceptional children* (2nd ed.). Dubuque, IA: William C. Brown, 1979.

Ulman, E. A new use of art in psychiatric diagnosis. *Bulletin of Art Therapy*, 1965, *4*, 91–116.

Williams, G., & Wood, M. *Developmental art therapy.* Baltimore: University Park Press, 1977.

Wilson, L. Theory and practice of art therapy with the mentally retarded. *American Journal of Art Therapy*, 1977, *16*, 87–97.

Winnicott, D. W. *Playing and reality.* New York: Basic Books, 1971, 1–25.

RECOMMENDED READINGS

Ayres, A. J. *Sensory integration and learning disorders.* Los Angeles: Western Psychological Services, 1972.

Cratty, B. J. *Perceptual and motor development in infants and children.* New York: Macmillan, 1970.

Finnie, N. R. *Handling the young cerebral palsied child at home.* New York: E. P. Dutton, 1975.

Freud, A. The concept of developmental lines. In Sapir, S. G. & Nitzburg, A. C.

(Eds.). *Children with learning problems*, pp. 19–36. New York: Brunner/Mazel, 1973.

Fukurai, S. *How can I make what I cannot see?* New York: Van Nostrand Reinhold, 1974.

Gantt, L. The other side of art therapy. *American Journal of Art Therapy*, October 1979, *19* (1).

Halpin, G., Halpin, E., & Torrance, E. P. Effects of blindness on creative thinking abilities of children. *Developmental Psychology*, 1973, *9* (2): 268–274.

Haworth, M. R. (Ed.). *Child psychotherapy*. New York: Basic Books, 1964.

Jung, C. G. *Man and his symbols*. New York: Doubleday, 1964.

Karnes, M. B. *Creative art for learning*. The Council for Exceptional Children, Reston, Virginia 22091, 1979.

Lindsay, Z. *Art and the handicapped child*. New York: Van Nostrand Reinhold, 1972.

Lisenco, Y. *Art not by eye*. New York: American Foundation for the Blind, 1972.

Rodriguez, S. *The special artists' handbook: Art activities and adaptive aids for handicapped students*. Englewood Cliffs, NJ: Prentice-Hall Inc., 1984.

Roth, E. Choosing an appropriate candidate for art therapy among emotionally disturbed-mentally retarded children. In L. Gantt, et al. (Eds.), *Art therapy: Expanding horizons*. Baltimore: American Art Therapy Association, 1979.

Selfe, L. *Nadia: A case of extraordinary drawing ability in an autistic child*. New York: Harcourt Brace Jovanovich, 1977.

White, B. *The first three years of life*. New York: Avon Books, 1975.

SECTION IV

APPLICATIONS OF THEORY

It is all well and good to read about different theoretical approaches to art therapy, and to be stimulated by different styles of thinking and of working. But what is the practitioner to do with all this information? Is it best to select one primary orientation? Or is it wiser to use whichever one seems right at any particular moment?

Elinor Ulman's chapter reminds us of the dilemma faced by early art therapists, who felt a need to choose between *art as therapy* (espoused by Edith Kramer) and *art psychotherapy* (developed by Margaret Naumburg). Given these two approaches, both grounded in Freudian theory— one with the emphasis on *art* and one with the emphasis on *therapy*— which direction should the clinician take? Unlike those who saw the two approaches as incompatible, Ulman has insisted for the past quarter of a century that they are not, and she has integrated them in her own theory of art therapy. However, as she details in her chapter, to choose any one road is to sacrifice what might be gained by traveling another; it is not possible to follow more than one simultaneously.

Harriet Wadeson, who entered the field a little later, describes her dilemma as she gradually learned about the many different ways of viewing human beings and psychotherapy. In her chapter on an *eclectic* approach to art therapy, she gives a clear account of how she came to know and to value diverse theories, and how she solves the problem of *which* one to use *when* in her clinical work. Many art therapists, perhaps a majority, approach their work in the fashion described by Wadeson, shifting gears as the situation seems to require. In fact, it seems to me that most art therapists are primarily *pragmatic* in their orientation, doing whatever seems to *work best* most of the time.

In addition to these two chapters, which describe ways of applying

275

more than one theoretical orientation to work in art therapy, there is also a concluding chapter, in which I first review some attempts on the part of others to describe the theoretical state of affairs in our field. Consideration is then given to the importance in theory selection of both participants in the therapeutic situation: the patient and the therapist. Finally, I go on to discuss the pros and cons of choosing one primary orientation versus utilizing two or more, according to what seem to be the most significant variables.

15

Variations on a Freudian Theme: Three Art Therapy Theorists

Elinor Ulman

. . . any particular scientific outlook represents only one possible way of organizing the raw material under consideration [but] . . . one often gets the impression that one theoretical outlook is *the* correct one. . . . one seldom hears acknowledgement that the organizational symbols behind one's outlook are, to some extent, subjectively chosen. We select our conceptual framework not only on the basis of intellectual judgment but also because it is congenial to our way of thinking and because the type of clinical work that follows from it suits our personality. Being aware of this subjectivity . . . introduces a welcome tentativeness . . . (Deri, 1984, p. 18).

Inspired by the above quotation from Deri, I shall try to look into the connection between the theoretical ideas and the personal value systems of three writers on art therapy: Margaret Naumburg, Edith Kramer, and myself. By doing so I hope to promote among art therapists that "tentativeness" that Deri saw as welcome for the psychoanalysts she was addressing. All three of these authors claim, to varying degrees, intellectual descent from Freud, but differences among them have helped to shape the development of art therapy in several different directions.

I shall begin by saying very briefly what I think may be the salient features of Freudian theory that some people find congenial and that

This chapter has also been published as an article in *The American Journal of Art Therapy*, 1986, *24*(4).

arouse the misgivings of others. Then I shall recapitulate some early definitions of art therapy put forward by Naumburg, Kramer, and Ulman. (I shall refer to myself sometimes in the first and sometimes in the third person, depending on the context.) Third, I shall speculate about personal factors that may have entered into the choice of beliefs adhered to by each of these three theorists. And last, I shall present case material to illustrate my own preferred methods and to dramatize the complexity of the issues that must sometimes be faced when circumstances dictate the choice of a particular approach to art therapy.

SOME FEATURES OF FREUDIAN THINKING

What are the key features of Freudian theory that tend to determine people's choice of Freud as a guide to understanding themselves and other people and to shaping therapeutic interventions? (The answer to this question will tell us at the same time a good deal about the subjective attitudes and beliefs of those likely to choose Freud as a mentor.)

Fundamental, I believe, is the concept that conflict is inherent in the nature of man. The human need for reconciliation of opposing internal forces has been recognized under many non-Freudian guises. Traditional symbols such as original sin give way to Freud's new metaphor—the epic struggle of ego and id.

Many people shrink from what they perceive as the harshness of the view that conflict is inborn, preferring to believe against all odds that every individual is born good, but in generation after generation that goodness is somehow distorted by wicked parents or by wicked society. (But who made society?) To some of us, however, it seems that recognizing how hard it is to grow up into a good human being makes for a feeling of compassion toward ourselves and others. It is much less discouraging to view one's own struggles as one's share of man's fate rather than as signs of one's own inborn inferiority or victimization on the part of evil parents or society (the collective parents).

Another aspect of Freudian thinking that attracts some people as much as it repels others is related to the concept of sublimation. The theory of sublimation postulates that humanity's great achievements—in art, science, and heroic self-sacrifice as well as more everyday civilized social behavior—are fueled by sexual and aggressive energies. Is the thought that out of the dungheap springs the rose cause for disgust or for amazed admiration? For those who find Freud's thinking congenial, the idea of sublimation does not denigrate the rose on the basis of its humble origin; rather, it recognizes in the rose a testament to miraculous transformation.

Inner conflict and sublimation are only two particular facets of Freudian thinking that quite understandably are rejected by many people. Both can be looked upon as corollaries of Freud's basic discovery: the key role of the unconscious in human life. This concept, too, is rejected by many. The thought that one is truly *un*aware of a very important—even power-ful—part of oneself is frightening and therefore not easy to accept. Acceptance entails, among other things, a high tolerance of ambiguity.

Insofar as the three art therapists we are considering ascribe to Freud's views, we can assume considerable common ground among them, whatever their differences.

THREE THEORIES OF ART THERAPY

Naumburg

Although both Naumburg and Kramer relied on psychoanalytic insights, the divergence between these two theorists (in the areas of both practice and theory) tended to widen in the course of time. A knowledgeable friend once remarked that Naumburg took the psychoanalytic patient off the couch and stood him in front of an easel. The consequences of her doing so were far-reaching. In Naumburg's own words, art therapy as she practiced it based

> . . . its methods on releasing [the unconscious by means of] spontaneous art expression; it has its roots in the transference relation between patient and therapist, and on the encouragement of free association. It is therefore closely allied to psychoanalytic thera-py . . . (Naumburg, 1958a, p. 516).
> . . . Treatment depends . . . on a continuous effort to obtain [the patient's] own interpretation of [his or] her symbolic designs. . . . The images produced are a form of communication between patient and therapist; [they] constitute symbolic speech (Naumburg, 1958b, p. 561).

Here I want to state parenthetically my opinion that Naumburg's professed application of psychoanalytic techniques in art therapy is not to be taken entirely at face value. In particular, she speaks somewhat loosely of *free association*; what she reports sounds more like *conscious interpretation* by her patients of their art products. They are not asked to make the difficult attempt to abandon censorship of speech that is demanded of the analysand. Likewise, what she terms *transference* often sounds more like a *therapeutic alliance* between herself and a patient.

Naumburg (1958a) cited the advantages of introducing painting and clay modeling into psychoanalytically oriented psychotherapy as follows:

First, it permits the direct expression of dreams, fantasies, and other inner experiences that occur as pictures rather than words. Second, pictured projections of unconscious material escape censorship more easily than do verbal expressions, so that the therapeutic process is speeded up. Third, the productions are durable and unchanging; their content cannot be erased by forgetting, and their authorship is hard to deny (p. 512). Fourth, the resolution of transference is made easier. "The autonomy of the patient is encouraged by his growing ability to contribute to the interpretation of his own creations" (p. 514). Thus, art is seen as an added ingredient that makes possible an improved and streamlined psychoanalytic procedure; Naumburg viewed art therapy as a primary as well as an adjunctive form of treatment. The client's experience of the creative process is not even mentioned at this point as a benefit of the kind of art therapy Naumburg had come to advocate.

But it was not always so. About a dozen years earlier Naumburg had written:

> A vital implication [of] studies . . . made on children's art expression as an aid to diagnosis and therapy is that imaginative, creative expression is, in itself, a source of growth and sustenance as well as a language of communication in the life of every individual . . . (Naumburg, 1947/1973, p. 89).

Kramer

Kramer's basic ideas have more in common with those of the earlier than of the later Naumburg. Throughout her writings Kramer finds in art itself the explanation of the art therapist's special contribution to psychotherapy. She went beyond Freud himself in her use of "the insights of Freudian ego psychology to elucidate the problem of quality in art" (Kramer & Ulman, 1977, p. 22), but her understanding of the healing quality inherent in the creative process is firmly based in Freudian personality theory. In an early formulation (Kramer, 1958) she described art as " . . . a means of widening the range of human experiences by creating equivalents for such experiences" (p. 8). Using these equivalents the artist can choose, vary, and repeat what experiences he will. He can reexperience, resolve, and integrate conflict. Throughout history " . . . the arts have helped man to reconcile the eternal conflict between the individual's instinctual urges and the demands of society" (p. 6). But the conflicting demands of superego and id cannot be permanently reconciled. The art therapist makes creative experiences available to disturbed persons in the service of total personality. He must use " . . . methods compatible with the inner laws of artistic creation" (p. 6).

It is to be remembered that three of Naumburg's four books on art therapy had already appeared when Kramer published her first book on the subject in 1958. Later, practices stemming from Naumburg's "dynamically oriented art therapy" (the title of her last book, 1966) came to be known as *art psychotherapy*, and Kramer herself coined the phrase *art as therapy* to define her work (1971). When I began to work on my own definition of art therapy in 1961, these terms were not yet current, but I will use them retroactively in discussing later developments.

Ulman

Almost a quarter of a century has passed since my first attempt to define art therapy in such a way as to encompass both art psychotherapy and art as therapy. In Ulman, 1961, I stated my belief that " . . . the realm of art therapy should be so charted as to accommodate endeavors where neither the term art nor the term therapy is stretched so far as to have no real meaning . . . " (p. 19).

I designated

. . . therapeutic procedures as those designed to assist favorable changes in personality or in living that will outlast the session itself. . . . Therefore, specialized learning that leaves the core of the personality untouched is not part of therapy. . . . The art therapist often must tolerate defensive or escapist uses of art materials but this is never his goal (p. 19).

I then offered a very condensed definition of art:

Its motive power comes from within the personality; it is a way of bringing order out of chaos . . . chaotic feelings and impulses within, the bewildering mass of impressions from without. It is a means to discover both the self and the world, and to establish a relation between the two. In the complete creative process, inner and outer realities are fused into a new entity. . . .

The proportions of art and of therapy in art therapy may vary within a wide range. The completion of the artistic process may at times be sacrificed to more immediate goals. Stereotyped, compulsive work used to ward off dangerous emotions must sometimes be permitted. Communication and insight may take priority over development of art expression. On the other hand, where no fruitful consolidation of insight can be foreseen, the exposure of conflicts may be deliberately avoided in favor of artistic achievement. (p. 20).

DISCUSSION

Younger readers need to be reminded that in the 1950s it was relatively easy for Naumburg and Kramer each to assert that her own views and procedures represented all that art therapy was or ought to be. But as early as 1961, when I first put forward what was intended as a comprehensive definition of art therapy, it seemed clear that no discussion of psycho-analytically based art therapy could afford to ignore the divergent ideas of both these thinkers.

Although Naumburg and Kramer both leaned heavily on Freudian personality theory as the basis for understanding people's psychological needs, they saw the implications of Freudian theory for the *practice of art therapy* quite differently. Kramer subscribed more fully to Freudian *principles*, but it was Naumburg who emulated the psychoanalyst's *techniques*. Kramer developed her own methods of eliciting the most effective possible art, in the name of therapeutic gains for her young clients.

SUBJECTIVE FACTORS IN THE DEVELOPMENT OF THEROY

What personal attitudes of Naumburg, Kramer, and Ulman are likely to have played a part not only in their general choice of Freudian views but also in their development of art therapy theory on the basis of those views?

Contrasts Between Naumburg and Kramer

Naumburg, who was born in 1890, grew up in New York, where her immigrant father had become a successful businessman. Her parents were of their time, and it was left to Margaret's generation to rebel against the rigid conventionality of their late-nineteenth-century beginnings. Perhaps this helps to account for the embattled quality evident throughout Naumburg's writings. In both her early career as an educator and her later career as a therapist, she tilted against the establishment, whether academic or psychiatric (Thomas Frank in Detre et al., 1983, p. 114).

Naumburg's education and experience seem to have helped incline her toward eclecticism. (She was a critical thinker who made her own synthesis of ideas from various sources, not an idea-hopper flitting from one theoretical notion to another.) Perhaps it was just chance that Naumburg's first experience with personal analysis was with a Jungian; Jungian ideas were certainly important in her early thinking about art therapy (Naumburg, 1950, pp. 15–34). She later undertook treatment with a Freudian psychoanalyst, and it was largely from Freudian sources that she subsequently derived her techniques: associative work, attention to transference, and the liberation of repressed material. In fact, she acknowledged primary indebtedness to Freud, Jung, and Harry Stack Sullivan (Thomas Frank in Detre et al., 1983, p. 114; Naumburg, 1953, p. 3).

Kramer was born about a quarter of a century after Naumburg. Her early years were spent in pre-Anschluss Vienna. Many members of her family and their friends were engaged with one or another of the arts. Her parents were unconventional people who had rebelled against their own families' middle-class values. Some of their associates were among the younger members of Freud's early circle. Thus, Kramer was familiar early in her life with psychoanalysts and their ideas. Later her own analysis was along orthodox Freudian lines. While she is open to the later theoretical developments springing from ego psychology, Kramer has never subscribed to any of the schools of thought that repudiated substantial portions of Freud's teaching.

A very important key to the ideas Kramer and Naumburg espouse lies in the place held by *art* in the life of each. Kramer is first and foremost an artist; painting has been the abiding passion of her entire life. Small wonder, then, that artistic sublimation, which has been such an important reward of her chosen lifework, should appear as the cornerstone of her beliefs about what makes art therapy work. Her primary commitment to art also helped to make her happy with the role of adjunctive therapist, for unlike that of a primary therapist, this role left her free to devote four out of every 12 months exclusively to painting. (Some adherents of Kramer's general thinking do not agree with her view that art as therapy is an adjunctive therapy, that it cannot stand alone as a primary form of treatment.)

Naumburg knew a great deal about art and art history, and her responses to the art of her own time were knowledgeable and sensitive (Thomas Frank in Detre et al., 1983, pp. 112–113). Also, she undoubtedly learned much from observing the work of her sister, Florence Cane, at the Walden School (Cane, 1951/1983). Thus, Naumburg was able to introduce the teaching of art into her work as a therapist when she deemed it appropriate (see, for example, Naumburg, 1966, p. 131). She also recognized that art therapy often enhanced the quality of a patient's art because it released the same unconscious forces operative in all art (Naumburg, 1953, p. 7). Most of the illustrations she chose for her art therapy publications are expressive artworks—far different from the impoverished stick figures that today sometimes suffice (or are even encouraged) in art psychotherapy.

Despite Naumburg's understanding of art, her primary identity was not that of an artist. She has been described as "an educator who became a psychologist and an art therapist" (Carolyn Refsnes Kniazzeh in Detre et al., 1983, p. 115). Naumburg came to view art therapy as an independent mode of treatment that offered numerous advantages over the "talking cure," where treatment depended entirely on verbal exchange. In her later years she yearned for recognition as a psychotherapist, especially in psychoanalytic circles. The role of primary therapist, with its implied responsibility 365 days a year, suited her to a tee, for *art therapy* was in any case central to her life.

Ulman's Background

My own personal history and inclinations were, of course, likewise influential in the development of my beliefs about art therapy. I am about five years older than Edith Kramer, and we entered the art therapy field at approximately the same time.

I grew up in Baltimore. My parents were middle-class liberals, and most of their associates were teachers and professional people. I was the first member of the immediate family to become an artist; painting was my first profession and my main occupation for about eight years. In 1966, explaining my emphasis on particular aspects of art therapy, I wrote, "When I started working in a psychiatric clinic in the early 1950's, I envisioned myself as a potential art *teacher*, not as an art *therapist*" (p. 9).

I add today that my landing in a psychiatric setting at all was fortuitous. I was an artist but, having become blocked in my painting, was earning my living in ways unrelated to art. Homesick for the world of art and artists, I looked for a career with a legitimate relation to art even if I remained unable to resume being a painter myself.

I went on (in 1966) to say the following:

> Guided by the new approaches to art education enunciated by such writers as Florence Cane (1951) and H. Schaefer-Simmern (1948), I wanted to be the kind of art teacher I wished I had had. Naumburg stood alone at that time as a spokesman of psychoanalytically oriented art therapy. I did not feel qualified to follow in her footsteps, but was pleased and excited when some of the clinic patients led me a little way along that road. A much larger number of my patients, however, did not try to translate the symbolic content of their pictures into words, yet it seemed to me that they too were getting something valuable from their work in art that nothing else could supply. . . . It was eight years later that Edith Kramer's book *Art Therapy in a Children's Community* [1958] was published. . . .

Kramer analyzed from the vantage point of Freudian theory the place of the arts in the emotional economy both of the individual and of society. The subtle relationships between psychoanalytic and artistic insights began to come clear to me, and I was provided with theoretical backing for my unarticulated feeling that my functioning as an artist-teacher and an art therapist were not so far apart (p. 9).

At this point I need to mention other personal factors that have helped determine my thinking. First I had entered analysis shortly before my first foray into art therapy. The three analysts I eventually saw, though to varying degrees unorthodox, gave their primary allegiance to Freud. Certainly, my hours on the couch were not devoted to the discussion of rival psychological theories or rival philosophies of life, but it seems likely that my analysts' attitudes exerted influence in my eventual adoption of a generally Freudian outlook.

Second, though I drifted into art therapy specifically because I was a frustrated painter, I am as much a word person as a visual person. My talent and taste for literary expression are at least equal to my talent and taste for the visual arts. I found the world of verbal psychotherapy fascinating and wanted to develop an understanding of art therapy that embraced Naumburg's ideas as well as Kramer's.

Having welcomed Kramer's exposition of the psychological and social functions of art, I made my own formulations concerning the place of the arts in human development.

In the terminology of Susanne Langer, the business of the arts is to give form to feeling, and this is the basic method whereby man creates his world. Every child needs to be an artist insofar as he must find a means to conceive himself and the world around him and to establish a relation between the two. . . . But the task does not end with childhood, and the arts serve throughout life as the meeting ground of the inner and outer worlds (Ulman, 1971, p. 93).

Later, I elaborated further on the same theme:

Cultural history and the developmental history of each human being alike bear witness to a universal inclination toward the arts as a means of reconciling two conflicting demands: the need for emotional release and the need to discover order and impose organization. . . . The artistic process calls on the widest range of human capacities. Like maturation in general it demands the integration of many inescapably conflicting elements, among them impulse and control, aggression and love, feeling and thinking, fantasy and reality, the unconscious and the conscious. . . . The function of the arts has been explored in terms of numerous theories. . . . The common thread uniting these many views is recognition of the inherently integrative character of the arts, that is their power to unite opposing forces within the personality and to help reconcile the needs of the individual with the demands of the outside world. . . . True mastery of life's tasks depends upon a disciplined freedom, whose model may be found in the artistic process (Ulman, 1977, p. 14).

Thus, it should be clear that I came to art therapy from my own experience with *art*, and it should come as no surprise that my enthusiasm for art as therapy happens—for this very personal reason—to be greater than my enthusiasm for art psychotherapy.

However, I recognize the validity of these two applications of psychoanalytic theory to art therapy practice. Art psychotherapy and art as therapy can exist side by side in the same room at the same time, or in the work of the same therapist at different times. In my own life as a clinician I moved between the two, using art as therapy where I could and shifting to art psychotherapy where the situation seemed to call for it.

ART AS THERAPY WITH ADULTS

The following two case vignettes are intended primarily to make clear what I mean by art as therapy and why I have found so much satisfaction in it. At the same time, this material may help to counter a widespread notion that art psychotherapy is for grownups and art as therapy is for children. (Kramer's strong identification with art as therapy and child art therapy appears to have contributed to this mistaken impression.)

Mary*

Mary readily became interested in using art materials. She had no extraordinary aptitude for art, had very little formal education, and showed no signs of unusual intelligence or skill in the use of words. Her first few years she had lived on a farm, then had grown up in an orphanage. She was in her late twenties when I met her in the psychiatric ward of a general hospital; she had been diagnosed as a paranoid schizophrenic, but soon after her admission to the hospital, her more florid symptoms abated.

Figure 1, however, suggests the severity of her illness. In it we can sense the horrifying self-denigration and the violent extremes of her sexual

---

*Some of this case material was published in a slightly different form in Ulman, 1966, and Ulman, 1971.

Figure 1

ambivalance. Other early drawings reflect the childhood stereotypes that she brought to the renewed experience of using art materials. Like Figure 1, they were characterized by extreme rigidity, a quality she came to recognize and deplore in her art.

Gradually, Mary's work lost its symptomatic qualities and took on the decorative charm of folk art. At first proud of such productions, she later disparaged them as "too proportionate," her term for the stiffness and "hardness" she had come to dislike as much in her work as in her personality.

Figure 2 was painted when Mary had been in the art therapy group for about three weeks. She and I were equally excited about it. I took pleasure in her new-found grace as she stepped back to decide where her picture needed another flower. She joyfully declared, "It's the first thing I've ever done in my life that isn't *neat*." She went on to talk about her restaurant

Figure 2

job. She and the other waitresses drove each other frantic because she went into a tailspin if the salts and peppers she had arranged in a certain way were moved around.

Mary developed pride in the originality of the many pictures she made without models or any direct assistance from me. In the beginning, she would beg me to do her work for her and would get very angry at my unwillingness to do so. Then, almost in the same breath, she would accuse me of not letting her do anything her own way. Now she was sorry that her brutal ex-husband wasn't around to see her artwork. "He never thought I could do *anything*," she said. "He took my mind away from me. But it started in the orphanage. In the orphanage everything was thought for us, even time. I have no meaning of time."

Thus, we see that through art, Mary caught a glimpse of her own worth and capability. The flower picture taught her, as well, that she could relinquish her obsessive-compulsive defenses without precipitating disaster. Instead, the free play of feeling, controlled and channeled into her art, allowed her to function more effectively than she ever had before.

Mary's pictures suggest another sacrifice we sometimes make when we opt for art as therapy. The closer the work done comes to *art*, the less its diagnostic value is likely to be. "Bad art always invites speculation about the artist and good art never does" (Kramer & Ulman, 1977, p. 21). Mary's early work, as shown in Figure 1, is a raw, easy-to-decipher presentation of symptoms. Figure 2, on the other hand, tells no more about her than that, at a given moment, she was able to function fully in artistic terms.

What is true in the small world of art therapy is also true in the large world of art.

> Daydream art, self-serving autobiographical apologias, and unintended revelations of pathology inevitably invite speculation about their authors' problems and motivations. Great art, on the other hand, invites us to think not about its author and his experiences, but about our own experiences and ourselves. . . . Every great work of art has a life of its own quite separate from the biography of its maker (Kramer & Ulman, 1977, p. 21).

Mary's story gives justification to the frequently made claim that art can serve the expressive needs of inarticulate people. Janet, on the other hand, was adept in the use of words but used them mainly in the service of defense. Her experience exemplifies the usefulness of art in cutting through the emotional smokescreen some highly verbal people are able to erect.

Janet*

Janet's story is like Mary's in that it exemplifies the aspect of art therapy that depends less on interpretation than on the experience of a special kind of functioning. The artistic process itself is a momentary sample of effective living, providing an invaluable glimpse into modes of thought and action that have wide application outside the artistic realm. Furthermore, an art therapy client may derive potentially useful insights from art experiences neither designed for nor subjected to analysis of their symbolic implications.

Janet's work illustrates this kind of therapeutic art experience. She was a pretty, intelligent, young alcoholic woman. Before joining the art therapy group at the clinic where I was working, she had made many attempts

---

*Some of this case material was published in a slightly different form in Ulman, 1966, and Ulman, 1971.

to learn about perspective and to discover rules that would help her achieve "correct" graphic representation. She was justifiably dissatisfied with the tight, flat landscape she made on her first visit. She was trying, she said, not to get lost in details, not to be overprecise; as a result, her picture turned out to be at the same time both vague and overworked.

My first intervention with Janet was to introduce her to rhythmical exercise and scribbling as a way of searching for more inwardly derived, less conventional imagery (cf. Cane, 1983, pp. 56–80). Figure 3 shows a drawing developed from a scribble about a month after Janet started

Figure 3

attending the art therapy group. The strength, movement, and depth she was now able to achieve constituted an artistic accomplishment. Janet herself translated this into psychological terms, saying, "For the first time I really know what my therapist means when he says I must learn to trust my intuitions." In these words she acknowledged a new experience of inner freedom and a new awareness of modes of action more effective than her habitual overintellectual attempts at planning and controlling her life.

Janet mentioned that the scribble had suggested to her a dress form and that she had placed it in her own preferred position, inside a window looking out. She thus spontaneously called attention to symbolic details that identified the figure as a self-image, but the picture's most significant symbolic association was never talked about. One of Janet's legs had been amputated when she was still a child; her disability dated back to a congenital malformation and was at the root of many severe problems. Janet and the clinical staff were well aware of these ramifications. Their symbolic expression in the dress form, full of life yet immobilized, impaled on its single peg leg, offered Janet little new insight on a conscious level. It seems likely, however, that Janet's enthusiasm about this esthetically transformed self-representation helped her at an unconscious level to better accept her mutilated state.

In another connection Janet remarked, "I'm all id and superego," and indeed the observation was apt—the id drunken, violent, promiscuous; the superego wearing an Alcoholics Anonymous halo and a mask of sweet devotion to helping others. In her experience with art, Janet found at last and recognized some moments of successful ego functioning.

Figure 4 was painted more than a year after the dress form. Its loneliness and chill not only say something about Janet, but also evoke a similar mood in many others. At a modest level, Janet here achieved the quality of art.

Like many adults, Janet readily translated into words the insights derived from her art experience. Insight often accompanies the changes brought about in adults by art as therapy, even though the therapist has not set insight as a goal. We note that in Janet's case it was the formal qualities or abstract character of her pictures that spoke back to her, confirming what she had experienced while making them. Subject matter was relatively unimportant.

This kind of spontaneous verbalization of new insights happens frequently with adults who use art as therapy, but is far less likely to occur with children. Thus, the line between art as therapy and art psychotherapy is more likely to become blurred when we consider art therapy with adults than when we are discussing the practice of art therapy with children.

Figure 4

Possibly this is another reason for the relative neglect of and ignorance about art as therapy with adults.

THE CONSEQUENCES OF THERAPEUTIC CHOICE

Sometimes circumstances other than the needs of a given client dictate the choice between art psychotherapy and art as therapy, and every choice entails a sacrifice of whatever lies along and at the end of the road not taken. Sometimes an art therapist is free to choose within a wide range—a range whose limits are set only by her own capabilities. At other times choices are limited by many factors, including availability of personnel, money to pay for their time, institutional policies, and a myriad of others.

Greta

To dramatize the consequences of choice between art as therapy and art psychotherapy, let us consider two pictures by Greta, a good-looking, sun tanned, blonde woman in her early thirties. She came to the day hospital where I was working only a few hours a week. She was told, in my absence, about an opening in the art group. Greta enthusiastically agreed to the four-week commitment to weekly attendance, the rule that the staff and I had set.

Unfortunately, the staff member who introduced Greta to the various therapeutic activities available did not know enough about either art or art therapy to explain to Greta how different this particular group was from a regular art class. In keeping with the nature of the entire program—it consisted of numerous group activities constantly subjected to group discussion—and because I was available for very few hours each week, we had arrived at a structure we thought would make the most of the limited possibilities. At each session, the group agreed on a theme suggested either by me or by one of them. Art work was then limited to 45 minutes, after which the paintings were tacked up and subjected to group discussion. Thus, in setting the stage for art psychotherapy, we had made it very unlikely that art—and hence art as therapy—could flourish.

On Greta's first visit, the group agreed on an idea presented by one of their number. Draw the animal you would like to be if you were born back on this earth as an animal other than human. Greta was furious about the regimentation, the strict time limit, and the pressure to discuss the pictures and listen to the comments of others. Figure 5 is the eloquent expression of her rage. She called it a "bird of paradise" and claimed to see nothing in it but the beauty to which she aspired! A group member identified it as "the terrible tyrant of the classroom." Evidently he sensed—as I did—that Greta's tightly controlled ferocity was largely directed at me.

It was apparent that the art-psychotherapy character of the group had accidentally revealed the great potential value that art as therapy might have had for Greta. Half regretting that I could not transform the setting into one more congenial to her, I nevertheless looked forward with great interest to further experiences of her power for vivid graphic expression and wondered whether the group would permit her to maintain the massive denial with which she had greeted her first revelation of feeling.

Figure 5

I was never to find out. Greta managed to evade the next three sessions of the art group; corralled by a staff member into meeting her obligation, she showed up for the last session before the Christmas break.

Knowing how hard the holidays often are for people suffering from mental breakdown, I assigned this topic: Try to put into a picture your feelings about the upcoming holiday. Greta was subdued and withdrawn, obviously depressed, quite different from the rather arrogant bird of paradise of our first encounter. She worked slowly, and in itself her weak drawing with all its international Christmas greetings (Figure 6) expressed little.

By this time a change had taken place in the day hospital schedule, and the time devoted to drawing by the art group (which accommodated no more than eight clients at a time) was immediately followed by a meeting of the entire day hospital community—about 30 clients and all the staff members who were available to attend. We decided to carry the artworks to the meeting and pin them on the wall, where they might attract the attention of others and become the focus of the larger group's discussion.

In this setting the role of leader was usually taken over by a young psychiatrist who was a great confronter. He zeroed in on Greta's six-pointed star, asking why she chose a Jewish symbol to hang from her Christian tree. For a few minutes Greta tried to maintain that the Star of David was simply easier to draw because it could be constructed out of two triangles. Dr. Miller pooh-poohed this excuse, he and Greta both knew she could easily draw a five-pointed star.

Figure 6

Suddenly, the floodgates opened. Greta started by telling the community about her father. He had been a fairly high official in Hitler's Germany; as a child Greta knew him only as the warmer and more loving of her two parents. Now, as an adult American with many Jewish friends, she could not come to terms with the knowledge that this beloved parent had been responsible for the death and torture of many innocent Jewish victims.

Then she turned to the special meanings that Christmas had for her. It was on Christmas that her sister had been almost killed in a skiing accident and her mother had coldly withdrawn, leaving all the responsibility on Greta's young shoulders. And what about the loving father? He had been jailed after the war and was awaiting trial for his crimes when, just a year before her sister's accident, he was found hanging in his cell on Christmas Eve.

Dr. Miller was famous for not permitting community members to leave the meeting no matter how urgently they pleaded. Having finished her story, Greta asked if she could leave. Dr. Miller, rendered speechless like the rest of us, merely nodded. The whole group seemed stunned. As we stared at Greta's weak, empty little Christmas cryptogram, I'm sure I wasn't the only one to think of the red heart hanging from the tree as linked with Greta's father hanging in his cell.

This cathartic outpouring was entirely new in the day hospital staff's experience with Greta. It seemed to have resulted from the Christmas theme assigned in art therapy in keeping with the methods of art psychotherapy.

Greta's time in the hospital's 30-day treatment program was almost over, and I did not see her again. From the two experiences we had, there is no way to guess which art therapy approach would have yielded more benefit to Greta. Only one thing is sure: Under the circumstances at the day hospital, she couldn't have both. We had made our plans with the hope of offering the best we could to the greatest number of clients; inevitably, this was not always the best possible treatment for every client all the time.

CONCLUSION

I hope this backward glance at the work of three art therapy theorists will encourage a rising generation of art therapists to become acquainted with the broad range of art therapy practices and to maintain the flexibility that will enable them to choose the best available method in their work with each individual client.

In 1961 I remarked that:

when we talk about cause and effect, art therapists are in the same boat as the rest of psychiatry—mostly at sea. If favorable changes occur we don't know exactly how much an esthetically valid painting or how much a dramatic new spoken insight had to do with it. (Ulman, 1961, p. 19).

Freudian-based art therapy, as it has descended and evolved from the theoretical and practical differences among Naumburg, Kramer, and Ulman, presents great possibilities for favorable change. Yet, we must also face up to the limitations of therapeutic work whatever its theoretical basis. It has been remarked that the net achievement of psychological treatment in general has been to cure the healthy and maintain the sick.

Accepting this as a realistic expectation of our endeavors is perhaps less cynical than it seems at first blush. The sick may be maintained in the desperation of an old-fashioned back ward or in the dignity of a day hospital whose program may offer art therapy among other beneficial opportunities. It is a mistake to underestimate the vast amelioration that may take place short of cure.

REFERENCES

Cane, F. *The Artist in Each of Us* (Revised Ed.). Craftsbury Common, VT.: Art Therapy Publications, 1983. (Originally published, 1951.)

Deri, S. K. *Symbolization and Creativity*. New York: International Universities Press, 1984.

Detre, K. C., Frank, T., Kniazzch, C. R., Robinson, M. C., Rubin, J. A. and Ulman, E. (1983). Roots of art therapy: Margaret Naumburg (1890–1983) and Florence Cane (1882–1952), a family portrait. *American Journal of Art Therapy*, 1983, *22*, 111–123.

Kramer, E. *Art therapy in a children's community*. Springfield, IL: Charles C Thomas, 1958.

Kramer, E. *Art as therapy with children*. New York: Schocken Books, 1971.

Kramer, E., & Ulman, E. Postscript to Halsey's 'Freud on the nature of art.' *American Journal of Art Therapy*, 1977, *17*, 21–22.

Naumburg, M. *Schizophrenic art: Its meaning in psychotherapy*. New York: Grune & Stratton, 1950.

Naumburg, M. *Psychoneurotic art: Its function in psychotherapy*. New York: Grune & Stratton, 1973.

Naumburg, M. Art therapy: Its scope and function in *The clinical application of projective drawings* by E. F. Hammer. Springfield, IL: Charles C Thomas, 1958a, pp. 511–517.

Naumburg, M. Case illustration: Art therapy with a seventeen year old girl in *The clinical application of projective drawings* by E. F. Hammer, Springfield, IL: Charles C Thomas, 1958b, pp. 518–561.

Naumburg, M. *Dynamically oriented art therapy: Its principles and practice*. New York: Grune & Stratton, 1966.

Naumburg, M. *An introduction to art therapy: Studies of the "free" art expression of behavior problem children and adolescents as a means of diagnosis and therapy* (Revised Ed.). New York and London: Teachers College Press, 1973. (Originally published, 1947.)

Schaefer-Simmern, H. *The Unfolding of Artistic Activity.* Berkeley and Los Angeles: University of California Press, 1948.

Ulman, E. Art therapy: Problems of definition. *Bulletin of Art Therapy*, 1961, *1*(2), 10–20.

Ulman, E. Therapy is not enough. The contribution of art to general hospital psychiatry. *Bulletin of Art Therapy*, 1966, *6*, 3–21.

Ulman, E. The power of art in therapy. In I. Jakab (Ed.), *Conscious and unconscious expressive art—Psychiatry and art*, Vol. 3. Basel, Switzerland: S. Karger, 1971, pp. 93–102.

Ulman, E. Art education for the emotionally disturbed. *American Journal of Art Therapy*, 1977, *17*, 13–16.

16

An Eclectic Approach
to Art Therapy

Harriet Wadeson

In responding to the editor's invitation to contribute to this book, my secretary typed that I would be happy to write a chapter on "The *Electric* Approach to Art Therapy." I didn't correct the letter, but added in the margin that this is indeed highly charged work. And so it is. The power of an eclectic approach is the personal nature of its development. Nothing is taken for granted. It is not simply because I believe that many theories have something to offer, nor that any one theory may be too limiting— although I find both to be true—that I choose to be eclectic and encourage my students to be so as well. My rationale is far more fundamental, far more intrinsic to my convictions of what therapy is and what it is about.

The instrument of the therapy is the self of the therapist in concert with the self of the patient. Our basic tools are not paint or brushes any more than they are words. Whatever happens in art therapy occurs within the container of the transference relationship (psychoanalytic theory: Moore & Fine, 1968). Margaret Naumburg (1966) was particularly emphatic in making this point. I believe, as well, that the therapeutic endeavor is a creative enterprise. Since the selfhood of each therapist is unique, each clinician's creative work in this realm will bear the imprimatur of that self, with all its life experience influencing each moment of the therapeutic relationship. Just as my painting will be different from yours (even though we may have attended the same art school), so we will practice therapy differently, each according to our own style, even though we may share similar views of psychodynamics and treatment objectives.

Each existing theory orients us somewhat differently. No doubt these theories were developed in consonance with the unique needs and life experiences of their authors. It follows, therefore, that if we are to make the most of *our* own unique potentialities, it is up to us to select and synthesize from among the many theories and treatment models available to us in accordance with *our* needs and world views.

It is important to note that this is an active and ongoing process. Being eclectic does not mean slipping into a ready-made garment and going to work. The process requires far more creativity. We may select a hat from one store, a sweater from another. We hope the shoes won't clash with the rest of the ensemble. We might outgrow them or discard a style that pinches for one that is more comfortable. It is in this way that we create ourselves as art therapists. Nevertheless, it is not necessary for us to weave our own garments. We can select ready-made slacks and shorten them only if they are too long. To switch metaphors, we don't have to reinvent the wheel.

When we look at the theories that we wear, however, we must recognize them for what they are. They are not skin or blood or bones. They are made up to serve a purpose. For example, there is no such thing as an id. (Have you ever seen one?) There is only a concept. If that concept helps us to organize our understanding, then it is useful. On the other hand, if we are referring to ''repressed'' aspects of the ''self'' that are more encompassing than ''basic drives,'' we may find the Jungian ''shadow'' a useful concept to express our understanding.

An eclectic approach is a more difficult road. It requires choices. There isn't a unified system into which the complex data for understanding and changing human dynamics can fit. Nevertheless, for me it is the only way. It is consonant with my belief that therapy is growth, and that growth is a mystery. The art therapist participates with the client in the client's growth. And the art therapist must grow as well. An aspect of that growth is the continuing search for understanding, the ongoing refinement of one's thinking. This is an active process of attending to all possible influences, including new ideas and theories.

And the mystery? Ultimately the process of growth is a mystery to us. It is a continuation of the process of creation. As an art therapist I am in a position of awe in relation to that process. As a searcher and a seeker in the understanding of human creation and growth, I must be open to new possibilities.

MY ECLECTIC LAYER CAKE

In a brief chapter such as this, it is not possible to present a full description of the eclectic synthesis that informs my view of art therapy at this time. The best way to summarize it appears to be an historical review of the layers of my own theoretical development.

As I have stated elsewhere (Wadeson, 1980), I began with Father Freud during teen-age baby-sitting stints at the home of my-uncle-the-psychiatrist. I had never dreamed dreams could be so illuminating (Freud, 1900). When I began working at the National Institute of Mental Health, the neo-Freudians who reigned supreme were being joined by the systems folks who were researching family dynamics, which they later published (Bowen, 1961). I read Jung (1959) but found him too spiritual. Later, I was ready for him. I was working with adolescents at the National Institute of Mental Health (NIMH) then and leaned on Erikson's (1950) developmental model.

During the midsixties I began venturing forth from NIMH and a medical model into more humanistic realms. I read in existential philosophy (Heidegger, 1962, 1964; Jaspers, 1952, 1963; Kierkegaard, 1957) and began to replace the idea of psychic determinism with the notion of individual responsibility for creating one's life. I began to see perception as an active, selective process. This view was more hopeful, and therapy took on new dimensions and possibilities for me. I suppose I was always a closet phenomenologist, but in conjunction with existentialism it took on new validation (Boss, 1958). When I changed projects at NIMH and moved from affective disorders to acute schizophrenia, my immediate interest was to try to understand what it was like to be schizophrenic. There are plenty of observations by others of acute schizophrenics, but I wondered what it was like for *them*. So I directed my research to the phenomenology of schizophrenia (Wadeson & Carpenter, 1976). Art therapy was a natural channel for the expression and reification of the inner experience.

Consonant with an existential view was a shift from viewing the patient as object. It became increasingly apparent that the patient was not a constant with a fixed symptomatology. There were patients who behaved very differently in their art therapy sessions with me than they did with their psychiatrist or in the dayroom. Since most of the patients with whom I worked were diagnosed psychotic and were free of medication for research purposes, the shifts in their behavior were often quite dramatic. I began to see how much influence the therapist has. It became clear to me that I could not understand my sessions with patients without exploring my half of the equation. I began to scrutinize the therapeutic relationship.

From a practical standpoint, I found Fritz Perls' (1969) Gestalt therapy helpful. Attending to the messages my body was sending me, I became more self-aware in this endeavor. This was particularly useful during art therapy sessions. For example, I began to notice that at times my eyes would go out of focus. I came to recognize that this signaled boredom or apathy on my part and was almost always related to the patient's enacting some distancing maneuvers. Now, the moment my eyes go out of focus, I interrupt the patient and inquire about what's going on.

I find Gestalt therapy's concept of "disowned parts" an interesting companion piece to the concepts of "projection" in Freudian psychoanalytic theory and of the "shadow" in Jungian analytical psychology. Taken together, these three constructs round out a significant area of psychopathology or malfunctioning. The three ideas do not contradict one another, but rather are complementary, each adding a dimension to our understanding of what happens to those aspects of ourselves we find difficult to accept.

Of the major triumvirate of psychoanalysis, humanistic psychology, and behaviorism, I find the latter the weak sister. And yet I borrow from that approach too. I believe that there is never a session in which I do not use positive reinforcement with my patients. And particularly around sexual issues with couples, I am likely to use some behavioral approaches for restructuring the interaction.

In more recent times I have focused on group dynamics. I find art expression especially valuable in both reflecting and advancing group process. The art activity makes everyone a group participant. Yalom's articulation of group therapy theory and practice has been especially clarifying for me (1975, 1983). Promoting experiences of universality through the commonality that can be readily viewed in the content of the art productions, and the exploration of the here-and-now through art expression, make the marriage of group therapy and art therapy a dynamic union.

Finally, there are two significant influences that form the matrix of human experience and are sometimes overlooked in theories of psychotherapy. One is the physiological. Much of the research at NIMH with which I was affiliated resulted in significant correlations between biochemical variables and psychopathology. Given this information, coupled with epidemiological studies pointing to genetic links for certain clinical syndromes, the possibility of hereditary predispositions in mental illness is a very strong one.

The second influence is societal. It is so pervasive that it is difficult to define briefly. Hopefully, two examples will suffice. It seems to me that most emotional problems stem from feelings of inadequacy or of unworthiness of love. In our society children are usually raised in an isolated nuclear family, are often pushed to achieve, and are seldom cherished just for being who they are. Child rearing is different in many other cultures where an extended family, as well as parents, dote on the growing child. In our culture, therefore, child-rearing patterns along with economic pressures and rapidly changing social values may contribute to emotional disturbance. Whereas the first example deals with etiology, the second deals with disposition. No matter what the treatment, the proof of the therapeutic pudding must come later, in the world in which the patient lives. In some instances, a child may have to return to hostile parents or an adult to the unemployment line. So it does seem obvious to me that both physiological and societal factors must be recognized in our understanding of the people we treat and the treatment we undertake with them.

In sum, I have only alluded to the sources for the content of my eclecticism. Hopefully, the following examples will provide a view of how they come into play in the clinical situation. Please bear in mind, as you view them, that an eclectic approach is not a fragmented one. The pieces that come together from diverse sources must integrate as a whole if the art therapist is to have a basis for understanding the therapeutic process and directing it in a meaningful way.

AN ART THERAPY EXAMPLE

Susan, a bright, capable teacher, was a member of a private practice art therapy group of eight women. In the third month of treatment, the group was discussing their feelings toward me, spearheaded by Susan, who at 34 was amazed by how childlike she felt in relation to me. Others were also animated in expressing their feelings, so I suggested that they all draw pictures of their relationship with me. Figure 1 is Susan's.

She spoke of feeling very young, wanting my protection, affection, and approval, and represented herself as a child close to me with my arm around her. The figure on the right came as a surprise and represents her defiance and anger at being a dependent child. I am no longer with her, and she is larger. I asked her if she was willing to act out her picture and she agreed. First, she assumed the position of the child and I put my arm around her. Then I sat down and she assumed the position of her larger self. She commented that she felt nervous and sort of frightened in the first position, and that the second position felt much better.

Fundamental to an understanding of the theoretical frameworks that I utilized in conceptualizing and dealing with this event in Susan's therapy is a recognition of the facilitating function of art expression. Although Susan had recognized uncomfortable feelings in relation to me prior to her drawing, it was the pictorial image formation process that brought into awareness an unexpected side of her feelings. Therefore, it is important to bear in mind, as a foundation to the approaches to be discussed, the power of art expression as a ladle for dipping into the unconscious

Figure 1

soup. With that as a basis, I will discuss the various theoretical frameworks from which I approached this episode in Susan's therapy:

1. *Freudian Psychoanalytic*. The subject is transference. In her reaction to me, Susan recognized the parallels to childhood relationship to authority and the adaptations that evolved. The therapeutic situation plunged her into feelings of dependency that she had not experienced in some time.

2. *Gestalt Therapy*. The technique I used in asking Susan to "enact" her picture is drawn from Fritz Perls' dreamwork (1969). His view is that the objects in a dream are all self-representations, and clients can best process their dreams by "becoming" the objects in them and thus reown "disowned" parts. I believe art expressions may be viewed and worked with in the same way. In Susan's case, the enactment deepened the "owning" of her feeling states, forming a synergy between the imagistic and the kinesthetic.

3. *Jungian Analytical Psychology*. Both the dependent child and the angry defiant adult bear elements of the Jungian concept of the "shadow" (Jung, 1964). Both these aspects of "self" were un-

acceptable to Susan and were usually repressed, causing her difficulty by being unacknowledged. By bringing these shadow elements into the light, Susan was able to work with them, rather than to be unconsciously subverted by these denied aspects of self.

4. *Developmental*. In Susan's picture and its processing, we can see her move from dependent child to defiant adolescent. By working with her "shadow," she was eventually able to grow into an adult in relation to me, no longer dependent on my approval and no longer angry. She was also able to see me more realistically.

5. *Existential*. Susan recognized her responsibility for her feelings. She was quick to see that her feelings emanated from her perception of me, rather than from anything I was doing to her. With this recognition of herself as the creator of many of her life experiences, she also recognized her power to change them.

6. *Group Therapy Theory*. In Yalom's view (1975, 1983), group therapy should be based on a theory which postulates that humans learn and develop in the context of interpersonal relationships (Sullivan, 1953). It follows, therefore, that individuals can best learn about themselves by examining their relationships with others. There is no better place than group therapy for obtaining this sort of feedback in the here-and-now. Often history taking in groups is not necessary, as the group becomes a social microcosm in which its members display their relationship patterns in the ongoing group interactions. Furthermore, the group often provides an awareness of the universality of one's experience, so that its members feel less negatively unique, less isolated, less alone. Such was the case for Susan in this instance. The pictures made by other group members at this session also displayed dependency and/or anger toward me. The social microcosm aspects of Susan's behavior were represented in her risk taking. It was she who opened the sensitive subject of feelings about the therapist early in the group's life. This was the first time anyone had enacted a picture. Not everyone was willing to be as open or risk as much during this session as Susan did. She demonstrated some of her very significant interpersonal strengths.

LOCKED INTO THEORY

In the next example, my intention is not to erect a straw man to knock down, but rather to present a somewhat extreme example of the problem of being theory-bound. Please bear in mind that the purpose here is not to disparage the use of a well-integrated theory, but rather to point out the problem of narrow adherence.

I was giving an art therapy presentation to a hospital psychiatric staff unfamiliar with art therapy. The senior psychiatrist was particularly impressed by Figure 2, a depiction of a delusion drawn by Vickie, a young woman diagnosed acute schizophrenic. Prior to entering the hospital, she had the repeated experience of a "big black man, a killer" stalking her in a back alley. By drawing a picture of him, she was able to explore her delusion more fully and make more sense out of her confusion over what was real and what was not. Furthermore, the drawing communicated an experience that had previously remained private for this withdrawn young woman. Its expression in imagery and our subsequent discussion of the picture and the experience markedly undercut the isolation of this patient who, prior to hospitalization, had remained shut in at home alone for several months.

But the senior psychiatrist had other ideas about the picture. He saw it as a penis within the vaginal canal. It seemed to me that his classical analytical training influenced him to seek out only sexual symbolism. Is this really the picture's deeper meaning? How do we know? I believe these questions confront us with larger issues of how we approach our work: how we understand the imagery presented to us, the resultant understanding we gain of our clients, and what outcomes these understandings shape in the way we develop treatment goals and the way we relate to our clients. The psychiatrist who interpreted Figure 2 as an image of sexual intercourse probably would have had a different sense of the patient's dynamics than I did. Perhaps he would have conducted the treatment differently and would have related to her around an interest in uncovering repressed sexual conflicts.

I believe it is important to meet clients where they are (fundamental to social work theory and others), and to build an empathic bridge (Kohut, 1959) between the patient and myself. In Vickie's case this bridge served to reach the island of isolation she had created for herself. Bridging this sort of isolation is particularly important for psychotic patients whose delusional, idiosyncratic ideation separates them from the basis of a consensual reality to which others ascribe. Furthermore, the empathy of the art therapist often provides the "corrective emotional experience" (Alexander & French, 1946) that is a basis for a humanistic approach to therapy.

But suppose the psychiatrist's interpretation is correct? An important foundation in my commitment to an eclectic approach is that I have found no single theory that can fully explain unconscious processes. There are no indisputable answers. We can no more claim that the psychiatrist's interpretation is erroneous than we can say that it is correct. So how do we find out?

Figure 2

As a phenomenologist, I would rely on the patient's experience, first through imagery, then through fantasy. I would utilize free association (Freudian), active imagination (Jungian), perhaps enactment (Gestalt and psychodrama), and so forth. I would make use of many tools from many therapeutic approaches, capitalizing on those to which the client responded most readily. Ultimately I would probably recognize that some areas would still remain shrouded in mystery, but my experience as an art therapist has taught me that there is so much that the art expression provides that it is not necessary to make speculative leaps into insubstantial interpretations.

This conclusion leads me into another concern about being locked into theory. The internal consistency of a theory enables the clinician to arrive at a relatively neat and comprehensible formulation of a client's psycho-dynamics. Of course, the problem is that sometimes the client is made to fit the theory rather than vice versa. Having a dynamic formulation may relieve the therapist's anxiety and can serve as a platform on which to erect the therapeutic work. It is more difficult to remain open to many possibilities and to recognize that the data are never all in.

This sort of openness to possibilities, this working with hunches rather than more solid formulations, may be easier for art therapists than other clinicians. As artists, we may be characterized by some of the attributes Frank Barron (1968b) has found exemplified by creative people, particularly a tolerance for ambiguity and a preference for complexity. Therefore, with the recognition of the essential complexity in every human existence and a tolerance for the ambiguity in a situation in which we are presented with an abundance of data (images, statements, behavior), my hope is that my anxiety will not push me to premature closure in an attempt to fathom my client's problems. I believe an eclectic approach encourages me to cast my net widely for the many sources of knowledge that may inform my understanding, and to take the time to weave a synthesis of ideas. Hopefully, an eclectic approach also prevents me from coming to premature formulations based on what I may have found to be a tried and true theory.

TOWARD FUTURE ART THERAPY THEORY

Art therapists have utilized various theories of human development, psychopathology, and psychotherapy to inform their work. Often we adapt our work to these theories or we adapt these theories to art therapy. Many recognize a need for a theory of art therapy that would integrate human psychology, creative art expression, and the meaning of visual imagery.

A brief glimpse of artwork by a psychiatric patient may indicate some of the directions for future theory. Figures 3 and 4 were drawn by Craig, a young man diagnosed paranoid schizophrenic and hospitalized at the National Institute of Health's Clinical Center, where I worked with him. Craig had been dragged into the hospital by seven policemen and was considered dangerous by the staff. His shaggy appearance and suspicious and menacing glances added to the effect. Artwork was an important outlet for him, and although his pictures expressed "secrets" he feared revealing, his love of drawing and the communication it made possible lessened the isolation his idiosyncratic ideation created.

Figure 3

The two pictures reproduced here were made prior to Craig's hospitalization. He stated that Figure 3, delicate traceries on notebook paper in pencil and blue ink, was drawn "in a shit house" when he was working at a factory. Figure 4 was also drawn on notebook paper with pencil and blue ink. He described it more fully, saying that it was himself. The underneath part is "strong and grasping," the sphere is "selfless" and represents his "mind." He explained that the roots are holding the sphere and that basically the underneath shows "control" of the body over the mind. "In order for the mind to exist, the body controls or comforts it," he said. (For additional examples of Craig's artwork, see Wadeson, *Art Psychotherapy*, 1980, pp. 140, 153, 154, 155, 156, 157, 159, 160, 161.)

An art therapy theory would be able to account for many aspects of Craig's art-making activity. First, there would be an understanding of why

Figure 4

and how a very psychotic patient did not decompensate further as so
many others did upon hospitalization. It was clear that making art, in and
of itself, was a stabilizing process for Craig.

   Second, Craig's frightening physical aspect, his fear that people would
take his "secrets" from him, and his elaborate delusional system alienated
him from others. But his art created a bridge for him. Staff and patients

were intrigued by his pictures and showed their interest and often their admiration. But even more significant was the opportunity art therapy sessions provided Craig. It was in this context that he began to build trust through my interest in the meaning of his imagery. In his pictures he portrayed an elaborate inner world of strange beings and unearthly land-scapes. The isolation experienced by delusional patients cannot be overem-phasized. An art therapy theory would note art's potentiality for bridging.

Most obvious, of course, an art therapy theory would facilitate the understanding of imagistic expression. There would be recognition of the delicacy and loving care that this fearsome, often wild-looking young man devoted to Figure 3. Evident also in this picture is some of the control of which he spoke in reference to Figure 4. This latter drawing is an interesting contrast to the former. The upper tree is quite truncated in comparison to both the more conventional tree of Figure 3 and the un-usual underpart of the second tree in Figure 4. This underground aspect is original, creative, and bizarre. The artistry in art therapy, it appears to me, is the art therapist's ability both to encourage art expression and to facilitate the patient's relating to it. In this case, although Craig had been fearful of disclosing his private meanings, sufficient trust had developed between us for him to associate to his picture quite freely.

But even with his somewhat unclear explanation, how do we under-stand such an image? Hopefully, an art therapy theory might provide direction. For the present, we note the power and importance of what is underground, what is hidden from view. Craig has related this portion of the picture to control. He has spoken of mind and body, but the locus of control is unclear from what he says. The roots appear to grasp and to be quite separate from the portion of the tree above ground. We gain a sense of Craig's struggle for control, both from the content of this picture and from the style of all his pictures. We see the separation, both graphi-cally and thematically, between the upper and the lower. We see a young man with a highly original creative energy who has had difficulty getting along in the world, who has managed to frighten almost everyone—family, employers, hospital staff—almost everyone except his art thera-pist. Even a famous psychiatrist renowned for his writings on schizo-phrenia, who served as consultant to our ward, was afraid Craig wanted to kill him and would not see him alone. I found Craig gentle, sensitive, a very caring human being. What might an art therapy theory tell us about this discrepancy?

Finally, there is the question of creativity. How does it move us? What is the healing nature of art making? Certainly it operated for Craig. And what is the nature of a therapeutic relationship that has creativity at its center? Perhaps this phenomenon allowed me to know an aspect of Craig that others didn't see.

THE SELECTRIC ELECTRIC

I have strayed from "An Eclectic Approach . . . " only to return to it. My hope is that as we develop our profession and gradually build what will come to be art therapy theory, we will learn from and integrate whatever wisdom we may. There are many paradigms, more than one lens through which to view our complex world. They enable us to see a number of different relationships within the "reality" we are attempting to understand.

I hope this chapter has made clear that I believe theory to be an essential foundation to our work. An eclectic approach respects the contributions of many theorists and enables the clinician to draw on many sources of knowledge. It places a great deal of responsibility on the therapist to form a functional synthesis, integrating theories with one another and applying them to practice in the most efficacious way.

For those who feel a need for art therapy to have its own theoretical base, I believe this book begins a process for developing and drawing together the various strands that can be woven into an art therapy theory. We look to the articulation of knowledge of human growth and behavior, to metapsychological viewpoints, to formulations of psychopathology, to treatment rationales. We have a rich heritage for a foundation. To that we must add an understanding of what is unique to art in therapy: expression in images, working with art materials, the client-therapist relationship around art making, the place of creativity in art therapy. It is an exciting challenge.

For starters, I would like to return to the thoughts of my typist. I highly recommend her Selectric-Electric approach to art therapy.

REFERENCES

Alexander, F., & French, T. *Psychoanalytic theory: Principles and application*. New York: Ronald Press, 1946.

Barron, F. *Creativity and personal freedom*. New York: Van Nostrand Reinhold, 1968a.

Barron, F. The dream of art and poetry. *Psychology Today*, 1968b, *2*:7.

Boss, M. *The analysis of dreams*. New York: Philosophical Library, 1958.

Bowen, M. The family as the unit of study and treatment. *American Journal of Orthopsychiatry*, 1961, *31*, 400–460.

Erikson, E. *Childhood and society*. New York: W. W. Norton, 1950.

Freud, S. *The interpretation of dreams* (1900). New York: Modern Library, 1950.

Heidegger, M. *Being and time*. London: SCM Press, 1962.

Heidegger, M. *Existence and being*. Chicago, IL: H. Regnery Co., 1964.

Jaspers, K. *Reason and anti-reason in our time*. New Haven, CT: Yale University Press, 1952.

Jaspers, K. *General psychopathology*. Chicago, IL: University of Chicago Press, 1963.

Jung, C. *Basic writings*. New York: Modern Library, 1959.

Jung, C. *Man and his symbols*. Garden City, NY: Doubleday & Co., 1964.

Kierkegaard, S. *The concept of dread*. Princeton, NJ: Princeton University Press, 1957.

Kohut, H. Introspection, empathy and psychoanalysis. *Journal of the American Psychoanalytic Association*, 1959, 7, 459–483.

Moore, B., & Fine, B. *A glossary of psychoanalytic terms and concepts*. New York: The American Psychoanalytic Association, 1968.

Naumburg, M. *Dynamically oriented art therapy: Its principles and practice*. New York: Grune & Stratton, 1966.

Perls, F. *Gestalt therapy verbatim*. Moab, UT: Real People Press, 1969.

Sullivan, H. S. *The interpersonal theory of psychiatry*. New York: W. W. Norton, 1953.

Wadeson, H. *Art psychotherapy*. New York: John Wiley & Sons, 1980.

Wadeson, H., & Carpenter, W. Subjective experience of acute schizophrenia. *Schizophrenia Bulletin*, 1976, 2, 302–316.

Yalom, I. *The theory and practice of group psychotherapy*. New York: Basic Books, 1975.

Yalom, I. *Inpatient group psychotherapy*. New York: Basic Books, 1983.

17

Conclusion

Judith A. Rubin

The question of which theoretical framework(s) any art therapist ought to adopt is not unique to me or to this book. From the first volume of the first periodical in this newly emerging discipline, thoughtful workers have been concerned with the problems of selection among different points of view (Ulman, 1961). As soon as a national organization was formed, arguments about the proper qualifications for registration as an art therapist reflected these concerns, especially in regard to how much a qualified practitioner ought to be an artist, and how much he or she should be a therapist. Although many have debated, often with considerable heat, the identity of the art therapist, most agree with the broad-based definition offered by Ulman: that *art therapy* ought to be applicable to any endeavor that genuinely partakes of both art and therapy (Ulman, 1961, p. 13), which leaves considerable leeway for a variety of viewpoints.

At the second meeting of the national organization in 1971, one of the contributors to this book noted that there were then "a variety of approaches that utilize different remedial frameworks of personality theory" (Garai, 1971, p. 1) He went on to state, however, that "only a few sporadic and rather tentative attempts have been directed toward the development of a more coherent and testable theory of art therapy . . . " (*Ibid.*). And he concluded that "no coherent, broad, scientifically sound and verifiable theory has yet emerged" (*Ibid.*). He then went on to propose humanistic psychology as a more appropriate framework for art therapy than psychoanalysis, a position he continues to espouse in Chapter 11 in this volume.

At the next meeting of the American Art Therapy Association (1972), another practitioner underlined "the need for good theory," as well as the fact that "a theory of art therapy, as such is not yet possible." This person even went so far as to imagine the possibility that "it may not occur later" (!) She suggested that "until it does, we must in the meantime draw theoretical positions from aesthetics and the various theories of personality for the framework in which to try many approaches to the practice of art therapy" (Hodnett, 1973, p. 77). The speaker expressed the opinion that "humanistic psychology offered a 'better fit' for the aims of art therapy . . . than psychoanalysis." At one point, however, she imagined a possible accommodation between the two: "perhaps both psychoanalytic and humanistic theories of personality will eventually be utilized together in some sort of tandem or leap frog manner in the process of art therapy, shifting gears from one to the other as the patient/client's needs are met and understood" (*Ibid.*, p. 78).

During that same conference (1972), one of the contributors to this volume organized a panel discussion entitled "Integrating Diverse Techniques with Divergent Theoretical Operations." Arthur Robbins moderated a discussion among four individuals who presented cases in which each had used a different approach: group interactional, psychoanalytic, Gestalt, and behavioral. And two years later, the general session of the convention was a symposium on the "Integration of Divergent Points of View in Art Therapy," which included presentations by four contributors to this volume (Levy et al., 1974). In his introduction to the discussion, moderator Bernard I. Levy pointed out a potential pitfall of attempts at synthesis: "While divergent viewpoints can be 'integrated' as a conceptual act and even rationalized with an eclectic philosophy, the rationale must not be so broad as to espouse laissez-faire. Integration of divergence need not mean that 'anything goes'" (*Ibid.*, p. 13).

Three years later (1975), one of those to whom Levy had referred in his introductory remarks as beginning the difficult work of defining the field (Betensky, 1973) offered phenomenology as a more appropriate framework for art therapy than psychoanalysis. Mala Betensky, another contributor to this volume, stated that "our body of theory is slender, our research meager, and our method still in need of development. This unrest is a welcome sign of a search for a conceptual basis for art therapy." She went on to say that the current state of affairs in our discipline reminded her of Pirandello's play *Six Characters in Search of an Author*," "except that the art therapists in search of a philosophy will have to be their own authors" (Betensky, 1975, p. 1). Betensky suggested that "what we are searching for in order to develop art therapy into a discipline will have to be elaborated from the empirical stuff of which art therapy was originally created." She then went on to demonstrate the shortcomings of psychoanalytic theory and the assets of phenomenology as a more appropriate framework for what happens in art therapy (cf. Betensky, 1976).

Six years later, Arthur Robbins again addressed the relevance of different theories, presenting a paper entitled "Integrating Diverse Theoretical Frameworks in the Identification Process of an Art Therapist," which was discussed by another contributor to this book, Mildred Lachman-Chapin (1982). In his presentation, Robbins vividly described the typical dilemma of a recent graduate of any of the masters degree programs in art therapy: "You . . . have been exposed to various theoretical viewpoints that you struggle to synthesize and integrate their inherent polarities." Not only is this conceptually difficult, but, as the speaker pointed out, "many of these constructs are alien and very removed from your experience as an artist" (1981, p. 1).

The question of how to relate one's identity as an artist to one's identity as a therapist has always been critical for art therapists. As Bob Ault, second president of the national organization, had asked in a talk four years earlier, "If someone shook you awake at 3:00 in the morning and asked 'Are you an artist or a therapist?' how would you answer?" (1977, p. 53). And as Robbins put it in his presentation, addressing the recent graduate: "You do not want to see yourself as a psychotherapist. The smell of paint and sense of excitement about the art room moves in your arteries and you have a strong identification with your fellow artists. Consequently, you search for constructs that resonate with your experience as an artist, as the technical notions of psychotherapy seem alien and have the ring of jargon" (1981, p. 2).

In that presentation, Robbins struggled to find a way for the art therapist to create "a synthesis of your art background and a clinical knowledge of psychiatry and psychology" (1981, p. 12). The solution he proposed was a creative response to the patient: "You feel and see as well as move with the complex melodies and rhythms of your patient's pathology, and you are not limited or defined by a particular theory" (1981, p. 13). He concluded: "Theory, then, becomes something that is very much organic and part of you and is not used as a defense to interfere with your experience of your patients. In fact, with each therapeutic encounter, we rediscover the theory with fresh eyes, even though somewhere in the back of our consciousness we have carried within us a psychiatric sophistication. . . . Theory then is an emotional, cognitive integration that is mediated through the process of assimilation and accommodation" (1981, p. 14).

By thus viewing the use of different theories in a spontaneous, creative fashion, Robbins felt that he could achieve his goal of synthesizing his artist and psychologist identities: "There still remains the core of me that is the artist that has merged with the psychologist and discovered a new sense of wholeness and professional mastery" (*Ibid.*). In a recent issue of one of the journals in our field, Robbins further clarified his fantasy of how to integrate the two facets of art therapy: "We require a complex theory of treatment that integrates psychodynamics and aesthetics. . . . Psychological theory must be recast into the language of art so that psychodynamics can be felt and comprehended within a nonverbal frame" (1985, p. 68) In other words: "We must find creative means to translate psychology into the language of art" (p. 69).

In an article published the following year based on his 1981 presentation, Robbins clearly stated his preference for exposure to multiple orientations: "Art therapy can be cast in many different frames depending on any number of factors" (1982, p. 1). He also concluded the paper by saying "how important it is for art therapists to respect the differences in theory and approach and to learn from one another" (1982, p. 8). Emphasizing the importance of responding openly to each individual, he wrote: "My professional identity as an art therapist is no longer static, but ebbs and flows with each session and patient" (1982, p. 8).

The *patient* variable may, in fact, be as important as the *clinician* variable in the theoretical equation developed by each art therapist. Robbins, in both versions of the above paper, explains that he felt a need to look beyond art therapy theories stressing sublimation, largely because of experiences with psychotic and borderline patients who were unable to sublimate successfully. And Lachman-Chapin, in her commentary on Robbins' talk (1982) as well as in her own presentation to art therapists of new theoretical ideas (1979), emphasizes the special relevance of self psychology for work with those whose problems are primarily narcissistic. Similarly, Rhyne remarks in her chapter that the confrontational and demanding approach of Gestalt art therapy is not for those whose psychological state is too fragile. Along parallel lines, it has already been noted that the more prescriptive and structured approaches described in the third section of this book grew out of work with severely handicapped populations.

The editor of a collection of chapters on different types of psychotherapy expressed a related idea a quarter of a century ago: "One source of difference between schools of psychotherapy that is often overlooked and which needs to be made explicit is the difference in types of patients on which the founders of the different schools based their initial observations" (Stein, 1961, p. 6). After citing some well-known examples (like Freud seeing hysterics and Sullivan schizophrenics), he went on to draw the logical conclusion: "With these differences in basic data and sources of observation, it is not surprising that each school should develop its own special theory and technique." It therefore also makes sense that "one school might well have a good deal more to say about one specific type of patient than another" (*Ibid.*, p. 7)—or, one might add, about one aspect of a patient rather than another (cf. Frances, Clarkin, & Perry, 1984).

Within his lifetime, Freud's theories about the mind developed and changed and were further elaborated and modified by his followers. In 1973, two psychoanalysts (Gedo & Goldberg) published a book called *Models of the Mind*, in which they suggested that there was a "need for different theories to deal with different sets of empirical data." They even went so far as to "propose that no single theory is fully sufficient to order even one set of clinical observations" (p. 172). One implication of their study is that different models fit different patients, as well as the same patient functioning at different developmental levels (cf. Rothstein, 1985).

A recent book by a psychologist elaborates a similar application of such principles, referring also to current developments in psychoanalytic theory. Entitled *Listening Perspectives in Psychotherapy* (Hedges, 1983), the book clarifies the importance of being able to hear a patient's communications in terms appropriate to their source. The author, Lawrence Hedges, defines *listening perspectives* as different "clinical frames of reference," which provide a "backdrop" for hearing patients' verbalizations. In addition to understanding what is being said, art therapists also need to develop an appropriate set of *looking perspectives*, so that we can look each time in a way that is truly consonant with the process and/or product in front of us.

Certainly, each person being seen in art therapy is unique, and it makes sense that a theory and technique most appropriate to a psychotic adult might not be best with a neurotic child. In spite of the following joke, it is also true that not every patient seen in art or any form of therapy comes of his own volition or is truly motivated to do the hard work involved in redefinition of the self: "How many shrinks does it take to change a light bulb? One, but the light bulb has to really want to change!" And it is also important to remember that not all "shrinks" are either interested or talented in changing light bulbs. In other words, as important in choice of theory as the nature of the patient is the personality of the clinician. Equally relevant for both parties in the therapeutic situation is "cognitive style," the related dominant mode(s) of thought and expression, elaborated recently in the hypothesis of "multiple intelligences" (Gardner, 1983).

In both chapters dealing with the problem of selection among different theories, the authors stress the significance of individual style. Both Ulman and Wadeson note that just as theoreticians develop ideas that fit their personalities and ways of working, so one's way of being a therapist must be synchronous with one's authentic self. It is really impossible to "put on" any approach that does not "fit" comfortably.

We need to be careful, however, that the theory we espouse does not conceal unrecognized needs or conflicts within ourselves. In a talk opening the 1978 Art Therapy Association conference, I presented the following elaboration of such thoughts:

> Since I believe that unconscious fantasies and strivings are ubiquitous, the only sensible thing to do is to acknowledge their existence, and then to examine our work, how we do it, and what we say about it, in the light of what we know or suspect about our personal hidden agenda. For what we say, I believe, is as capable of such analysis as what we do. It is all too easy, especially if one is articulate, to find or create a theoretical rationale for almost any therapeutic stance. . . . And, to the extent that our theory, as well as our practice, is determined by forces of which we are unaware, then it is no more than a verbal externalization of our own intrapsychic issues. To the extent that we have, usually through personal therapy, come to know and to accept these forces, we can hopefully be in charge of them, and can try to evaluate them more objectively, in the light of what we know and understand about the human and artistic needs of those with whom we work. Only after this step of self-analysis, are we ready to think or talk about the mature and creative use of the self in art therapy. (Rubin, 1979, pp. 1–2)

I went on in that presentation to suggest that "the next step toward that goal is to be open-minded . . . about how one perceives what is happening, how one approaches the patient, and what one does in response" (p. 2). However, an *open* mind is not an *empty* one; as the situation requires, it is a mind open to seeing and hearing what is being presented, perhaps through various theoretical lenses. It certainly makes sense that the more familiar one is with different possible ways of seeing and hearing, the more likely it should be to truly see and hear what is actually there.

Of course, there are times when we simply cannot perceive the signal, like the pitch of animal sounds that are beyond the range of human hearing. More often, however, we could see and hear what is there, but are unable to do so because we do not know a frame of reference (a theory) that would make it possible. One goal of a book like this one is to increase the number of "lenses" art therapists are able to put into their clinical "frames," to multiply the number of "listening and looking perspectives" potentially available to each clinician, so that he or she can receive, perceive, and conceive as well as possible when dealing with different patients at different times.

One of the best collections of thoughts about different theories of mental functioning is *Maps of the Mind* by Charles Hampden-Turner (1981), a literate scholar whose avowed preference for a humanistic per-

spective does not inhibit his ability to sympathetically and humorously
describe a variety of mental maps. He reminds us, in his Introduction, that
"maps vary according to the point of view" and cites the wonderful tale
of the "six wise men, all blind who came across an elephant, and tried
to discern its shape. . . ."

Six wise men of India
An elephant did find
And carefully they felt its shape
(For all of them were blind).

The first he felt towards the tusk,
"It does to me appear,
This marvel of an elephant
Is very like a spear."

The second sensed the creature's side
Extended flat and tall,
"Ahah!" he cried and did conclude,
"This animal's a wall."

The third had reached towards a leg
And said, "It's clear to me
What we should all have seen instead
This creature's like a tree."

The fourth had come upon the trunk
Which he did seize and shake,
Quoth he, "This so-called elephant
Is really just a snake."

The fifth had felt the creature's ear
And fingers o'er it ran,
"I have the answer, never fear,
This creature's like a fan!"

The sixth had come upon the tail
As blindly he did grope,
"Let my conviction now prevail
This creature's like a rope."

And so these men of missing sight
Each argued loud and long
Though each was partly in the right
They all were in the wrong. (pp. 9–10)

Of course, as Hampden-Turner hastens to point out, the poem "simpli-
fies our problem by assuming there *is* a lumpy, three-dimensional animal

'out there.''' He then suggests that "mind is even more elusive because the sensors and the sensed overlap" (p. 10). Although it is probably not true that each theorist discussed in this book had as partial a perspective as the blind men, the essential veracity of the parable is sufficient to justify its inclusion.

Moreover, in spite of the multidimensional value of multiple lenses, there is also much to be said for the enthusiastic embrace of at least one well-known and well-digested approach. In the Conclusion to a recent collection of chapters on different personality theorists, the authors agree:

> The notion of a general synthesis or integration usually communicates to the student the need to be cautious, take all points of view into consideration, and to avoid emotional involvement with a particular, one-sided position. . . . Contrary to this conception, we recommend strongly that students should, once they have surveyed the available theories of personality, adopt a vigorous and affectionate acceptance of a particular theoretical position without reservation. Let the individual be enthusiastic and imbued with the theory before beginning to examine it critically (Hall & Lindzey, 1977, p. 705).

Not only does such an embrace of a single theory make sense logically, it makes even more sense psychologically, in regard to the individual therapist. A Gestalt therapist once wrote,

> A person must find a theory which is sympathetic to his best talents, whether they be interpretive, poetic, directive or such. If he doesn't do so, he will be inept, or more likely, phony. . . . The primary question about the "rightness" of a style is whether one accepts responsibility for the consequences he evokes and is skillful in facing them. . . . Certainly, psychologists should be aware of the unlikelihood of discovering *the* single technique of psychotherapy (Polster, 1966, p. 5).

In regard to the search for the single or best "technique," in art therapy as in other forms of psychotherapy, I am reminded of Hanna Kwiatkowska's delightful presentation at a Symposium noted earlier (Levy et al., 1974). She told of her long fight with the editor of the university catalog over the letter "S," explaining: "One of the courses I teach is consistently listed as 'Techniques of Art Therapy,' a distinction the editor refused to understand or honor." She went on to explain the reason for her objection: "My strong conviction is that *the only technique of art therapy is the technique of relating to a patient through art*" (p. 17) Kwiatkowska felt that the numerous "technical maneuvers" then exploding on the art therapy scene stemmed largely from clinicians' anxiety about what would happen if things were left open. I agree and also wonder whether many art therapists do not genuinely misunderstand the medical model and feel it to be their responsibility to provide specific tasks. Whatever the cause, the reader would do well to look carefully at the specific technical approaches described in this book. No matter what the orientation, even the most prescriptive are carefully designed to promote the patient's own creative participation in the making of his or her art.

Technique, however, is a much more subtle thing than techniques. Whether an art therapist openly espouses a theoretical stance or insists that he or she is atheoretical; whatever is done (the "technique" employed) implies some underlying theoretical assumption(s). As in the title of a recent journal article, "Brother, Can You Spare a Paradigm?" there is *always*, even if unacknowledged, a "Theory Beneath the Practice," the subtitle of the paper (Pearse, 1983). Or, to put it another way, "Clinical judgments and activities flow organically from concious or preconscious theoretical premises, rather than the other way around" (Deri, 1984, p. 218).

There has been considerable resistance within our field to theorizing, perhaps because those who prefer to think visually are less comfortable with thinking verbally. Perhaps, too, there are "transferences" to theory, both positive and negative, based on experiences with therapists, teachers, or supervisors in the individual's past. If the transference is positive, the theory espoused by that person might be idealized, but if it is negative, a specific theory—or *all* theories—may be viewed in an agnostic or atheistic fashion (cf. Rangell, 1985).

It is also true that the patient comes to therapy "with a theory of pathogenesis of his symptoms. With his words and speech [and art] the patient conveys not only a description of what he suffers, but his own diagnoses and explanatory theories of his [illness]. . . . These explanations, the patient's theories, are not to be ignored but to be used as data, which not uncommonly go some distance toward insight" (Rangell, 1985, p. 81). Although none of the authors in this volume specifically address the patient's "theory," most suggest or imply that the patient's ideas and associations to his art must be taken seriously.

In this generalization about something common to most of the chapters, I have been what psychoanalyst Arnold Cooper would call a "lumper." During a discussion on the relation of theory to technique, Cooper referred "to the distinction between 'lumpers' and 'splitters' [and] noted that we can at any moment, and with a particular end in view, decide whether we are interested in differences in technique or in how all techniques are at bottom the same" (Richards, 1984, p. 600). Whether "the search for common ground" is really more appropriate than "the examination of differences" (*Ibid.*) at this point in the development of art therapy is not clear to me. I believe I tend to be a "lumper" by inclination, tending to see commonality more than distinctions among the various approaches. Perhaps it is that aspect of my thinking which has led me to see important learnings in a wide variety of theories and techniques, like those described in this book.

In any case, I believe it would be appropriate at this point to briefly note some of those commonalities which seem apparent to me, though the reader may well have come away feeling differently. First, all of the contributors to this volume have found a way to integrate their previous training and experience with their chosen theoretical approach to art therapy. Betensky, for example, was trained as a clinical psychologist and has been able to incorporate techniques like the house-tree-person drawing series and the Rorschach inkblots into her work as an art therapist. Kramer's work as a teacher of art must have influenced her choice of sublimation as the primary goal of art therapy, wherein the promotion of good-quality creative products would be consonant with both effective treatment and fine education.

Robbins, a sculptor, and Lachman-Chapin, a painter, refer to a need to integrate their identity as practicing artists with their role as art therapists. Perhaps this need enhances their interest in the visual, preverbal elements in psychopathology and in theories that deal with such early issues. Similarly, Silver has utilized her experience as an art educator/researcher in her particular approach to the training of cognitive skills through art therapy. Aach and Kunkle-Miller have selectively utilized their training in child development, special education, and rehabilitation in creating their developmental approach to art therapy. Ulman's chapter, detailing the roots of three art therapy theories, makes this same point in more depth.

In addition to finding ways to incorporate (rather than to discard or put aside) previous experiences, all of the contributors have been rather creative in utilizing their chosen theories. Sometimes they have applied the ideas in a novel way, as with Roth's "reality shaping," or Rhyne's integration of ideas about cognitive constructs with her training as an artist and a Gestalt therapist. The inventiveness of Aach and Kunkle-Miller is evident not only in the techniques they have developed, but also in their ways of *thinking* about what to do with their multiply handicapped clients. There is nothing Kohut wrote that would predict Lachman-Chapin's specific idea of drawing with the patient, though it is indeed a kind of "mirroring." Just as she has gone beyond her primary theoretical source to another thinker, D. W. Winnicott, she has also amplified *his* idea of shared squiggles, so that she is experimenting with a novel way of using her artist-self in her work as a therapist (cf. Winnicott, 1971).

This tendency to be inventive and to go beyond the primary theoretical resource is seen in many of the contributors to this volume. Kramer, for example, long after her initial statement of the theoretical importance of sublimation for art therapy, explored in yet another realm—ethology—additional meanings and implications of her position. Garai, though he began his writings by referring primarily to those psychologists known as "humanistic," like Maslow, has found it necessary more recently to move beyond, into the thinking called "holistic," the authors coming from a variety of disciplines. And Wadeson reminds us, in her chapter on an eclectic approach, of the importance to art therapy of both biology and environment, two areas acknowledged, but largely ignored, by most theories of psychology and psychotherapy.

In addition, all of the contributors seem to agree on at least two things: (1) the importance of the image and (2) the complexity of both person and process in art therapy. And whatever the relative emphasis on art and therapy in any author's conception, all include a consideration of both. Some of the approaches are rather intellectual and logical, some are more emotional and intuitive, but all involve an attempt to integrate both feeling and thought in the art therapeutic process. Some also make explicit their conviction that any viable theory of art therapy which might eventually evolve ought to include both elements of this hybrid discipline, as well as the special relationship between them.

As noted in the Introduction, and in a recent book, "The development of a valid theory about art therapy is a more demanding task, yet perhaps the most important . . . of all. For, if we are unable to account for our effectiveness in a logical and communicable way, we will continue to be viewed as either charming romantics or hopeless airheads, depending on the bias of the perceiver. . . . I am not suggesting that most clinicians are interested in becoming theorists, any more than I would expect most therapists to like doing research. But I do think that art therapists, once they have learned to do their work artistically, have a responsibility to those they may train, advise, supervise, or inform to be able to understand theory in their own field and in related disciplines . . ." (Rubin, 1984, pp. 144–145). It is hoped that this book will be a step in that direction, and that it will make the journey somewhat less confusing than it might have been without any theoretical "maps" to define the pathways.

REFERENCES

Ault, R. Are you an artist or a therapist? A professional dilemma of art therapists. In Shoemaker, R. H., & Gonick-Barris, S. E. (Eds.), *Creativity and the art therapist's identity*. Baltimore, MD: American Art Therapy Association, 1977, pp. 53–56.

Betensky, M. *Self-discovery through self-expression*. Springfield, IL: Charles C Thomas, 1973.

Betensky, M. Phenomenology: A theory of art therapy. Unpublished manuscript presented at the American Art Therapy Association Conference, November, 1975, 11 pp.

Betensky, M. The phenomenological approach to art expression and art therapy. *Art Psychotherapy*, 1976, *4*, 173–180.

Deri, S. K. *Symbolization and creativity*. New York: International Universities Press, 1984.

Frances, A., Clarkin, J., & Perry, S. *Differential therapeutics in psychiatry: The art and science of treatment selection*. New York: Brunner/Mazel, 1984.

Garai, J. E. The humanistic approach to art therapy and creativity development. Unpublished manuscript presented at the American Art Therapy Association Conference, October, 1971, 10 pp.

Gardner, H. *Frames of mind: The theory of multiple intelligences*. New York: Basic Books, 1983.

Gedo, J. E., & Goldberg, A. *Models of the mind: A psychoanalytic theory*. Chicago: University of Chicago Press, 1973.

Hall, C. S., & Lindzey, G. (Eds.). *Theories of personality*, 3rd Ed. New York: Wiley, 1977.

Hampden-Turner, C. *Maps of the mind: Charts and concepts of the mind and its labyrinths*. New York: Macmillan, 1981.

Hedges, L. E. *Listening perspectives in psychotherapy*. New York: Jason Aronson, 1983.

Hodnett, M. L. A broader view of art therapy. *Art Psychotherapy*, 1973, *1*, 75–79.

Kwiatkowska, H. Y. Technique versus techniques. *American Journal of Art Therapy*, 1974, *14*, p. 17.

Lachman-Chapin, M. Kohut's theories on narcissism: Implications for art therapy. *American Journal of Art Therapy*, 1979, *19*, 3–9.

Lachman-Chapin, M. Discussion of Arthur Robbins' paper: Integrating diverse theoretical frameworks in the identification process of an art therapist. In Di Maria, A. E., et al. (Eds.), *Art therapy: A bridge between worlds*. Falls Church, VA: American Art Therapy Association, 1982, pp. 88–90.

Levy, B. I., Kramer, E., Kwiatkowska, H. Y., Rhyne, J., & Ulman, E. Symposium: Integration of divergent points of view in art therapy. *American Journal of Art Therapy*, 1974, *14*, 12–17.

Pearse, H. Brother, can you spare a paradigm? The theory beneath the practice. *Studies in Art Education*, 1983, *24*, 158–163.

Polster, E. A contemporary psychotherapy. *Psychotherapy: Theory, Research & Practice*, 1966, *3*(1), 1–6.

Rangell, L. On the theory of psychoanalysis and the relation of theory to psychoanalytic therapy. *Journal of the American Psychoanalytic Association*, 1985, *33*, 59–92.

Richards, A. (Reporter). Panel: The relation between psychoanalytic theory and psychoanalytic technique. *Journal of the American Psychoanalytic Association*, 1984, *32*, 587–602.

Robbins, A. Integrating diverse theoretical frameworks in the identification process of an art therapist. Unpublished manuscript presented at the American Art Therapy Association Conference, October 1981, 16 pp.

Robbins, A. Integrating the personal and theoretical splits in the struggle towards identity as an art therapist. *The Arts in Psychotherapy*, 1982, *9*, 1–9.

Robbins, A. Working towards the establishment of creative arts therapies as an independent profession. *The Arts in Psychotherapy*, 1985, *12*, 67–70.

Rothstein, A. (Ed.). *Models of the mind: Their relationships to clinical work*. New York: International Universities Press, 1985.

Rubin, J. A. Opening remarks. In Gantt, L., et al. (Eds.), *Art therapy: Expanding horizons*. Baltimore, MD: American Art Therapy Association, 1979, pp. 1–2.

Rubin, J. A. *The art of art therapy*. New York: Brunner/Mazel, 1984.

Stein, M. I. (Ed.). *Contemporary psychotherapies*. New York: The Free Press of Glencoe, 1961.

Ulman, E. Art therapy: Problems of definition. *Bulletin of Art Therapy*, 1961, *1*(2), 10–20.

Winnicott, D. W. *Therapeutic consultations in child psychiatry*. New York: Basic Books, 1971.

Index